Financial Modelling in Corporate Management

Second Edition

Edited by
JAMES W. BRYANT
Sheffield City Polytechnic

JOHN WILEY & SONS
Chichester · New York · Brisbane · Toronto

Library of Congress Cataloging-in-Publication Data:

Financial modelling in corporate management.
Includes index.
1. Corporations—Finance—Mathematical models.
I. Bryant, James W., Ph. D.
HG4012.F54 1986 658.1'5'0724 86–32446

ISBN 0 471 91476 2

British Library Cataloguing in Publication Data:

Financial modelling in corporate management.
—2nd ed.
1. Corporations—Finance—
Mathematical models 2. Industrial
management—Mathematical models
I. Bryant, James W.
658.1'5'0724 HG4026

ISBN 0 471 91476 2

Typeset by Activity Ltd., Salisbury, Wilts
Printed in Great Britain by St. Edmundsbury Press, Bury St. Edmunds

List of Contributors

LEO BRESSMAN, Manufacturers Hanover Trust Company, New York, USA.

JAMES BROWNE, Port Authority of New York and New Jersey, New York, USA.

JAMES BRYANT, Sheffield City Polytechnic, Sheffield, UK.

JOHN COLEMAN, Health Care Plus of America, Wichita, USA.

IAN CRAWFORD, TAC Construction Materials Ltd, Manchester, UK.

JOHN DOLBEAR, Blue Circle Industries plc, Aldermaston, UK.

JOHN DROBNY, Port Authority of New York and New Jersey, New York, USA.

PAUL FINLAY, University of Technology, Loughborough, UK.

JOHN GRINYER, The University, Dundee, UK.

JOHN HOLLAND, University of Glasgow, Glasgow, UK.

BARBARA JACKSON, Harvard Business School, Boston, USA.

FRANK KAMINSKY, University of Massachusetts, Amherst, USA.

CORNELIUS DEKLUYVER, University of Virginia, Charlottesville, USA.

S. V. LE, California State University, Long Beach, USA.

ALASDAIR LONIE, The University, Dundee, UK.

STEPHEN LYUS, Imperial Group plc, Bristol, UK.

RANDY MCGLADE, Interstate Electronics Corporation, California, USA.

JOHN MACGREGOR, EPS Management Consultants, St Leonards, Australia.

G. A. McNally, University of Canterbury, Christchurch, New Zealand.

John Precious, Tioxide Group plc, London, UK.

Tony Rands, Oxford Centre for Management Studies, Oxford, UK.

Jae Shim, California State University, Long Beach, USA.

Benson Shapiro, Harvard Business School, Boston, USA.

Cheresse Smoot, California State University, Long Beach, USA.

Bob Vause, Oxford Centre for Management Studies, Oxford, UK.

Peter Whyte, Imperial Chemical Industries Ltd, London, UK.

Contents

PART 3 MODELS IN ACTION

PART 4 MODEL TEMPLATES

PART 5 OPPORTUNITIES FOR MODELLING

Preface

This is a book about practical financial modelling which is intended as an introduction for anyone concerned with financial management, whether as a manager or as an analyst, and whether as a practitioner or as a student. It presents, within a structured framework, a collection of chapters which cover all aspects of the subject, from an introduction to the basics of modelling, through sections describing the practice of modelling and giving examples of some of the models which have been created, to presentation of some model templates and modelling opportunities from which the reader may draw inspiration for model development. Throughout, the text has been informed by the belief that, to be of any real value, the narrative is best provided by those who have themselves been intimately involved in the practice of the subject, and so the contributors are drawn from that growing band of experienced financial modellers who have helped to make the subject such an essential part of modern financial management.

It is now over twenty years since the advent of interactive computing facilities stimulated the development of the earliest financial planning systems. The succeeding years have seen the rapid take-up of the idea by organizations of all sizes, and the marketing of a wide range of computer-based corporate modelling services. The first edition of this book, conceived almost a decade ago, was able to present a balanced picture of the state-of-the-art at the start of the 1980s, and filled a noticeable gap in the existing financial modelling literature, which at that time was almost totally confined to specialist journal articles or computer software sales materials. Since then a number of other books have been published dealing with the subject at a theoretical level, reviewing the use being made of models, or simply focusing on specific computerized modelling systems, but there still appears to be a need for a pragmatic introductory guide for the interested newcomer.

This updated text, which reflects recent developments in the subject area, maintains the practical perspective of its predecessor (which one reviewer mysteriously claimed was 'excessively down to earth'!), while building selectively on its strengths. Thus, there are new chapters describing experiences of modelling in a variety of organizations, and detailing the actual models produced, as well as new contributions of a review nature. Throughout, a sharper distinction has been made between the 'wood' and the 'trees' of modelling, and this should be especially useful in helping the novice to appreciate the core of each application described. As before, it is to be hoped that the accounts of practical modelling work will do something to dispel the remaining mystique which regrettably still surrounds the use of modelling methods in financial decision-making, and thereby open up the area to all whom it should concern.

The book is addressed to a number of audiences. First, it should provide a broad introduction to the field of financial modelling for the accountant or non-specialist manager alike. Secondly, it should be of educative value to that dramatically growing body of students in accounting, business management and related subjects by providing a comprehensive coverage of one of the most significant areas in contemporary organizational control. And thirdly, it should help to widen the perspective of those already engaged in modelling work, both in financial and other contexts, and suggest potential fields of application within their own organizations.

Acknowledgement by name of all those who contributed, directly or indirectly, to the shaping of this book is an impossible task; indeed to do so would inevitably lead to invidious and probably meaningless distinctions being made. It is rather the outcome of a process which began for me in a parental home dominated by accountancy; which continued through training in operational research and subsequent internal management consultancy in industry; and which is now maintained by my work in business education. At every stage, there have been individuals who have provided professional or personal support, guidance and encouragement, and it is they who have really made a publication possible. It is the very least that I can do to dedicate this book to them in gratitude.

JIM BRYANT

Sheffield
September 1986

Editor's Introduction

Management arises from uncertainty and the contemporary response to uncertainty is planning. In any setting, it is because there are choices to be made, decisions to be taken, directions to be determined, that a planning process, however defined, is necessary. A family unit choosing where to take the next vacation, a community group deciding how to run a leafleting campaign, a company board determining whether a divestment should be made of a subsidiary; all these are faced with the challenge of uncertainty, and uniquely each tries to handle its affairs in such a way that the unknown abstract future becomes a desirable concrete present. The simplest, but most dangerous, response to uncertainty is to ignore it; to pretend it does not exist, and to act accordingly. More productively, uncertainty may be recognized and attempts made either to work with it or else to reduce it; in both cases, reflection about the nature of a situation and the gathering of relevant information are likely to be crucial aspects of the resulting process. Financial modelling is an activity that has been developed to help those willing to confront uncertainty to gain a better understanding of the financial aspects of the choices with which they are faced, so that they may more effectively plan for those systems and organizations for which they are responsible.

Consider the following situations:

- In a multi-product food company, management wish to examine the financial impact of changes in commodity prices and labour costs, and the implications of alternative marketing and distribution policies.
- A shipping company requires a procedure to ease the preparation of budgets so that changes in cargo flows and fleet movements can be rapidly re-evaluated, and reports on individual ships, routes and onshore facilities can be generated to monitor performance.
- The economics of oil exploration and production for a company operating in the North Sea must be assessed, and a system is therefore needed which will be capable of handling the complex financing arrangements involved and the taxation implications of alternative strategies.

- Head office of a multinational conglomerate wish to investigate manufacturing location options and associated future investment strategy in the light of exchange rate fluctuations and anticipated unit cost differentials.

In each case, a financial model might be used to aid and inform managerial decision-making, by permitting the detailed testing of choices and policies prior to any actual decision being taken. Such models make it possible to 'live through' any number of potential futures, without the attendant risks, in a learning mode which not only enhances managerial judgement concerning the decision in hand, but usually also develops generalizable insights about the organizations and systems for which planning is being carried out.

The basis of all financial modelling is the representation of the relationships among financial variables, and between these variables and other measures of corporate activity. It is the fact that such relationships can be defined quite independently of the actual numbers involved, that makes financial modelling possible. Thus, the revenue which a soft drinks company obtains from sales of canned beverages is defined as the number of cans sold multiplied by the unit price of each can, irrespective of how many cans are involved. The simple identity that Revenue equals Sales Volume times Unit Price is a (very basic!) financial model, and could be used in any trading company. However, more realistically, it is the recognition that the financial structures which underlie decision-making in most organizations can be built up from sets of such simple identities that gives value to the financial modelling concept.

Most usually today financial models are computer-based because of the complexity and extent of the calculations involved in most worthwhile applications. Thus a representation of the logic of relevant accounting identities is first established within the computer, and can then be used repeatedly to investigate the outcomes of policy options as embodied by alternative input data sets. There is a wide variety of ways in which this interaction with the computer can be handled and it is the software in use which determines how 'friendly' or otherwise a particular implementation will be. The spectrum ranges from the simplicity of stand-alone microcomputer-based spreadsheet programs (essentially large two-dimensional sheets of columnar analysis 'paper') to the power of mainframe-based multi-dimensional modelling packages complete with sophisticated reporting facilities and linked on-line to corporate or other databases. In nearly all cases, however, today's systems are not the arcane province of computer buffs but are open to the non-specialist user: hence this text, an attempt to introduce the content and methodology of modern financial modelling practice to the general reader.

And so to the contributions which follow. These have been organized into a number of distinct sections each of which deals with a separate aspect of financial modelling activity. The sequence of sections is such as to lead from the more elementary expository material, through succeeding descriptive elements based on case applications, to more speculative and theoretical material in the final part. Within each chapter, detailed results and supporting materials have been relegated to appendices so that the central message in each case can show through clearly.

In Part One of the book, the fundamentals of financial modelling are described at some length, so that the concepts and terminology used in the cases which constitute the bulk of the remainder of the text may be made clear. Chapter 1 provides a context for this exposition by outlining a few of the features of modern financial management which have stimulated the development of modelling methods in the finance area. Some of the techniques which have evolved in recent years to cope with an increasingly complex managerial situation are also covered, and this should be helpful for those readers who are less familiar with modern finance methodologies. In Chapter 2 the basic concepts of financial modelling are presented using simple examples, and some specific modelling techniques are expounded. Additionally, the computerization of models is explained in a way which should aid readers who may be chary of computer-based approaches. The third chapter provides an overview of the historical development and future prospects for financial planning models, and provides the reader with a picture of current practice that forms an invaluable backdrop to the later case material. Finally in this section, Chapter 4 provides through the use of a classification of the various types of package on offer some guidance for the prospective buyer.

Part Two of the book is concerned with the practice of financial modelling and contains accounts of experiences in implementing modelling systems within a range of organizational settings. In many ways this material provides the key to successful modelling work since it is as often through the process of modelling as through the output of the models themselves that management gains those insights which represent the major spin-offs of the activity. This part begins with an intriguing and refreshingly honest account, in Chapter 5, of the succession of phases which financial modelling work has passed through in a major UK company. This is nicely complemented by the description given in the following chapter of the design and implementation of a planning model in a relatively young capital-intensive company in New Zealand. However, not all corporate planning exercises are as successful, and Chapter 7 provides some cautionary advice through the medium of a further case history, this time set in a medium-sized consumer goods manufacturer. The last contribution in this part approaches the same issues of implementation from a different direction by coupling an account of model-building in a finance house with some methodological guidelines for model development based on action research.

In some ways the core contributions in the book are those found in Part Three, since it is here that accounts are given of some typical applications of financial modelling methods. The first of these accounts, in Chapter 9, of budget modelling provides an ideal starting point, since it is precisely with such an application that many organizations begin their involvement with corporate models. The creation of budgetary or short-term planning models leads in many cases to the wish to look at the related issues of financial management and control from a fresh perspective. Hence, the coverage of a long-term planning model in Chapter 10 is, as can be learned from the narrative given there, a natural succession to the opening contribution. Chapter 11 is a case study of work carried out in the development of a suite of planning models using a specific modelling system. It is interesting to compare these first three contributions to this part of the book with each other, because of the three distinct perspectives on modelling which they provide: Chapter 9 is by a management accountant, Chapter 10 by an internal operational researcher and Chapter 11 by an external management consultant. The emphasis moves, in Chapter 12, from the more operational and tactical issues so far covered to those involved in strategic planning; in this chapter, a description is given of some models which are used for investment appraisal of proposals for corporate expansion in a major UK company. The final contribution in this part is also concerned with investment appraisal, but this time approaches it through the application of a simulation approach involving probability estimates to the evaluation of options for industrial development in a US public agency.

All of the contributions in Part Four are also based on practical applications of financial modelling, but they differ from those given in the previous part by presenting the work in the form of focused modelling frameworks, which the reader may well be able to adapt to problems in hand. For this reason, less detail of the actual models is provided than in the earlier studies. This part begins with the presentation in Chapter 14 of a comprehensive system for financial planning in health maintenance organizations, which gives not only a clear description of the contextual planning process, but also a good account of the use of sensitivity analysis on the model output. The contributions in Part Four are a deliberately diverse collection and so it is no accident that Chapter 15 shifts attention to a quite different area: that of determining in a marketing setting the product range to be offered for sale, by systematically examining the financial implications of alternative policies. Once again the stress changes in Chapter 16, which deals with one of the commonest problems facing small businesses; the management of cash flow. Models are presented to illustrate how some measure of control can be achieved. Chapter 17 concludes Part Four with an account of a menu-driven modelling system which has been developed to permit the effective management of asset/liability portfolios by financial institutions, though its general principles may be of use in other sectors.

The last part of this book is more openly speculative in nature and contains two contributions of a more academically developed character which lie at the interstices of financial theory, accountancy practice and developmental modelling. These are presented in the belief that they point the way forward to the more sophisticated modelling applications of the 1990s, when a closer partnership may be struck between accountancy theory and financial modelling practice, and when today's 'advanced' modelling concepts will be regarded as commonplace. In Chapter 18 the role of dividend growth as a strategic variable in an uncertain environment is stressed, and complemented by modelling examples, while in Chapter 19, the particular problems facing managers in multinational corporations are examined through a number of models concerned with investment and financing policies.

Overall, the intention has been to provide the reader with a structured introduction to financial modelling. It is to be hoped that this book transmits not only the principles and methods of the subject, but also gives an appreciation of the benefits of the approach and of its potential for effective management. If it also conveys some of the interest and excitement of working in the field, then that is no bad thing.

PART 1
FUNDAMENTALS

Financial Modelling in Corporate Management, 2nd Edition
Edited by J. W. Bryant

1

Corporate Financial Management

JAMES BRYANT

1.1 Corporate Financial Objectives

The subject of corporate objectives has attracted much attention in recent years as the importance of an organization's interactions with its environment and of the welfare of the individuals and groups of which it is composed have been more generally recognized. This has meant that the historical tendency to consider corporate objectives in purely monetary terms has been supplemented by the use of broader goals including measures of social welfare. One of the principal features of this change of emphasis has been a widening of the working definition of the boundaries of corporate responsibility. For example, in the opening of a new factory not only must its potential as a revenue-generating unit providing financial benefits for employees and shareholders be examined, but the impact it will have on the locality in which it is to be sited has also to be considered; this may include the physical effects of manufacturing processes on the natural environment, the economic effects of the additional wealth created on the local business community, and the social effects of migration and housing development on the character of a neighbourhood. This new perception of the role of corporate management brings with it more and conflicting demands on an organization's resources and new constraints on the deployment of those resources and so makes the process of management more complex.

Despite the broader view of corporate objectives now held in many organizations, the financial objectives of most continue to be stated implicitly if not explicitly in terms of relatively unsophisticated measures. The assertion, to be found with slight variants in most texts on financial management, that the purpose of financial control is to direct an organization towards such traditional targets as profit maximization has only recently been challenged. Indeed much of accounting methodology is concerned with the creation of conventions to provide unambiguous statements of corporate profitability. The cynical may argue that the provision of good working conditions, community benefits or efficient product servicing are simply means to the ultimate ends of organizational economic growth through the generation of profits, but this is too superficial and one-sided a view for the management of business enterprises in contemporary conditions. At the very least, recent worldwide economic instability and the accompanying inflationary tendencies have led to a shift in emphasis for many firms from profit to related metrics such as economic value, reflecting a greater concern for the long-term net benefits of financial policies for the ownership interests of the corporation. In other firms the narrowness of the shareholder benefit criterion of financial performance has been challenged by the 'stakeholder theory' of corporate objectives which reflects the responsibility, mentioned earlier, of an organization towards all those 'stakeholders' with which it significantly interacts; these include not only shareholders but also moneylenders, suppliers, debtors, customers, employees and the general public. This view leads to the alternative financial objective of maximizing net social consumption, where this is defined as the value of the total consumption that an organization makes possible less its own consumption. Social disbenefits resulting from an organization's activities have a negative effect on such a measure while other cash flows such as wages paid to employees have a positive effect. A broader measure of this sort has the advantage of embracing the system-wide effects of management decisions, but unfortunately the methodology and databases required for its use remain to be fully developed. Financial management today is therefore in the uneasy position of continuing to work with measures that are exact but which are recognized as being inadequate for corporate decision-making, while the new broader measures have still to be soundly defined and practically established.

1.2 Financial Aspects of Corporate Activity

Despite the uncertainties which have been stated about the choice of appropriate financial objectives, the management of corporate activity cannot be 'put on ice' until this issue has been resolved. How then do corporations operate to achieve their financial targets? Organizations function in financial terms by using long-term funds to support activities which will generate short-term gains. Financial management therefore involves the control of two interacting cash-flow cycles as illustrated in Figure 1.1. Cash is raised from capital markets and is invested in assets required for operations; these facilities are used for the production of goods and services and the products traded to provide a cash flow for future organizational growth as well as to repay market liabilities. The capital cash-flow cycle has an enabling function and involves interchanges between the organization, sources of funds such as moneylenders

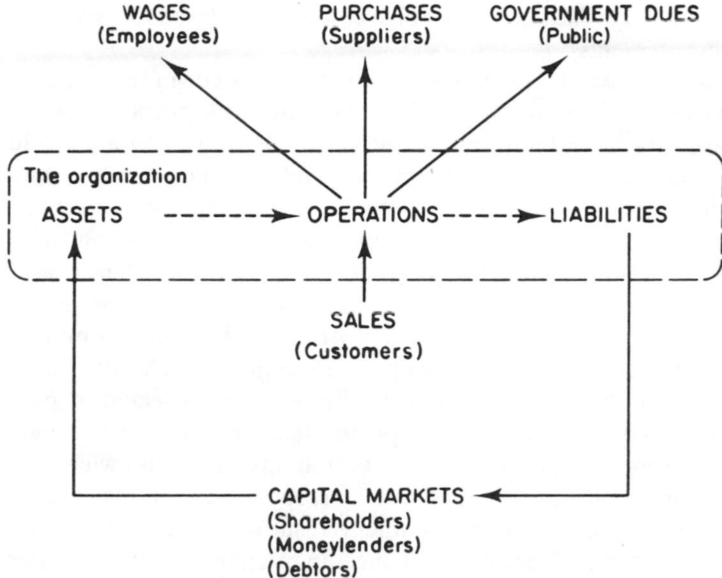

Figure 1.1 Organization cash-flow cycles

and shareholders, and investment opportunities such as debtors. The trading cash-flow cycle made possible by the capital base involves the organization in transmitting earnings from product sales to employees as wages, to suppliers for purchases and to the government for the provision of a wider economic infrastructure. The stakeholders referred to earlier have been explicitly indicated in these cycles which identify their roles.

Despite the strong interaction between the capital and trading cycles, these two aspects of financial management are conventionally held apart and may even be the responsibilities of two separate functional elements within the finance department of an organization. Thus a financial controller may be primarily concerned with the trading cash flows, while a corporate treasurer handles the financing of operations by dealing with external sources of capital. The central problem of purposeful financial management is the provision of integrated control for the two cash-flow cycles, in order to achieve overall corporate goals.

1.3 Financial Decision-making

The process of financial management involves the direction of a corporation towards its financial objectives but within the constraints imposed by other corporate aims. This process involves the taking of decisions which have financial implications for the organization. Decision-making can only properly be regarded as a cyclical process which can be considered to have a number of interacting elements.

Financial decision-making arises when events occur in the choice environment; these may be either internal or external to the corporation. Examples might be a change in bank rate or the compilation of monthly product sales statistics. Detection of such events depends crucially on the monitoring capabilities of the finance function which in turn depends on what features of the environment are regarded as important and on the availability of information relating to these features. Thus it is only in recent years that the energy budgets of organizations have received much attention as the cost of energy has become an increasingly important debit item. Incoming information is evaluated in accordance with a concept or model of the perceived situation. If a substantial mismatch with what is expected is present the information may either be rejected or supplementary evidence sought before the process proceeds further. If a substantial mismatch with what is desired is present then a problem has been formally recognized. This may occur because of a change in the choice environment resulting from earlier decisions or external forces; for example, a change in pricing policy or exchange-rate fluctuations may have had a harmful effect on sales. Alternatively the desired state may be modified because of changes in corporate objectives or perceptions: a target level of profitability might, for instance, no longer be regarded as adequate.

A variety of solutions to a problem is usually generated, although this may include a 'no-action' option. These solutions are attempts to reduce the mismatches detected and are most likely to involve changes in the perceived situation, although it is possible that the financial goals may be altered instead. For instance a corporation which discovers that it has inadequate funds to finance a new development may issue shares or debentures, raise loans or bank overdrafts or discontinue existing unprofitable activities; alternatively the new development plans may be modified or abandoned so that the funds are no longer required. Problems range from those which are repetitive and familiar to the novel and unique, and the effort involved in solution generation varies accordingly, possibly involving problem re-formulation in an iterative manner. Additionally, solutions may be suggested at a number of levels and the choice of an appropriate level may be at least as difficult as the selection of a particular solution at that level. Thus a high level of debtors in a particular market may be tackled by introducing a tighter debt-monitoring policy to pressure customers, by using a factor to handle debt-collection activities, or by moving out of that particular market; within each of these levels several options may exist.

The next stage in the decision-making process is the evaluative comparison of alternative solutions so that a selection can be made. This evaluation involves again the use of models which predict the outcomes of the options under consideration. Such models may be complex mathematical formulations or simple rules of thumb. Consider the example of anticipating dividend levels for property and mining shares over the next five years; this may interest a portfolio analyst. At one extreme detailed mathematical models relating dividend policies to macro- and micro-economic factors may be developed; at the other extreme it may be assumed that dividend levels in one sector would be double those in the other. Both of these predictive methods involve models, although the level of explanation offered is very different. Provided that a uniform set of measurement scales is available for comparison of the predicted outcomes and provided that a procedure for selection based on these scales can be arrived at, choice of a course of action is possible. Common measurement scales employed for investment appraisal include payback period and rate of return and the corresponding selection procedure is simply the choice of the option giving the minimum or maximum value respectively. However, selection of a solution is rarely such a straightforward matter, as a multiplicity of scales is normally involved in each assessment. Thus in addition to the criteria for capital budgeting suggested above, non-monetary considerations such as the creation of goodwill with a particular supplier may come into play. When a choice of solution has finally been made it is expressed in the form of an action-plan and implemented. The consequences of this choice are then subjected to the normal monitoring procedure so that further corrective action can be taken if necessary.

The decision-making process poses a variety of problems for financial management and some of these have been suggested above. Further difficulties are associated with the tradeoffs that have to be made between incommensurable variables in the evaluation of existing or proposed policies, the handling of uncertainty in projected outcomes and the presence of time lags in cash flows which can have a great impact on the levels of balances held. Constraints on the choice of solutions considered range from those imposed by legal or economic conditions, to those based on humanitarian or ethical grounds, or to others resulting from internal or external political wrangling. It is the handling of these and other features which forms the substantive subject matter of the practice of accountancy.

1.4 Management Accounting Activity

The process of financial management and control has greatly increased in complexity as the social and technological context in which organizations operate has become more dynamic. In many cases too the sheer size of organizations has posed new problems of internal control, and the development of management information systems has been of paramount importance in coming to terms with these difficulties. Nevertheless the basic concern of the finance function remains the monitoring and recording of financial transactions, the analysis and forecasting associated with financial decision-making and the management of cash flows on a continuing basis.

Financial accounting, the stewardship of a business involving the maintenance and interpretation of historical financial records, remains a major part of the accounting function. In recent years, the advent of computer-based book-keeping and auditing systems has released management time for the less mundane aspects of financial accounting. In particular, it has led to a concern with the principles of financial record maintenance rather than exclusively with the techniques involved. Thus, with the additional stimulus of world economic conditions, inflation accounting has been a topic of widespread interest involving the formulation of new conventions for financial reporting.

The developments in decision accounting have been no less marked. A range of analytical techniques has been developed and now forms part of the corpus of knowledge expected of the qualified practitioner. Advances in the general area of business forecasting as well as in the more specialized areas of operational research methodology have provided an input that is increasingly valued in financial analysis. In addition, new measurement concepts such as discounting procedures have lent precision to the comparison of alternatives. Largely because of these innovations, it has been possible to push planning horizons forward into the future in accordance with the contemporary need for adequate lead times for effective management decision-making.

The purpose of control accounting is the short-term guidance of an organization to achieve performance in line with planning targets. Here too there has been a twofold impetus given by advances in technology and methodology. The former has made it possible to obtain rapid feedback of information about the consequences of operating decisions and gives potential access to instantly updated databases reflecting the current financial situation at any time. The latter has introduced a number of new measures for performance monitoring in the form of control ratios ultimately derived from the science of cybernetics.

Overall, financial management is concerned with the provision and interpretation of information about business performance and with the use of financial projections to guide future actions. The methodologies used have developed rapidly in recent years and an even greater subtlety of representation is likely to be achieved in future as the more mechanistic aspects of accounting practice are taken over by electronic information-handling systems. A range of widely accepted techniques and methodologies has evolved to deal with the more common accounting problems, several of which have been mentioned above, and these will be considered in more detail in the remainder of this chapter. However, before this is done, it will be helpful to provide a context for the discussion.

At any time, a corporation may be characterized by a number of *state variables*. These variables are selected features which are considered to be of importance both in describing its current position and also in understanding its behaviour through time. Financial management is primarily concerned with

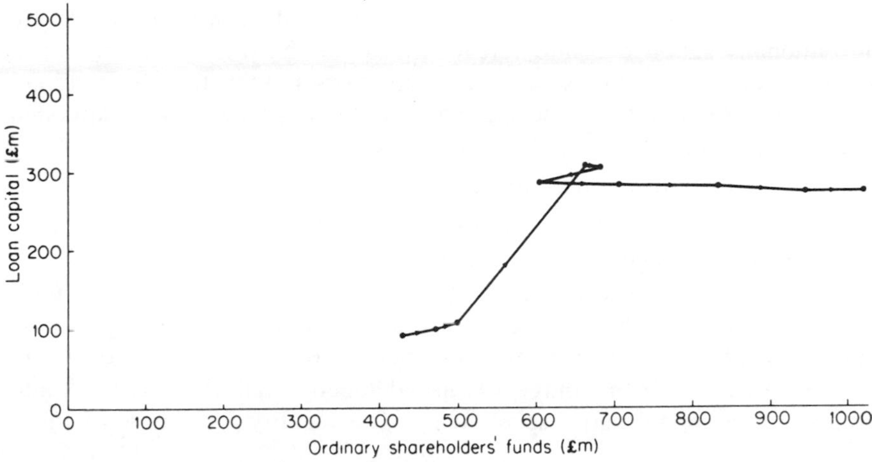

Figure 1.2 System trajectory for Imperial Group Ltd (1969–78)

state variables such as those that appear as balance-sheet items like asset valuations or bank overdrafts. Corporate activity changes the values of these variables with time. It follows that the financial development of an organization can be represented by a record of the changes in the values of its financial state variables. As an example, consider just two financial variables, loan capital and ordinary shareholders' funds. Then changes in the financial situation can be represented by the graph in Figure 1.2 which shows the values of these two state variables over a period of ten years for a major UK conglomerate. The path traced out by joining the points corresponding to successive annual values of the variables is called the *trajectory* of the corporation in the state space defined by the two chosen financial characteristics. In practice a large number of financial state variables would be considered, but the concept of a trajectory in a state space is one which can usefully be generalized to such cases even if a diagrammatic representation is no longer possible.

1.5 Financial Reports

Accounting reports, which summarize the activities of a corporation over a period of time and which provide statements of the financial situation at particular dates, are routinely used for management purposes, as well as being required by external agencies. The three most familiar, which will be discussed here, are the balance sheet, flow of funds statement and profit and loss account.

The balance sheet presents a 'snapshot' of a corporation at a given date and therefore corresponds to a single point on the corporate trajectory. This snapshot includes as variables the deployment of funds within a company and the amounts of those funds derived from different sources. The former are the assets of the organization, the latter are the liabilities and net worth. Assets are conventionally subdivided into categories such as fixed and current assets, stocks and debtors; liabilities into loans, creditors and taxation due; and net worth into share capital and reserves. Thus the balance sheet may be expressed concisely by the identity:

assets = liabilities + net worth.

Since all funds deployed must necessarily have been obtained from somewhere, the balance sheet inevitably balances.

Movement along the corporate trajectory is explained by the flow of funds statement which describes changes in balance-sheet items. Net changes in the application of funds, again normally subdivided into different asset groups, are balanced by changes in the sources of funds detailed as in the balance sheet into liability, share capital and reserve items. The identity for a flow of funds statement is:

Δ assets = Δ liabilities + Δ net worth

where Δ stands for 'net change (during a specified period) in' the term it precedes.

The profit and loss account is a more detailed report that explains changes in just one of the balance-sheet items, the retained profit, which forms part of the company's reserves. This account is therefore an expansion of part of the flow of funds statement, and describes changes over a period of time arising from profits or losses arising from corporate activity. The following identity explains this relationship:

Δ net worth = Δ share capital and capital reserves + Δ retained profit,

where

Δ retained profit = revenue − expenses − net interest − taxation − dividends.

These relationships between the three financial statements are illustrated in Figure 1.3.

The double-entry system which underlies conventional accounting practice ensures that all sources and applications of funds are separately recorded and thereby provides a sound basis for auditing. In this system, each transaction is recorded as a credit entry in the giving account and as a debit entry in the receiving account. Thus if an asset is acquired for cash, the cash account contains a credit entry of the amount paid while an asset account contains a debit entry of the same value. Double-entry methods also make possible the detailed analysis of the interests of the owners in a business and so facilitate evaluation of past policies.

It is principally because of the double-entry system that an historical cost convention has been adopted, and this has been found to have severe

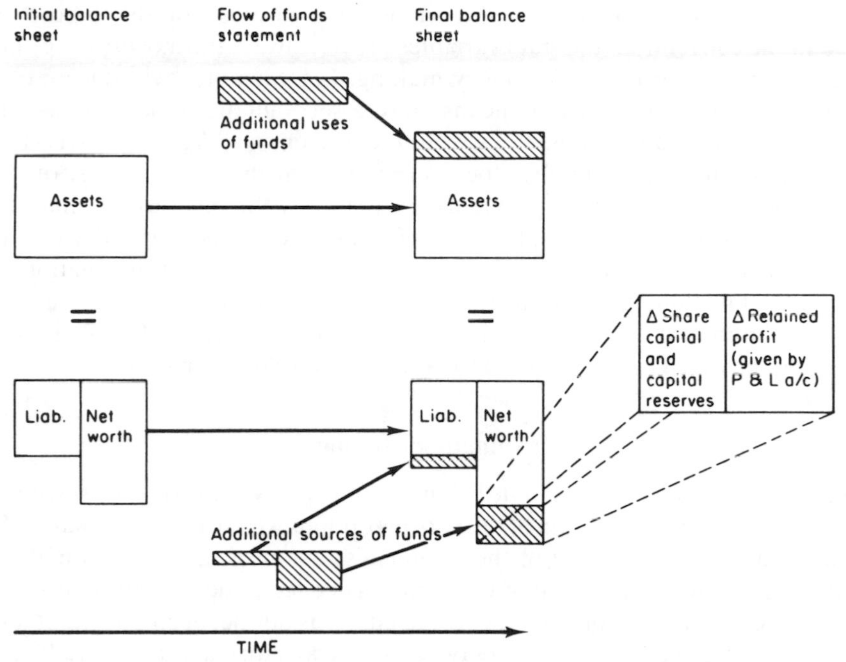

Figure 1.3 Financial statement relationships

deficiencies in times of high inflation. The recording of assets at acquisition cost and the application of depreciation to this figure means that adequate provision is not made for their replacement if inflationary tendencies have pushed up the cost of such replacements. Additionally, profits will be overstated on an historical cost basis if inflated revenues are matched against the corresponding expenses which generated them. That is, there will be a difference between the actual costs incurred on goods sold and the costs of replacing those goods at the time of sale. For these reasons, new conventions have recently been suggested which attempt to present a more helpful picture of the financial position of an organization than traditional reports can give.

Currently, inflation accounting information is presented in the form of reports which supplement rather than replace the historical accounts. Adjustments are made to depreciation and cost of sale figures to reflect current costs, and a proportion which reflects the ownership share of these adjustments is then deducted from the historically calculated profit to produce the profit figure under the current cost convention. The adjustments themselves are generally based on price indices, supplemented by other valuations as necessary.

Financial reports either express the position of an organization in a financial state space or the movement of the organization along its trajectory in this space during some period of time. However, because of the nature of accounting conventions the state variables are not always the most appropriate ones to be used as a basis for policy-making. For example, the concept of a business as a going concern means that asset valuations do not usually correspond to the amount that they would realize on sale. Again, conservative conventions are used whereby stocks are valued at the lower of cost or net realizable value. Additional problems are posed by the inclusion in financial reports of cash flows taking place in different time periods, and the way in which current and non-current items are handled, especially in relation to corporate taxation, presents further problems for analysis. These features make it important to expose with the utmost clarity the methodology and conventions which have been used to prepare financial statements.

1.6 Evaluating Alternatives

One of the central problems of decision-making in any context is the selection of a method for the evaluation of the various options which may be available. In general, as was pointed out in the earlier discussion of the decision-making cycle, a multiplicity of measurement scales is needed to define the state space used to assess each option. However, the choice is not between one point and another in this space but rather between one trajectory and another. If, for instance, a share issue is being contemplated, this does not only have implications for a corporation at the time when the issue is actually made, but by altering the capital structure it will affect the course of corporate development thereafter. In financial management it is therefore necessary to compare the paths taken through time under alternative policies in terms of selected financial variables.

Adequate quantitative techniques have not yet been devised in any area of decision-making to deal with the evaluative comparison of alternative state-space trajectories. In general, two procedures are applied to simplify the comparison process. One is to reduce the state space to a single dimension, commonly by working with a weighted combination of the various measures. To take a simple example, if broad policy issues are being considered, the total turnover of a product group may be considered rather than the sales volumes of individual product lines: turnover is in fact the sum of the sales volumes weighted by the product-line prices (i.e. Σ (price $\times$ volume) over all lines). The second procedure is to eliminate the time dimension by performing a weighted summation over successive points on the trajectory. Frequently, this summation takes the form of a discounting routine which systematically reduces the weight given to values more distant in the future. These two procedures may be carried out in either order, but if both are used they result in the options being reduced to single points on a scale from which a choice may be made directly.

The use of a single, composite financial measure to characterize alternative policies is common. For instance, projects involving an initial capital investment which generates revenue in later time periods can be described in terms of the cash outflows and inflows which are expected to take place. The use of measures of this sort is in principle straightforward, although there may be considerable scope for professional argument in estimating individual figures. However, such analyses are not intended to, and cannot, take account of aspects of a policy which cannot be expressed in monetary terms. While it may legitimately be argued that this is inevitable, as accounting is only concerned with events that can be measured in monetary terms, it can lead to an appraisal being conducted exclusively using these variables and ignoring other features which are more difficult to measure. The application of a more broadly based single measure along the lines of cost-benefit analysis is a possible solution to this difficulty.

Condensation of a set of figures on one or more financial variables measured through time, to a single point, commonly invokes the concept of the time value of money. This principle is a recognition of the fact that the basic monetary unit is not a homogeneous one; £1 today is not equivalent to £1 at some past or future date. This is because today's £1 could be invested to yield a larger sum in the future, and so its worth is not only its current face value but also the future flows which it can generate. Inflation reinforces this tendency, since £1 can be used to buy more today than £1 will do in the future. Conventionally, values n years in the future are translated into today's terms by dividing them by a discount factor,

$$(1 + r)^n,$$

where r is the discount rate used. Using discounting methods a project history can be represented by a single figure and thus easily compared with other options.

A number of criteria have been developed for financial appraisal of alternatives, mainly in the context of capital budgeting studies. To illustrate these criteria, consider a project which is expected to produce the cash flow pattern shown in Figure 1.4(a). After an initial outlay, the project generates a growing cash inflow which rises to a peak and then slowly declines up to the time horizon of the appraisal, A. This pattern may be discounted at some chosen rate to reflect the time value of money, and the corresponding discounted cash flow is also shown in the figure. The basic cash flow (CF) and discounted cash flow (DCF) patterns are not a convenient form for appraisal purposes, and it is usual to work instead with the cumulative cash flow (CCF) and cumulative discounted cash flow (CDCF) respectively. The graphs of these two series, illustrated in Figure 1.4(b), plot the total CCF and CDCF up to the corresponding point in time since the initiation of the project. The simplest and one of the most commonly used appraisal criteria, the payback period, defined

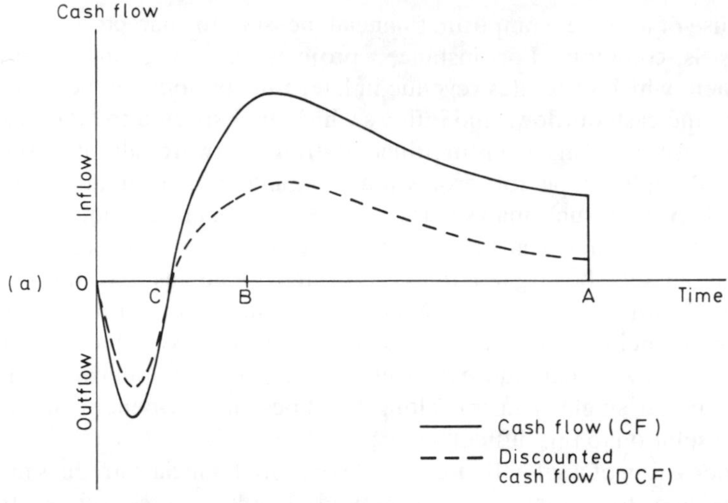

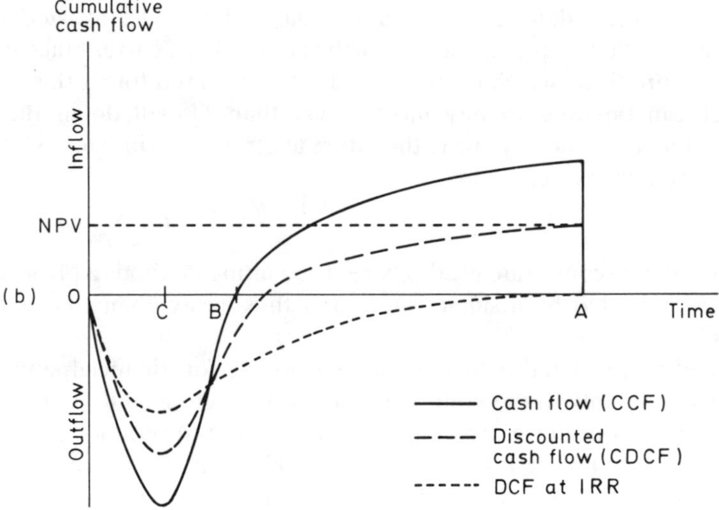

Figure 1.4 Discounted cash-flow concepts

as the time required for a project to generate sufficient cash inflows to cover the initial investment, is simply point B in Figure 1.4(b), since it corresponds to the time when the CCF reaches zero. Unfortunately payback period does not provide a measure of profitability, but rather indicates a project's liquidity: it also has the limitation that cash flows after time B are ignored. For these and other reasons the rate of return is frequently employed. Basically this is the average earnings from a project expressed as a fraction of the average capital employed. If, in the example, it is assumed that the initial cash outflow represents the capital investment in the project, then the rate of return corresponds to the ratio of the area under the cash-flow graph between C and A in Figure 1.4(a) (which is the total cash inflow from the project), to the area above the cash-flow graph between O and C (which is the capital investment in the project), and multiplied by $(2/T)$, where T is the life of the project, OA (to perform the necessary averaging). The rate of return ignores the timing of cash flows, a disadvantage which is overcome by the use of discounting methods. Straightforward application of a discount factor produces the net present value (NPV), defined as the present value of a project's net cash flows, discounted at a chosen rate, r, to the start of the project. This corresponds to the terminal value of the CDCF as illustrated in Figure 1.4(b). While there may be some difficulty in selecting an appropriate value of r to calculate the NPV, there is much to be said in favour of the calculation of an absolute monetary value as a measure of project worth. The alternative discounting criterion is the internal rate of return (IRR) defined as that rate, r, which will make the NPV of a project zero: the CDCF at the IRR is also shown in Figure 1.4(b). The IRR is probably the most widely used appraisal criterion today, and it certainly provides in a single figure a measure of profitability which takes account of the cash-flow pattern in time, but it can produce problems when more than one value of r makes the NPV zero. A further measure intended to overcome the shortcomings of other discounting methods is the profitability index, defined as the ratio of the present value of the cash inflows divided by the present value of the cash outflows. The abundance of assessment measures demonstrates the lack of agreement about the most critical features of investment alternatives. More generally it illustrates the difficulties of reducing a complex, dynamic, multidimensional situation to a single figure and the problems of interpretation that arise.

1.7 Monitoring Performance

The essence of management is control. Financial managers attempt to direct an organization towards its financial objectives. That is, they attempt to steer along a desirable corporate trajectory in their chosen state space towards some identified goal. More realistically, the goal is unlikely to be so precisely defined as to be a specific point in the state space. For instance, there will not be a unique combination of asset value, sales turnover and distributed profit that is considered satisfactory. Instead there will be certain regions that are regarded as being desirable and others that are regarded as being undesirable ones to enter. Taking profit margin as an example, where this is defined by the net profit as a proportion of sales, the undesirable region may be described by a target ratio below which the value should not fall. If there is also a minimum

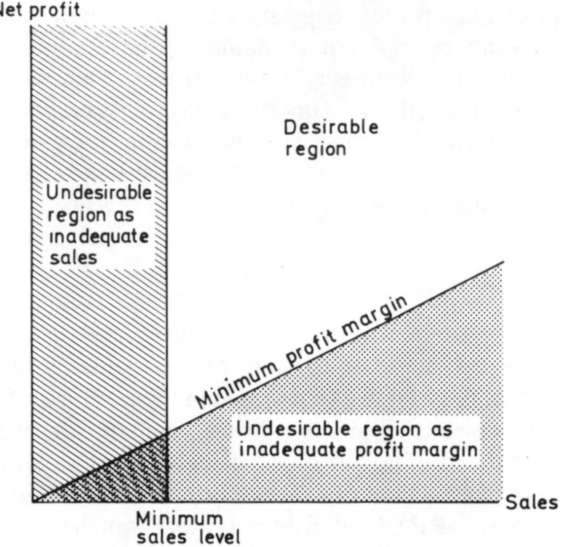

Figure 1.5 Financial objectives in a state space

level of sales turnover required, then the two regions in the relevant state space could appear as in Figure 1.5, where the unshaded area is considerable as desirable in terms of the two stated requirements; of course, much of this area may be unattainable in practice for other reasons. This concept of regions in a state space is realized in practice by two common accounting devices, budgets and control ratios.

Budgets are used mainly in short-term planning and specify a point in a financial state space which has been chosen through a comprehensive forward-planning exercise as representative of the desired target region. The variables used to define the state space are the expenditures and incomes anticipated under each of a large number of budget heads. Thus, based on assumptions about future economic and trading conditions, sales forecasts are made and from these the associated costs of production, selling and administration are found. Taken in conjunction with capital budgets relating to fixed assets, inventories, debtors and creditors, these are then used to obtain an overall cash flow budget which is usually expressed in standard financial report format.

The use of a budget as a control device is normally achieved by the analysis of the variances or divergences found between the actual and the budgeted figures under each budget head. Now each budget item is a monetary amount based upon two components: a quantity and a valuation. The quantity, often physically measurable, is the level of the variable measured and the valuation is an economic statement of the worth or cost of the variable being set at this level. For example, a budgeted labour cost is based upon a number of man-hours worked and an hourly wage rate; a budgeted sales revenue is based upon a sales volume and a unit price; and a budgeted overdraft charge is based upon an overdraft level and a bank interest rate. Variances for a budget item can stem from one or both of variances in quantity or value. Thus if a budgeted quantity, q, and value, v, are used to derive a budget item, $q.v$, and if individual variances of Δq and Δv occur for quantity and value respectively, then as the actual amount observed is,

$$(q + \Delta q)(v + \Delta v) = q.v + \Delta q.v + q.\Delta v + \Delta q.\Delta v$$

the divergence from the budgeted value is $(\Delta q.v + q.\Delta v + \Delta q.\Delta v)$. Conventionally the first term is called the quantity or volume variance and the remaining two terms are referred to as the value, price or cost variance depending on the context. Once variances have been calculated, it remains to determine if they are important and whether they indicate that control action should be taken. It would obviously be laborious to investigate the causes of every variance and so it is usual to employ a screening criterion to highlight the most significant items. This may take the simple form of a fixed percentage divergence from the budgeted value for any item. For instance, if an actual amount is ± 5 per cent from the budget amount it may be separated out for further study. Alternatively, more technically complex methods may be used based upon the use of statistical control charts. In this approach, the historical fluctuations of the variable concerned about its average level are used to define limits beyond which any variations should be investigated. A control chart to monitor a particular budget item could appear as in Figure 1.6, where the limits indicated are values that will be transgressed by chance on the percentage of occasions stated: that is there is only a 5 per cent or 1 in 20 chance of obtaining a value beyond the 95 per cent limits and this may suggest that any such instances should be investigated. Finally, it is necessary to determine what action, if any, should be taken as a result of any significant variances detected. Generally the variances themselves will suggest the nature of any remedial activity, but if they are due in large degree to changes in external circumstances beyond managerial control no action may be required except perhaps the preparation of a revised budget. This is a restatement of the methods of dealing with identified mismatches in the decision-making cycle described earlier in this chapter.

The discussion of budgets has suggested the use of variances or differences as control measures. However, there are some circumstances in which budget/actual ratios can be more powerful. Ratios have the advantage of being independent of the original units of measurement and this can be helpful for comparison purposes. Such comparisons can be extended beyond the scope of budgetary control to the assessment of wider financial structuring by the use of control ratios. These ratios, which are extensively used in long-term planning,

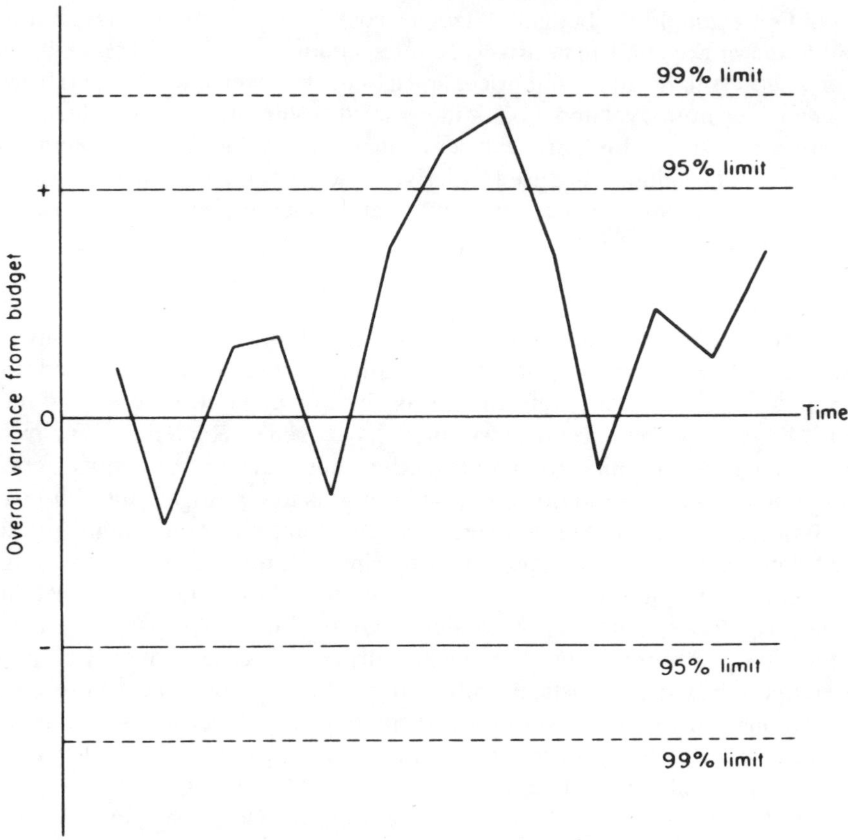

Figure 1.6 Variance control chart

trace the relationships between different financial variables rather than between intended and observed values of a single variable.

Various hierarchies of control ratios have been developed which may be used to explore different aspects of an organization's financial performance. However, the ratios that have been found of practical benefit are fewer in number than the multitude that have been advocated by theoretical texts, and fall into three main subject areas: profitability, managerial performance and solvency. The first group relates the profit achieved to the sales turnover and assets employed and also indicate the return obtained by shareholders. The second group measures aspects of management control including the outcome of credit and inventory policies and the cost-effectiveness of administrative activity. The final group of ratios indicates the short-term liquidity and the long-term solvency of an organization. Examples of some of these measures and their behaviour over a period of time are given in Table 1.1. Immediately

Table 1.1 Control ratios for Cadbury-Schweppes Ltd (1970–78)

Measure and control ratio		1970	1971	1972	1973	1974	1975	1976	1977	1978
Profitability										
Return on capital	$\frac{\text{Operating profit}}{\text{Assets employed}}$ (%)	13.2	15.2	16.8	15.5	15.0	15.1	15.1	15.1	15.2
Capital turnover	$\frac{\text{Sales}}{\text{Assets employed}}$	1.78	1.90	1.95	1.87	2.20	2.07	2.16	2.25	2.49
Profit margin	$\frac{\text{Operating profit}}{\text{Sales}}$ (%)	7.4	8.0	8.6	8.3	6.8	7.3	7.0	6.7	6.1
Managerial performance										
Credit policy	$\frac{\text{Sales}}{\text{Debtors}}$	5.08	5.48	5.17	5.24	6.10	7.10	6.16	6.81	7.40
Inventory policy	$\frac{\text{Sales}}{\text{Inventory}}$	4.00	4.51	5.11	5.40	4.19	4.74	4.62	4.49	5.26
Structural policy	$\frac{\text{Current assets}}{\text{Fixed assets}}$	1.14	1.12	1.36	1.02	1.19	1.28	1.42	1.60	1.54
Solvency										
Short-term	$\frac{\text{Current assets}}{\text{Current liabilities}}$	1.53	1.58	1.61	1.43	1.35	1.73	1.80	1.90	1.87
Gearing	$\frac{\text{Loan capital}}{\text{Ordinary share capital}}$	0.28	0.29	0.52	0.39	0.55	0.70	0.94	1.08	1.35

apparent for the figures given are the gradual decline in profit margin despite improved managerial performance, and a change towards a more highly geared structure brought about by attractive long-term loans. To emphasize the relationship between these ratios and the concept of the corporate financial trajectory it may be pointed out that the final ratio in Table 1.1 is equivalent to the slope of a line drawn from the origin to a point plotted in the coordinate system of Figure 1.2, which was also based upon loan and ordinary share capital. The actual tabulated figures thus correspond to a trajectory which would gradually curve upwards if graphically displayed in this manner. As in budgetary control, decisions about the nature of any action suggested by changes in the values of control ratios depends upon the threshold level of change considered as significant and upon the interpretation of reasons for movements in the state space.

Financial Modelling in Corporate Management, 2nd Edition
Edited by J. W. Bryant

2

Concepts and Techniques of Financial Modelling

JAMES BRYANT

2.1 Nature of Financial Modelling

The concept of a financial state space, which was introduced earlier, can be used to describe concisely the principal activities of management accounting. Briefly these are to identify where an organization is in the state space at any time, to record how it reached that point, to predict in which direction it will move under the various options available, and, when action has been taken, to monitor subsequent progress and to explain any divergencies from the forecasted path. That is, management accounting is concerned with the historical and possible future trajectories of an organization in a financial state space, as seen from the particular point on that trajectory corresponding to the present time.

The three main aspects of management accounting, financial accounting, decision accounting and control accounting, which have already been discussed, are intended to deal respectively with the past trajectory, the future trajectory and the monitoring of the present position in the state space. In principle the mechanics of these three functions is not difficult, and simply demands record-keeping procedures coupled with some kind of predictive capability. However, the practical requirements in an organization of even modest size are usually considerable, and it is only in recent years with the development of computerized accounting procedures that such functions as the keeping of ledgers, the preparation of invoices and the handling of the payroll have ceased to absorb an inordinate amount of company time. Such applications of the ability of computers to perform mundane repetitive tasks following simple rules have gained wide acceptance, but it has taken rather longer for activities involving more than basic record keeping to be dealt with in a similar way. It is, however, in such areas that computerized methods have the greatest potential benefit, since while it is of considerable value if invoices can be despatched swiftly or the manpower used to prepare wage slips can be reduced, it is likely to be of even greater long-term value if strategic or tactical decisions influencing future prospects can be better informed. This latter role is one which financial modelling methods are intended to fulfil.

The idea of a financial model can best be introduced by considering an example from one of the established areas of computer application mentioned above; the payroll. The net salary which an employee receives is based upon a gross figure which is adjusted downwards by various deductions and upwards by various allowances in any period. Considered from the employee's point of view the net salary is therefore related to the gross salary by the following identity:

$$\text{net salary} = \text{gross salary} - \text{deductions} + \text{allowances}.$$

This simple statement relates a number of financial variables to one another. It does this without reference to any specific numerical values which net salary, gross salary and the other variables may take, but expresses the general structure of the relationship between these four elements. Thus, given particular figures for the gross salary, deductions and allowances, the net salary could be calculated according to the rule which the identity above provides. A statement of this sort which embodies the relationship between financial variables may be called a financial model.

In practice, of course, the relationships between financial variables of interest to management, and indeed even those of interest to people as individuals, are usually far more complex than those given in the last example. The example itself is a gross simplification, since several highly aggregated variables have been included. For instance, the deductions from salary probably comprise income tax, health insurance and pension fund contributions. In turn, the tax figure involves all the intricacies of current government revenue regulations in its calculation. Now these further details could also be expressed in the form of identities. A model which explains the calculation of deductions might therefore appear as follows:

$$\text{deductions} = \text{income tax} + \text{health insurance} + \text{pension contribution}.$$

It would obviously be possible to continue in this manner, setting down further equations which described the calculation of the variables on the right-hand side of this equation from other more fundamental variables. Thus the deduction for pension contributions might be simply a percentage of the gross salary. However, it can become rather difficult to handle a set of interrelated models or equations of this type when the level of detail increases. This is where the use of a computer which can be programmed to hold such sets of relationships in its memory is advisable.

Essentially, computers are machines in which sets of instructions can be stored and used to manipulate incoming information to produce an output information stream. The means by which this is achieved, involving as it does the alteration of the electrical state of component parts, is of little concern to most users, and these so-called hardware aspects will not be discussed here. On the other hand, it is helpful to have some appreciation of the nature of software, the conceptual as opposed to the physical means by which information manipulations are carried out.

Most computers are built as general-purpose machines without any particular application in mind. That is, they simply have the general ability to manipulate data in accordance with a set of instructions, but specific instructions to be used are not present. The general ability is provided by the hardware through appropriate electronic circuit design, while the sets of instructions have to be provided by the user as software whenever the machine is employed. The software is in the form of computer programs; sets of instructions written in a highly stylized form which are simultaneously intelligible to user and computer. The stylized nature of these programs, which are written in languages having their own strictly defined grammar, is necessry because computers can in fact only carry out a very limited range of operations and the user's intentions have to be translated unambiguously and rapidly into an appropriate form for these operations to be executed. Once a program has been provided, a computer can then be used to carry out the manipulations which the program dictates, on any data which the user may care to input, and to produce the results of these calculations as an output stream.

How might a simple financial model be handled by computer? Reverting to the salary calculation example above, it is apparent that the first equation given constitutes an instruction for the calculation of the net salary from the other variables. If suitable translation facilities are available within a computer for this equation as it stands to be acceptable as a valid set of instructions, then it would suffice as a computer program to carry out the desired calculation. All that would then remain would be to inform the computer of the values taken on any particular occasion by the variables gross salary, deductions, and allowances, and to request it to output the calculated value of the net salary. If the more detailed version of the example, in which the deductions are split down into three components, is considered, then the program comprises the two equations given, and input values are now required for the following variables: gross salary, income tax, health insurance, pension contributions and allowances. Very crudely, this is the basis of computerized financial modelling.

Practical financial models are not necessarily confined, as is the example chosen above, to variables relating to a single time period. Frequently the values of a financial variable in one period are related to the values of other variables in later periods. For instance, credit-card purchases made by an individual in one month may be invoiced in the next and any balance remaining unpaid at the end of that period will be charged with interest. In general such inter-period transfers occur with any variables where a balance is passed on from one period to the next.

Even if models are being handled by computer, they still have to be constructed or defined by the user first, and it is helpful here to have a form of representation that is more immediately comprehensible than a vast set of identities. The most commonly used representation, and one which is visually appealing, is the so-called operations tree diagram. In such a diagram the arithmetic relationships between financial variables are expressed by symbols used in conjunction with a tree-like structure which links the individual variables. The idea of an operations tree is best illustrated by example, and so Figure 2.1 gives the tree corresponding to the salary example which has been discussed in this section. The compact form of the representation makes it ideal for handling large models and it is also useful as a device for communicating models to new users. Some conventions which may be used in drawing up diagrams are given in Table 2.1.

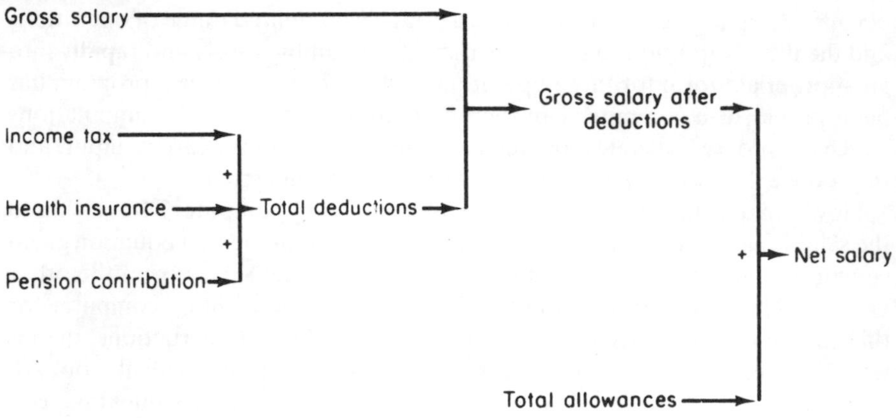

Figure 2.1 Simple financial model: the salary example

It is useful to have a means of representing the broad structure of very large operations tree diagrams. For this purpose a flow diagram can be used which illustrates the relationship between sub-models or modules, each of which contains a large number of calculations and each of which corresponds to a section of the overall operations tree. An example of such a flow diagram which illustrates a planning model is given in Figure 2.2. Thus, for instance, one sub-model in the flow diagram is concerned with the calculation of interest charges from details of debt capital and interest rates. In such diagrams, arrows represent the flow of information from one module to another without specifically indicating any algebraic relationships involved.

Table 2.1 Basic operations tree conventions

Operations tree	Equivalent identity
Arithmetic 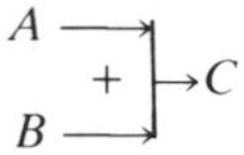 $A \rightarrow$ / $+$ $\rightarrow C$ / $B \rightarrow$	$C = A + B$ Also equivalent forms for subtraction (−), multiplication (*) and division (÷)
Inverse operation 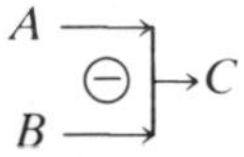 $A \rightarrow$ / $\ominus$ $\rightarrow C$ / $B \rightarrow$	$C = B - A$ (i.e. variables are read upwards) Also equivalent form for division (⊖)
Constant term $A \rightarrow$ / $+$ 2^{*} $\rightarrow C$ / $B \rightarrow$ 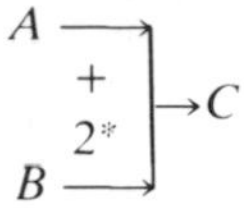	$C = A + (2^{*}B)$ Also equivalent forms for other arithmetic operations
Time shift 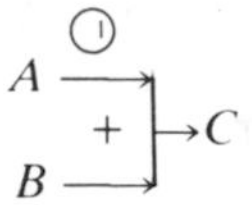 (1) $A \rightarrow$ / $+$ $\rightarrow C$ / $B \rightarrow$	$C_t = A_{t-1} + B_t$ Also equivalent forms for positive time shifts
Summation 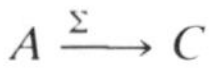 $A \xrightarrow{\Sigma} C$	$C = \sum_i A_i$ (i.e. summation over all A_i) $\sum_t$ denotes summation over time periods
Change 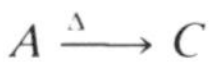 $A \xrightarrow{\Delta} C$	$C = A_t - A_{t-1}$ (i.e. change in A between times t and $t - 1$)
Discounting 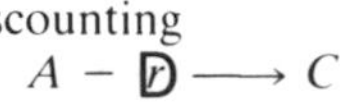 $A - \boxed{r} \longrightarrow C$	$C_t = \dfrac{A_{t+t'}}{(1 + r)^{t'}}$ (i.e. A discounted at rate r to time t)

2.2 From Basics to Practice

Financial modelling is conceptually a very simple process. However, the fundamentals discussed above have been elaborated upon in practical studies so as to provide models that more faithfully reflect financial structures, and which are more flexible and efficient in use than would otherwise be the case.

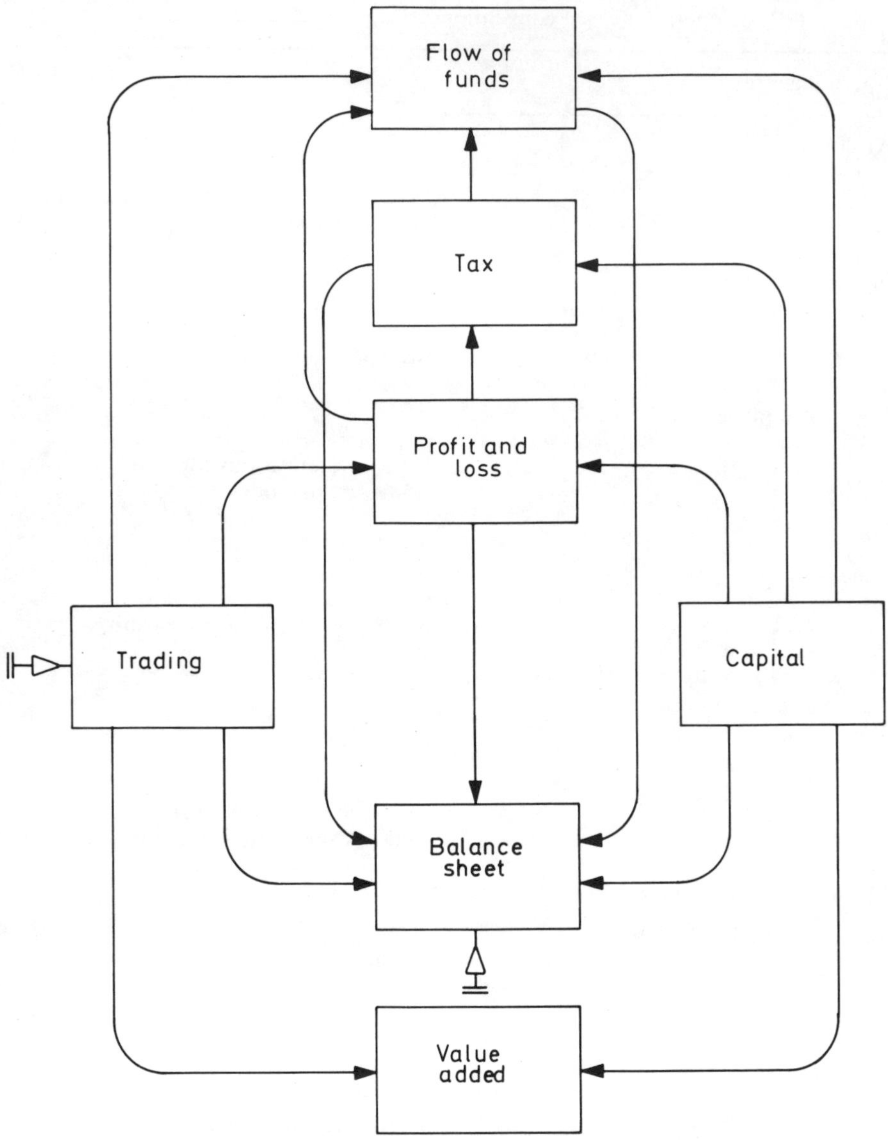

Figure 2.2 Planning model: module interrelations

Some of these elaborations relate to the structuring of models while others relate to their content, and these two areas will now be considered in turn.

Two aspects of model structure can be identified which will be termed here microstructure and macrostructure. The former refers to the nature of the relationship between financial variables and is depicted by the operations tree:

the latter refers to the relationships between modules and is depicted by the flow diagram. To a large extent it is possible to discuss developments of these two aspects independently, despite their obvious interrelationship.

The operations tree diagram was introduced as an attractive way of showing the form of what are essentially arithmetic relationships between financial variables. These range from simple addition and subtraction to the use of discount factors. However, quite commonly there are also logical relationships between variables. For example, dividend restraint regulations may limit the increase paid over a previous year's level. Other logical functions may involve the use of conditional statements; for instance, if cash balances fall below a certain level, then new loans may be raised. Such logical statements can often be attached as appropriate to an operations tree diagram.

The other aspect of microstructure which needs to be further examined is concerned with the evaluation of variables in an operations tree. In the examples given so far the process of evaluation is straightforwardly a matter of moving progressively through a tree from the 'roots' to the 'trunk' calculating successive variables. However, there are many instances where this is not possible. Taking the simple salary example of Figure 2.1, how can the calculation be carried out if pension contributions are not as suggested earlier a proportion of gross salary, but instead a proportion of net salary? This would mean that net salary would have to be found for the pension contribution to be calculated, but that the former could not be evaluated until the latter was known. The solution to this apparent impasse lies in the simultaneous evaluation of both variables, which can be carried out by trial-and-error methods or, more rigorously, by the use of mathematical techniques to solve the implied set of simultaneous equations. This form of interdependence between variables is called recursion and is commonly found in the finance sector, for instance in the relationship between the demand for loans and loan interest rates. The presence of recursive relationships is apparent from an operations tree diagram, as completed loops will be observed.

Turning next to the macrostructure of models, elaborations here are concerned mainly with the efficient functioning of a model, rather than with any features that are mandatory for logical reasons. It may be useful to be able to recalculate or modify portions of a model while leaving the remainder as it is. These portions may correspond to the modules identified in a flow diagram, or they may be at an even higher level of aggregation. Thus, if the method of calculation of depreciation in Figure 2.2 were to be altered, it would be desirable not to recalculate those parts of the flow diagram which are unaffected by the change. This intention can be achieved by the division of the model into self-contained elements. Such modularization of a model is largely dependent on the software available, an aspect of modelling that will be discussed in later sections of this chapter.

The content of the models which have so far been present is of the simplest kind, being both deterministic and non-optimizing in character. By deterministic is meant that they have the property that all the variables included are precisely specified by a single value. In practice, input variables in particular may only be available in the form of uncertain estimates, and it is important that this uncertainty is preserved in the calculation of any later dependent variables. The use of probabilistic estimates of this kind is the subject of risk analysis, a technique which is expounded further in a later section, where the concept of optimization is also outlined. Briefly, optimization is an essential feature of financial modelling when the achievement of predetermined targets, possibly within constraints on the values of certain variables, is required. This may, for instance, be found in models where a specified rate of dividend growth is sought within a context which restricts the capital structure of an organization. By the inclusion of probabilistic values a model becomes non-deterministic (or stochastic), while the provision of target-seeking capabilities makes it an optimizing model. Either or both of these extensions of the basic model content described before may be needed in an application. However, as a footnote it may be added that currently the majority of practical models still do not incorporate these extensions.

2.3 Numerical Data in Modelling

Financial models describe the relationships between financial variables, so that the changing values through time of these variables can be traced. A model only represents the structure of financial relationships and to 'bring it to life' it must be supplied with numerical values, in much the same way that a geographical map needs a scale if it is to be used to measure real distances. These input values determine the usefulness of a model since the old computing maxim 'garbage in–garbage out' obviously applies.

Depending on the structure of a model, input numerical values may have to be supplied for the whole period of the time path of interest, or they may only be required initially to give the starting position of the financial trajectory. The former type of model can be termed the open-loop type since the output values do not influence the inputs, which may be estimated externally to the model before it is used. Consider as an illustration the model in Figure 2.3(a) which calculates the trading profit on a product for successive time periods. As it stands this is of the open-loop type with values of such variables as unit price, advertising and unit costs being provided as management estimates for each period. By contrast a closed-loop model requires variable values only for initialization purposes. Thus in the example, the unit price might for instance be found as a fixed proportional increase on the corresponding figure for the previous time period, as shown in Figure 2.3(b), so that once the value for the first period has been stated, the others follow directly. In more complex

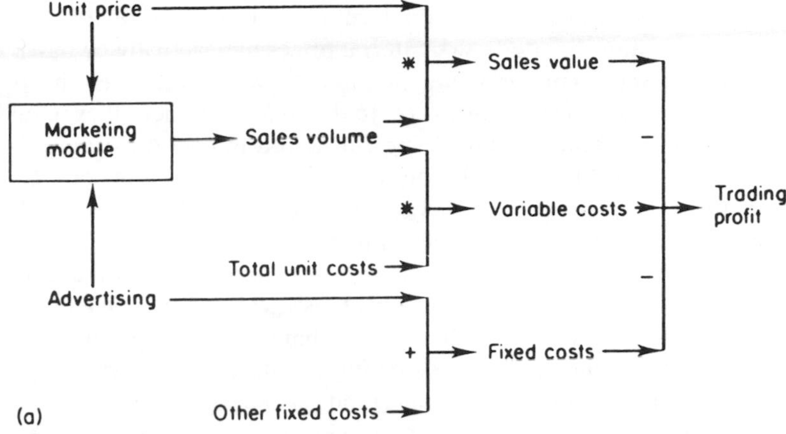

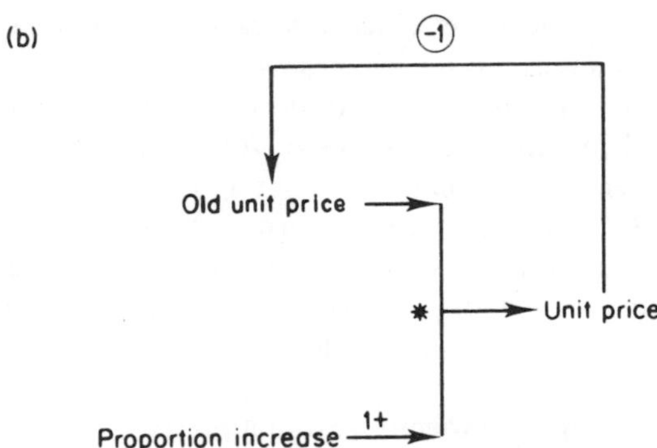

Figure 2.3 Simplified trading profit model

closed-loop models the value of a variable in one period may depend on the values of a number of variables in earlier periods. Using the same illustration again, the unit price might then be modelled as dependent on not only previous prices but also on the level of sales achieved or profits made in earlier periods. These three types of model, open-loop, single-variable closed-loop, and many-variable closed-loop, require different approaches when numerical values are introduced and these will be dealt with in turn below.

Any procedure used to provide predetermined data values for input to an open-loop type of financial model can be described verbally, even if this description consists of no more than stating that values are random guesses made by the company finance director. On closer inspection it is usually found that such subjective estimates for a variable in successive time periods are not independent values, but that some rough rule is being used to relate the values to each other. Thus estimated raw-material prices may actually be based on a notion that a fixed compound rate of increase will occur over the period concerned. If such calculations were to be made explicit they could be incorporated in the model itself, being calculated in each time period from previous values, and the model would then be a closed-loop one for this variable. Open-loop structure is therefore associated with those variables for which no such relationships are made explicit. In particular it is associated with those input data values derived from external sources where the estimates given are trusted, but where the quantitative justification for them is not known or is irrelevant to the purposes of the model in hand. An example of this kind of data might be government estimates for future interest rates, which could be used as direct model input. Direct data input also occurs importantly when a model is being used interactively by a decision-maker who wishes to explore the effects of alternative future values of a particular variable. In this case values tested relate to some hypothesized future scenario and need have no further formalized justification. However, in a sense this is really a closed-loop example, with the user closing the loop, since interactive use implies that output values influence the values of input variables tested later.

Turning next to models with an implicit closed-loop form, a wide range of techniques can be employed to generate a series of forecasted values for a particular variable. These techniques may, as suggested above, either be incorporated in the model itself, or else be used externally to provide an input data sequence for the variables concerned. However, the range of methods which can be used within a model is naturally restricted by the facilities of the modelling system being used, and so external calculation may sometimes be unavoidable.

The simple forecasting technique, subjective estimation, has already been mentioned. Management may postulate, for example, a fixed linear growth rate for a variable on the basis of past experience and expert knowledge of future trading conditions. If y_t represents the value of the variable to be forecasted at period t, then this can be formalized as the model,

$$y_t = y_0 + at,$$

where y_0 is the initial value of the variable and a is the growth expected in each period. A second example is provided by the compound growth of the price model of Figure 2.3(b), where if y_t now represents the price at time t and a is the proportional increase each period,

$$y_t = y_0(1 + a)^t$$

or equivalently,

$$y_t = y_{t-1}(1 + a).$$

The latter expression is in a so-called recursive form, each value in the series being related to the corresponding value for the previous period. What is subjective about the method of forecasting being discussed is the estimation of the growth rates, a, in the above models. However, there exist more sophisticated techniques for estimating such model parameters.

Statistical methods can be used to find model parameters which provide a 'best fit' to historical data for a variable. These same parameter values are assumed to hold good in the future and so the models can be used to make forecasts for any coming period. Obviously trial and error methods could be used to find suitable parameter values for a specific model, but statistical results produce immediately the best-fit values and so are preferable. The range of models which can be treated in this way extends far beyond the simple examples given so far, to those incorporating powers of the forecasted variable such as the quadratic model,

$$y_t = y_0 + at + bt^2,$$

and others incorporating decay factors such as the sigmoid form,

$$y_t = \frac{a}{1 + be^{-ct}}$$

where a, b, and c are all parameters to be estimated. This curve-fitting approach as outlined assumes that a suitable model can be found and that the series of values is likely to continue to follow a well-behaved mathematical function. Consideration of many series encountered in practice shows that such behaviour is exceptional.

An alternative type of forecasting model formulation is provided by the range of time series smoothing techniques. These consist of a variety of models which relate, using functional forms of varying complexity, the value of a variable to earlier values on the assumption that an underlying pattern exists and will persist into the future. Linear weighting models are the simplest in this class of techniques and are typified by the relationship,

$$y_t = \sum_{i=1}^{T} w_i y_{t-i},$$

where the w_i are parameters which given different weights to the T historical data values considered relevant to the forecast for period t. If these weights are all identical, then a moving average is effectively being calculated, while a commonly used model in which the weights are related to each other in a geometric manner is termed exponential smoothing. More complex models must be used if a series exhibits any trend or cyclical fluctuations over time but the principle remains the same. The weights to be used, which are the parameters of this type of model, are again calculated to provide the best fit to a set of historical data.

A possible objection to the models so far presented is that they incorporate fixed parameter values and so are inflexible in their behaviour over time. Adaptive forecasting models surmount this limitation by incorporating parameter values which alter as a data series develops. For instance, the method called adaptive filtering uses a linear weighting model as described above, but systematically recalculates the w_i after each new forecasted value is found in the light of any discrepancies from the actual values recorded. The subsidiary model for recalculating the w_i is fitted from historical data and can then be used for predictive purposes. This self-correcting feature enables adaptive models to perform well in tracking data values and in generating future estimates.

One of the inevitable problems of statistical forecasting concerns the choice of a good model to use. This choice has to be made by examining the ability of the alternatives to fit historical data and also by considering the plausibility of the models' form. The fit is usually measured by summing either the absolute or the squared values of the discrepancies between the actual values and those produced by the model over the period for which historical figures are available. A best-fit model can then be found by trying a variety of forms. As an alternative to this rather haphazard approach, so-called Box–Jenkins methods provide a structured rationale for selecting a suitable model from a large family of generalized formulations. The question of plausibility is a largely subjective one but, for instance, it would be nonsensical to adopt a model incorporating long-term exponential sales growth in a market where a limit on potential sales was considered to exist.

Many-variable models take the discussion into the arena of explanatory or causal modelling. In the present context these are usually econometric in character, relating the values of economic variables to each other through mathematical functions. Such models attempt to explain changes in one variable in terms of changes in variables that are believed to have contributed to those changes. The structuring of explanatory models requires an intimate knowledge of the processes being described, but can give far more satisfactory results than the consideration of an isolated time series. The financial model of Figure 2.3(a) needs a causal model in the box labelled 'marketing module', which predicts sales from the unit price and level of advertising used. This model may be of the simple linear form:

$$s_t = a_0 + a_1 p_t + a_2 A_t$$

where the sales in period t, s_t, is related to the price p_t, and advertising expenditure, A_t, using three constant parameters a_0, a_1 and a_2: a_1 is probably negative, the others positive. Values for the parameters could be estimated as usual by finding a good fit to historical data. Such a crude model would probably be a poor predictor of sales and in practice non-linear functions recognizing the possibility of saturation advertising, of consumer's memory of past advertising, and of varying demand elasticities, might be required.

Attractive as the prospect is of developing detailed models that really explain changes in the value of a variable some notes of caution must be made. Firstly, the presence of an apparent association between variables does not imply any causal link. For instance, sales may be related to advertising not because the latter causes the former but because advertising budgets may be set on the basis of earlier sales, thus giving rise to a self-perpetuating relationship. Secondly, it is easy to allow enthusiasm in model-building to get out of control, thereby creating enormously complicated structures. The purpose of modelling must continually be borne in mind and models based on a principle of parsimony, new explanatory variables being added only if they provide better explanatory power. Finally, caution must be exercised if predicted values lie at or near the extreme historical data values used to fit the model parameters. In explanatory modelling, as indeed in any of the other approaches mentioned above, it is useful to provide a quantitative measure of the uncertainty associated with any predicted values. This is a point that will be taken up in some detail later.

It is apparent that a wide range of forecasting techniques is available and this range can bewilder the intending modeller. The choice of approach depends on the nature of the forecast required. Key features to be considered in providing forecasts for financial models are the time horizon, level of detail, desired accuracy and ease of calculation. For example, curve-fitting methods are seldom appropriate for long-term forecasting, for which explanatory models are likely to be more successful. There is often a trade-off to be made between accuracy and detail in calculation, and the uncertainty associated with data input to the forecasting procedure chosen may render complex modelling irrelevant. Perhaps the most important feature of any technique of forecasting is that the user has confidence in it; without this, the predictions of the financial model with which it is employed will always be regarded with scepticism.

2.4 Advanced Modelling Techniques

Risk Analysis

The fact that models need not be deterministic was mentioned in an earlier section when the content of models was being discussed. It seems eminently sensible to recognize that the future is uncertain by building stochastic models. However, the incorporation of uncertainty can be positively misleading if care is not taken in model formulation, and so this sub-section aims not only to outline the principles of risk analysis but also to point out the hazards that await the unwary modeller.

Predictions of the values of any financial variables will normally be uncertain, and this uncertainty can conveniently and conventionally be represented using a probability density function. Such a function is illustrated in Figure 2.4(a) and indicates the uncertainty associated with an estimate of

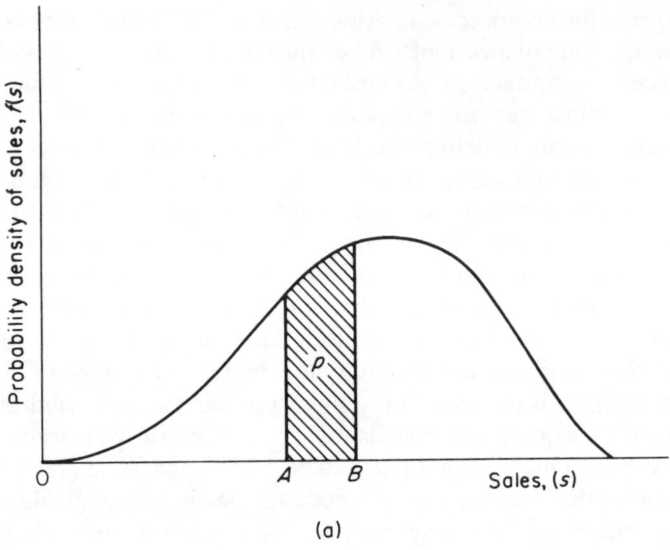

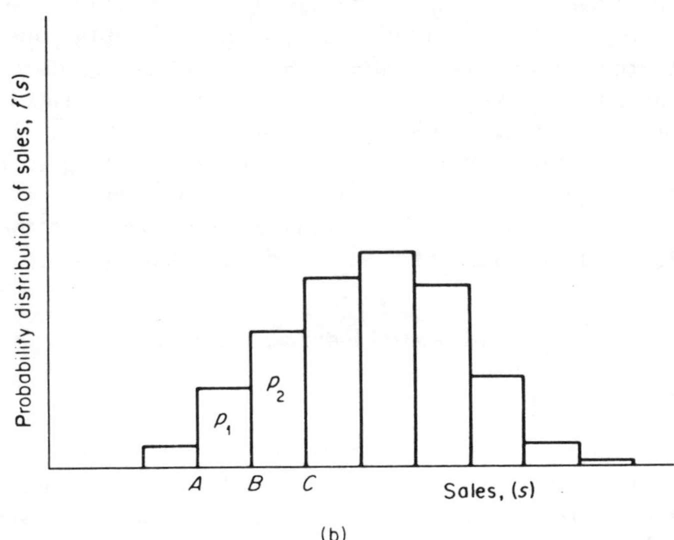

Figure 2.4 Examples of: (a) probability density function; (b) probability distribution

the sales of some product during a specified period of time. The probability of the sales level falling within a given range of values is indicated by the area under the curve between the corresponding points on the horizontal sales axis. Thus the hatched area is the probability of achieving sales between A and B in amount. This probability, p, is a number between zero and one (the total area under the curve is unity), and can be thought of as the proportion of times in a large number of realizations that values between A and B would occur. Alternatively or additionally it can be thought of as indicating the strength of belief an assessor has of obtaining values in this range, given that zero on the probability scale represents impossibility and one represents certainty. A probability density function can be specified for a variable by stating its functional form and the values of its parameters. For instance, the familiar bell-shaped curve of the Normal distribution may often be considered appropriate to represent the uncertainty in financial variables. If it is chosen, then the precise form is given by stating its two parameters, the mean and variance, which respectively indicate the average level of the variable and its spread about this average value. The large range of statistical distribution models available can represent almost any desired form of probability function.

Values of financial variables following standard distribution models will usually be produced by the more formal forecasting techniques discussed earlier. Thus causal regression models will probably generate a series of forecasted values each of which is taken as the mean of a Normal distribution whose variance is also given. However, the more subjective methods of producing forecasts are likely to express uncertainty in a less mathematical manner as a so-called probability distribution. Here, rather than the variable concerned being regarded as continuously variable, ranges are considered and estimates are then attached to these ranges which indicate the probability of occurrence of the corresponding values. Figure 2.4(b) gives an illustration of a probability distribution: here p_1 is the probability of sales falling between A and B, p_2 of their lying between B and C. Estimates which can be depicted as probability distributions can be elicited from managerial decision-makers provided that it is made quite clear what the probabilities represent. Difficulties in understanding the concept of probabilities in this connection and of interpreting the distributions are the main reasons why the risk analysis approach has not been more successful or more widely used.

Uncertainty, however it is expressed in the data input to a financial model, is transmitted through the model structure to the other variables. If a single uncertain variable were involved in a model while all the other variables could be specified exactly, then it would be quite easy to calculate the effect of the uncertainty at any subsequent stage of calculation. For instance, uncertainty in the 'other fixed costs' variable of the model in Figure 2.3(a) gives rise to the same level of uncertainty in the trading profit figure to which it is related by simple arithmetic. If, however, a number of variables are uncertain, then the evaluation of later variables becomes very difficult. Figure 2.5 gives a slightly simplified version of the previous model in which not only fixed costs but also sales volume and unit costs are expressed in probabilistic terms as shown by the

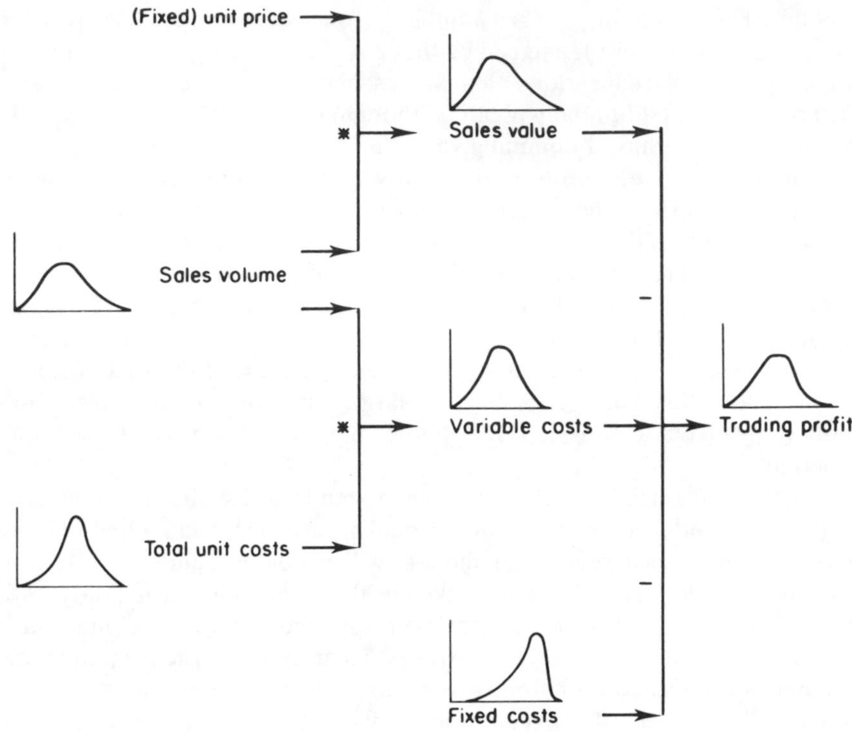

Figure 2.5 Trading profit model with uncertainty

corresponding distributions. Sales value will have a distribution identical with that of sales volume, since the former is simply the latter multiplied by the constant unit price. By contrast, the distribution of variable costs is complex as both sales volume and unit costs are uncertain. The complications which develop in more extensive models can easily be appreciated.

How can the distributions of variables which are dependent on uncertain input values be found? It is theoretically possible to use advanced statistical methods to derive the distribution of a variable which is a simple arithmetic function of two or more other variables whose distributions are known. However, in any but the simplest examples this is a very difficult procedure, and so a quite different approach using so-called Monte Carlo methods is invariably used. This approach can best be understood by remembering that one interpretation of probability density functions or distributions is that they indicate the proportion of times that an event will occur in a large number of repetitions of the variable concerned. That is, if it were possible to run repeatedly through the single time period, whose sales volume distribution is as shown in Figure 2.5, then this distribution would be built up from the frequency of occurrence of different sales volumes observed. Conversely, the distribution can be used to mimic or simulate the possible sales volumes that would occur in repeated realizations of a time period. A simulation of this sort uses a structured procedure to select random values from the distribution, and as the selection is purely random, over a large number of such selections the distribution of occurrence of the different values corresponds to the distribution from which this random sample of values is being taken.

This process of random selection can be carried out for each input variable in a model and for each set of variable values on a particular realization the values of dependent variables can be found. Thus a randomly selected sales volume and a randomly selected unit cost from the respective distributions could be used to calculate a sales value and variable costs value for the model in Figure 2.5. Taken with a fixed-cost figure also selected by a similar randomizing method, these will yield a trading-profit value for this particular realization or run of the model. Repetition of this process gives different sales volume, unit cost and fixed-cost figures from the input distributions and a different trading-profit figure. In a large number of such repetitions, the full spread and shape of the input distributions is represented and a distribution is also generated for the calculated variables; sales value, variable costs and trading profit. In this way distributions can be found for any variables output from a financial model.

The method of simulation which has been described so far could produce results that are seriously in error. This is because it has been assumed that the selection of random values for different input variables is carried out quite independently. In practice, variables are likely to be strongly interrelated. Thus in the model of Figure 2.5, there may be a relationship between sales volume and costs, since higher sales levels may make possible longer production runs with lower associated costs. It would therefore be quite inappropriate if a randomly selected sales volume at the upper end of the distribution were coupled with a cost figure also at the upper end of the distribution. The presence of such correlations between variables must always be taken into account and explicitly used to constrain the values of related variables selected in each simulation run. Not all financial modelling systems have a facility to make the modelling of such dependency relationships straightforward. A distinct but similar note of caution must be made if autocorrelations are likely to be present for any variable. Autocorrelations are relationships between the value of a variable in one time period and the values it held in earlier periods. It is easy to see that, for instance, a simulation in which prices oscillated violently up and down from period to period might not be at all realistic, and changes that involve 'set up' or 'break down' charges would probably also be avoided. A satisfactory simulation model must be able to incorporate such temporal interrelationships if it is to produce sensible results.

Interpretation of the output of a model when it is in the form of probability distributions can be problematic. The distribution tells the user the chances of output variables falling in any range of values of interest. It is then a question of managerial judgement to select, as a basis for action or further analysis, a value that is regarded as satisfactory, given the level of risk or uncertainty calculated as associated with this value. For example, a trading-profit value from the model of Figure 2.5 might be used as the basis of a new product-development decision. It could be that management would not be willing to take the risk of the project yielding profits at the lower end of this distribution with the probability calculated. Considerable expertise may be required in the interpretation of the output of risk analyses and in deciding where it should be employed, and this can be a barrier to its use.

Much has been written, a lot of it critical, about the use and advantages of risk analysis. The benefits are that it allows explicit consideration to be taken of uncertainty in the predicted values of input variables. It avoids the rather crude assumptions often made when traditional contingency provisions are used to indicate variability in estimates. And it can be more accurate than simply using average values for all variables without taking account of the probable asymmetry of errors about the mean. However, the concepts underlying it have seldom been clearly understood by managers, and so the advantages are not seen to outweigh the additional computing costs that stem from running a model one hundred or more times. Despite this, risk analysis is being used increasingly in capital investment appraisal studies and it is likely to gain acceptance in other fields as familiarity with the method develops.

Optimization

Financial managers may be content to use financial models as a convenient way of calculating the consequences of alternative scenarios. It is undoubtedly the case that used in this way models can save much time and effort and enable a wider range of alternatives to be explored. However, often little thought is given to the selection of the scenarios to be investigated. Further, the alternatives chosen in this fairly arbitrary manner usually differ mainly in terms of low-level policy variables such as product prices or sales forecasts, rather than in terms of the higher-level variables such as dividend rates or liquidity ratios with which management might more properly be concerned. What is needed is a structured approach to the selection of scenarios for financial model evaluation, and this is what optimization methods can offer.

In the last chapter, when the monitoring of performance was being discussed, the idea that organizations attempt to remain within a region in a financial state space, bounded by limits corresponding to their financial goals, was suggested. At the level of strategic decision-making, these goals might relate to capital structure or shareholder policy. Conventional, non-optimizing financial models trace out the trajectories that would be obtained in scenarios which differ mainly in the values of low-level decision variables, and these paths are then examined to see how well they lie within the pre-designated desirable region. Such models usually incorporate very simple rules of thumb so that, for instance, in any run of the model the changes in loan capital from one period to the next may match the change in financial requirements, rather than the loan capital changes more realistically being a definite part of management policy, which will instead constrain and modify the requirements themselves. In an optimizing model, corporate goals, usually expressed as high-level control variables, are given as constraints on the trajectory which must always be recognized, and the best trajectory which fulfils these conditions is then calculated. Financial policies are therefore input directly as constraints in this form of modelling, rather than the results of a model being examined retrospectively to see how well financial goals are satisfied.

Selection of a 'best' trajectory which satisfies financial goals has been stated as the objective of an optimizing model, but the criterion to be used has not been considered. In a sense this question returns the discussion to the opening remarks in this book about corporate objectives, although in those optimizing models which have been developed the maximization of the present value of the shareholders' equity has often been used as the objective function. However, it is unwise to allow discussion of optimizing models to become dominated by the choice of an objective function, since a model of this sort may best be used by testing different objective functions and seeing how sensitive results are to such changes.

Now that the purpose and broad approach of optimizing models have been discussed it is appropriate to outline the way in which they can be used. Most optimizing models take as input, policy constraints over the period of interest together with forecasts of exogenous variables such as interest or tax rates. An optimal financial plan is developed, normally using the technique of mathematical programming, and is presented in the form of standard financial reports which indicate the values required of key financial variables such as dividend payments and working capital levels. Further 'what if' runs of the model may then be carried out with different policy constraints; for instance the minimum working capital ratio may be raised. The net effect is a series of financial plans each of which represents the best possible strategy in terms of the selected objective function, rather than the set of haphazardly chosen plans, which might be produced by a non-optimizing model, with trajectories wandering in and out of the region delimited by corporate goals.

It would be misleading to end here without mentioning that optimizing models have so far failed to obtain wide acceptance among financial managers. Instead their main uses have been in the more limited areas of production and marketing planning. Indeed many financial modelling systems have no optimization facilities in any case. Nevertheless optimization does appear to be a technique which can beneficially direct the focus of management attention to issues of strategic importance instead of allowing it to become attracted by minor problems of a tactical nature, and it is likely that wider use will be made of it as these benefits are more generally recognized.

2.5 Options in Financial Model Building

The financial model-building concept involves more than the abstract formulation of the models themselves. Equally important, and stemming from the almost invariable use of computers as the basis for the calculations, is the context for model building in the form of the software and hardware used. The options available in this area complicate considerably the simplistic picture drawn earlier, in which it was glibly stated that models written in equation form using conversational English might be 'understood' as instructions by a computer. Furthermore no limits on the scale of calculations carried out and no constraints on the effort involved in model building were suggested: indeed these factors were not even indicated as worthy of consideration.

As soon as the decision has been taken to proceed with a financial modelling exercise in some area, management is confronted by a number of subsidiary choices which must be made before the actual model-building process begins. These choices, which relate to the mode of implementation of the proposed model in terms of computer-based resources, affect the form of subsequent developments and are also important constraining factors when the system has been completed and is in everyday use. Essentially, the choices concern the logistics of model development and the qualities of the modelling medium used.

Models can be 'custom-built' or bought 'off-the-shelf'. Any model-building activity makes manpower demands in terms both of time and expertise, and choices depend on the resources available. Ready-made models require the least manpower investment, but their general nature means that any deviations from the standard form can be difficult if not impossible to handle. Such models, in the form of complete computer programs, are of value to small firms who lack software development personnel but their inflexibility has caused many users to turn to custom-built modelling, increasingly as the modelling systems available have become more readily comprehensible without specialist training being required. Modelling systems are 'high-level' languages which permit the user to construct a model to desired specifications ('high level' means that sophisticated translation facilities exist which allow the user to address the computer in a close approximation to normal English, whereas 'lower-level' languages are more formal and mathematical in nature, closer to the machine code with which the computer actually works). A wide range of modelling systems are marketed, some being available for internal company development, others only through the use of external consultancy services. As an alternative method of producing custom-built systems, standard, general-purpose, computer-programming languages not specifically intended for financial modelling can be used, but these normally require the use of specialist staff which can be a handicap when it comes to implementation. Whichever option is taken up as the means of developing a model, it can be seen that the logistic support required and the properties of the model constructed are intimately interrelated, and trade-offs between the various benefits provided have to be made. These trade-offs have been much debated elsewhere, but perhaps the best approach for the intending user is to discuss the particular application with as many users and representatives of the different options as possible.

Their very nature implies that the development of financial models necessitates the involvement of personnel who understand the financial structures being described. The translation of these structures into computer programs of any sort requires mastery of the syntax involved in the particular programming medium chosen and so may often be carried out by specialists with operational research or data-processing training. However, as only a capacity for the logical application of clearly stated rules is needed, such a background is by no means mandatory, and recently developed modelling systems are intended to dispel the mystique often introduced through the use of programming experts, by permitting financial managers without previous programming experience to construct their own models without difficulty. Model construction today may be time-consuming or tedious but it is unlikely to pose severe intellectual problems.

Different modelling media have different potentialities and shortcomings depending on features which they offer the user. Model structure and model content are both constrained by the quality of the software used. The importance of being able to use a modular structure has already been mentioned and related to this is the ability to link otherwise separate models. Such linking is often achieved by the use of intermediate files of data held on electronic disc. The ability to access disc files may also facilitate linking a financial model with a generalized management-information system. It is of evident value if data input values for a financial model, for instance sales forecasts projected from historical values taken from the sales ledger, can be obtained directly. Model linking for the consolidation of company accounts into group financial statements or for consolidation at other levels is also a frequently desired feature. Considering next the content of models, this is evidently limited by the presence or absence of facilities for carrying out discounting, forecasting, tax calculations, risk analysis, simulation and other operations which may be required. However, it is also limited in a far more fundamental sense by such factors as the size of model which can be handled in terms of the number of variables and time periods used. Attractive output facilities like the drawing of histograms or graphs can do much to make results more immediate for a user, and even the ease with which tabular output in varying formats can be produced may be of critical importance in a particular application. In finding a way through the bewildering range of features offered by competing financial modelling systems it is probably helpful to employ one of the many checklists which have been published on this subject. This topic is taken up more fully in Chapter 4 below.

2.6 Use of Financial Models

Applications of financial modelling are as diverse as the range of financial decisions with which managements are faced. Models to aid in the construction of corporate budgets and for subsequent use in budgetary control are one of the most common points of entry of an organization into the financial modelling field. Experience with these models may then lead into the development of longer-term corporate planning models, typically looking about three years ahead at broader issues of company policy. Investment appraisals and financial analyses carried out as an adjunct to production and marketing planning are other common areas of application. Surveys suggest that a wide range of organizations, both public and private, have found models useful in each of these fields of application. The next chapter reviews these uses in more detail.

Depending on the purpose of a model, the level of detail in its structure varies. Models may be characterized as being 'bottom up', 'top down' or 'middle up' models. The first type was historically the earliest developed, and typically may be used to calculate cash-flow statements from fundamental information at a very high level of detail. Some applications of this sort in manufacturing industry have taken as input data basic production details and the models have depicted the physical flows of materials which are then converted into monetary units and used to prepare financial reports. 'Top down' models in contrast operate at a high level of data aggregation and may be used in long-term corporate planning exercises. They are usually closely related to existing financial reporting systems, and generate information for strategic decision-making. Both 'bottom up' and 'top down' models have been found wanting in practical studies because of difficulties in integrating them into the decision-making process. Recent innovations in computing have made feasible the development of 'middle up' models by managers themselves, which operate at an intermediate level of detail and to some extent get over the deficiencies of earlier model types.

The purpose of financial modelling has been stated as being to provide information support for tactical and strategic financial decision-making. Perhaps the main advantage of using this methodology is that it enables management to explore a larger number of alternatives than would otherwise be possible. The implications of these alternatives can then be calculated in detail, allowing full account to be taken of interrelationships between variables, and showing at any desired time intervals the position attained on the trajectory through the selected financial state space. The 'middle up' model has developed as an approach to modelling which makes the maximum use of the educative potential of models. By interacting with and evolving their own models, managers enter into a symbiotic relationship with the computer, which enhances by an order of magnitude their capabilities in financial decision-making.

Financial Modelling in Corporate Management, 2nd Edition
Edited by J. W. Bryant
Published by John Wiley & Sons Ltd.

3

The Use of Corporate Planning Models: Past, Present and Future*

JAE SHIM AND RANDY McGLADE

3.1 Introduction

Corporate planning models are of recent origin in comparison with the more standard tools of business managers and analysts. Since the 1960s, planning models have advanced from an obscure concept for large corporations to a credible tool for planning in a broad size-range of companies. The proliferation of planning models has been due largely to the increasing availability of computers over the last twenty years, which quickly enhanced the applications and practicality of modelling for all types of business. This chapter provides an overview of the concept, developments and future of corporate planning models.

3.2 Definition and History of Modelling

Definition

The definition of a planning model varies somewhat with the scope of its application. For instance, financial planning models may have a very short planning-horizon and entail no more than a collection of accounting formulae for producing pro forma statements (Kingston, 1977). Corporate planning models are often considered a separate kind of model in which the quantitative and logical interrelationships among a corporation's financial, marketing and production activities are simulated (Naylor, 1976). In this sense, the model has greater utility because any of the coordinated subroutines composing the comprehensive model may be isolated for narrower applications. Therefore,

*First published in *J. Opl. Res. Soc.*, **35**, 885–894 (1984). Reproduced with permission.

the definition of corporate planning model in the present discussion includes any type of planning model (e.g. financial, accounting, production, etc.), since financial and physical modules can be combined to form larger routines (Power, 1975). Planning models can be categorized according to two approaches: simulation and optimization (Hammond, 1974; Power, 1975). Simulation models are attempts to represent mathematically the operations of the company or of the conditions in the external economic environment. By adjusting the values of controllable variables and assumed external conditions, the future implications of present decision-making can be estimated. Probabilistic simulation models incorporate probability estimates into the forecast sequence, while deterministic simulation models do not. Optimization models are intended to identify the best decision, given specific constraints. The typical framework for financial planning models is discussed in a later section.

History of Models

Naylor (1983) places the rudiments of corporate modelling in the early 1960s with the large, cumbersome simulation models developed by major corporations, e.g. AT&T, Wells Fargo Bank, Dow Chemical, IBM and Sun Oil. Most of the models were written in one of the general programming languages (GPLs, e.g. FORTRAN) and were used for generating pro forma financial statements. The models typically required several man-years to develop and, in some cases, never provided benefits sufficient to outweigh the costs of development. Financial models were considered an untested concept, suitable only for those corporations large enough to absorb the costs and risks of development.

Important advancements in computer technology in the early 1970s provided the means for greater diversity and affordability in corporate modelling. Interactive computing facilities allowed for faster and more meaningful input/output sequences for modellers; trial-and-error adjustments of inputs and analyses were possible while on-line to the central computer or to an outside timesharing service. The advent of corporate simulation languages enabled analysts with little experience with GLPs to write modelling programs in an English-like programming language (e.g. EXPRESS, SIMPLAN and XSIM). By 1979, nearly every Fortune 1000 company was using a corporate simulation model.

As companies gained experience in developing basic, deterministic simulations, renewed effort was directed toward consolidating and integrating smaller models into the larger corporate models first attempted in the 1960s. Furthermore, certain companies were attempting the more difficult optimization models and were increasing predictive power by using econometric models to link their simulations with product markets and the external economy. Early successes with the simpler models led to a boom in modelling, but an increasing number of failures in more ambitious projects soon moderated the general enthusiasm. As the economy entered a recession and became more unstable (less predictable), the weaknesses in the rationale underlying many corporate models were revealed. Managers realized that the purpose of a model must be well-defined and that the end-users should be involved in its development. Although the bad experiences of the mid-1970s have jaded some executives against models to the present day, most veterans of the period have developed a realistic attitude toward the capabilities of models and are employing recent advancements in techniques to construct more serviceable models.

3.3 Current Practices of Modelling

Surveys of Corporations

Several surveys of financial model-making in US and UK firms have been conducted over the last fifteen years. The firms represented a broad cross-section of industries and services, with sales ranging from one million to over one billion dollars annually. The specific purposes of the surveys varied somewhat between researchers, but each was designed to estimate the general acceptance and development of corporate financial modelling. While different sample sizes and populations prevent pooling the results, it is instructive to discuss important issues and common findings.

The earliest survey results, reported by Gershefski (1969), revealed that 63 (20 per cent) of 323 firms sampled in 1968 were working with corporate planning models. Naylor and Schauland (1976) found that 253 (73 per cent) of 346 firms were using or developing corporate planning models in 1975. Recent surveys by McLean and Neale (1980) and by Klein (1982) indicated that 85 per cent of companies surveyed (410 and 204, respectively) were using some type of financial model. The results indicate that corporate financial modelling has become a common tool in US business firms (Table 3.1).

Table 3.1 Results of surveys for the use of corporate planning models

Author	Sample size (responses)	Companies using or developing models
Gershefski (1969)	323	63 (20%)
Naylor and Schauland (1976)	346	250 (72%)
McLean and Neale (1980)	410	246 (60%)
Brightman and Harris (1982)	237	126 (53%)
Klein (1982)	204	175 (86%)

Among the reasons cited by corporations for using planning models were (1) economic uncertainty, (2) shortages of resources, (3) diminishing increase in productivity, (4) international competition, (5) tight money and inflation, (6) political upheavals (affecting foreign operations), (7) environmental problems, and (8) new business opportunities (Naylor, 1976). There was general agreement that models enabled managers to run alternative analyses and to adjust decision variables, while reducing the time needed for report writing. The many possible applications of corporate planning models are listed in Table 3.2; financial forecasting/planning and pro forma balance-sheet statements were the most common applications at most companies. The models proved to be useful tools in 'what-if' analysis, sensitivity analysis, simulations, best/worst case scenarios, goal seeking, optimization and report preparation (Klein, 1982).

Table 3.2 Applications of corporate planning models

Financial forecasting	Construction scheduling
Pro forma financial statements	Tax planning
Capital budgeting	Energy requirements
Market decision-making	Labour contract negotiation fees
Mergers and acquisition analysis	Foreign currency analysis
Lease versus purchase decisions	*Utilities:*
Production scheduling	Load forecasting
New-venture evaluation	Rate cases
Manpower planning	Generation planning
Profit planning	
Sales forecasting	
Investment analysis	

A consistent finding among the surveys was the involvement of top management in successful modelling efforts. Naylor (1976) and Klein (1982) found that in 50–90 per cent of the companies using models, upper managers (e.g. President, Vice-President Finance, Controller, Treasurer, Executive Vice-President) participated in the definition and implementation of the model. The background of the participants in Klein's survey was predominantly in finance, followed by computer science and accounting. Grinyer and Wooller (1975) found a predominance of operational researchers in their sample. The end-users of the models were usually strategic planning groups, the Treasurer's department, and the Controller's department.

The only detailed figures on actual developmental costs of modelling were supplied by Naylor (1976). The average costs (labour, computer time, materials) in 1975 for developing a model in-house with no outside assistance was $82 752. The average costs to firms that received help from outside consultants was $29 225, with markedly shorter development schedules.

Ironically, most executives believed that outside consultants were too expensive and avoided hiring them (Grinyer and Wooller, 1975; Brightman and Harris, 1982; Klein, 1982). Furthermore, Ang and Chua (1980) reported survey results showing that two-thirds of the faulty, discontinued corporate models had been developed in-house, yet only three of 31 companies hired outside consultants on subsequent efforts.

Despite the growing diversity of modelling techniques available, the vast majority of corporate models encountered in the surveys were basic, deterministic simulations. Probabilistic considerations were seldom incorporated into the models by any but the largest corporations. As recently as 1983, Naylor (1983) found that no firms were using optimization models as a planning tool. Evidently, the accuracy of optimization models, as well as their clarity to upper management, must improve before they receive significant use.

Attitudes and Problems

The reluctance of many firms to experiment with corporate planning models derives chiefly from a fear of the unknown. Confusion over what models are and how they are used precludes serious investigation of their potential benefits. Sherwood (1977) summarized the myths that discourage managers from considering models:

1. Models are complicated—On the contrary, most effective models are fairly simple structures, incorporating only the essential processes of the problem under investigation. The maths involved is often basic algebra and modeling languages reduce complex terminology.
2. The company is not large enough—Models do not consist solely of comprehensive simulations. Some of the most frequently utilized models center on a limited number of key relationships.
3. We do not own a computer—Models are being designed for use on inexpensive personal computers, and outside time-sharing services are available.
4. We do not have any modellers—Modern planning languages have so simplified the modeling process that even a novice quickly becomes competent. Outside consultants are also available for assistance.

Attitudes of initiates towards modelling have progressed from the rather deteriorated outlook of the mid-1970s to today's more optimistic viewpoint. The past trend probably explains the general negativity of earlier results reported by Higgins and Finn (1976) in their literature review of top management attitudes in the UK toward modelling. In summarizing the activities making up the senior executive's role, the authors concluded that most of the manager's duties involved behavioural, interpersonal communication problems requiring this direct ministering. The majority view of managers emphasized that models could not capture the essential complexity of the organization and ignored the political/behavioural issues. In the few areas where a model could prove useful, the executive had insufficient time to learn how to apply it. At that time, the picture of an executive seated at a computer and engaged in problem analysis was unrealistic. The ultimate finding, however, was not a wholesale abandonment of corporate planning models among managers but the delegation of modelling analysis to lower managers. Thus, models seemed destined to become strictly a middle-management tool.

Contemporary with that study, Grinyer and Wooller's survey showed the importance of obtaining top management's support to assure success in any model-making project. However, top managers in over 50 per cent of the companies sampled believed their models had improved forecasts; 31 per cent were undecided. More encouraging results followed. Wagner reported that upper management in his survey not only requested that models be built, but participated in their development. The finished products received a high average utility rating (1 to 5, 5 best) of 3.9. A similar evaluation in 1980 by top management at 410 US firms (annual sales exceeding $100 million) yielded a 4.95 rating (7 being best) for their computer-based planning models. None of the CEOs considered the models useless. Klein (1982) found evidence of significant cost savings through modelling with one Vice-President of Finance reporting a $600 000 savings through use of a financial planning model.

The growing acceptance of planning models has enabled managers and technicians to identify areas requiring improvement and to formulate criteria for success. Optimization models are one technique in need of refinement. Optimization models are inscrutable 'black boxes' to those managers who have had no part in the modelling effort (Power, 1975). Naturally, top management has little confidence in forecasts produced by a model they cannot understand. The need to monitor a suite of financial and non-financial variables precludes the construction of simple optimization models.

There were no serious limitations of modelling noted by respondents in Naylor's 1975 survey. The criticisms were directed at the inflexibility of some models, poor documentation by the model builder and excessive input data requirements. Aggarwal and Khera (1980) identified several points of inflexibility in most models. Models usually simulate only one cause-and-effect relationship, whereas multiple effects are often present. Similarly, the intended results of a control action may be accompanied by unintended results. In that instance the desirability of the two consequences must be compared on a common utility scale. When several consequences of a decision are separated in time, a means for making intertemporal comparisons is required, analogous to a discount rate in capital budgeting. Such techniques are rarely available in practice.

The reasons for discontinuation of corporate planning models in 31 of the largest US corporations were reported by Ang and Chua (1980). The majority of firms sampled were industries, followed by retailers, transporters, utilities, banks, finance and insurance institutions. The 31 firms having discontinued models were only 27 per cent of the total sample of 113 corporations. Twenty-nine of the 31 models were designed for producing pro forma financial statements, and were discontinued within three years following construction. The various reasons for the rejections are listed in Table 3.3; the common justifications were model deficiencies and human problems in implementation. Three of the prevalent reasons (inflexibility, lack of management support, excessive input data requirements) are familiar shortcomings discussed earlier. The need for management's support for successful model-making cannot be over-emphasized; their role as champion of the effort is essential for company-wide acceptance of the final product. It is interesting to note from Table 3.3 that excessive development time and costs were not a basis for rejection.

Table 3.3 Reasons for discontinued models (Ang and Chua, 1980)

Lack of sufficient flexibility
Lack of adequate management support
Excessive amounts of input data required
Replaced by a better model
The need no longer existed
The model did not perform as expected
New management de-emphasized planning
Poor documentation
Lack of user interest
Excessive development costs
Excessive operating costs
Excessive development time required

A novel insight on success factors in modelling was provided by Simon, Lamar and Haines (1976). The authors asserted that the modeller must understand that management's expressed need for a particular model may be specious; the modeller must perceive from the manager's behaviour, rather than from his verbal request, the type of model needed. If an incorrect determination is made, the model may never be implemented. Two of the five categories of uses for models outlined in the study were legitimate and straightforward: Type I models are simulation/optimization techniques and Type II models condition data for easier utilization. When the modeller perceives that management's objectives are not consistent with those of Type I or II models, one of three alternative choices is implied:

Type III: merely subterfuge for establishing a data link, forcing one part of the organization to channel information to another;
Type IV: a means of supplying formal rationale for decisions reached in the past;
Type V: a means of establishing a manager's reputation—simply a remake of a previously successful model.

A table of management behaviour was provided by the authors as a guide for modellers in determining the type of model implied in the original request and in subsequent feedback.

3.4 State-of-the-art and Recommended Practices

The acceptance of corporate planning models has resulted in many firms establishing planning departments, responsible for development and implementation of planning models. The structure of the typical corporate financial model is an integration of smaller modules used by each department or business unit for planning purposes. Figure 3.1 shows a flowchart of a comprehensive planning model driven by a series of functional models which may be used either on a stand-alone basis at the business-unit level or consolidated and used by upper management (Naylor and Mansfield, 1977).

Optimal procedures for assembling effective models are still much at the discretion of the individual planning department, but useful guidelines have been published. Suggestions offered by Hammond (1974) serve as practical considerations in evaluating the timeliness of a proposed modelling project and

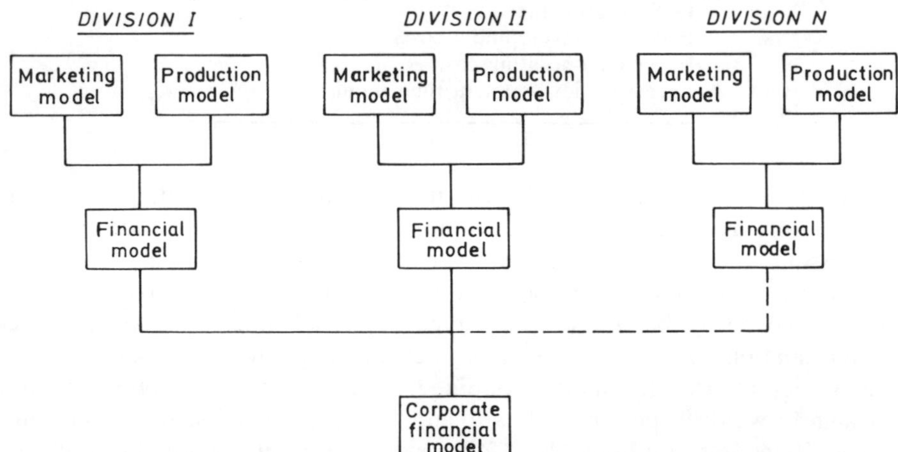

Figure 3.1 Typical structure of a corporate planning model (Naylor and Mansfield, 1977)

in guiding the project. He suggested that the modelling effort could be divided into ten stages of activities:

(1) Determine which process(es) can be modelled effectively.
(2) Decide whether to use a model.
(3) Formalize the specifications of the model (e.g. inputs/outputs, structure, etc.).
(4) Prepare a proposal.
(5) Conduct modelling and data gathering concurrently.
(6) Debug the model.
(7) Educate the prospective users.
(8) Users validate the model.
(9) Put model into use.
(10) Update/modify the model as needed.

Hammond cautioned that several iterations between certain stages may be necessary and that several failures may be obtained before a valid model is obtained. He also provided a list of prerequisites for modelling and control factors for success (Table 3.4).

Table 3.4 Success factors in modelling (Hammond, 1974)

Uncontrollable prerequisites
Operations understood, data plentiful
Relevant data accessible
Budgets, plans and control systems are well-defined, understood
Modellers have management's support
Management scientists accept responsibility for implementation
Similar innovative techniques used in the past
Manager and modeller share status and background

Controllable factors
Involve potential users in development process
Define model's goal explicitly
Input and output are in familiar formats
Company procedures modified little, at first
Look for common management problems to model
Start simple and keep it simple
Allow for ample judgemental inputs
Be realistic about planning time and expected results
Put a manager (not a modeller) in charge
Define roles clearly
Demonstrate part of model early on
Build model within users' organization
Develop expertise to manage and update model
Provide ample documentation

Kingston (1977) defined the anatomy of the contemporary financial model as being composed of five parts: the documentation supporting the calculations, input assumptions regarding future periods, the projections and decision points leading to the forecasted values, managerial (financial) ratios, and graphics displaying information from decision points. The forecasting systems utilized depend upon the breadth and planning horizon of the model; typical methods include market research and Delphi method, time trends, moving averages, Box–Jenkins, and various causal methods, such as leading indicators, life-cycle analysis, regression, etc. (Naylor and Mansfield, 1977; Patterson and Walter, 1980).

Forecasting methods should be reviewed periodically by an independent party to ensure that the techniques have not become outdated. This can be determined only by maintaining a current management information system (MIS), which provides data to econometric models of the external environment. The critical importance of external data in determining company strategy is the central theorem of MIS. Thus, planners make assumptions about the business environment for a particular planning horizon, based upon the output from the MIS. The information is combined with internal data to prepare demand forecasts, and the results can be input to a planning model or used to check the validity of forecasts produced by current techniques (Patterson and Walter, 1980).

Planning and modelling languages (PMLs) have been a major incentive in involving higher management in modelling. General programming languages, such as FORTRAN, are seldom used in current models; oddly, COBOL, the 'business language', has never been used extensively in modelling. The advantages of PMLs are steadily edging out GPLs: models are built more easily, with shorter development and data-processing times, are more easily understood by upper management, and are periodically updated with enhancements from the vendor (Brightman and Harris, 1982). Today, over seventy PMLs are available at reasonable cost, including EMPRE, FINPLAN, VISICALC, BUDPLAN, MULTIPLAN and 1-2-3.

A further convenience offered to companies looking into modelling is pre-made planning packages sold by software vendors. The packages have often been criticized for their inflexibility, but the newer models allow for more user specificity. Analytical portfolio models are commercial packages that tell a conglomerate how to distribute resources across the portfolio of profit centres. Boston Consulting Group, Arthur D. Little and McKinsey have developed models that categorize investments into a matrix of profit potentials and recommended strategies, e.g. cash flow/hold and collect (Naylor, 1983). A model for profit impact of market strategy (PIMS) is offered by the Strategic Planning Institute. The package is a large, multiple regression model used to identify the optimal strategy in a given business environment. Similar packages are likely to proliferate in the future as more companies are forced to use decision models to remain competitive.

MIS and Personal Computers

The analytic and predictive capabilities of corporate planning models depend in large part upon the supporting database. Information technology has advanced to the point that databases consist of logico-mathematical models and highly integrated collections of data, derived internally and external to the firm. The databases are now called management information systems (MIS) or decision support systems (DSS) because they store the data and decision tools utilized by management (Burch and Strater, 1974; Chacko, 1979).

A primary value of the MIS's large storage capacity for data is the potential to model more accurately the external economy and to forecast business trends. Managers are finding that effective long-range planning depends primarily upon a thorough understanding of their competitors and the forces at work in the market-place. A considerable body of data is required to develop insight into the competitive environment. Information derived from within the company has little strategic value for those purposes; thus the collection of external data should be emphasized (Young, 1981; Rucks and Ginter, 1982). As a result, the relevance of information to future conditions is the standard by which input of data to the MIS is controlled.

Once the strategic data have been stored in the mainframe computer system, managers need quick access to the database and a means for inputting alternative data sets/scenarios into the econometric models. Only recently have such activities been made possible by the development of communication links between mainframe systems and personal computers (PCs). Many of the applications of the mainframe–PC connection involve rather basic analyses, such as accounts payable, receivables, general ledger, etc. However, internal financial planning packages (e.g. EPS, IFPS and SIMPLAN) are currently available, as are external timeshare services, such as Dow Jones, Lockheed's Dialog and The Source (Ferris, 1983).

The outlook for the next few years indicates an increasing integration of the microcomputer with the mainframe. A recent survey of over 100 organizations showed that 67 per cent of middle management and 22 per cent of top management of non-data-processing departments were using personal computers (Data Decisions, 1983). The results evidence significant momentum at the top of corporate management for the use of PCs. The future demand for sophisticated modelling capabilities on PCs should intensify the need for mainframe connections.

Corporate planning software packages for PCs are already proliferating. Applications now available range from cash flow analysis and budget projections to regressions, time series analysis and probabilistic analysis (Miller, 1983). Kennedy (1983) recently listed 116 software packages for financial/business analysis on the IBM PC; many were suitable as corporate planning models. The trend in PC technology is aimed toward implementing as many mainframe, analytical capabilities onto the microcomputer as the market will support.

3.5 The Future of Corporate Planning Models

The interest in obtaining corporate models is likely to continue, and Naylor (1983) predicted some of the near-term trends. The concept of the 'strategic business unit' as an object of analysis may prove to be unviable. There has been no consistent definition of an SBU, and most models treat them as independent of one another; this may not be accurate. The SBU is typically forced into short-term profit making (rather than long-term development), eventually sapping its vitality. Consequently, an improved rationale may cause models to build around a different grouping of profit centres.

We can expect to see an increased linking of portfolio models with corporate simulation and optimization models (Naylor and Tapon, 1982). Modelling software will become more modular, in order to perform limited analyses or comprehensive projections. More software will be written for microcomputers, graphics will improve, and modelling languages will become more user-friendly. The future of modelling is somewhat assured because it is intimately linked with the continued expansion of the computer market. Though shake-outs may frequently occur among hardware manufacturers, planning models will always have a market as software writers improve their understanding of the planner's needs and produce more efficient decision-making tools.

3.6 Conclusion

The reputation of corporate planning models has improved significantly from the bad experiences of the early 1970s. As tight economic conditions and intensified competition required managers to formulate more effective strategies, the advantages of modelling became more apparent. The use of models is now less threatening to upper management, owing to the flexibility and simplicity of present techniques. As modelling success stories become more common, managers of all-sized firms can be expected more readily to lend their support to in-house modelling projects or to the purchase of ready-made systems.

References

Aggarwal, R. and Khera, I. (1980). 'Using management science models: a critique for planners', *Managerial Planning*, **28**, 12–15.

Ang, J. and Chua, J. (1980). 'Corporate planning models that failed', *Managerial Planning*, **29**, 34–8.

Brightman, H. J. and Harris, S. E. (1982). 'The planning and modeling language revolution: a managerial perspective', *Business*, **32**, 15–21.

Burch, J. G. and Strater, F. R. (1974). *Information Systems: Theory and Practice*, Hamilton, Santa Barbara, California.

Chacko, G. K. (1979). *Management Information Systems*, Petrocelli, New York.

Data Decisions (1983). 'Micros at big firms—a survey', *Datamation*, **29**, 160–75.

Ferris, D. (1983). 'The micro-mainframe connection', *Datamation*, **29**, 126–41.

Gershefski, G. W. (1969). 'Corporate planning models—the state of the art', *Managerial Planning*, **18**, 31–5.

Grinyer, P. H. and Wooller, J. (1975). 'Computer models for corporate planning', *Long Range Planning*, **8**, 14–25.

Hammond, J. S. (1974). 'Do's and don'ts of computer models for planning', *Harvard Business Review*, **52**, 110–23.

Higgins, J. C. and Finn, R. (1976). 'Managerial attitudes towards computer models for planning and control', *Long Range Planning*, **9**, 107–12.

Kennedy, J. (1983). 'Financial applications', *PC World—Annual Software Review*, pp. 324–40.

Kingston, P. L. (1977). 'Anatomy of a financial model', *Managerial Planning*, **26**, 1–7.

Klein, R. (1982). 'Computer-based financial modelling', *J. Systems Management*, **33**, 6–13.

McLean, E. R. and Neale, G. L. (1980). 'Computer-based planning models come of age', *Harvard Business Review*, **58**, 46–54.

Miller, J. L. (1983). 'Business management', *PC World—Annual Software Review*, pp. 368–80.

Naylor, T. H. (1976). 'Conceptual framework for corporate modeling and the results of a survey of current practices', *Opl. Res. Q.*, **27**, 671–82.

Naylor, T. H. (1983). 'Strategic planning models', *Managerial Planning*, **30**, 3–11.

Naylor, T. H. and Mansfield, M. J. (1977). 'The design of computer based planning and modeling systems', *Long Range Planning*, **10**, 16–25.

Naylor, T. H. and Schauland, H. (1976). 'A survey of users of corporate planning models', *Mgmt. Sci.*, **22**, 927–37.

Naylor, T. H. and Tapon, F. (1982). 'The capital asset pricing model: an evaluation of its potential as a strategic planning tool', *Mgmt. Sci.*, **28**, 1166–73.

Patterson, F. S. and Walter, J. D. (1980). 'Planning models and econometrics', *Managerial Planning*, **28**, 11–15.

Power, P. D. (1975). 'Computers and financial planning', *Long Range Planning*, **8**, 53–9.

Rucks, A. C. and Ginter, P. M. (1982). 'Strategic MIS: promises unfulfilled', *J. of Systems Management*, **33**, 16–19.

Sherwood, D. (1977). 'Business computer models—dispelling the myths', *Accountancy*, **88**, 44–6.

Simon, L. S., Lamar, C. and Haines, G. H. (1976). 'Managers' use of models', *Omega*, **4**, 253–63.

Wagner, G. R. (1979). 'Enhancing creativity in strategic planning through computer systems', *Managerial Planning*, **28**, 10–17.

Young, R. C. D. (1981). 'A strategic overview of business information systems', *Managerial Planning*, **29**, 28–37.

Financial Modelling in Corporate Management, 2nd Edition
Edited by J. W. Bryant

4

Computer Packages in Financial Modelling

PAUL FINLAY

4.1 Introduction

Over the last 15 years, planning personnel have been heavily involved in obtaining financial modelling facilities for the organizations in which they work. During this time their role has changed as shown in Figure 4.1, so that today a major role is that of investigating the software products available.

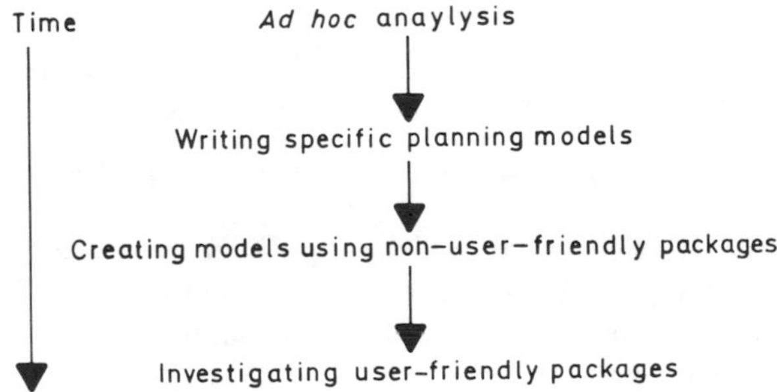

Figure 4.1 The changing role of planning personnel in obtaining financial modelling facilities

Although financial modelling packages are used widely in the UK, there are still many companies about to make their first acquisition. Again, companies with experience of one package may feel the need to upgrade, or to acquire other, complementary packages. Thus the acquisition rate for financial modelling packages remains high, with a very large number of packages to choose from: Grinyer and Wooller (1975) describe around 80 packages, while the *Directory of Software* published by the National Computing Centre's

Microsystems Centre (1985) lists over 100 packages currently available on microcomputers. Planners need help in clarifying how best these offerings match the needs of their organizations.

With so many packages it does not make sense to start off by attempting a detailed investigation of specific packages: what is first required is an identification of the broad characteristics of classes of package. Such a classification will then allow an organization to select the type of package that best fits its particular needs, with subsequent detailed investigation limited to packages within the chosen class and taking account of the special organizational requirements. It is with the primary classification that this chapter is concerned: with describing the wood rather than the trees.

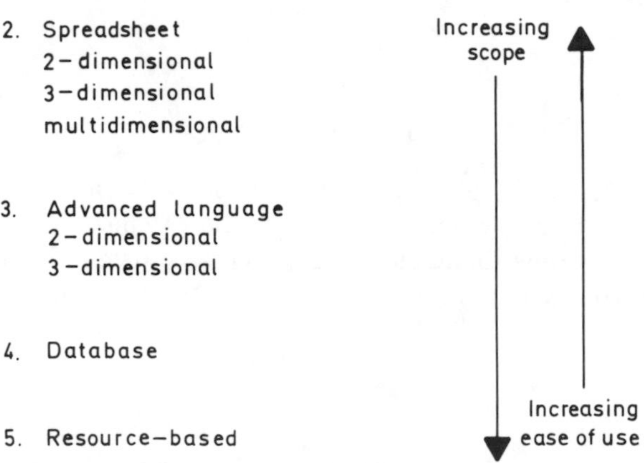

Figure 4.2 Classes of financial modelling package

Five broad classes of financial modelling package have been identified and these are listed in Figure 4.2 along with their subdivisions. They are listed roughly in order of increasing scope which, unfortunately, tends to be associated with decreasing ease of use. Note that the categorization is not totally watertight: sometimes one characteristic would place the package in a different category from that corresponding to its general properties.

Before discussing the characteristics of each class, it is worth pointing out that even the simplest package can often be used to tackle complex problems, but this demands considerable effort and skill. This requirement rather defeats the purpose of buying a package. Consequently in the following discussion only those capabilities that can be obtained in a straightforward manner will be listed.

In the remainder of this chapter, as different types of financial planning software are discussed, a large number of specific contemporary packages are mentioned. These are listed in Exhibit 4.1 in the Appendix to this chapter, where sufficient details are provided for readers wishing to obtain copies for themselves for use or appraisal. As each package is introduced in the text, it is referenced by a number in parentheses: this number corresponds to the reference number in the list in Exhibit 4.1. Naturally the library of financial planning software is being added to all the time, and so the list must be taken as purely indicative of what is currently available, rather than being in any way comprehensive.

The inclusion of a package in the list should not be taken as implying any recommendation of the software concerned; nor should the omission of a package be taken as an implied criticism of any relevant materials on the market in the corresponding category.

4.2 Dedicated Packages

Computer models consist of the rules of the game (the logic) and the associated data. Dedicated packages differ from all other types of package in that their main offering is not a framework within which you can do your own thing with the logic, but rather a set of completely defined routines covering whole areas of accounting and finance, such as investment appraisal and the production of company accounts. Thus the user does not have to worry thinking about the model logic and report specifications as these are predefined: his only concern is to insert data in response to computer-generated prompts. Use of the package is thus 'prompt driven'.

PLANALYST (1) is a good example of this genre, and is geared to financial analysis and projections. The screen prompts the user for some input, perhaps for employee costs or numbers, for which there are several options. The user makes his selection and inputs the values. The system remembers the options selected and adjusts later menus accordingly. Boardroom quality standard reports that are available include a Balance Sheet, a Profit and Loss Account, Cash Flow Statement, Productivity Analyses and a wide range of financial ratios.

Although it is sometimes possible to create non-standard outputs using dedicated packages, this is usually rather difficult. Dedicated packages have their greater appeal to managers who want computer assistance in performing well-defined activities and who have little time or computer expertise. TK!SOLVER (2) provides investment appraisal, ratio analysis, depreciation and other financial modules. SystemBuild (3) offer a library of around 40 programs suitable for use with LOTUS 1-2-3 (4) and SYMPHONY (5) (see spreadsheet packages below). This library includes modules for cash-flow forecasting, investment appraisal and fixed asset records and depreciation calculations.

4.3 Spreadsheet Packages

A spreadsheet is the electronic equivalent of a large piece of paper divided into rows and columns. A typical small spreadsheet package offers 63 columns and 254 rows, while LOTUS 1-2-3 for example, offers 256 columns and 2048 rows—a total of 524 288 cells. However, the size of the computer memory may restrict the usable size. Into each cell can be inserted text, data or a formula. A very simple financial model as it might appear using a typical spreadsheet package is shown in Figure 4.3(a). Figure 4.3(b) shows the other 'side' of the spreadsheet giving the input data and the rules of calculation (the formulae). On some spreadsheets (such as SUPERCALC (6)) a few keystrokes also allow the user to switch from the display of Figure 4.3(a) to that of Figure 4.3(b) and vice versa. To be able to see and to print out the formula and input data as in Figure 4.3(b) is an exceedingly useful facility when building models and validating them. Note that the formula is cell-specific: for example, for 1986 the formula 'Revenue = Sales × Price' has been inserted into the spreadsheet as B6 = B4 * B5, where B4, B5 and B6 are the cells containing the values of Sales, Price and Revenue for that year.

While almost all types of package now offer a form of spreadsheet for data input and for showing results, what differentiates a spreadsheet package from the others is that the logic has this 'cell-specificity'.

A complete matrix, even a small one of 63 × 254 cells, is far too large to be shown on a computer screen and thus a portion of the spreadsheet must be chosen for viewing at any one time. The computer screen may thus be regarded as a 'window' which can be used to view any chosen portion of the imaginary piece of electronic paper residing at the back of the computer. This 'windowing' is shown in Figure 4.4.

The simplicity of spreadsheets is their greatest strength. The traditional way an accountant would build a financial plan is reproduced closely, and the printout reproduces exactly what is seen on the screen. The typical manuals that accompany the software are generally clearly written and most users should be constructing simple models within an hour of starting with a package.

Spreadsheets are ideally suited to activities where a series of calculations are to be performed frequently, often with a little modification: e.g. product costing, simple budgeting and investment appraisal.

Although a marvellous tool for such applications, the spreadsheet is barely adequate for sophisticated modelling. It gives insufficient help with data input: for example, it is often necessary to 'spread' a value across several time periods, or to extrapolate according to a given growth rate. Spreadsheets do not offer this facility nor the capability to carry out a full sensitivity analysis. They are weak in dealing with complex data structures, and this militates against their successful use in handling corporate modelling issues. Thus they tend to be used in 'stand-alone' applications.

	A	B	C	D	E	F
1			HOLDTITE ADHESIVES PLC.			
2						
3	YEAR	1986	1987	1988	1989	1990
4	SALES	1500	1600	1750	2000	2100
5	PRICE	3	3	3.5	4.5	5
6	REVENUE	4500	4800	6125	9000	10500
7	UNIT LABOUR COST	1	1	1	1	1.5
8	UNIT MATERIAL COST	1.5	1.5	1.6	1.7	1.8
9	UNIT VARIABLE COST	2.5	2.5	2.6	2.7	3.3
10	TOTAL VARIABLE COST	3750	4000	4550	5400	6930
11	CONTRIBUTION	750	800	1575	3600	3570
12	FIXED COSTS	500	650	760	850	1000
13	====================	==========	==========	==========	==========	==========
14	PROFIT	250	150	815	2750	2570
15	====================	==========	==========	==========	==========	==========

(a)

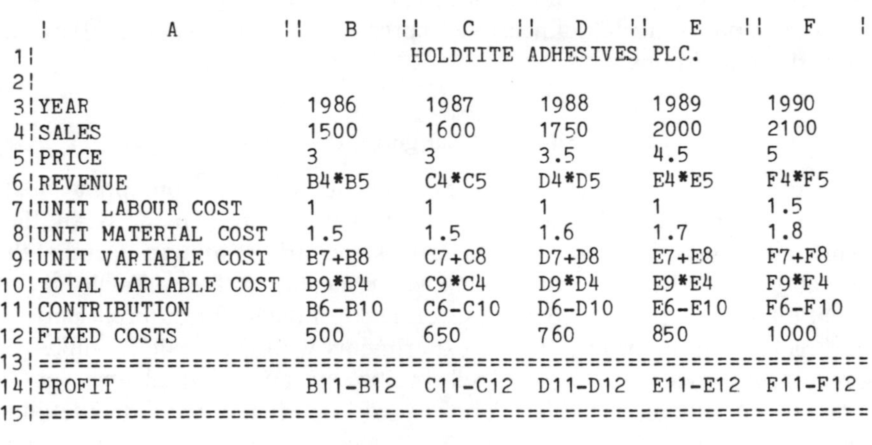

	A	B	C	D	E	F
1			HOLDTITE ADHESIVES PLC.			
2						
3	YEAR	1986	1987	1988	1989	1990
4	SALES	1500	1600	1750	2000	2100
5	PRICE	3	3	3.5	4.5	5
6	REVENUE	B4*B5	C4*C5	D4*D5	E4*E5	F4*F5
7	UNIT LABOUR COST	1	1	1	1	1.5
8	UNIT MATERIAL COST	1.5	1.5	1.6	1.7	1.8
9	UNIT VARIABLE COST	B7+B8	C7+C8	D7+D8	E7+E8	F7+F8
10	TOTAL VARIABLE COST	B9*B4	C9*C4	D9*D4	E9*E4	F9*F4
11	CONTRIBUTION	B6-B10	C6-C10	D6-D10	E6-E10	F6-F10
12	FIXED COSTS	500	650	760	850	1000
13	====================	==========	==========	==========	==========	==========
14	PROFIT	B11-B12	C11-C12	D11-D12	E11-E12	F11-F12
15	====================	==========	==========	==========	==========	==========

(b)

Figure 4.3 A simple financial model as it might appear using a typical spreadsheet package. (a) Input data and the results. (b) Input data and the formulae

Until 1985, spreadsheet packages were solely two-dimensional with good examples being LOTUS 1-2-3, SYMPHONY and SUPERCALC. With such packages, models were invariably constructed with time along the horizontal axis (columns used as time periods) and with rows designated as variables. The complexity of several products or several companies was catered for by replicating down the spreadsheet or by using different files. This was not altogether satisfactory since it did not fit easily with how the data is viewed and could lead to problems of consistency. Now three-dimensional spreadsheets

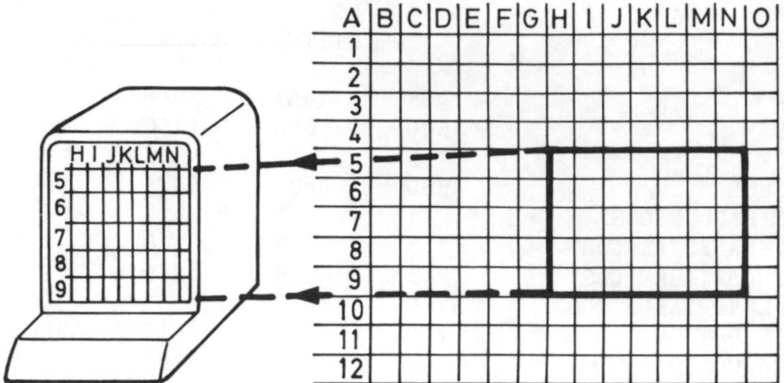

Figure 4.4 A typical spreadsheet window and display

are available in which the third dimension can be likened to the leaves of a book or as depicted in Figure 4.5. Examples of three-dimensional spreadsheets are BOEINGCALC (7) and REPORTMANAGER (8).

An example of a multidimensional spreadsheet is VP-planner (9) which offers five dimensions.

4.4 Advanced Language Packages

These packages provide more than the framework available from spreadsheets by offering a high level language in which to write financial models. Another term for such packages is 'separate logic package', arising from the fact that the logic and data are kept separate, except when calculating. The rationale for this is that the same logic may apply to several sets of data—for different parts of the organization or from different experiments with the model. Unlike the spreadsheet packages the logic is cell-specific, but applies to all time periods unless specifically restricted. Straightforward English may be used in defining the logic (e.g. the expression 'Revenue' = 'Sales' × 'Price' is acceptable) which enables the models to be self-documenting—a not insignificant feature when it is realized that formal planning is generally carried out only spasmodically, and the ability to regain a firm understanding of a model built during the previous planning period is very important. An example of the logic for a simple financial model written using an advanced language package is given in Figure 4.6.

Advanced language packages offer full data modelling thus easing data input. Extensive predefined financial routines, for example facilities for sensitivity analysis, allow many options to be investigated easily. For example, a 'targeting' facility is available whereby 'what must?' questions may be answered, e.g. 'What must Sales be in order that the Profit will be £4m?' Together with the ability to produce 'Boardroom Reports' and a graphics

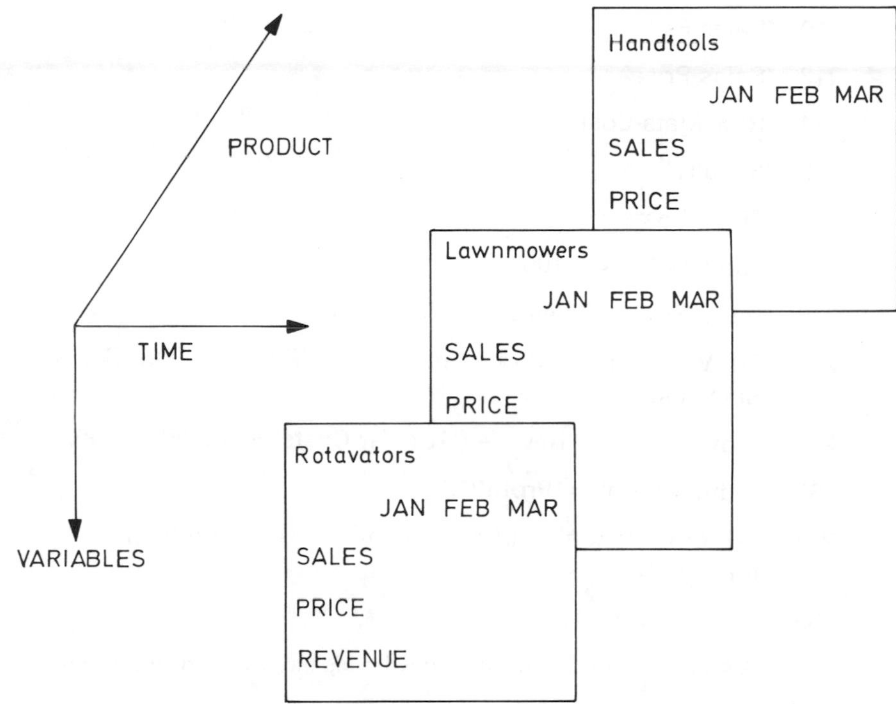

Figure 4.5 Three-dimensional modelling, with PRODUCT as the third dimension

capability, separate logic packages provide a very sophisticated modelling tool. They can also be 'black-boxed', which permits the package also to be used operationally as well as for planning.

Two very powerful advanced financial modelling packages are FCS (10) and MASTER MODELLER (11). On a smaller scale is FASTPLAN II (12). Another package is PLUSPLAN (13), which, however, fits rather uneasily into this category. Its unique features are its adherence to accounting jargon, its basis in double entry bookkeeping and its general 'auditor-friendly' approach. PLUSPLAN has certain facilities for ensuring that accounting consistency is maintained, and offers full accounting consolidation. All of the packages mentioned above offer what is basically two-dimensional modelling. FINAR (14) is an example of an advanced language package offering three-dimensional modelling.

4.5 Database Financial Modelling Packages

Database Financial modelling packages are the most recent type of package to be developed. They are not to be confused with database packages (such as

```
210  'Sales Est'
212  'Sales Price'
214  'Raw Mats Cost'
216  'Royalty'
218  'Fixed Costs'
220  'Lab Cost' = 4.0/100
226  'Sales Rev' = Sales Est' * Sales Price'
228  'Tot Var Cost' = ('Raw Mats Cost' + 'Royal' + 'Lab Costs') *
     'Sales Est'
230  'Profit' = 'Sales Rev' — ('Tot Var Costs' + 'Fixed Costs')
232  'Profit/Month' = 'Profit'/12
234  '%Profit Change' = ('Profit'-'Profit'Lag1.)/'Profit'Lag1
      for 2. to 3
235  ;234 = 0.0 for 1.
```

Figure 4.6 A simple financial model developed using the advanced language package FCS

dBASE) but have been developed along database lines specifically for financial modelling. Although the concepts may be a little difficult to get used to, this type of construction allows the modeller great freedom. He does not need to specify the exact form of the model at the outset, but instead is called upon simply to specify the basic features of the model: its dimensions, elements and the logic that links the variables—plus, of course, the data.

For example, a company selling several products in several regions might create a model with the dimensions of product, cost, region and time. Elements for each dimension would be specified (for example, London, Leeds and Glasgow for the dimension 'Region'; January, February, March, etc. for the dimension 'Time'). It is then possible to report on any two dimensions—costs against time for the production of bolts for London say, or products against costs for the London region for the whole year. This is illustrated in Figure 4.7, using FINAL (15).

A further attraction of database financial planning packages is that it is not necessary to specify the sequence of calculation (which is necessary with all other types of package) since they are powerful enough to work out an appropriate sequence for themselves. Thus the rules of logic can be written in any order.

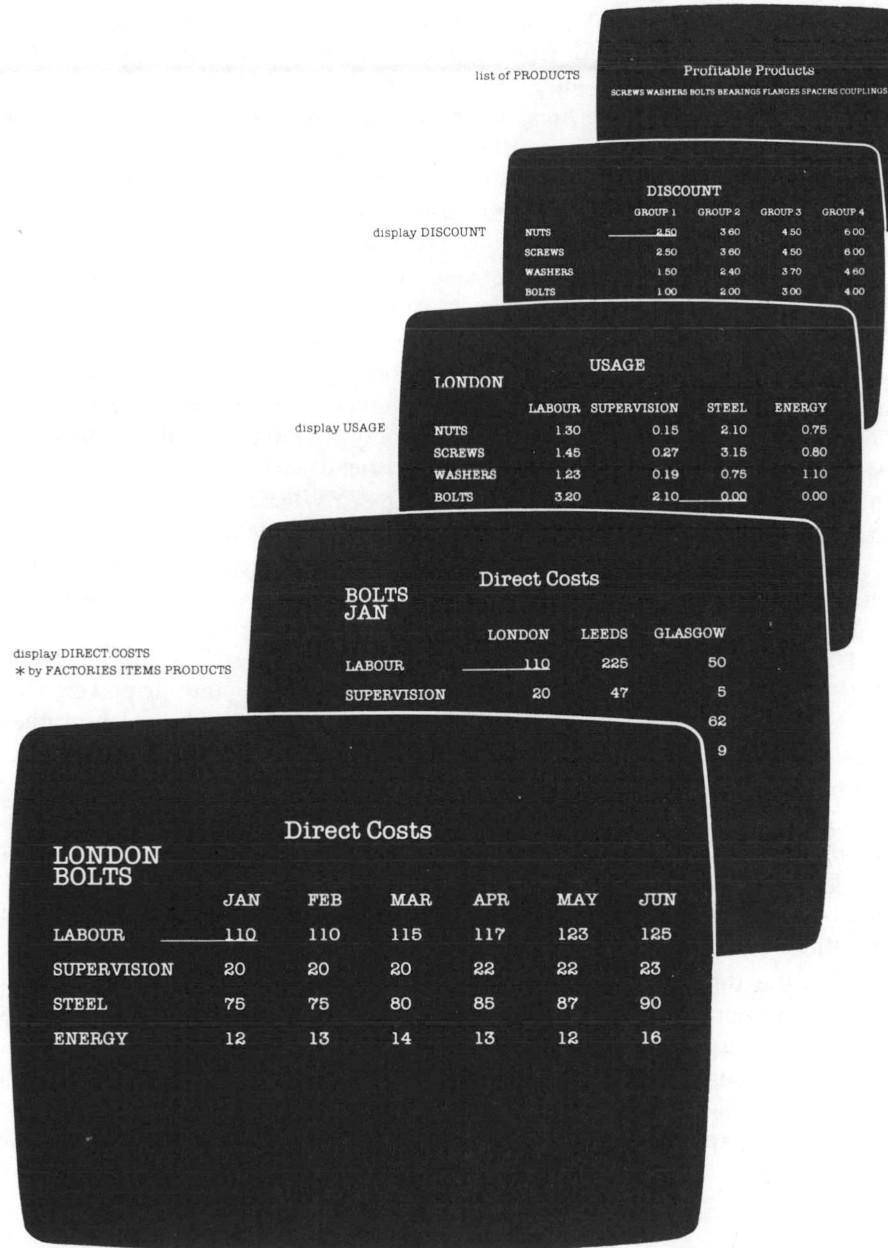

Figure 4.7 Different views of the data

FT.MONEYWISE (16) is perhaps the easiest of these packages to get started with since it looks at first sight to be a three-dimensional spreadsheet with its rather fixed data entry format. The package offers what is termed a Moneybook consisting of 67 pages. These pages are of several types, the most important ones being the modelling, graphic and presentation pages. The modelling pages consist of a matrix of 168 rows and six columns. All six columns are always shown on the screen and, rather unusually, represent variables rather than time. The rows are associated with time, with 12 time periods visible on the screen at the same time. The rationale of this method of input is that this is the only satisfactory way of ensuring that all the data associated with the very common twelve-month planning horizon are all visible on the screen at one time. It is into the modelling pages that the user would place input data (normally columnwise) together with the rules of calculation. The presentation and graph pages contain information to be output which can show any relation between the data. The speed with which reports can be prepared is one of the great assets of FT.MONEYWISE. Another is the facility to carry out data modelling—being able to extrapolate and interpolate data very easily, and for the user to see visually the effects of arithmetic and geometric incrementation. The package, however, does not offer a sophisticated sensitivity analysis facility.

FT.MONEYWISE is a small database package. Perhaps the largest is SYSTEM W (17) which tends to be very demanding of computing power. This package offers a very wide range of facilities but its price and its rather complicated model building means that it is only really suitable for the large corporate user having computer expertise on hand.

EXPRESS (18) and FCS-MULTI (19) are other database financial modelling packages offering a wide range of facilities, but again requiring skilled users. FINAL offers fewer facilities but is much more user-friendly than SYSTEM-W, EXPRESS or FCS-MULTI. FT.MONEYWISE, FINAL and EXPRESS are available in microcomputer versions.

The large database financial modelling packages find their greatest use with corporate users where the volumes of data are substantial, where the data structures are complex and where the number of 'views' of the data are numerous. Corporate budgeting and reporting systems are areas where such packages are likely to come into their own. Corporate users are likely to have a corporate IT resource, which is just as well as these packages are not for the uninitiated.

4.6 Resource-based Packages

An important factor to realize with financial modelling packages is that they are something of a misnomer. They *are* financial modelling packages, but they are also able to be used for the planning and control of resources other than money. In fact, there is a great deal to be said for using a common modelling tool in the modelling of non-financial resources, and linking this to a financial model.

All financial planning packages will support non-financial resource modelling to some extent. What has been achieved with ATPLAN (20) for process industries is to develop an integrated hierarchy of three levels of model. At the lowest level, the use of non-financial resources is modelled: at the second level costs are married to the resource usages calculated at the lower level to produce cost data. Finally, the results from the cost model are automatically fed to a financial planning model (and this could be one of the packages already described).

The great attraction of resource based systems is that many of the major functional areas in an organization can gain experience of using the same planning tool. This in itself should encourage the debate between interested parties in the planning process. ATPLAN is the only package known to the author that is explicitly designed for resource base planning in this way.

4.7 Conclusion

Outlined above are the characteristics and scope of five major classes of financial modelling package. This classification is aimed at helping direct the activities of people involved in package selection.

The cost of software varies widely and this might be considered an important constraint on acquisition. However, the purchase price of software is likely to be only a small portion of the total cost of developing and implementing systems. The costs after the purchase of the software—in training, maintenance and so on—are often hidden but they are nevertheless real. Perhaps the rule of thumb should be to pay somewhat 'over the odds' for the software itself, since this is likely to reduce substantially the overall costs of systems development when compared with those associated with bending a package that does not have the required facilities in an easily usable form.

References

Grinyer, P. H. and Wooller, J. (1975). *Corporate Models Today: a New Tool for Financial Management*, Institute of Chartered Accountants in England and Wales, London.

National Computing Centre (1985). *Directory of Software*, NCC Microsystems Centre, London.

Appendix to Chapter 4

Exhibit 4.1 Contemporary Software Directory

The following list is UK-oriented but many of the packages are available worldwide.

(1) PLANALYST, Computer Financial Models, Suite 20, Moreland House, 80 Goswell Road, London EC1V 7DB (01-253-6738).
(2) TK!SOLVER, Software Arts Inc., 27 Mica Lane, Wellesby MA02181, USA. (From Byteshops, Head Office 0480-218812.)
(3) SystemBuild, 13 Market Place, Market Deeping, Peterborough PE6 8HD (0778-342341).
(4) LOTUS 1-2-3, Lotus Development Corporation, 161 First Street, Mass., 02141, USA (From Byteshops, Head Office 0480-218812.)
(5) SYMPHONY (as for (6)).
(6) SUPERCALC, Sorcim Corporation, 405 Aldo Avenue, Santa Clara, CA95050, USA (From Byteshops, Head Office 0480-218812.)
(7) BOEINGCALC, Boeing Computer Services (Europe) Ltd, PO Box 173, St Martins House, 31–35 Clarendon Road, Watford, Herts WD1 1ED (0923-49611).
(8) REPORTMANAGER, Sapphire Systems Ltd, 1–3 Park Avenue, Ilford, IG1 4LU (01-554-0582).
(9) VP-planner, Paperback Software Int., 2612 Eighth Street, Berkeley, Ca. 94710, USA. (From Direct Computers Ltd, Bessemer Drive, Stevenage SG1 2DX 0438-310160.)
(10) FCS, Thorn EMI Computer Software, EPS Consultants, Boundary House, Boston Road, London W7 2QE (01-579-6931).
(11) MASTERMODELLER, Planning Sciences Ltd, Colonial House, 35 Church Road, Barnes Village, London SW13 (01-741-9620).
(12) FASTPLAN II, Comshare Ltd, 32–34 Great Peter Street, London SW1P 2DB (01-222-5665).
(13) PLUSPLAN, Deloitte Haskins and Sells, PO Box 207, 128 Queen Victoria Street, London EC4P 4JX (01-248-3913).
(14) FINAR, Corporate Modelling Consultants, 46 Chagford Street, London NW1 6EB (01-262-1021/6).
(15) FINAL, D. M. ENGLAND and Partners Ltd, Tudor House, 24 High Street, Twyford, Berkshire RG10 9AG (0734-342666).
(16) FT.MONEYWISE, Moneywise Software Ltd, 226 Sheen Lane, London SW14 8BR (01-878-8585).
(17) SYSTEM-W, Comshare Ltd (as for (14)).
(18) EXPRESS, Management Decision Systems Ltd, Old Crown, Windsor Road, Slough, Berkshire SL1 2DL (0753-822456).
(19) FCS-MULTI (as for (12)).
(20) ATPLAN, Atkins Planning, Woodcote Groves, Ashley Road, Epsom, Surrey.

PART 2
THE PRACTICE OF MODELLING

Financial Modelling in Corporate Management, 2nd Edition
Edited by J. W. Bryant

5

An Experience of Corporate Modelling*

JOHN PRECIOUS

5.1 Introduction

This chapter describes the experience gained in the field of corporate computer model-building by one organization over a period of about eight years. Throughout, an emphasis has been placed on the practical aspects of the work: how we approached the technique from first principles; the errors which have been made; and the successes which we feel have accrued. There will be companies which have different or more rapid progress to report, but it is probable that the lessons learned at Tioxide are fundamental and of general relevance to any organization embarking on corporate modelling.

The development process is described below in three parts, the first dealing with the initial four years of work, while the other two cover the later phases of modelling carried out during a further succeeding four-year period. These sections were each written at the end of the respective four-year development period which they describe, and so there is added poignancy in the remarks made at the end of Section 5.2 which describe the then anticipated developments, as opposed to the reality described in Section 5.3. It was felt to be instructive to retain this historical dimension rather than to produce a single discussion of the whole modelling programme written with the benefit of hindsight, because it illustrates quite dramatically how perceptions of the growth and value of specific corporate models can change for reasons that are not always easily anticipated.

*Parts of this chapter are reproduced by permission of the publisher from J. R. Precious and D. R. Wood, 'Corporate Modelling: When Success Can Be a Long-term Forecast', *Accounting and Business Research,* Autumn 1975, 254–72.

5.2 When Success can be a Long-term Forecast

This section reviews the first years of corporate modelling at British Titan Ltd. (later renamed Tioxide Group Ltd). There are three clearly defined phases through which we progressed, and these are described below *as seen at the conclusion of this part of the work.*

Phase I

The process of model building by computer began some four years ago, shortly after finalization of the group's five-year plan. The decision to take our first tentative steps in building an 'in-house' corporate model was made before the experience of compiling this particular plan by hand had receded into the memories of those concerned. That experience (at least to the accounting function) could probably best be summarized as: mass calculation, analysis, compilation and consolidation—repeated several times, to test forecast revisions—which, manually, is a time-consuming process. It was therefore logical to conclude that use of the company's computer should, by the very time saved, allow a much closer look at the key variables through the medium of sensitivity analysis. Thus followed our first acquaintance with the Prosper programming package.

So the decision was made; but how to begin? And promptly, our first mistakes: we chose to approach the task by straightforward transcription of the recent plan, using the accounting schedules to prepare an outline flowchart. We had unknowingly made two fundamental errors:

(1) We assumed that, by and large, each succeeding reappraisal of medium- and long-term plans would fit the format devised for the most recent manual assessment.
(2) We devoted a relatively small amount of time (approximately two weeks) to the preparation of logic diagrams.

In other words, reduction of the accounting man-hours became the major objective. It did not, of course, follow that the resultant model would be particularly appealing in a practical sense to anyone other than accountants. Had we been content to merely simplify our own involvement in subsequent reviews, then in some ways the project could have been considered a partial success. But this was not our sole objective, it was not even the most important. We wanted to build a model which could be used by corporate planners to test the broader strategic aspects of possible courses of action open to the group. In this respect, the model was a failure.

Further, our first corporate model was inflexible. Most of its drawbacks resulted from a combination of this and the two major policy errors mentioned above, all of which were the direct result of our inexperience in this planning technique.

By the time the project was eventually complete, we had assembed a formidable list of items requiring amendment or improvement, which effectively meant a total program overhaul. Some of them are outlined below:

(1) The program was written as one complete model.
It is not difficult to envisage the impact of this decision upon run time and paper: excessive consumption of both. So for example, to observe the effect of a change in sales prices on trading profits, we had to resign ourselves to a twenty minutes wait whilst the model ran from start to finish. Compared with the process of manual adjustments, this is of course an insignificant period. But when a computer is operational for many of the 24 hours in a day, working to closely defined schedules, time assumes a premium rating: one-third of an hour used in this manner equates to a waste of resources.

Thus we learnt the value of time spent in planning a program, and how the use of a number of submodels can help to accelerate the results of sensitivity analysis.

(2) The opportunity to use the results of a series of instructions and forecasts in a different area of model was not used to the full.

Another example may best illustrate this point. The group's manufactured end product demands considerable investment in raw material stocks. To calculate the usage of cost of each raw material, assembly of the relevant stock accounts will obviously be necessary. But when complete, this process will also show the investment in raw material stocks at each period end—which in itself is a major element of working capital, necessary for the compilation of cash flows and balance sheets.

Because we elected to construct trading accounts, cash flows and balance sheets independently of each other, we did not take programming advantage of this obvious financial link. The result was a less efficient model than might otherwise have been the case, and once more the reason was lack of pre-program planning.

(3) There was only one way in which a sales forecast could be calculated. The chosen method was to assume that finished product stocks would equate to a fixed number of weeks' sales (based on past experience), and with a known production capacity, sales would be the balancing figure. The principle was, of course, perfectly sound. But a planning model which does not offer any alternative means of constructing a key forecast is taking too much for granted: inflexibility again.

(4) The standard of output presentation was poor.
Some figures had been subject to rounding up procedures, but others contained two or three places of decimals. The impact on a casual observer

would no doubt have been bewildering; but to those concerned with some measure of detail, irritation may have led to despair.

Most long-term planning models result in a considerable output of information when run in full. By giving minimum attention to print-out formats, we did not assist any subsequent analysis of the results.

Naturally, there were more errors in this first model, but a lengthy catalogue has an air of repetition. We feel the above to be a representative and possibly useful selection to anyone interested from a practical viewpoint.

Of design successes (other than the fact that the model was capable of operation, however inflexibly), three are perhaps worth passing mention:

(1) The raw materials of importance in the manufacturing process were assumed to be key determinants of factory cost; all other materials and services were consolidated into two summary headings.

An obvious decision—though it would have been equally simple to make numerous additions in portraying an 'accurate' factory cost statement. But we felt that the model, when operational, should be able to display effectively possible future trends in the business over a maximum ten-year period. Consideration of detailed factory costs in this context simply yields a model with an excessive number of input forecasts, whose claims to greater accuracy are largely illusory.

(2) Calculation of working capital levels was also made on the basis of isolating key elements.

Another hardly less than obvious remark. So for the same reason outlined in (1)—that it is always tempting to err on the side of detail in pursuit of the 'most accurate' result—we isolated the major elements of the company's investment in working capital. The annual movement in each largely governed the movement in working capital as a whole. As may be expected, the analysis showed that stock (finished product, raw material only) and trade debt were the determining factors. The remaining assets and liabilities had either relatively static levels or fairly predictable cyclical movements.

(3) There was a page selection print-out facility.

Item (4) above gave the major negative presentation error; this facility helped at least to minimize the discomfort. Thus, for example, to see the effects of an adjustment to sales prices (in terms of revenue, trading profit and cash flow) required only five of the more than forty pages to be printed. It was unfortunate that the construction of the model still necessitated operation of the complete program, despite the diminution in requested print-out volume.

Phase II

It was after a year of comparative inactivity in the model-building field, that serious thought was given to the development of our limited experience to date. This time we approached the problem in a rather less insular way. In conjunction with the data-processing manager, a report was prepared for the group financial controller which proposed a revised and expanded modelling system, for the eventual use of all companies in the group. It explained the proposals under four main headings:

objectives;
benefits;
outline structure;
implementation and costs;

with three accompanying appendices:

detailed structure;
key data elements;
a comparison of available modelling systems on the market.

It may be of interest to summarize the objectives and benefits of the system as they were seen at that time.

Objectives

(1) Assist management in the evaluation of long-term plans, using inter-linked computer-based models to evaluate, and where possible optimize, profits and cash flow.
(2) Enable subsidiary plans to be produced in local currencies prior to conversion and consolidation into sterling.
(3) Provide detailed evaluation of sales and production forecasts; profit and loss accounts, balance sheets, cash flows, operating ratios and statistics, to be the minimum financial statements.
(4) Show separately the effects of inflation.
(5) Allow for the optimization of certain specified functions.
(6) Either incorporate or have access to a minimum of ten (preferably twenty) years' historical statistics, to enable regression analysis to be carried out where requested.
(7) Anticipate the necessity for new factories or extensions to those already in existence, and indicate where any increase in productive capacity could be undertaken, based on the available input data.

The remaining objectives were viewed in terms of implementation, running costs, and ease of operation.

(8) Assemble a flexible structure with at least a five-year life expectancy.
(9) Keep the installation costs to a minimum, but without compromising achievement of the objectives as a whole.
(10) Be easy to maintain and develop, yet fast and efficient in operation (i.e. extensive use of disc storage).
(11) Enable alternative strategies to be evaluated without compromising original or basic data.
(12) Allow full acceptance and modification of data, with subsequent results displayed through computer terminals.
(13) Be capable of accepting as input data available information from other computer systems using the projected database.
(14) Incorporate alternative methods of data input through which the system may be activated.
(15) Ensure, if requested, that selected data and results be displayed through the various stages of operation.

Benefits

(1) Would enable evaluation of long-term plans to be carried out throughout the year.
(2) Make more time available for detailed study of the results of alternative courses of action.
(3) Enable the present five-year view to be enhanced by a further five-year period, thus allowing the investigation and development of potentially more far-reaching strategies.
(4) The provision of individual self-contained subroutines to encourage greater participation by line management, in both the concept and formulation stages of the long-term planning process.

Heady stuff! And to be at all comprehensible a structural outline of the complete model was required.

In summary, the following were the important aspects contained in this part of the report.

Outline Structure

(1) There were to be three major areas of operation which could broadly be classified as marketing, production and finance.
(2) The complete model was to be operational in five individual, but linked, levels:

Level 1 Profit and loss accounts
Balance sheets

Cash flows
Ratios and statistics

Level 2 Summarized sales and production forecasts (in the form of trading accounts).
Level 3 Detailed marketing and production forecasts.
Level 4 Optimization of marketing and production capacities.
Level 5 Determination of world demand for the product.

(3) The model was to be designated as a hierarchical structure, level 1 being the 'highest' and level 5 the 'lowest'. But it was recognized that in the interests of flexibility, there had to be provision both to transmit data and forecasts from one level to any other specified level (not necessarily in sequence) and to commence at any desired point. To be satisfactory, this effectively required that the upward sequence from level 5 to level 1 could be dispensed with if attention was to be directed to a particular planning area. It was therefore envisaged that a 'link data file' between each level and the next would give effect to these or any other operational circumstances requested.

An additional facility to be made available through these linking files was an overwrite option. In other words, as data progressed towards level 1, a user could make amendments to the result sequence by direct input of alterations or additions at each level. This was to ensure that the changed results or forecasts would be used thereafter in later levels of the model.

(4) There would be a similar set of submodels for each company in the group in levels 1–3. This was seen as simplifying the process of consolidation in levels 1 and 2, when programming commenced.

(5) Output data from all stages of the model would be available in either horizontal or vertical form, i.e. by function or company.

Although this completed the system in outline, some further amplification of the distinguishing characteristics in levels 2, 3 and 4 may assist clarification of the operational areas in the report.

Level 2: Summarized Sales and Production Forecasts

(1) At this stage, a clear forecast relationship would have been established between sales and production functions throughout the group. The statistics could have been derived (through a logical operational sequence in the model, having commenced at level 5) or directly input at some intermediate stage through a link data file.

(2) Level 2 would be the highest point in the structure where consideration of production and sales could be made in units of each (the profit and loss accounts in level 1 would assume a statutory accounts format). It

therefore follows that this would also be the highest level wherein a contribution gap could be deduced from independent sets of data.
(3) Both sales revenues and production costs would be expressed in summary form.

Level 3: Detailed Marketing and Production Forecasts

(1) Seen as an intermediate stage between the global supply/demand formulation at levels 4 and 5 and subsequent corporate trading results at level 2.
(2) This subroutine would thus be primarily concerned with the evaluation of sales within group companies, by sales or marketing characteristics.
(3) The construction of a production cost forecast differentiating between variable and fixed costs would be made at this point.

Level 4: Optimization of Marketing and Production Capacities

(1) Expected to be a marketing oriented subroutine where production capability would be a limiting factor. Thus, a marketing strategy (either directly input or developed at level 5) beyond productive capacity would be satisfied by the model automatically taking note of the shortfall, and suggesting a construction location/programme based on previously input parameters, e.g. group strategy, cost of capital, availability of funds, production costs, etc.
(2) The marketing programme established, and feasible within the above constraints, maximization of group contribution would be attained by the distribution of sales and production targets to each manufacturing source, having regard to the appropriate costs and revenues existing at each.

The proposal was subsequently accepted and the project began soon after. We had thus progressed to

Phase III

Output Specification

It was clear from the outset that with a (relatively) far more ambitious project under way, the original corporate model should be retired to the archives of experience. Clearly, to have attempted to amend the program would have taken more time than to write a new one.

This decision made, detailed output specifications were drawn up as a first step towards ultimate programming. During the course of this process, information gaps were discovered relating to the requirements of levels 4 and 5, such as to render their specification incomplete. As a result, and because each level would be programmed individually, it was decided to concentrate on levels 1–3 in the first instance.

Logic Diagrams

Although we already had composite output specifications for these areas, we determined that detailed logic diagrams should be drawn from them before programming work commenced (an early lesson remembered!) This approach may not meet with the general approval of those experienced in data processing or corporate modelling activities. Nevertheless, we felt that the analysis had been worthwhile for the following reasons:

(1) The links to and from other levels and/or subroutines are clearly established.
(2) Forecast number usage is consequently restricted. The effects of providing for alternative courses of action and sources of input are properly evaluated.
(3) The programming function is simplified since objectives are clearly stated.
(4) Testing of programs and location of program errors is facilitated.
(5) Basic system design errors are readily evaluated, and the impact of their correction easily seen, prior to any program modification which may be necessary.

Programming

Work commenced after certain fundamental program criteria had been established:

(1) We elected to program the first three levels for one company alone. The remaining companies' comparable models and subroutines would thereafter be installed either by total or selected duplication of this 'base' model.
(2) Level 3, containing much of the model's component detail, was the logical beginning.
(3) Provision for the use of trend and adjustment factors would be accommodated in the programs, but they would not be displayed in the subsequent print-out. (This simply meant that if any part(s) of the output tabulations were required for publication in the ensuing group plan, presentation would not be affected by extraneous detail.)

(4) Where a company had more than one factory, the profitability of each would be assessed in addition to that of the company as a whole.

Level 3

Almost immediately after commencement, some of the logic assumptions were in question. During the early programming stages of major raw material (MRM) manufacturing cost, a problem had arisen concerning the evaluation of each material's usage. Originally, it had been the intention to calculate a weighted average price based upon the costs of opening stock and subsequent annual purchases. Unfortunately, this involved the use of program structures which, in operational terms, only served to slow the program down. Considered in the context of the model as a whole, a desirable solution appeared to be valuation at the current year's purchase price: financially conservative in times of inflation and operationally faster.

The next contentious programming area which we encountered was also reminiscent of the original corporate model: calculation of sales, production and stock levels of finished product.

It will be recalled that one method only was previously available. Mindful of this serious shortcoming, we therefore proposed the following options for user consideration:

(1) Input: sales, production and first year's opening stock.
Calculate: production.
(2) Input: sales, closing stock and first year's opening stock.
Calculate: production.
(3) Input: sales and first year's opening stock.
Calculate: closing stock (as x weeks' sales) and production.

In all cases, input could be either direct or from level 4 (when completed).

The final reference to programming experience at this level of the structure concerns the assessment of fixed manufacturing costs, and in particular, a manpower planning facility.

As a result of time constraints, we were not able to conduct the background analysis which we felt the subject warranted: that is, a separate subroutine for each factory payroll. In these circumstances, we made provision for only one category of process labour, which therefore had to represent a weighted average of all relevant employee grades. Nevertheless, we suggested that a forecast compiled from this undesirable base at least recognized that costs of (salaries and) wages depend on numbers employed, as well as annual increments. Therefore, any proposed increase in production should display a sharp rise in the company's manpower investment if the resultant forecasts are to retain credibility.

Within three months all programming and subsequent testing of the completed level 3 had been accomplished.

Level 2

Once again, a flaw in the output specifications was quickly uncovered—this time in the calculation of depreciation and government grants.

We had presumed an instruction sequence operational here, immediately prior to compilation of the detailed trading account. But this overlooked the logical sequence which began in level 3 with the construction of individual factory and company profitabilities, where net depreciation is naturally a significant item of fixed cost.

We therefore had no alternative but to reopen level 3 and accommodate these amendments—a straightforward process which demonstrated (if demonstration was required) the inherent flexibility of a model comprising a series of individual subroutines.

Yet another departure from plan was also made when we determined that compilation of 'detailed' trading working capital was a more feasible proposition at this stage than the previously envisaged level 1. The decision centred upon the degree of sophistication to be expected when considering certain strategies. For example, a ten-year assessment of outline data, which may be expected to take place within the boundaries of the first level, was thought unlikely to use anything more complex than an *ad hoc* estimation of total annual working capital movement. On the other hand, we reasoned that a view which began with summarized forecasts of sales and production units could well require a comparative assessment (at least) of the significant working capital elements.

Phase III had begun at the start of a year and July saw the completion of level 2. All this enabled us to complete the programming for level 1 well before the end of the year.

Up to Date and Beyond?

It is fortunate that continued development has not progressed as we expected. There have been a number of reasons for the slow down, but by far the most significant is the perennial complaint of many in commerce and industry: staff shortages. It is to our immediate benefit that within the recent past, steps have been taken to alleviate the situation, and we anticipate that much (if not all) of the backlog will have been eliminated before the end of this fourth year since modelling began.

However, the above slightly despondent air is not to imply cessation of progress over the past year and a half; that would be far from true. We have managed to complete almost all the programming and subsequent testing of programs for other group companies, including the modifications which were necessary from the basic model described above. Disc storage space has been allocated for each, and the models are expected to be installed within the next two months.

To complete the first major segment of this second corporate modelling system therefore only requires the establishment of a consolidation routine at level 1; level 2 consolidation is already operational.

With an enlarged availability of resources the outstanding parts of level 1, 2 and 3 will be speedily assembled and tested. In conjunction with colleagues in the Planning, Marketing and Data Processing Departments, we would anticipate completion of level 4 before the end of this year.

Of the original proposal, this would leave only level 5 to successfully conclude the project. However, it is now thought likely that work in this sphere will be deferred in favour of an additional submodel at level 1. A program written during the last few months has already been the subject of some development work directed towards the establishment of corporate financial returns and objectives for the future. Its successful completion and addition to the present structure would, we believe, usefully enhance the Group's assessment of its long-term objectives, and the strategy which might be employed in their achievement.

As in much work of a development nature, the end of a project may signal the beginning of new or related investigations. So with this company's approach to corporate modelling. We feel that with the resources at hand, two years represents the long-term—the sort of time-scale to be expected for completion of all the above outline proposals. It will be interesting to see, next year, if we managed to achieve our objectives.

5.3 ... But Long-term Finance Forecasts are Usually Wrong

The last section described some four years' work in corporate financial model building, ostensibly aimed at simplifying and improving the group's long-term planning process. Paradoxically, in view of these preceding circumstances, a disinterested observer could well conclude that one form of purgatory had been exchanged for another. For here was a catalogue of almost unremitting gloom laced with a series of conspicuous failures. Nevertheless, a note of cautious optimism was struck towards the end of the review: Utopia appeared to be just around the corner; even the future was 'more readily discernible', at least within the organization.

But experienced corporate modellers would not have been deceived. The signs would have been recognized for what they were—another false dawn: within a year, the large UK model that was to form a prototype for the remainder of the structure had already gathered its first layer of dust on a shelf to which it had been ignominiously consigned. It was there for the same reason that any other development project will always fail—if the work becomes an end in itself to the exclusion of the needs of the market place or, as here, the end-users.

This second instalment in the department's experience also measures four years. Apart from the inauspicious beginning sketched above and some eighteen months of desolate aftermath it is actually possible to claim a first significant success.

After recording the practical experience to this point the earlier barren years will be contrasted with later more productive ones, using published material for comparison in the next section, to see whether any satisfactory conclusions can be drawn to account for some of the bizarre results which have accrued.

It is not intended that the reader be denied a second opportunity to survey further modelling calamities at leisure. Indeed, the display must be candid if lessons are to be learnt. And if those new to—or less experienced in—the field can successfully avoid some of the traps, their work will be the better for it, and recounting the latest instalment in this particular saga will have served its purpose.

There are again three clearly defined phases through which the work has progressed. The aim is still to be practical, even though there is not a particular model structure to focus upon. This is because the salutary lessons are in the reasons for eventual success—and in particular, why the vision of so many years ago should have taken so long to materialize.

Phase IV

Early in the fifth year since work commenced there was an expectant air amongst those building—or merely waiting upon—the second large-scale group financial model. At least, that was the impression gained by the two staff members in the North of England responsible for its development. Indeed, when one-half of the team was given a permanent position in the London-based Group Finance Department (of the recently renamed Tioxide Group Ltd) it was not even then immediately apparent that the department had lost any enthusiasm for the project which it had first requested. Of more pressing need—or so it seemed at the time—was how to successfully complete the development work with an enforced geographical separation of staff to contend with. The only answer seemed to be to continue as before. Why should distance be anything other than a minor practical irritant?

However, as the year wore on, it became clear that its earlier promise had been evanescent. Progress was ever more difficult to achieved. Other priorities both in London and the North were encountered; and modelling lost. The workload of the Group Finance Department was increasing, and though completion of the model was an accepted part of the new environment at the outset, its importance relative to other tasks steadily declined.

There were two principal reasons for this regrettable but ineluctable development: first, the group's management accounting system was materially changed; and second, when viewed from the centre, the model-building progress to date was by no means as successful as it had seemed to be from the subsidiary, only a few months before.

Ironically, the preceding progress report had correctly—but quite unwittingly—noted this development in its penultimate paragraph. For at the time it was observed that:

> it is now thought likely that work in this sphere will be deferred in favour of an additional sub-model at level 1. A program written during the last few months has already been the subject of some development work directed towards the establishment of corporate financial returns and objectives for the future. Its successful completion and addition to the present structure would, we believe, usefully enhance the Group's assessment of its long term objectives, and the strategy which might be employed in their achievement.

Stripped of all sentiment, this simply meant that the package in course of preparation was not going to meet user requirements. Consequently, work had begun separately in London on a model which would do so. The matter of user involvement in the model-building process—one of the key requirements for success—had in effect been blithely ignored by the modelling team for at least the previous two years.

Shortly after this realization had dawned, it required no great sense of prescience to conclude that further work on the model structure would be futile. Its own size had eventually ensured its technological and practical downfall. It had been difficult enough to accept the almost imperceptible progress since the previous year on a second ambitious project. But this was as nothing to the feeling of desolation which followed the inescapable conclusion that here was another spectacular and resounding failure. Which would probably have been a suitable point to have closed this whole, sorry financial model-building story, had it not been for a series of events—unconnected with the modelling process—which occurred during that same year, for they ushered in the era of third-generation long-term financial-planning models.

Phase V

The first development of significance was another change in the Group's planning systems. The previous annual process of compiling a long-term plan—a financially orientated document of some complexity and considerable detail—was to be replaced by a strategic plan. The difference lay not in the choice of words—the old ways merely refurbished—but in fundamental concept. Detail was recognized for what it often is at the top of a planning hierarchy: spurious accuracy to fill a void left by the absence of realistic assumptions or any feasible alternatives.

This strategic plan would comprise a series of statements resulting from the assessment of perceived alternative courses of action. Its compilation was to focus on four main areas of the business: marketing, production, finance and personnel. And the emphasis would be placed on a careful review of the past and current environments, before the underlying assumptions for the forecast period were selected.

The second and most significant development in this context was a task for the Group Finance Department from the Board: to prepare, at three levels of confidence, ten-year projections for the pigment-producing companies, and the Group, showing forecast profit and loss accounts, cash flows, balance sheets and resultant ratio analyses. Quickly.

Without prior warning, this request had the instantaneous effect of concentrating departmental minds on an objective, output reports and time-scale which allowed no margin for failure. So the first problem was fundamental: how to begin?

There appeared to be only three alternative approaches:

(1) By hand—with full potential for a clerical exercise in which both content and consumption of time were awesome to contemplate. Or,
(2) Use the (unfinished) Prosper model. The portents here were no less awesome, since the model had to be finished (in areas where work had not even begun) and tested, before the process of feeding in base data could begin. The previous two years' work hardly suggested that a successful final outcome could be foreseen with confidence.

Which left only,

(3) Try another modelling language, better suited to the particular task. But which one? Grinyer and Wooller (1975) had listed 38 financial modelling systems in their survey. How could available systems be ranked to satisfy Tioxide's criteria?

After a good deal of thought and outside consultation, the field was narrowed down to two languages: Planmaster and FCS. The choice was difficult, because both had competing attributes. But eventually it was apparent that Planmaster had the edge in this particular application for the following reasons:

(1) Quick initial comprehension and ease of use thereafter
The given circumstances placed a high premium on time. It was important that the operating principles of the chosen language could be easily

grasped, and that its subsequent use should be comparatively straightforward—even for the relative novice. Designing and building the model was clearly going to be difficult enough. But to have saddled this process with an unwieldy (or low-level) language would almost certainly have courted failure. This language had remarkably few rules to learn, which thus ensured speedy development. (If it is suggested that there is an analogy here with building a house—which may be completed slowly by traditional means, using several different skills acquired over the years; or quickly by use of prefabrication, which requires fewer skills acquired in much less time—then the analogy is solely concerned with relative completion times. There is no implied suggestion of better or worse structural permanence.)

(2) Rule changes automatically resorted and validated before model updates
An efficiency advantage. Certain languages required specific editing, i.e. direct replacement of logic or commands by the user within a model structure. Furthermore, it could not always be taken for granted that the other systems would generate automatic error reports if changes were incorrectly programmed.

(3) Structural changes made with ease
It does not necessarily follow that a fundamental change in a model's structure—for example, the installation of a new company or product line—will be accomplished with ease. Indeed, it is possible that the reverse circumstances may apply. At the very least, this could mean a considerable loss of time while a model is being built, and it would certainly affect the efficiency of maintenance and development work which must inevitably follow.

(4) Built-in consolidation facility

(5) Automatic currency conversion
Both factors simplified the construction process and made for ease of use thereafter. The initial directive required that full consolidated results be included in the presentation. These attributes of the language strongly—and correctly—influenced the final decision.

But the process of analysis and comparison also revealed some disadvantages which, though considered of minor importance at the time—since accomplishment of the task in hand was the overriding criterion—would not have been ignored under any other circumstances.

(1) Costly to run
This derived partly from the fact that the language was only available through a time-sharing bureau, and partly from its mode of operation. The end result of the combination meant that any forecast of design and running costs had to be speculative—in fact, a guess—and it must be admitted that none was ever made.

(2) Static rules
Which meant that a total re-sort was necessary whenever changes were made. Though arguably inefficient, there was no doubt that this meant a greater use of computer time. In other words, the model was going to cost more to build and run.

(3) Less flexible report format compared with FCS
But the (exclusively financial) output requirements meant that this was of negligible importance. Within a small group of similar operating companies, the format for one profit and loss account or balance sheet almost certainly satisfies the remainder, with minor modifications.

So, the advantages of Planmaster outweighed its disadvantages, and the whole package was considered superior to FCS. (But it is essential to remember this record is portraying the respective attributes and drawbacks—*as seen at the time*—of two competing modelling languages, for a particular task, about to be attempted by a particular company. It did not follow that the same decision would necessarily be taken by another company in the same or differing circumstances. Nor even that the same decision would be made by this company today.)

However the next year, after a short period of training which followed system selection, the way was clear to flowchart the required structure; and thereafter to begin programming the model itself.

As with all previous experience to date in the company, there was only one person deputed to the project on a day-to-day basis. But this time, an attempt was made to secure effective insulation from the rest of the department's responsibilities; and of course, there was no geographical separation of staff to contend with. Needless to say, this did not work to perfection in practice, but a good deal of application and week-end work soon saw considerable progress being made.

It would not be unduly cynical to ask *how* this 'considerable progress' came to be made, in view of what had gone before. The main reason was force of circumstance: apart from the fact that this was a much higher-level language than the ICL Prosper of earlier days, it was clear from the start that there could be no concession to detail in the model structure. The built-in variables would have to be fewer than in either of the two previous model attempts—provided always that this criterion could be reasonably substantiated—if only to shorten the odds on success. In the event, statistical research of the recent past suggested that there were five variables which mattered more than any others in providing a satisfactory financial explanation for the results which had been posted by the manufacturing companies. Subsequent confirmation of these relationships and their quantification for each company meant that this latest suite of models had an excellent fundamental core on which the whole structure could be built. And with rather more confidence than had previously been the case.

From this point onwards, the only question of significance was whether the remaining time available would be sufficient to ensure completion of the models and their adequate testing, whilst still allowing for the assembly of live data for final report generation. Surprisingly enough, the target was achieved with time to spare. But even now, some years later, the day can still be savoured which first saw the production of a complete set of reports to the original specification—if only because there had been times during the years of failure when success was a word whose very existence had seemed in doubt.

Whilst reflecting that any financial modelling system which not only worked but was also in use in the company either gave cause for some celebration, or else served only to confirm the law of averages—depending upon the observer's viewpoint—there can be little doubt that completion of this project within three months was meritorious in its own right.

To the surprise of many—not least those directly concerned—this was all the time that was required from beginning to end. In fact, the Board's request which began the whole process had arisen from its last meeting of the year in mid-December; system reviews culminated in selection of the Planmaster package in the first week of the following January; and the first complete print-out of results was produced in the middle of March.

5.4 The Years in Retrospect

It is always tempting to allow success to blind failures, and never more so than in the case of Tioxide's financial modelling experience. But this would do less than justice to the earlier miguided years of honest endeavour. Besides, if a change of approach can have such a fundamental effect on system building expectations, then it must be possible to discern reasons for the interest of others contemplating use of the technique for the first time. Indeed, if there are none, who could confront a learning curve of these proportions with equanimity?

In fact, there are some very clear conclusions to be drawn. But beforehand it would perhaps be instructive to take account of the views of others. Whilst so doing, a consensus of opinion may be discerned on how to build models successfully—or at least how to lessen the likelihood of failure.

As Mann (1978) noted, models are not new, and to some may even be thought prolific, so there has been an increasing amount of literature devoted to the topic in recent years. Whilst the references which follow are claimed to be illustrative in a Tioxide context, their selection is strictly subjective. Nevertheless, the reader is invited to conclude that where there is a sufficient similarity in content or emphasis, then the opinions are not to be lightly ignored.

Mann observed that the effective use of practical models in a company's long-term planning process was rare, but suspected that this was only partly a function of the lack of success:

> Nor are models always useful. Over the years many have been constructed merely to satisfy the desires and aspirations of the model-builder, or to enhance the power of the computer. Problems were chosen where a solution was not necessarily of benefit to management

He then cited two golden rules:

> (1) The model must be related to the real needs of the managers who are responsible for the running of the business. The model-builder must work closely *with* the manager, to understand his problems, to find a solution for use *within* the existing planning processes.
> (2) The model must be simple, it must avoid the pit of size. This can be achieved by constructing a system on the modular approach, building a step at a time.

The same general lack of successful integration of models into the planning process despite dramatic increases in usage of computer-based planning models since the beginning of the last decade, was noted by Naylor (1977). These failures severely limited the usefulness of models as planning tools. Yet little attention had been given to the problem of tailoring the model to the company's specific planning requirements. Naylor suggested that there were six steps to ensure successful integration:

(1) Review the planning environment. Begin with the organizational structure (of the company); then its management philosophy (management's attitude towards formal planning and the use of models in the process); and finally, the business environment and the planning process itself.
(2) Specify the planning requirements of individuals in the company: the type of report required and the questions to be answered; the business strategies to be followed in future years.
(3) Define the goals and objectives for planning—as required by management.
(4) Evaluate the existing planning resources. Only when a company has reviewed its planning environment requirements and resources could,
(5) Design of an integrated planning and modelling system, and,
(6) Strategy for integration of the planning model into the planning process,

be successfully accomplished. And in considering the latter, Naylor warned that a management education programme in the system's use would be necessary, while recommending that a modular building approach be taken, which tied performance to specific timetable dates.

In concluding their survey, Grinyer and Wooller (1975) remarked that:

> our visits to companies with corporate models showed us again and again that the crucial factor is enthusiasm for the corporate model among top management (and especially senior financial management). Other conditions for success exist ... but this is the one of overriding importance

However, their own experience and published literature suggested that there were six main interrelated conditions for successful modelling. (The absence of any three tended to produce failure):

(1) Sponsorship and continued support given by top management.
(2) Top management understands and has confidence in the model, and places at least some reliance on its results.
(3) The model meets specific management decision-making needs.
(4) Input data are readily available and not voluminous.
(5) The model is embedded in the planning process—used as a matter of course.
(6) Proper documentation has been kept throughout development.

If the past is to be examined before the future is contemplated, Hammond (1974) cautions against undue reliance upon empirical evidence—at least in model-building—if it is assumed that historical relationships or data would be maintained in future. (This point had in fact been taken in the Tioxide experience described above. Analyses of past results were certainly undertaken to *identify* five variables and their interrelationship within each company; but it was not henceforth assumed that they would remain at constant levels during the ensuing forecast time periods.)

Hammond elicits a ten-step process in the conception, creation and use of models in the planning process. In the first instance, it is necessary to decide where a model may be useful and only then whether to use it. Given that there will probably be a need for the release of significant resources in the company—both time and money—then a formal proposal should follow definition of the input and output specifications. It is then almost inevitable that program testing will require data collection, the results of which may question the program logic or even the fundamental concept that the model seeks to reproduce. Users have two important roles throughout: first, they must be educated and their acceptance of the model obtained, preferably to include contribution in its design; and second, they must be responsible for program validation prior to use. Finally, use of the model or passage of time must create the need for maintenance, whether of error correction or development to suit the needs of the business.

Several factors are noted to help the model-builder ensure success. The following selection is from a comprehensive list:

(1) Keep to established company procedures (at first) and use familiar input/output formats.
(2) Start and stay simple in concept. 'Companies should beware of channelling effort to the development of a mammoth model before understanding has been firmly established by both managers and modellers and scope and feasibility have been made clear'.
(3) Beware of optimistic delivery dates—plan for the fact that programs always take longer than expected.
(4) Aim to produce some managerially useful results as soon as possible.
(5) Ensure continuous update of the model once it has been built, and maintain high standards of documentation throughout.

Higgins (1980) lists a number of practical aspects which must be heeded in developing and implementing corporate models. Noting that the prospects for successful innovation and continued use of the model are enhanced if the project has been commissioned by top management, he considers that a relatively simple structure is usually preferable at first to gain full comprehension. Then managers could be expected to have sufficient belief in the model to use its results and ensure that it becomes an integral part of the planning process. Indeed 'senior managers should be encouraged to use real-time corporate models directly ... '

Higgins also observes that:

> as an organisation gains experience in model-building, it will be well advised to develop a suite of models rather than a unique, large model. A modular structure illustrates the general issue of flexibility or versatility of corporate models. ... Flexibility of logic implies that the model can accommodate major changes in organisational structure, e.g. the creation of new divisions or subsidiaries, without the need for reprogramming.

And finally, whilst reviewing the progress of management information networks in a marketing context, Schewe (1974) defined a few key directives for a successful system:

(1) 'Gain top management support.
First and perhaps foremost, top management must be given *tangible* evidence of the value of the ... system.' There must be total commitment

from top executives within the firm and this should be obtained by provision of immediate and tangible returns on the firm's system investment.

(2) 'Set reasonable system objectives.'
The degree of technical sophistication should be related to the needs of the company;

(3) 'Build the system over time, not over night.'
Begin simply and work slowly towards greater complexity.

(4) 'Gain user involvement.'
The system must be user-orientated; it should begin with the manager's perception of the decision environment and related information needs. There must be user involvement in the building process: participation throughout the design and implementation stages should facilitate both knowledge of the system and its early acceptance.

(5) 'Provide system users with sufficient training.'
And to this end, avoid jargon so that communication is at the user's level and thus fully comprehensible.

Although this last article is concerned with an information system for marketing, on the same subjective basis which governed selection of all quoted references within this Tioxide review, Schewe's pithy statements can be seen to encapsulate most of the recommendations for success noted by the other authors.

It should by now be reasonably clear to the reader why failure resulted from the earlier Tioxide attempts before an operationally satisfactory and usable structure was eventually devised. The first model simply broke every one of Schewe's system-building principles.

Sadly, the second effort fared little better. Its early stages flattered to deceive: the top management support gained by acceptance of the initial comprehensive report specification was clearly forfeited when there were no early tangible returns once modelling had begun. Eventually, the users lost interest in the project. Why? Because in retrospect, it can be seen that the crucial decision was the very first programming step: in choosing to begin at level 3 (the area of most component detail in that particular model) all possible hopes for retention of user goodwill were lost on two counts. First, the amount of detail involved was of no interest to them and second, it was inevitable that they would have to wait for *any* tangible return.

In contrast, the third attempt scored because the principles *were* observed. Certainly, the restrictive time allowance was in this sense a benefit—there had to be a reasonably early return if the task was to be completed in time. But the reader should not be misled: this success did not accrue following discovery and careful assimilation of all the above quoted material. With the exception of the book of Grinyer and Wooller (1975), none of the other sources were then known to exist! Which probably only goes to show that a final vital ingredient in any successful modelling venture is a substantial portion of luck.

Phase VI

In the opening paragraphs of this second corporate progress review, no mention was made of events following completion of the successful model. Until some time later from an innovative or design point of view, there was virtually no further progress—other than routine maintenance and development of the model program. However, it had long been apparent in Tioxide that a relatively small Group finance function convinced of the virtues of modelling must look to the technique to increase its departmental efficiency and effectiveness.

To this end, some two years after completion of the Planmaster model, a good deal of time was spent surveying the available modelling systems, for it was certain that a greater investment of computer time could only mean much greater expenditure of money. Since an ambitious programme had been planned—covering almost every aspect of the department's responsibilities from exchange exposure to statutory accounting—there was little doubt that a two- to three-year programme of modelling work could be expected. This in turn suggested that all models should be programmed in the same language, to enhance operational efficiency and prepare the way for an integrated Group management information system.

The time which had passed since selection of the Planmaster package had seen many changes in the available systems. So perhaps there is a certain amount of poetic justice in disclosing that the result of this later review recommended another change: away from Planmaster—to FCS. In the department's view, all the previous substantive drawbacks of FCS had been more than made good during the previous three years. Added to which the FCS software house was regarded as giving an excellent service, from its substantial staff base.

And so the saga continued. ... However, rather than going on to describe subsequent experiences with the in-house FCS system eventually implemented in this most recent phase of evolution, it seems more valuable to conclude this cautionary tale at this point with some more general comments. So whilst recognizing that the narrative has been devoted to the description of a model-building programme whose avowed aim has always been directed towards assisting the strategic planning process—no matter how implausible the results—it is well to remember that a successful model can never be a surrogate for selection of feasible alternatives, or indeed the conception of planning. Nor can it predict or state best answers, whatever they might be. Management must weigh and ultimately decide upon the available opinions, facts and forecasts within its own business environment. A successful model can only be a useful tool in the entire process; no more, no less.

Last words, then, to Drucker (1979) who had the following observations to make whilst considering what strategic planning is *not*:

> It is not a box of tricks, a bundle of techniques. Many techniques may be used in the process—but, then again, none may be needed. Strategic planning may require a computer, but the most important question—'what *is* our business?' or 'what *should* it be?'—cannot be quantified and programmed for the computer. Model building or simulation may be helpful but they are not strategic planning; they are tools for specific purposes and may or may not apply in a given case.
>
> Quantification is not planning. To be sure, one uses rigorous logical methods as far as possible if only to make sure that one does not deceive oneself. But some of the most important questions in strategic planning can be phrased only in terms such as 'larger' or 'smaller', 'sooner', or 'later'. These terms cannot easily be manipulated by quantitative techniques. And some equally important areas: such as those of political climate, social responsibilities, or human (including managerial) resources, cannot be quantified at all. They can be handled only as restraints, or boundaries but not as factors in the equation itself.
>
> Strategic planning is *not* 'the application of scientific methods to business decision ... ' It is the application of thought, analysis, imagination, and judgement. It is responsibility rather than technique.

You have been warned!

References

Drucker, P. F. (1979). *Management: Tasks, Responsibilities, Practices*, Pan, London.

Grinyer, P. H. and Wooller, J. (1975). *Corporate Models Today*, Institute of Chartered Accountants in England and Wales, London.

Hammond, J. S. (1974). 'Do's and don'ts of computer models for planning', *Harvard Business Review*, **52**(2), 110–23.

Higgins, J. C. (1980). *Strategic and Operational Planning Systems*, Prentice-Hall, London.

Linneman, R. E. and Kennell, J. D. (1977). 'Shirt-sleeve approach to long-range plans', *Harvard Business Review*, **55**(2), 141–50.

Mann, C. W. (1978). 'The use of a model in long term planning—a case history', *Long Range Planning*, **11**(5), 55–62.

Naylor, T. H. (1977). 'Integrating models into the planning process', *Long Range Planning*, **10**(6), 11–15.

Precious, J. R. and Wood, D. R. (1975). 'Corporate modelling: when success can be a long-term forecast', *Accounting and Business Research (20)*, 254–72.
Schewe, C. D. (1974). 'Management information systems in marketing—a promise not yet realised', *Management Informatics*, **3**(5), 251–5.

Financial Modelling in Corporate Management, 2nd Edition
Edited by J. W. Bryant
Published by John Wiley & Sons Ltd.

6

Developing a Corporate Planning Model for a Small Company*

CORNELIUS DE KLUYVER AND G. M. MCNALLY

6.1 Introduction

The use of corporate models for planning purposes has increased dramatically in the last few years. Recent surveys (Naylor, 1979; Naylor and Gattis, 1976; Higgins and Finn, 1977) suggest that the principal reason for this increase is a growing realization that better appreciation of future risk and uncertainty is a key factor in maintaining profitability. Energy shortages, government regulation, increased competition, fluctuations in monetary policy, and economic uncertainty generally are among the factors cited in this regard.

Corporate planning models developed to respond to these needs display a wide diversity ranging from detailed models of specific corporate functions (production, marketing, finance, etc.) to more aggregate models covering all functional areas. The last category, however, still appears to comprise a small fraction of all operational planning models (Borst, 1977).

The above surveys also reveal that corporate modelling is mainly concentrated among larger companies (Naylor, 1979), possibly reflecting the relative impact environmental variables exert on their operations, the sophistication of their top managements, or simply their willingness and ability to commit the substantial resources needed to develop, implement, and support a corporate planning model.

This chapter describes the development and implementation of a corporate simulation model in a different setting. The company concerned, Canterbury Timber Products, Ltd a medium-sized New Zealand producer of a medium density fibreboard product, is small by international standards with an asset

*Reprinted with permission from *Long Range Planning*, Vol. 15, de Kluyver and McNally, Developing a corporate planning model for a small company, © 1982 Pergamon Press Ltd.

base of $16 million and sales of around $10 million annually. Also, it is relatively young, having been founded in 1973 with commercial production starting as recently as 1976. As a result, the development of the model took place in an environment in which a substantial amount of managerial time and skill had to be committed to relatively routine early life 'survival' decisions.

This chapter documents some of the lessons learned, and experience gained, during both the developmental and implementation phases of this undertaking, thought valuable in placing computerized corporate modelling for smaller companies in perspective.

6.2 The Corporate Environment

Canterbury Timber Products, Ltd (CTP) produces and markets a range of medium density sheet fibreboards of different structural characteristics for a large number of 'end user' applications. Production utilizes local supplies of softwood indigenous timber, and the output is frequently used as a substitute for natural wood products, often with superior features to the equivalent natural wood form.

The production process, from 'chipped' logs to the completed boards, is characterized by a short time cycle, often as little as 30 min. The process itself is structured in terms of a number of distinct phases as depicted in Figure 6.1.

The company is organized as a single plant and administrative facility, and reflects a high volume capital intensive production environment. Given the current 24 hour-a-day, 7 days-a-week production schedule, the company finds itself in the position where expansion opportunities are limited to a duplication of plant/administrative facilities at some other location.

To manage existing operations, the company has built up a small, close-knit management team to guide the continuous, relatively repetitively-natured production process, the limited range of products, and the fairly small number of sales regions. This form of organization is summarized in the organization chart given in Figure 6.2.

The 'Customwood' products produced by the company are marketed both in New Zealand and overseas in countries including Japan, Singapore, Australia and Europe, reflecting the high quality reputation the product enjoys internationally as well as aggressive marketing policies forced by the relatively depressed economic positions currently faced within New Zealand.

The financial history of the firm is typical of that of young, capital intensive operations. Since its beginnings in 1976, the company has recorded substantial operating losses until early 1979, when the previous year's $0.8 million loss was transformed into a healthy $1.5 million profit. Although substantial operating losses during the first few years of operation are not unusual, they were accentuated in this instance by the depressed economic position of many end-users in the furniture and building industries, the need to establish a new market for this innovative product, the high fixed cost structure of the capital

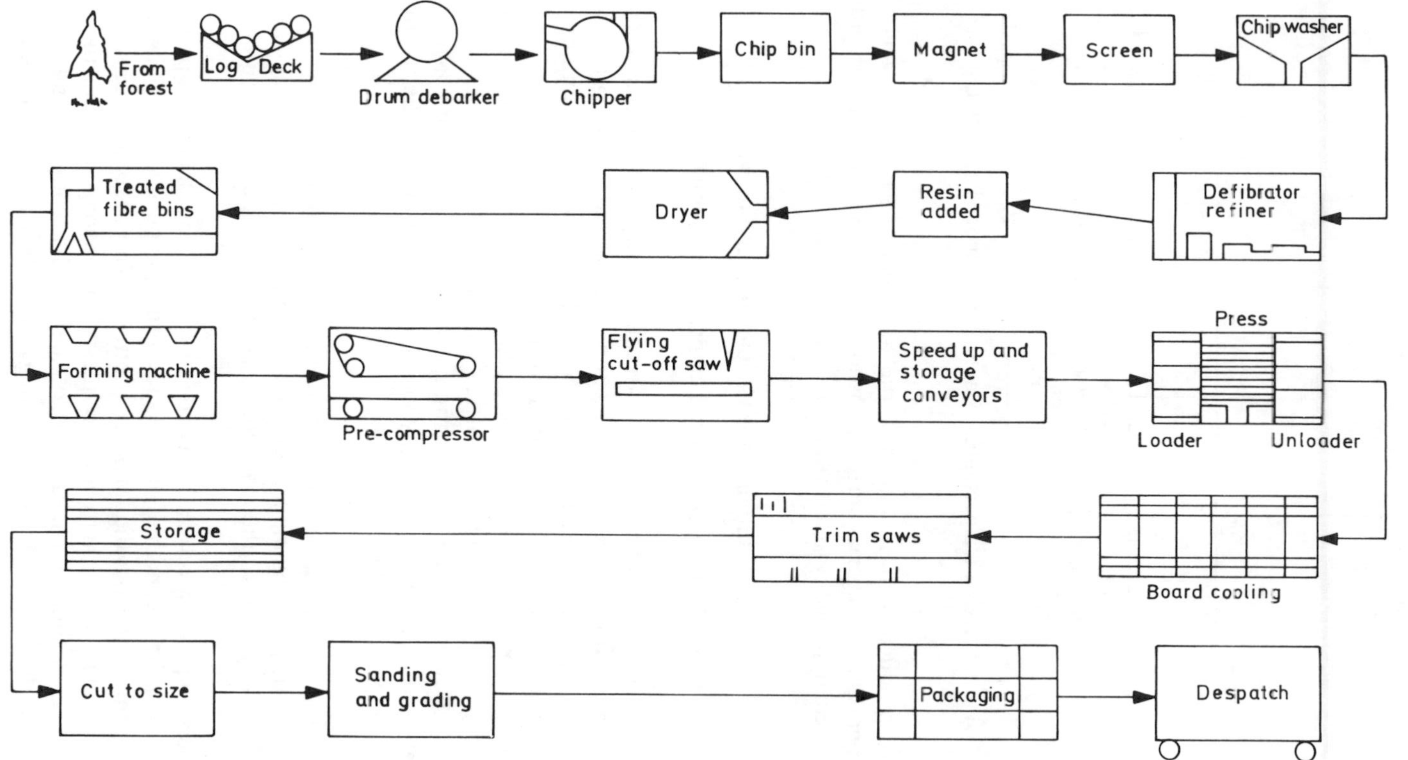

Figure 6.1 Production process

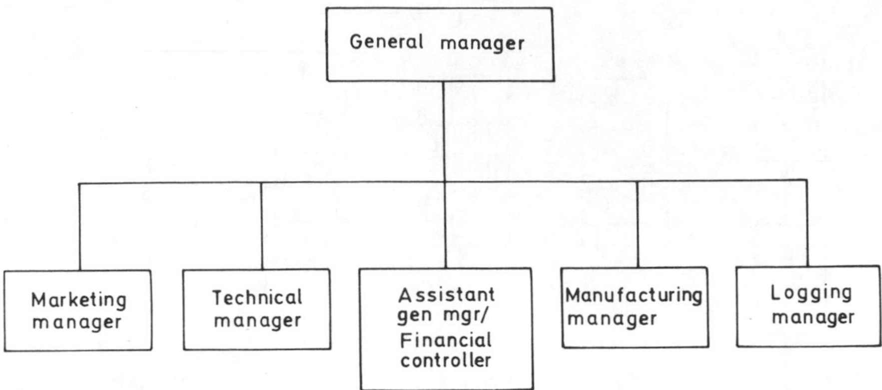

Figure 6.2 Executive personnel: Canterbury Timber Products Ltd

intensive product environment, and the long learning curve for technical, operational and managerial personnel who were relatively unfamiliar with the modern, technologically highly sophisticated production process.

6.3 The Evolution of the Corporate Planning Model

The development of the model evolved in three distinct phases:

(1) A simple model was formulated for examining the impact of changes in the sales mix, input costs and production rates on corporate profitability, following an initial request for back-of-the-envelope solutions to a number of desirable short-term profit positions;
(2) A full scale model was developed to produce a series of detailed corporate budgets for a planning horizon of 12–36 months;
(3) The full scale model was reformulated to accommodate longer term strategic moves by the company in response to proposals that corporate operations be expanded.

The first phase, while minor in importance when compared with the final, corporate-wide planning model developed, is important in that it signalled an awareness on the part of the management of the potential of computer-based corporate models.

The second phase was first discussed in 1977, and resulted in an operational model during the second half of 1978. The principal push for this phase in the development came from the financial controller who needed continuously up to date budget information to satisfy requests from management and the board of directors. Against a background of a limited accounting staff, rapidly changing product demand, and continuing instability in financial and economic conditions, the desirability of a flexible simulation model soon became evident. At this time, a primary requirement was to develop a system for efficient updating of budgets by rolling forward estimates for 12–24 months. As management continued to learn about plant capabilities, and as changes in inputs, production loss parameters, and efficiency ratings continued to show up, the concept of a static or forecast budget was inappropriate, even misleading. When coupled with changes in the product mix, pricing and local/export sales patterns, it became evident that a capability for rapidly executed, frequent budget revisions was needed.

One option open to the company was to contract one of the leading software systems for its budgeting and reporting. However, management decided it wanted more than many of the commercially available software packages could easily offer. In particular, while the company did not possess any substantial computing facilities of its own, it still wanted many of the in-house advantages such systems offer. Thus, it was decided to develop a model specifically designed for the company's needs using sales, production and cost data to generate a hierarchical system of reports of different levels of complexity and detail.

At this stage the company was still struggling to attain profitability as soon as possible and planning was done on a 24-month basis. This relatively short-term planning horizon is not unusual for young companies. Firstly, the company lacked sufficient forecasting history to provide a reliable base for detailed planning beyond this period; secondly, the focus of management was on achieving profitability within the time frame projected in its original prospectus to stockholders: thirdly, management was still learning about the plant's capabilities; and finally, the volatility of the environment in which planning took place would render any forecasts quickly obsolete.

The modification of the model to serve medium-term strategic planning purposes, a role for which most corporate models are developed, is relatively recent. As the reputation of 'Customwood' products continues to grow, capacity restrictions in the form of maximum plant utilization are increasingly being encountered. With the exception of maintenance down-time, the plant currently operates 24 hours a day and 7 days a week. Whereas for many large corporations plant expansion decisions are relatively routine, the required investment in this instance means a increase in total assets of 150 per cent making a detailed examination of this crucial decision imperative. Should unwarranted expansion occur, the financial consequences of servicing the increased capital requirements and the high fixed operating costs may have a severe impact on the future of the company. Conversely, if expansion is justified but does not occur, opportunities to capitalize on knowledge already acquired and substantially increase profitability would be lost to potential competitors.

The importance of this single decision was the principal reason for modifying the model to accommodate a longer planning horizon, increased aggregation of data by item and time period, and new technological and marketing relationships. The redesign was implemented in a format that allows the company to use the model in a strategic planning mode while retaining the option to employ the model as an operational planning tool using detailed data over a planning period of 12–24 months.

6.4 Structure of the Planning Model

The planning model, which integrates marketing, production and financial data, is organized in four modules representing the above three functional areas and a fourth 'report generator' module.

The marketing module processes a variety of revenue data from tonnage and price projections. These forecasts are generated separately since the limited data history available for forecasting has not proved sufficiently stable to warrant the addition of a forecasting capability, although this is envisioned in the future. The rapidly changing market share, market location, and heavy price fluctuations experienced to date favour the use of *ad hoc* forecasts where and when needed. Forecasts are generated in terms of:

- sales tonnes, by product line and by month/quarter,
- percentage breakdown by sales region, both export and domestic, by month/quarter, and
- prices per tonne, by product line, by sales region, and by month/quarter.

Detailed revenue projections are generated, as well as input data needed for estimating production requirements in the production module and projecting cash inflow in the cash module. Additionally, the marketing module serves a number of editing functions by printing exception reports when input data fall outside their predetermined 'reasonable' range.

The production modules uses sales input data together with processing constraints and requirements to generate a production schedule for the projected forward sales in terms of tonnes by product by period. Input requirements at this stage include (i) production/sales lags, (ii) production process loss parameters, (iii) raw material requirements ratios, (iv) manpower needs and constraints, (v) desired closing stock levels and (vi) plant capacity ratings and efficiency projections. In addition to generating a production schedule, this module also computes and summarizes raw material requirements to allow efficient forward ordering and projection of production losses and amounts of 'downgrade' product generated.

The orientation of the production module is toward obtaining feasible rather than optimal production schedules, primarily because at the upper ranges of plant capacity the use of optimization techniques does not yield substantial improvements over the use of more easily applied heuristic scheduling rules. Sample heuristics include:

- avoiding 'split production runs'; that is, the high incremental costs associated with production runs of less than 24 hours imply that it is economically advantageous to delay small production runs until closing stock requirements are breached and then schedule a minimum production run of 24 hours or more,
- the manipulation of 'press tonne operating rates'; that is, if in any given month the sum of projected forward sales and required stock holding exceeds planned operating capacity, press tonne operating rates are increased, work force schedules adjusted, and required stock holdings reduced to yield a feasible production schedule. The order and priority of these manipulations is established by management.

Further improvements in these heuristics are expected as the model is updated and as more sensitivity tests are carried out on the production variables. To date the continued operation of the plant at near capacity levels, however, has indicated that the heuristic approach followed is highly satisfactory, particularly in view of the limited capacity for improvement by the use of formal optimization techniques.

The cash module analyses the cash-flow and profit consequences of different sales and production projections. Additional inputs needed to prepare detailed profitability statements for short-term budgeting include (i) material input prices, (ii) marketing promotion, personnel and overhead costs, (iii) factory overheads, (iv) administrative expenses and (v) finance charges, supplemented with information regarding (vi) lags between expenses/revenues, and the associated cash outflows/inflows, (vii) fixed and variable components of manufacturing expenses and (viii) the basis for allocating overheads over time and apportioning manufacturing overheads across production lines. The latter supplementary data are essential if realistic unit costs estimates, cash-flow and profit/loss statements are desired.

In the course of the development of the model, it became apparent that reports on the cash-flow and profit implications of proposed decisions constitute a key output sought by the most senior management, whereas more detailed reports on unit costs and operating expenses are mainly used by middle management as a basis for comparison with actual expenditures incurred.

The method used to handle the vast amounts of input data needed to accurately describe the corporate environment reflects the basic philosophy that a planning model should be designed to allow the examination of a wide range of strategic alternatives. To accomplish this, input data are grouped into a 'base case' describing a 'most likely' future scenario containing all initial parameter settings, and a number of 'sensitivity data sets' enabling management to query one or more of the key parameter settings in the base case to monitor their impact on key output variables such as profit, unit costs, sales

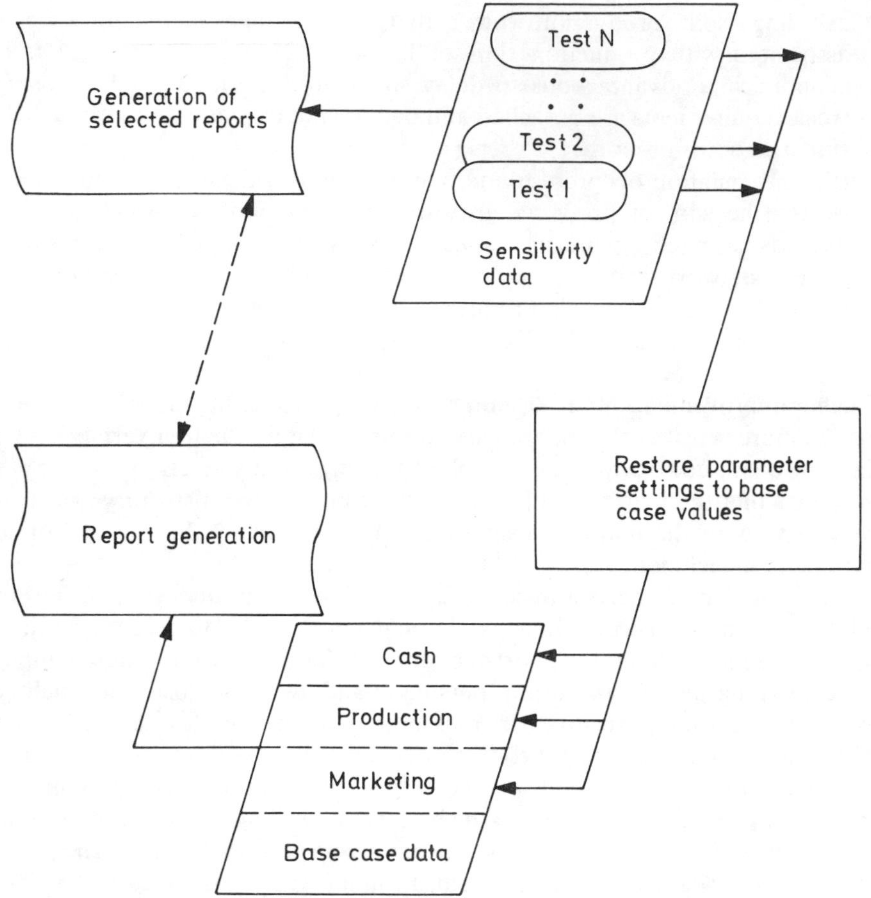

Figure 6.3 Model structure

revenue, production output or material requirements. As illustrated in Figure 6.3, the model is structured to sequentially perform a large number of sensitivity tests in this manner, thus increasing its real-time characteristic.

As revised data input estimates become available, periodic updating of both the 'base case' and 'sensitivity' data is performed to adjust agreed-upon plans, or, more generally, to maintain the representativeness of the model to corporate and environmental conditions.

The nature, content, and structure of reports generated can have a significant impact on management acceptance and use of a computerized planning system. Surveys by Naylor (1979) and Gershefski & Harvey (1970) suggest that information flexibility is a key requirement together with a familiar and easily grasped format of presentation.

All reports produced with the model are generated in a separate fourth print module, from which specific requests are made on a 'Chinese Menu' (i.e. by number) basis. This allows the construction of a hierarchy of reports by subject (e.g. sales, production, cash flow or profit/loss) at different levels of detail, thereby giving functional managers access to more detailed information while senior management can select reports containing aggregate data or specific key operating reports.

The various types of reports produced by the model are illustrated in Exhibit 6.1 in the Appendix to this chapter. They include:

(i) Sales reports:

- Input data editing: a restatement and analysis of key input data such as sales and price projections.
- Revenue reports: a statement of sales revenue by product line and time period for each of the sales regions served.
- Annual average price data: a trend analysis of past price data by product line.
- Revenue summary reports: summary statements of revenue projections for a group of product lines, domestic or export sales by time period.

(ii) Production reports:

- Input data editing: a restatement and analysis of key input data such as technological parameters, production constraints, loss parameters, etc.
- Production output reports: an analysis of planned tonnes of production, production losses, downgrade output, and material input requirements by time period.
- Production summary reports: aggregated production output data for all product lines, containing in addition to total production and loss estimates a projection of scheduled production days and hours needed to complete total projected production requirements.
- Production feasibility reports: an analysis of slack or shortfall in projected production hours, together with suggested heuristic adjustments to the planned production schedule to render it feasible.

(iii) Cash-flow/profit reports:

- Unit costs of production: an analysis of unit production costs separated into variable and fixed cost components, as a basis for 'marginal cost' pricing and related decisions.
- Profit/loss statements: A comprehensive analysis of proposed decisions and operating plans in terms of profit/loss. Revenue is separated into operating and non-operating categories, and costs are grouped along functional lines in detail to allow direct comparison with actual operating results for each month or quarter.
- Cash-flow reports: a detailed summary of the cash inflow and outflow implications of a proposed corporate strategy.

As the emphasis of the model shifted from the evaluation of detailed, shorter-term operating plans to mainly evaluating longer-term, strategic moves by the company, the structure of the model had to be adjusted accordingly. For example, an extension of the planning horizon from a three-year period to a seven-year period was accommodated by reorganizing both input and output data. In the current version of the model, the first twelve months are reported on in monthly figures, while the remainder of the planning horizon is treated with quarterly data. In addition, some sacrifices had to be made in terms of the level of detail that can be incorporated, while retaining sufficient detail to uncover significant trends. Finally, management attention has moved more closely to profit/loss and cash-flow reports rather than to more detailed budgetary reporting, now used elsewhere in the company.

In retrospect, this sequence of developments has proved advantageous in improving the authors' interface with the company. The knowledge and understanding of the company required to develop the shorter-term, budgeting-oriented planning model has enabled the authors to discuss various strategic issues with management in greater detail, thus eliminating many of the 'them and us' problems, so frequently associated with the use of external consultants.

The above sequence of developments also highlights the important difference between larger and smaller companies in terms of the relative significance of operational versus strategic planning. Surveys on the use of long term planning (McNally, 1979; Kumar, 1978; Denning and Lehr, 1972) confirm this. It appears, however, that many of the benefits attributable to long-range planning may be more easily available to smaller companies with computerized planning models having both strategic and operational components.

With respect to the second potential problem area, the degree of understanding needed of the company itself, of its structure, and of its functional and technological capabilities, it has been the authors' experience that problems of this kind are likely to be aggravated in the case of a relatively young company, particularly one of such a high degree of technological sophistication. Both management and operating personnel are continuously learning about plant capacity, relationships between production variables, the nature and causes of production losses, and the measurement of production output. In this environment, it is hard to agree on a basic model structure and 'reasonable' initial parameter settings.

However, on the positive side, the above problems forced a close working relationship in which both management and consultants constantly learned together. This, in turn, resulted in a better appreciation, on the part of management, of both the difficulties associated with constructing a corporate planning model, and of the relative importance of correctly representing material input requirements, processing losses, etc, for predicting output.

Finally, the degree of corporate support for a project such as this is a crucial variable in determining its success or failure. In this instance, the initial proposal for the development of a corporate planning model emanated from senior management itself. The fact that an initial appreciation of the capabilities of such a planning model was already present, coupled with the authors' involvement and implementation, including its coding and debugging, created a receptive environment favouring a successful application.

Although a high degree of receptivity was present, however, there remains a constant need to corporate personnel regarding problems that can be encountered, and time delays experienced, in establishing an operational planning model. Experience has shown that any suggestions that the model to be established can assist in the solving of a number of current problems should be discounted as soon as possible. With one or two man years constituting lower limits on development time, a failure to do so may cause management to become disillusioned, and worse, reduce further commitment to the project, either in terms of funds or time. Both management and consultants must view the development of the planning model in terms of a long-term addition to the corporate planning system.

6.5 Cost–Benefit Analysis

An evaluation of benefits derived from corporate models used for both short-and long-term planning typically includes the following dimensions:

- an ability to explore a larger number of alternatives,
- improved quality of decision-making,
- a higher degree of confidence in decision-making,
- more effective planning,
- availability of more timely information,
- a better understanding of the corporate environment.

Each of these benefits may result in corporate actions which yield a higher level of overall profitability. However, attempts to measure direct profit consequences attributable to the use of a particular planning system are likely to be spurious at best. In the authors' experience, it is more meaningful to interpret such general benefits in more specific if qualitative terms. For the case study described here, Canterbury Timber Products, Ltd has benefited from the use of the model in several ways as outlined in Table 6.1.

Obtaining these benefits is not, however, a costless process and two principal categories of costs; developmental and running/maintenance may be identified. The amounts and composition of these costs are very much 'situation specific' and it is difficult to generalize from this application alone. In particular, the already identified unique features of corporate age, model

Table 6.1 Specific user benefits

General benefits	Specific benefits to user
(a) Explore more alternatives	Examine a range of price/volume marketing strategies for the products and markets to assess the impact on cash flows and profits Cost implications of alternative technological possibilities and stocking strategies to meet production schedules
(b) Improve quality of decision-making	Modifications to production/marketing strategies are made in response to current cash flow and profit/loss data, not previously available Strategic decisions made with data from several scenarios
(c) More confidence in decision-making	Increased knowledge and certainty by management of short-term impact of changes to operating costs The model provides an assessment of unit cost implications, cash flow changes and profitability in a 'real time' response. Price revisions are made with confidence
(d) More effective planning	Ability to replan rapidly as important element for ensuring effective management action and performance. Real time redirection of resources to achieving corporate objectives Effective planning by testing and rejecting many possible corporate strategies. Improved planning without increases to management personnel The rolling forward to budget projections for a constant 12, 24 months horizon is performed as an integral part of corporate planning
(e) More timely information	Response time of 2–4 days (in batch mode) to an array of input data sensitivity tests, resulting in improved timing for management decision-making
(f) Understanding of the business	Management has a better appreciation of the impact of variables including overhead allocations and costs of operations on unit product costs Technical/production staff and marketing personnel appreciate the role of each group in the organization by interactive discussion sessions when preparing sensitivity data inputs for the model and when reviewing the reports generated

structure, continued use of external consultants and an evolving objective for the modelling exercise all contributed to the final costs.

Development costs consisted of consultants' fees for model design, programming and computer costs and an implicit cost of corporate executive time devoted to the modelling exercise. From the initial inquiry, through the development of the first simple model to the completion of the full scale planning model, direct costs were less than $5000. Executive time checking of model output and explaining technical aspects of plant operations took approximately 50–60 hours.

Costs of running and maintaining the model over its first two years of operations consist mainly of computer operating costs and consultants' fees for managing the model's use and incorporating minor modifications. The former, is incurred in extensive budgeting and strategic decision-making uses of the model, amounted to approximately $1200, while additional consultant fees were about $1500.

While the level of out of pocket costs may be lower for a company with its own computer facilities, the use of consultants by Canterbury Timber Products was essential. It avoided the need to substantially increase fixed costs for both data processing equipment and personnel and also provided the company with access to consultants whose experience and independent viewpoints have benefitted the company directly in the modelling process and indirectly in discussions of corporate operations.

6.6 Conclusion

The principal conclusion that can be drawn is that planning in this company is no longer a static, annual event. Rather, it comprises a continuous review process of alternative courses of action, in particular for the attainment of short-term corporate goals and improving the use of scarce financial, physical, and manpower resources. At the same time, the availability of the model has opened the doors to an examination of longer-term strategic moves without having to commit substantial personnel time, or having to suffer significant delays in obtaining information regarding the profit consequences of such moves. When viewed as a total system, it may be concluded that this smaller company has generated a planning capability, often associated only with larger corporations.

The experiences recounted here lead the authors to hypothesize that smaller, recently established firms may well be highly receptive to the development of computerized corporate-planning models, particularly in view of the dual role such models can play in this environment. Corporate politicking may well be less evident, interactions with the economic environment may not constitute dominant factors, and complexities inherent to larger corporations do not exist, while a small, enthusiastic management team striving to attain or maintain profitability constitutes an important supportive element for the successful implementation of new planning techniques.

References

Borst, D. R. (1977). 'Financial Modeling—a status report', in *Management Accounting: State of the Art*, University of Wisconsin, Madison.

Denning, B. and Lehr, M. (1972). 'The extent and nature of corporate long-range planning', *Journal of Management Studies*, February.

Gershefski, G. and Harvey, A. (1970). 'Corporate models: state of the art', *Management Science*, February.

Higgins, J. and Finn, R. (1977). 'Planning models in the United Kingdom: a survey', *Omega*, February.

Kumar, P. (1978). 'Long-range planning practices by U.S. companies', *Managerial Planning*, January/February.

McNally, G. M. (1979). *Cost and Management Accounting in New Zealand*, New Zealand Society of Accountants.

Naylor, T. (1979). *Corporate Planning Models*, Addison-Wesley.

Naylor, T. and Gattis, D. (1976). 'Corporate planning models', *California Management Review*, Summer.

Appendix to Chapter 6

Exhibit 6.1 Output reports

SALES INPUT REPORT UF-GRADE 07

	JUL	AUG	SEP	OCT	NOV	DEC	JAN	FEB	MAR	APR	MAY	JUN
TOTAL TONNES	3300.00	3800.00	4300.00	4050.00	4800.00	4000.00	4100.00	4500.00	4800.00	4900.00	4500.00	4400.00
EXPORT REG.1 %	100.00	100.00	100.00	75.00	75.00	50.00	50.00	50.00	50.00	50.00	100.00	100.00
EXPORT REG.2 %	0.00											
EXPORT REG.3 %	0.00											
EXPORT REG.4 %	0.00											
DOM.REG.1 %	40.00											
DOM.REG.2 %	30.00											
DOM.REG.3 %	20.00											
DOM.REG.4 %	10.00											
REGULAR %	100.00											
SPECIAL %	0.00											
EXP.PR.REG.1 $	430.00											
EXP.PR.REG.2 $	430.00											
EXP.PR.REG.3 $	470.00											
EXP.PR.REG.4 $	470.00											
DOM.RP.REG.1 $	510.00											
DOM.RP.REG.2 $	510.00											
DOM.RP.REG.3 $	510.00											
DOM.PP.REG.4 $	510.00											
DOM.SR.REG.1 $	410.00											
DOM.SP.REG.2 $	410.00											
DOM.SP.REG.3 $	410.00											
DOM.SP.REG.4 $	410.00											

SALES OUTPUT REPORT UF-GRADE 07

	JUL	AUG	SEP	OCT	NOV	DEC	JAN	FEB	MAR
TOT.EXP.REV. $	516000.	602000.	602000.	580500.	559000.	207500.	415000.	611250.	489000.
EXP.REV.RG.1 $	516000.	602000.	602000.	435375.	419250.	95000.	190000.	285000.	228000.
EXP.REV.RG.2 $	0.								
EXP.REV.RG.3 $	0.								
EXP.REV.RG.4 $	0.								
TOT.DOM.REV. $	1071000.								
DOM.REV.RG.1 $	428400.								
DOM.REV.RG.2 $	321300.								
DOM.REV.RG.3 $	214200.								
DOM.REV.RG.4 $	107100.								

SUMMARY UF STATISTICS

	JUL	AUG	SEP	OCT	NOV	DEC
REGULAR REV.	$ 1071000.	1224000.	1479000.	1377000.	1837500.	1837500.
SPECIAL REV.	$ 0.	0.	0.	0.	0.	0.
TOT.DOM.REV.	$ 1071000.	1224000.	1479000.	1377000.	1837500.	1837500.
EXPORT REV.	$ 516000.	602000.	602000.	580500.	559000.	207500.
TOTAL REV.	$ 1587000.	1826000.	2081000.	1957500.	2396500.	2045000.

ANNUAL STATISTICS

AVGE.PRICE EXPORT	$	439.58
AVGE.PRICE DOMESTIC	$	510.83
AVGE.PRICE OVERALL	$	475.21
WGHTD.PRICE EXPORT	$	417.88
WGHTD.PRICE DOMESTIC	$	510.96
WGHTD.PRICE OVERALL	$	487.71

(a) Sales reports

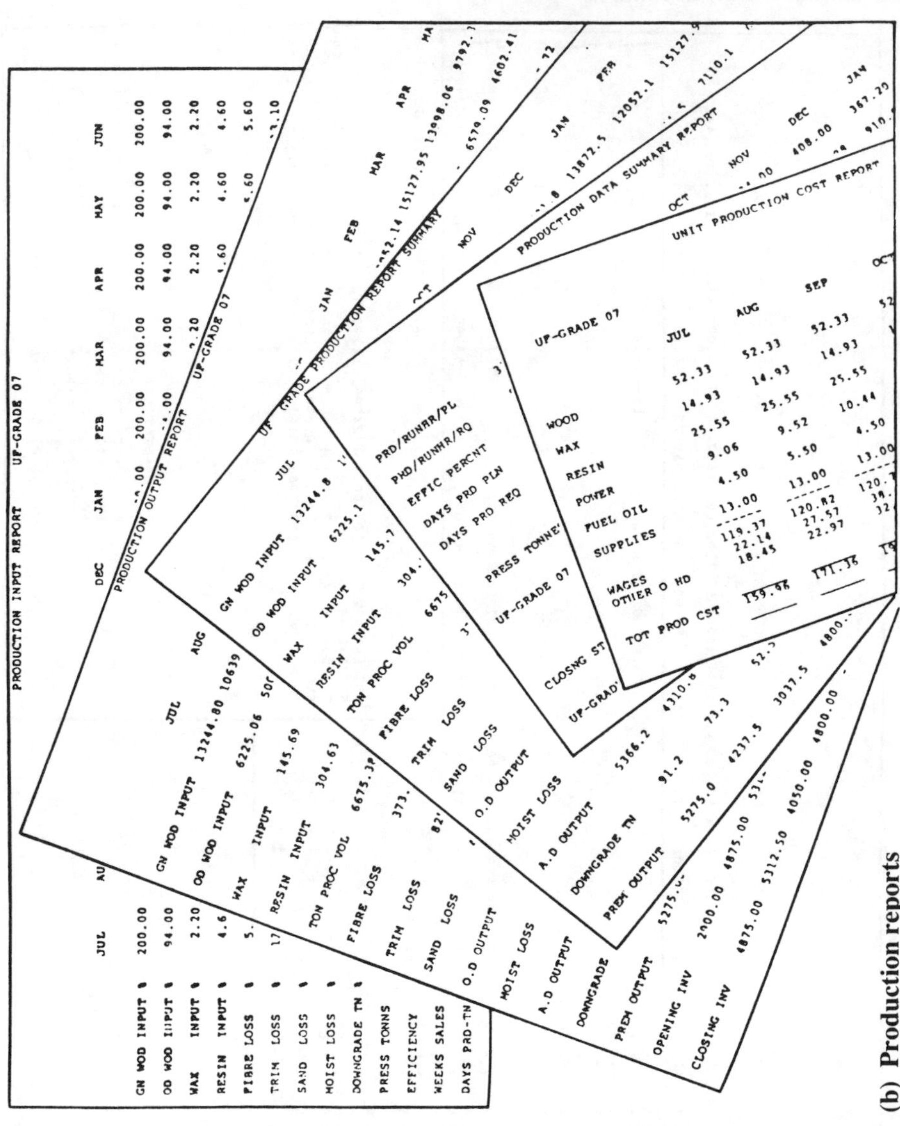

(b) Production reports

COSTS AND REVENUR REPORT

	JUL	AUG	SEP	OCT	NOV	DEC	JAN	FEB	MAR	APR	MAY	JUN
PRM.REVENUE	1587000.	1826000.	2081000.	1957500.	2396500.	2045000.	1980500.	2126250.	2307000.	2377000.	2230000.	2179000.
DWN.REVENUE	0.	0.	0.	0.	0.	0.	0.	0.	0.	0.	0.	0.
TOT.REVENUE	1587000.	1826000.	2081000.	1957500.	2396500.	2045000.	1980500.	2126250.	2307000.	2377000.	2230000.	2179000.
WOOD	280790.	225563.	161687.	255505.	159691.	216913.	294097.	255505.	320712.	296759.	207598.	136403.
WAX	80131.	64371.	46142.	72915.	45572.	61902.	83929.	72015.	91524.	84698.	59244.	38928.
RESIN	137084.	110122.	78937.	124740.	77962.	105899.	143581.	124740.	156574.	144880.	101351.	66593.
POWER	48637.	41038.	32248.	45158.	31974.	39847.	50468.	45158.	54130.	50934.	38565.	28759.
FUEL OIL	24159.	23709.	13905.	21974.	13733.	18655.	25292.	21974.	27581.	25521.	17854.	11731.
WAGES	118833.	118833.	118933.	118833.	162167.	162167.	162167.	162167.	162167.	162167.	162167.	162167.
SUPPLIES	69761.	56040.	40170.	63479.	39674.	53891.	73067.	63479.	79680.	73728.	51577.	33889.
OTHER O HD	99000.	99000.	99000.	99000.	99000.	99000.	99000.	99000.	99000.	99000.	99000.	99000.
TOT PROD CST	[illegible]	738676.	590923.	801604.	629773.	758274.	931601.	844937.	991369.	937578.	737355.	577477.
MARKET PROM			62769.	80205.	41846.	66256.	73231.	76718.	69744.	76718.	69744.	73231.
MKT REP EX			[illegible]	24179.	12615.	19974.	22077.	23128.	21026.	23128.	21026.	22077.
MKT WAGES			[illegible]	111068.	57940.	91752.	101410.	106239.	96581.	106239.	96581.	101410.
MKTO_HEA				28308.	14769.	23385.	25846.	27077.	24615.	27077.	24615.	25846.
MKT T[illegible]					[illegible]	201368.	222564.	233162.	211966.	233162.	211966.	222564.
ADM[illegible]						34103.	37692.	39487.	35897.	39487.	35897.	37692.
AD[illegible]						[illegible]	3231.	3385.	3077.	3385.	3077.	3231.
A[illegible]							37513.	39299.	35726.	39299.	35726.	37513.
								82171.	74701.	82171.	74701.	78436.
FI[illegible]									34188.	37607.	34188.	35897.
TOT FIN [illegible]										37607.	34188.	35897.
ACT FRGT CST	[illegible]										160000.	156000.
TOTAL COSTS	1295334.	1059274.										[illegible]
STOCK CHANGE	315926.	74968.	-241434.	[illegible]								
OPERATNG PFT	607591.	841694.	843874.	802034.	[illegible]							
NON OP.REV	0.	0.	0.	0.	0.	0.						
NON OP.COST	0.	0.	0.	0.	0.	0.						
NET PROFIT	607591.	841694.	843874.	802034.	1062773.	855633.	824194.	[illegible]				
NET FRGT CST	-4200.	-4800.	-5800.	-5400.	-7000.	-7000.	-6200.	-6000.	-7200.			7800.
SUNDRY DEBTR	1071000.	2682800.	2672400.	2950125.	3374650.	3695400.	3686750.	3578650.	3780350.	4085400.		[illegible]

CASH INFLOW AND OUTFLOW REPORT

	JUL	AUG	SEP	OCT	NOV	DEC	JAN	FEB	MAR	APR	MAY	JUN
OPR CASH IN	516000.	816200.	1489400.	1679775.	1971975.	1724250.	1989150.	2234350.	2105300.	2071950.	2077700.	2284300.
OPR.CASH OUT	362500.	1214061.	1014343.	858589.	1596271.	940107.	1052608.	1321934.	1159271.	1366702.	1381911.	1077689.
NET OPR FLOW	153500.	-397861.	475057.	821186.	375704.	784143.	936542.	912416.	946029.	705248.	695789.	1206611.
NON OPR INFL	0.	0.	0.	0.	0.	0.	0.	0.	0.	0.	0.	0.
NON OPR OUTF	0.	0.	0.	0.	0.	0.	0.	0.	0.	0.	0.	0.
NET CASH FLOW	153500.	-397861.	475057.	821186.	375704.	784143.	936542.	912416.	946029.	705248.	695789.	1206611.

(c) Cost and revenue statements

Financial Modelling in Corporate Management, 2nd Edition
Edited by J. W. Bryant
Published by John Wiley & Sons Ltd.

7

From Here to There and Back Again: a New View of the Planning Cycle*

Paul Finlay

7.1 Introduction

This chapter describes the approach to corporate planning that was taken over the five years to 1979 in a medium-sized UK company engaged in the production and marketing of consumer goods.

Firstly, it explains the mechanisms and organizational features of the planning activities that were undertaken—an area hitherto rather neglected in the literature (but see Currill, 1977)—and secondly it puts forward reasons for the limited success of the planning processes adopted.

The chapter is in four parts:

(1) A review of the state of planning in the company prior to the large planning effort made during 1976/1977.
(2) A description of the planning activities carried out during this period.
(3) A critique of this planning.
(4) A description of developments since 1977.

7.2 Corporate Planning Prior to 1976

The company is one of many within a Multinational Group. Its operations were supervised by a Supervisory Board located at Group Head Office which had overall corporate planning authority. It had a conventional formal organization with departments of Production, Marketing, Personnel, Accounting and Finance and Management Services.

*Reprinted with permission from *Long Range Planning*, **15**, Finlay, Introducing corporate planning in a medium-size company: A case history. © 1982 Pergamon Press Ltd.

In order that it could plan for the activities of all the companies in the Group, the planners within the Supervisory Board set guidelines for the company in which its expectations for the company were spelt out. These guidelines arrived in January of each year. In April the Supervisory Board then received from the company a preliminary briefing document setting forth a draft plan for the company covering the following three years.

After reviewing the preliminary briefing document, any necessary modifications would be incorporated into the Company Plan which was presented to the Supervisory Board in September. This fitted the company's financial year which ran from 1 October to 31 September.

In the years prior to 1976/1977, the main work of producing corporate plans had rested with the management accountants (although naturally the responsibility for the final plan and its ultimate transmission to Group Head Office lay with the Board). In this work the accountants were assisted by the Management Services Department, which had produced computer models to aid in planning. Three models were in use by 1976:

(a) A company summary model for forecasting profit and loss accounts, balance sheets and cash flows;
(b) A materials model to forecast raw material purchases and the associated variable costs for classes of product;
(c) A marketing model that allowed marketing area contribution to be calculated.

Although considered valid by the accountants and by Management Services Department, these models, and the use to which they were put, were not widely accepted in the company. Indeed the planning process itself was held by some departments as being far too financially oriented and controlled by financial personnel.

Whilst this rudimentary corporate planning was being developed, the company had been moving towards a positive commitment at Board level to the acceptance of a participative style of management. This trend, coupled with the dissatisfaction expressed by non-financial management about their lack of involvement in the planning process led to the initiation of a new and forceful direction to corporate planning. This occurred in mid-1976.

7.3 The Developments in Corporate Planning During 1976/1977

The Purpose of Planning

The first formal development in mid-1976 was the publication of the company's view as to the purpose of corporate planning. This was as follows:

(a) To identify decisions and actions that must be taken if a desired future is to be achieved (following pre-analysis and the evaluation of several such futures);
(b) To provide a basis for the communication of ideas during the planning process, and for the communication of this set of decisions, actions and results to those affected or influenced by them, and as a basis for subsequent control within the organization itself. In particular to link with the lower level planning of the Departmental Planning Teams (see below);
(c) To provide those to whom we are responsible, with a quantification of that future, for use in their own planning, and as a base for subsequent control, and to demonstrate to them that we are taking thought for the future.

Organizational Changes

To carry out this required planning, an organization different from the departmental organization was required. The first step in its construction was the identification of interests that were key to the survival and well-being of the company. The Core Interests so defined were:

(1) Marketing
(2) Profitability
(3) Productivity
(4) Employee relations
(5) Employee development
(6) External relations

A team was brought together to be responsible for the planning associated with each Core Interest. The leader of each Core Interest Group was normally the director most closely concerned with the area (e.g. the Marketing Director would head the Marketing Core Interest Group) The Managing Director would not normally be involved in a Core Interest Group where a departmental director would naturally take charge. Members of the team would include other involved directors, members of the departmental planning teams and at least one member of the co-ordinating team (see below). The membership of a Core Interest Group lay between four and eight.

The Board had overall responsibility for all planning activity within the corporate guidelines issued by the Supervisory Board and as leaders of Core Interest and Departmental Planning Teams, directors were individually responsible for these elements and for the consistency of their plans and *modus operandi* with other planning activities. The Board realized that it would not be able to devote sufficient time to the large task of creating the mechanisms needed for the participative planning envisaged or for the detailed control required. A team called the Co-ordinating Team was set up to take over responsibility for creating and operating the mechanisms by which the quantitative side of the plans would be computed, for identifying, publicizing and achieving resolution of any inconsistencies between them, for defining and monitoring the progress of plan formulation and reporting it to the Board.

Acting at one level below the Core Interest Groups were the Departmental Planning Teams. The responsibilities of the teams were defined by the departmental director concerned, although each department would be 'picking up' objectives/policies, etc. defined during the corporate planning phase. Whilst the composition of these teams varied considerably from department to department, members of the Co-ordinating Team were naturally included in their departmental team.

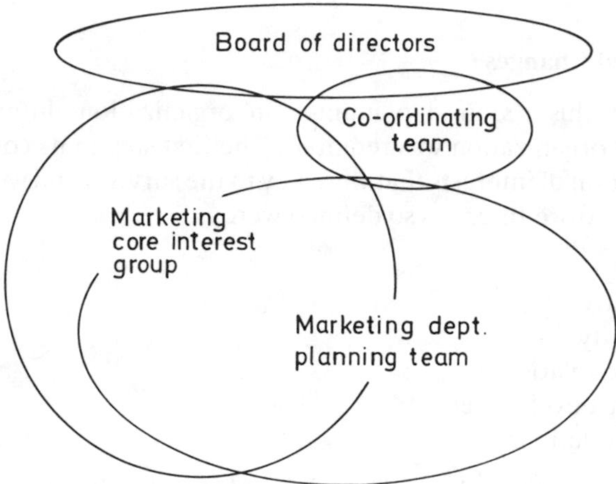

Figure 7.1 Membership overlap of planning groups

The relations between planning groups and the overlaps of membership that occurred are summarized in Figure 7.1 (for the sake of clarity only one Core Interest Group and its 'associated' Departmental Planning Team are depicted).

Formal Plans and Documents

The tangible end product of a phase of planning was the production of a plan. During the yearly planning cycle five formal plans were produced. These were:

(i) Skeletal Plan—a broad statement of the company's intentions broken down by Core Interest. It was produced in March with a time horizon of 3½ years (year 1 beginning in October). Its scope is wider than that of the Preliminary Briefing document (see below) to allow stronger links to Departmental planning.

(ii) Preliminary Briefing document—a document based on the Skeletal Plan, that satisfied the requirements of the Supervisory Board for its broad planning purposes.
(iii) Company Plan—a document covering the same ground as the Skeletal Plan but based on more detailed departmental planning. In its first year it was a summary of the more detailed Budget (see below).
(iv) Budget—a detailed financial picture of a financial year, with expected income and expenditure defined to the levels required for subsequent control.
(v) Company Action Plan—an extract from the Company Plan listing in chronological order the objectives to be attained during the current year, and breaking them down into the major sub-objectives as listed in the departmental plans. This then constituted the basis for ongoing control of progress towards those significant objectives not explicitly controlled by quantitative review against budget (for example control of the progress toward one negotiating period for all the Unions represented in the company).

Two further formal documents were produced. These were:

(i) *Guidelines*—a document issued by the Board to the Core Interest Groups and the Co-ordination Team, giving a company scenario and setting out its expectations by Core Interest and the constraints within which each Core Interest Group would operate to formulate its contribution to the Skeletal and Company Plans.
(ii) *Planning manual*—in which all relevant features of the planning process were documented, e.g. the definition of all terms used in planning; the composition of Core Interest Groups.

The link between these formal documents is shown in Figure 7.2.

Timings of Planning Activities

(i) *Rationale of timings*. The rationale behind the timings is that there is a broad measure of continuity in the company's activities from year to year so that the Company Plan produced in September of one year (say for example 1978) provides both the framework for the planning of activities for the next budget year (1978/1979) and the springboard for further strategic or outline planning (to cover years 1979/1980 and onwards). Thus budget year planning and outline planning proceed in parallel as two, fairly distinct activities both using the Company Plan as a base but concerned with different aspects of it.
(ii) *Main timings*. The sequence and timing of the main planning activities for the 1977-1978 planning cycle are summarized below.

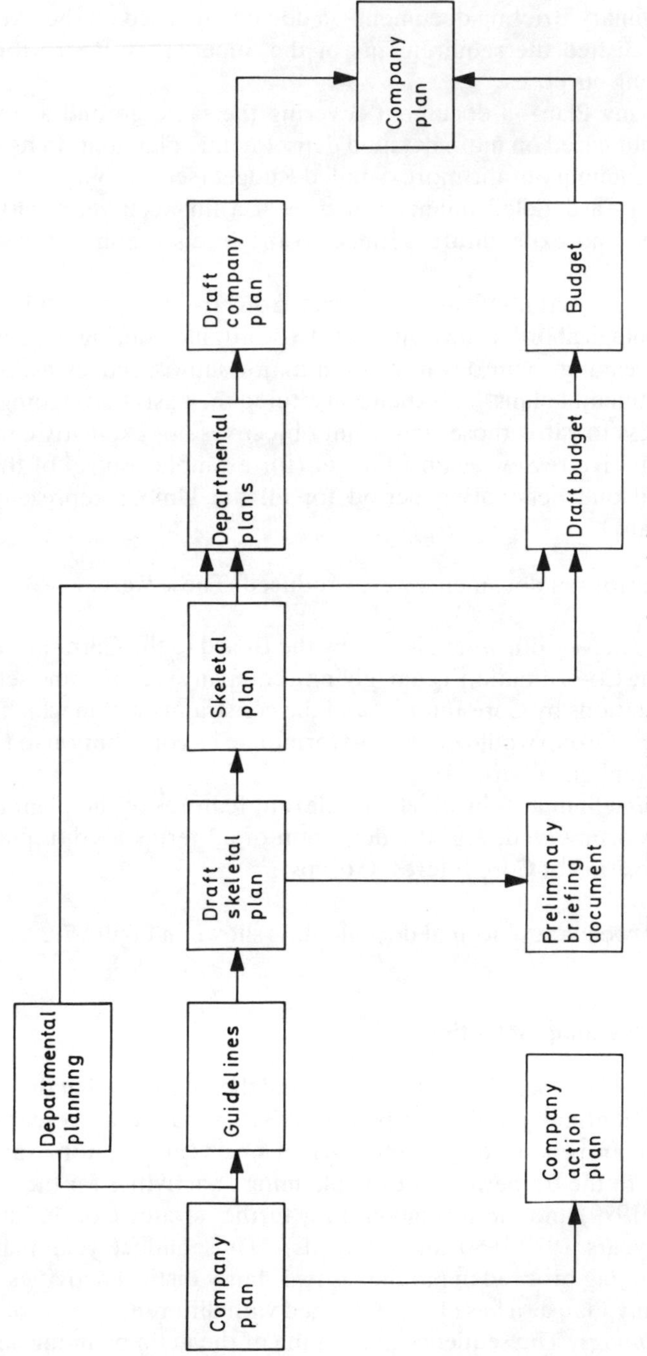

Figure 7.2 The link between formal documents

Date	
November 1977	Presentation to the Board of the Marketing Department's ten-year view.
December 1977	Board issues guidelines to Core Interest Groups.
January 1978	Board receives its guidelines from the Supervisory Board.
March 1978	Core Interest Groups send Skeletal Plan to Board.
	Board communicate required changes to Core Interest Groups.
April 1978	Skeletal Plan re-assembled with revisions and Preliminary Briefing document drawn up.
	Final Skeletal Plan and Preliminary Briefing document approval meeting of the Board. Preliminary Briefing document despatched to the Supervisory Board.
May 1978	Preliminary Briefing document presented to the Supervisory Board.
July 1978	First draft Company Plan produced. Core Interest Groups present Company Plan to Board.
Late July/early August 1978	Alterations made to Company Plan.
September 1978	Company Plan sent to the Supervisory Board.
	Company Plan presented to the Supervisory Board.

From this timetable it can be seen that there are two major phases in the planning cycle—that ending with the production of the Skeletal Plan (the Preliminary Briefing document merely consisting of extracts from it) and that ending with the production of the Company Plan.

The Development of Planning Mechanisms

From the foregoing it can be seen that the company wished to pursue a participative style of planning and one operating within a rather severe timetable. Having defined its Core Interests and the organization to go with it, it was necessary to develop mechanisms to aid the planning activities themselves and in the control of these activities. In particular it was necessary to have:

(a) A means of defining and controlling the sequence of activities necessary for the planning process;
(b) An appropriate means of eliciting expert knowledge and data from the relevant Core Interest Groups;

(c) A means of processing these data into comprehensive financial and physical pictures of the company and areas of activity within it, and to explore the sensitivity of the solutions to differing assumptions;
(d) A means of drawing together the qualitative and quantitative responses from all relevant groups.

The mechanisms involved for the first major phase of the planning cycle (ending in the production of the Skeletal Plan) are significantly different from those required for the second phase. Thus the two phases will be treated in turn.

Mechanisms for Producing the Skeletal Plan

The Guidelines issued by the Board in December set the framework within which the Skeletal Plan was to be constructed. The aim of the Guidelines was to allow all relevant expert knowledge and opinion within the company to be tapped and used in the planning process, whilst at the same time eliciting the small amount of data necessary to calculate the significant physical and financial consequences of any proposals put forward. And it was important that broad thinking would be positively encouraged and concentration on detail be suppressed.

This aim was achieved by constructing the Guidelines in two parts:

Part 1—a scenario specifying the company expectations and the assumptions and constraints within which those contributing to the Plan should work.
Part 2—a questionnaire split into two parts to: (a) elicit views on policies and philosophies, (b) gather specific sets of data.

The answers to part (a) of the questionnaire were used to produce the main 'qualitative' part of the Skeletal Plan, whilst the answers to part (b) were used, mainly as input to the computer models, in order to enable the calculations of the physical and financial consequences associated with the 'qualitative' part of the Plan. This procedure is depicted in Figure 7.3.

To structure the questionnaire it was important to identify, for each Core Interest, those issues where the policy adopted would be important to the performance of the company (rather than at Departmental level or below). An example should make this clear.

A very important issue for the company within the 'Productivity' Core Interest covered the purchase and storage of one type of raw material. By concentrating on corporate issues, four areas where policy statements would be needed were identified. These covered:

(a) The duration of stock to be held.
(b) Average quantity of the material to be used in the finished product.

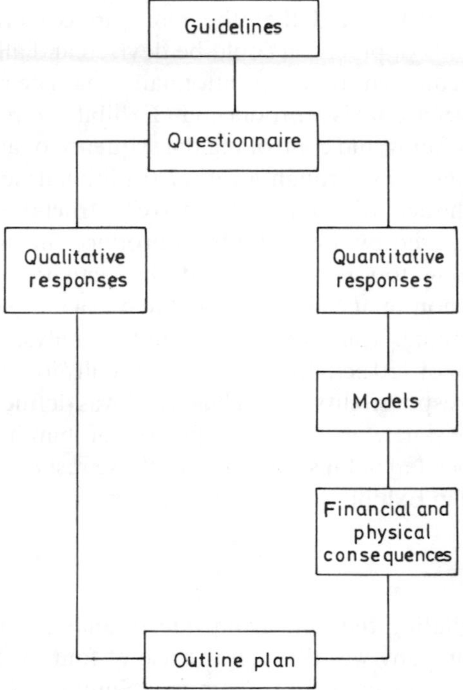

Figure 7.3 The place of the questionnaire

(c) Sources of the raw material.
(d) Expenditure on warehousing.

On these issues, broad policy statements were required with little quantification.

For part (b) of the questionnaire it was important only to ask for data that might affect corporate decisions, and at an appropriate precision. The precision required was determined by the following logic.

It was known from a review of past projections of sales, that the standard deviation of estimating was around 5 per cent. This meant that the spread in estimating the company profit was at least this size. The Board were exposed to the argument that little would be lost if the overall precision of the modelling process were such as to increase this uncertainty in profit estimation by 10 per cent—i.e. to 5.5 per cent. On this basis it could be shown that 'errors' of up to around 2 per cent of turnover could be accepted.

Armed with the Board's agreement to this, and knowing the approximate size of each contributory factor to the company's turnover, the precision needed of each element in the corporate financial plan could be calculated. For the important raw material this imprecision came to about £250 000 pa.

Knowing this £250 000 and that the main areas were as shown above, further requirements of precision could be devised and allotted to these main areas. Thus the second part of the questionnaire could be devised—the one for the important raw material is reproduced in Exhibit 7.1 in the Appendix.

The means of defining and controlling the sequence of activities necessary to the planning process was through a rather traditional network analysis. For historic reasons, the activities initially used to construct the network were those that had been required by accountants to produce financial plans. This was soon seen as being too restrictive and the activities were expanded to incorporate more non-financial activity and to mesh more easily with on-going departmental planning. The level of detail in the analysis can be judged from the fact that a total of 120 activities were individually identified.

To ensure that responsibility for each activity was defined, and the person or group responsible knew what was expected of him/it, a list of relevant activities and associated details were sent to those responsible. An example of this is reproduced in Exhibit 7.2 in the Appendix.

Computer Models

The means of collating the data from questionnaires to form the financial 'picture' of the company was through the use of four models. Three of these have already been referred to—the Company Summary Model, the Materials Model and the Marketing Model. These were modified slightly during the year and joined by a fourth model called the Personnel Model.

The Personnel Model was of a significantly different type to the other three models, in that it attempted a much more subtle modelling than their definitional modelling. For each department at each of the company's factories a model was derived relating the size of groups of employees to the volume of production of classes of product. In general, five groups of employees were identified in each department—managers, skilled employees, two types of unskilled employees and employees whose wage depended on measured output. Within a department an equation relating the size of each group with output was constructed for each group; labour costs were then determined by multiplying these numbers by the average company cost for the group and summing over groups. (In the case of employees where company cost per employee was related to output, a similar but more complicated calculation was necessary.)

With these four models, the quantitative consequences of answers to the questionnaires could be quickly assessed and collated, and the consequences of 'what if' questions could be explored.

The responsibility for checking on the consistency of the qualitative and quantitative responses from the Core Interest Group lay with the Co-ordinating Team. The mechanism for such activity was very simple. If inconsistencies were shown up in the returns (e.g. assumptions made by the Marketing Core Interest Group not agreeing with those made by Productivity Core Interest Group), the relevant Core Interest Groups were notified. As the time approached for submission to the Supervisory Board, this referral to a Core Interest Group was cut in favour of a direct approach from a member of the Co-ordinating Team to the most affected directly responsible company employee.

Planning Between Preliminary Briefing Document and Company Plan Production

The first year of the Company Plan evolved out of the detailed Departmental Planning that had, as its starting point, the previous year's Company Plan and, in exceptional circumstances, the Skeletal Plan. Thus, the last two years of the plan will normally be identical to those of the Skeletal Plan.

Cost information was obtained for the creation of the budget by distributing to all cost centres a cost-centre budget form. The entries of the budget form were of two types—for large expenditures (nine categories) the actual cost was to be entered; for all other categories non-inflationary *changes* over the past year to the nearest 5 per cent were asked for.

7.4 Critique of the Planning Activities of 1976/1977

The mainsprings for the changes in the corporate planning processes were the dissatisfaction of non-financial management with the dominance of financial management and financial considerations in the planning process, and the company-wide move to a more participative style of management. Thus a limited view of success or failure of the planning process might be judged by whether dissatisfaction was lessened and participation increased and effective.

The main points of the critique were:

(1) Although the Preliminary Briefing document was meant to give a very broadly-based view of the company's plans for the next few years, the planning associated with it and of the Skeletal Plan of which it was an extract were too detailed and polished. This was in spite of the acceptance of the logic underlying the consistency of precision described above. This seemed to be caused by the Board members responsible for presenting the Preliminary Briefing document to their bosses (the Supervisory Board) not having got agreement to the level of precision required. Working under such uncertainty as to what is required by one's bosses, it is natural to become precise and detailed, and also to amass a lot of even

more detailed back-up information should the presentation of the plan become sticky.

(2) The effort to form interdepartmental Core Interest Groups was only partly successful. An interchange of ideas between departments did take place, but since the composition of these teams were heavily biased in favour of associated departments (e.g. the Production Department providing many of the members of the Productivity Core Interest Group), the dominant department would generally work out a position prior to Core Interest Group meetings and the departmental view would prevail without much discussion. Thus the debate within the Core Interest Group that could have been so educative to the other group members was rather limited.

(3) The chairmen of the Core Interest Group did not seem to fully understand their responsibilities. This led to uncertainty as to the role of the Core Interest Groups.

(4) An obvious anomaly existed in that time pressures forced the company's Board to issue its guidelines before it itself had received guidelines from its boss—the Supervisory Board.

(5) The structure of Core Interest Groups tended to reflect a Head Office view, limiting the voice of the factories. This problem was encountered elsewhere by Currill (1977).

(6) The computer models had mixed fortunes.
The Marketing Model was used by Marketing Managers to help in their planning and was judged a success. The Company Summary Model was set up for the management accountants and financial director to use and satisfied their needs very well. The Materials Model was less successful. The main reasons for this were that the managers responsible for the purchase and storage of raw materials had only been peripherally involved in the creation of the model and had never had what to them was a satisfactory explanation of its workings. The problem was exacerbated by the fact that a computerized tactical planning model (more detailed but of lesser scope than the Materials Model) was already in existence and used to help in determining purchases of the most important raw material during the subsequent year. Management had grown to know and love this tactical model and when, not surprisingly, small discrepancies appeared between the expenditures forecast by the two models the Commodity Materials Model was denounced as 'wrong'—its results rejected. (The problem of gaining acceptance for the Materials Model was compounded by the unwitting use of different assumptions and different data when a comparison of the Materials Model and the second Model was made. Naturally enough, large discrepancies appeared, and time pressures prevented the reasons for the discrepancies being cleared up straightaway.)

(7) The Personnel Model was almost a complete disaster. It had been produced so that the manning levels and labour costs at the factories could be 'flexed' to follow changes in Marketing forecasts. (Without the model, it was a very time consuming business to obtain a revision of the manning levels from the factories.) The problem was that the objectives of the model were not sufficiently clear. Had the model been restricted to a planning tool rather than attempting also to provide a budgetary control mechanism it would have succeeded. Its failure must rest primarily with the failure of the business analyst to identify the problems effectively and not securing 'real' commitment from all end users. In the time available and with the organizational structure in the company this was very difficult to accomplish.

The basic problem was that the 'judgemental modelling' which was being attempted was far too sophisticated for practical use by the company. All the other three models were basically 'definitional models' in which all the rules were either widely accepted definitions or approximations to them. (Generally they were restricted to dealing with financial/accounting definitions.) In the Personnel Model, however, an attempt was being made to model a situation in which no one had thought in terms of explicit relationships. The idea of writing down an equation with symbols that would later have numbers attached was not understood and the implications to the company were not fully appreciated.

(8) The use of questionnaires designed to elicit both wide-ranging thinking and the necessary detailed data was a successful innovation in striking a balance between extrapolative and visionary planning (overcoming the problem cited in Currill, 1977) and mitigating the problems of data collection given in Hayes and Nolan (1974).

(9) The link up of questionnaires and models was not close enough and the models not easy enough to use to allow quick feedback of the results of proposals from the Core Interest Groups. Thus few iterations in the planning process were possible.

(10) The pace of development of planning was too great for the company to absorb (see discussion on models above).

(11) The management accountants, who had played the major role in producing the company plans prior to 1976/1977, retained the view that it is the financial statements in the plan that were important and that the planning process was rather inconsequential. One reason for this appeared to be that they looked to satisfy their functional 'bosses'. As the financial statements were all important they had to look right and this led to the accountants who were responsible for these statements 'reconciling' the data received from other areas within the company. In a sense they were correct to do this since incomplete or otherwise unacceptable returns were made by the Core Interest Groups, the relevant people

unobtainable and the accountants themselves had a reasonable grasp of the company's activities. However, this reconciling of the data is the very antithesis of planning which should allow a greater understanding of relationships by participants. These adjustments could only have been interpolations or extrapolations since in general the accountants did not have sufficient knowledge of markets or product trends.

(12) The link between operational data and that used in the planning models was tenuous. Although one can argue that if one is planning over a three-year time scale the exact state of play at the time the planning is taking place is rather inconsequential, many hours were expended arguing and determining exact stock positions, etc.—and taking the emphasis away from high-level thinking.

(13) The emphasis in the planning remained on the 'quantitative' (Core Interests (Marketing, Profitability and Productivity). However, the creation of the Company Action Plan was a very important step towards controlling not-directly quantifiable activities.

7.5 Developments After the 1976/1977 Planning Cycle

Given the nature of the large planning effort made in 1976/1977 it was felt worthwhile to seek an independent view of the planning activities and to this end an outside consultant was employed to review the situation. He concluded that the planning mechanisms were good and suggested *inter alia* that the company should organize itself along business area lines and should appoint a full-time Planning Co-ordinator. The business area suggestion was rejected (but introduced late 1979—see discussion below); the Corporate Planner was appointed mid-1978.

The company's momentum towards increased participation was continued by the appointment of a manager to assist in the development of company and departmental roles.

At the same time as the 1976/1977 planning was being undertaken, a separate team within the company was working totally independently on a project that was scheduled to come on stream in 1978, and would call for a production and marketing effort comparable with that currently being undertaken by the entire company. While this project team reported to the Managing Director the Supervisory Board was closely involved since the company itself would not have been able to support the cost of investment. Over a period of several months, there was discussion of how to treat this proposed activity—whether in or out of the formal company planning, how to apportion costs between current activities and those associated with the project, etc. Finally the project was (rather uneasily) incorporated within the operational planning framework, about two years after the project was begun.

Throughout 1977/1978 the company was preoccupied with the project and all other planning activities were considered of minor concern. Large modifications were needed to the Company Summary Model to incorporate this new activity and it was used extensively during this period. Interestingly, its ability to provide rapid analyses for management meant that a large amount of managerial time and effort was spent making minor adjustment to the figures rather than using the models to answer more fundamental 'What if' questions (also see the new factory discussion below). The Personnel Model was abandoned, with a promise to set up models of manning schedules on minicomputers at each factory. The reversion to manual calculation of factory manning levels was not at all successful: due to a near complete failure to co-ordinate head office and factory planning (the relevant Core Interest Group—the Productivity Core Interest Group—in fact never met) manning levels were produced by each factory on inconsistent bases with little apparent regard for the planning assumptions.

A fundamental shift in process took place during 1977/1978. This was caused by the priorities given to other Group activities and substantial changes in key personnel associated with the planning activities.

The accountants successfully exploited this situation to re-assert their dominance over the planning process. They proposed drawing up the Skeletal Plan at a very detailed level, but still submitting the higher-level Preliminary Briefing document to the Supervisory Board. This proposal was accepted by the Company's Board since it would enable Board members to answer detailed questions and reduce the difficulties in reconciling the Preliminary Briefing document and Company Plan. The advantage of concentrating on broad thinking had clearly not been accepted or understood by many managers during the previous year.

The planning emphasis now reverted to 'getting the figures right'. The qualitative aspect of the questionnaire all but disappeared and in some instances the questionnaires became computer input forms. Although planning was now effectively back under the control of accountants there was less 'reconciling' of the data due to the increased planning experience of the Core Interest Teams. When illogical data were produced, the accountants now sought to influence change at the data source.

In 1977/1978 a Planning Co-ordinator was appointed reporting to the Managing Director. Two meetings of the Co-ordination Team were held early in the 1978/1979 cycle but thereafter no more were organized and this body itself died through inaction. Questionnaires and the Core Interest Groups were quietly abandoned. Nevertheless planning continued on the basis of the planning timetable. The quantitative aspects of the plan were firmly under the accountants' control: not surprisingly since the models were outside the Planning Co-ordinator's control, being run and maintained for accountants by Management Services Department which was itself now part of the Finance Department.

By the end of 1978 a potential shortfall in productive capacity was foreseen for the early 1980s. A project team was set up to examine the feasibility of setting up a completely new factory in the UK. As with the project already mentioned, it worked in almost total independence of what was left of the planning process and mechanisms. (For example, the Planning Co-ordinator himself was not involved in the team.) The parallel with the 1978 project was quite close: the investment involved was too large for the company itself to underwrite, so the investment and hence the project was a Group project.

Ten work groups were set up to plan specific aspects of the project. Some of these groups were an abject failure, it being evident that in many cases the group chairmen did not understand their role, goals or constraints. There was little overall control of the groups nor was there adequate monitoring of the consistency of assumption being made.

Soon after the project started it was realized that a computer model was needed to provide a financial evaluation of the various proposed strategies. Senior management were persuaded that the project financial evaluation should be tackled using risk analysis. Although the principles underlying this technique were not generally understood, the scientific nature of the analysis impressed senior managers.

The model proved invaluable in co-ordinating marketing, production and financial assumptions. Once again, however, there was a preoccupation with detailed questions and little senior management direction regarding the basic methodology underlying capital investment decisions (e.g. inflated or 'real value' results, NPV, IRR or some other criterion, treatment of internal company transfer payments). In early 1979 the proposal to build a new factory was rejected, the Supervisory Board being sceptical about the projected sales growth and concerned about the magnitude of the investment.

During 1979 the company's financial position deteriorated sharply, and to cope with it the company decided to cut staff levels and move towards a more streamlined organization by undertaking a work rationalization programme. *Inter alia* this rationalization involved organizing the company around business areas (with representatives from accounting and personnel in each area group) and a move to place less reliance on committees with correspondingly greater individual responsibility. As a result of the reorganization, the managerial posts that had responsibility for planning co-ordination and for company and departmental role development were abolished; the Management Services Department analyst responsible for the planning models moved to supporting lower-level accounting systems. Control of the planning process was now firmly in the hands of accountants. Budgeting had taken priority over planning. In another guise Gresham's Law had triumphed once again.

7.6 Conclusions

The events described above took place over about four years. Within this time the company had gone through a complete cycle of planning activity and was almost back where it started—with emphasis on 'getting the figures right' and on budgeting rather than planning.

The broad reason for the regression may be summarized as follows:

(1) The intrusion of Group projects running in parallel with the main company planning process had very damaging effects on the credibility of the planning.
(2) Throughout there had been a tendency to underestimate very substantially the resources needed to develop and maintain the planning process and the associated mechanisms.
(3) As well as underestimating the resources required, the speed with which the organization could change its ways of thought was also grossly underestimated. Too much was attempted over too small a time scale.
(4) The accountants, who were influential in the company, never understood the planning process and did not understand the difference between data for planning purposes and those for operational control.
(5) The problem of level of detail had never been solved. Even when senior management issued clear instructions to proceed at a certain level of detail, the same senior managers, when presented with results, frequently asked questions that were themselves at variance with these instructions.
(6) There was too great a reliance on key personnel and too much depended on their abilities.

References

Currill, D. L. (1977). 'Introducing corporate planning—a case study', *Long Range Planning*, **10**, 70–9.

Hayes, R. H. and Nolan, R. L. (1974). 'What kind of corporate modelling functions best?', *Harvard Business Review*, **52**, 102–12.

Appendix to Chapter 7

Exhibit 7.1 Questionnaire for commodity X

Outline Plan: Questionnaire – Commodity X

In the COMPANY PLAN it was Stated that ....
(Repeat Here of Statements Concerning Durations, Inflation etc.) and in the CALCULATION OF PURCHASE QUANTITIES etc. the FOLLOWING DATA WERE USED (Statement of Data for Overall Product Characteristics)

Bearing in mind the COMPANY OBJECTIVES, would you state your Intentions Regarding Changes in the FOLLOWING OVER the next three Years, with ACCOMPANYING EXPLANATION

1. Policy on Commodity X Durations
2. Quantity of Commodity X Used per Unit Product
3. Policy on Proportions by Source
4. Storage Expenditure

Would you Please Complete the Table Below:

	1976/1977	1977/1978	1978/1979	1979/1980
1. Average Duration (to Nearest 0.2 Months)				
2. Cost Inflation (to Nearest 1%)				
3. Changes to Basic Recipes (to Nearest 1%)				
4. Changes in Storage Expenses (to Nearest £100,000 p.a. in 1976/1977 £)				

Exhibit 7.2 Individual planning activities

BUDGET PLANNING ACTIVITY PLAN, 1976

Name A. S. Smith Position: Production Acct

Event Ref. Nos.	Activity	Duration of Activity (Weeks)	Latest Finishing Date	Earliest Starting Date
54–72 et al	Branches informed of Changes in Inflation Rates	0.1	5 July	15 June
106–114	Production Team Agree Standard Costs	1.0	26 July	19 July
34–75	Other Manufacture Stds. Calculated	0.6	13 Aug.	1 June
116–128	Production Team agrees Fixed + 5-Y Branch Returns	1.0	16 Aug.	19 July
138–148	Production Team Prepare Commentary on Budget	1.4	31 Aug	23 Aug.
148–156	Production Team Finishes Commentary	0.4	2 Sept.	1 Sept.
162–166	Critique of Planning Cycle	2.0	22 Sept.	8 Sept.

1 Week is to be Taken as 5 Working Days

Financial Modelling in Corporate Management, 2nd Edition
Edited by J. W. Bryant

8

A Methodological Account of Financial Modelling

JOHN HOLLAND

8.1 Introduction

This chapter has two major themes. First, the broad outline of a managerial strategy for model development is outlined. Secondly, a detailed case study of financial model development and evolution in one company is employed to illuminate this strategy.

The chapter is divided into four sections. First, in Section 8.2, financial modelling by managers and academics is briefly discussed. In Section 8.3 the author draws from his research experience (Holland, 1978, 1981, 1986) in financial modelling, to outline a managerial strategy for model development and evolution. In Section 8.4 the implementation of this strategy in one company is described. This detailed case study traces the development from one simple budgetary model through to a sophisticated suite of linked investment, financing, and accounting models. Section 8.5 summarizes the strategy for financial model development and evolution, and its implications for managers and academics.

8.2 Financial Modelling

In the world of financial practice, managers have a tendency to use a pragmatic approach to decision-making. Such an approach concentrates on the search for rules of thumb which work with regard to planning problems and readily available data (Cooley and Copeland, 1975). Both Grinyer and Wooller (1975) in the UK and Naylor and Jeffress (1975) in the USA found that models generally used with this pragmatic mode of decision-making are normally deterministic financial report simulators.

Such accounting-based deterministic models give the manager little guidance in making important financial decisions and most of the work is done by the manager outside of the model in establishing the relationships between investment and financing decisions. These models are used to speed up routine aspects of data processing as the manager moves between problem solutions. Such movement is iterative in naure, as the manager moves by successive approximations, towards a 'satisfactory' solution. The models are, therefore, limited as financial planning tools because of their concentration on details and use of accounting frameworks.

These problems in managerial model building have been recognized by academic observers for some time (Carleton, Dick and Downes, 1972). The response of academics in the field of financial model building has generally consisted of a 'marriage' between the theory of business finance, and sophisticated management science techniques such as linear programming (see Holland, 1986, pp. 86–93) and Monte Carlo simulation. For example, Carleton (1970) has built a model for long-range financial planning. This model simultaneously chooses values for amounts invested, dividends paid, and debt/equity structure, within accounting, economic, institutional and corporate policy constraints, such that common stock price is maximized. This model is of interest because of the way in which the authors have tied together the theory of corporate finance and microeconomic theory of the firm into a mathematical framework and model that seeks optimal financial plans.

Myers and Pogue (1974) have also adopted this financial modelling approach by incorporating advances in capital market theory. Pogue and Lall (1974) suggested that: 'Models of this type are clearly going to play an increasingly important role in the formulation of corporate financial plans'. However, linear programming has been used sparingly by management. Some companies report starting with linear programming only to switch to simple report generators. Thus LP financial planning models have been mainly developed by financial theorists to develop and investigate theory, even though Carleton, Pogue, Myers and others may have initially wished to aid practitioners directly. Grinyer and Wooller (1974) suggested that the reasons for the low success rate of this approach, and the predominance of simulation models are that managers seem to find simulation models more intelligible and complex relationships can be represented more easily in simulation than in optimization models. In addition top managers often find it difficult, or politically inexpedient, to make objectives explicit, preferring instead to leave them implicit in the alternatives shown. In contrast optimization models require an explicit statement of objectives, while simulation models do not. Moreover, because estimates on which strategic decisions are based are liable to such wide errors, there is doubt as to the significance of a mathematical optimum based on them.

Many authors argue that the reasons why LP and other sophisticated OR techniques have proved unsuccessful in the past is because managers have not been sufficiently involved in building the model (Gershefski, 1969; Hall, 1973). Further reasons have been the independence of the model from the manager, and the fact that often the manager does not consider decisions simultaneously. Hence the manager believes that the LP model is taking major decisions without reference to him. He may understand relationships built into a model developed from his own ideas but because he is not part of the simultaneous solution process he finds it hard to accept the result. This is the case with all models of business situations but the paradox of the LP method is that its strength is also its weakness, i.e. the capacity to consider many decision alternatives simultaneously is beyond the manager and hence increases his scepticism.

Similarly managers may believe and understand the logical structure and solution search procedure of an LP model. However, they may object to the solution on the basis that they will often make or be forced to make single financial decisions without being able to change other major financial decisions. Managers would, therefore, like a capacity to 'behave', i.e. order the major decisions, in a way in which they may occur but which may not be logical *vis-à-vis* the theory of finance. This is essentially a simulation exercise.

Another management science approach which has proved popular in the academic financial modelling literature is risk analysis. This is normally seen as an embellishment of simulation modelling. However, as Grinyer and Wooller noted (1974) this modelling approach has also experienced problems in that early attempts to introduce probabilistic models had almost invariably failed to get management support. They argue that risk analysis may become more acceptable to management as they become more familiar with models. McInnes and Carleton (1982) also noted that most financial models did not directly address the issue of environmental uncertainty. However, they pointed out that the use of the models was central to the development of strategies to cope with uncertainty.

It appears that a central problem with LP financial planning models and with risk analysis and other similar normative models, is that they give too much guidance. The mathematical and financial theory is likely to be embedded in the model and the significant interaction between decision variables hidden from the manager.

8.3 A Managerial Strategy for Financial Model Development

There are, therefore, problems in financial model building in both the practical and theoretical context.

(1) Financial planning models based on financial theory and management science have proved too complex for managers to use.

(2) Simulation models currently in use are very simple and give little guidance to the decision-maker.

These problems have arisen in part because of the differing goals managers and academics have pursued in model building (Cooley and Copeland, 1975). Essentially managers are interested in improving the quality of decision-making through immediate application of financial models. Academics' immediate concern is to build financial models that are internally consistent *vis-à-vis* the theory of finance. Academics are generally interested in improving the quality of managerial decision-making in the long term through the development of fruitful theory and associated decision models. This has meant that most of the energies of academics have been employed in refining the theoretical constructs, and little attention has been given to implementation problems. Managers, in turn, have made little effort to pierce this abstract world of mathematical and economic thought.

The situation is a serious problem for both the 'state of the art' of financial model building and the advancement of a theory of financial decision-making. This is because within these abstractions lie extensive frameworks for thinking about financial decision-making. In particular these can provide useful decision guidelines when using and developing deterministic simulation models. For example, when linear programming is employed to solve the corporate investment plan the following issues are explicitly dealt with:

(1) Within a potential set of investment projects, there may be competition for resources in a period, and over many periods.
(2) Investment projects may themselves be a source of resources.
(3) The objective to be achieved is explicit and quantified.
(4) Other secondary objectives are expressed through non-violation of constraints.
(5) There is a valuation problem in the last period of the capital budget plan.
(6) The solution procedure finds the 'best' solution given the objective and constraints.

This list of ideas implicit in the linear progamming/corporate finance theory 'package' is one small sample of the store of concepts actually expressed in the 'package'. The problem for the manager is that in using normative models developed from the 'packages', he receives the whole 'package' at a time. However, a manager is more likely to choose and use the element of a package that is currently useful. The author would agree with criticisms of normative models, but would argue that the decision framework implicit in such models can be useful to managers, and influence the design of financial models in practice. Therefore, a key requirement is how to encourage managerial access to such frameworks, without their having to accept whole 'packages'.

McInnes and Carleton (1982) argue a similar point in their extensive empirical study of financial modelling in eighteen, mainly large international companies. They point out that there is considerable difficulty in constructing information within the firm which is meaningful in the normative framework of extant corporate finance theory. Such theory proposes that the financial planning problem be structured in global, *ab nova*, terms each time a financial plan is considered. This is extremely difficult in most enterprises where there are several different information and logic structures and where translation between them poses considerable complexities. Their evidence pointed to a substantial gap between theory and practice in the field of financial model building. A central issue here concerned the extraction of information from the monitoring and planning systems in a form amenable to an analysis conforming to the prescriptions of normative finance theory. This highlights the need for improved managerial insights into theoretical models and the need for researchers to study managerial financial decision-making logic and information structures.

To encourage this interaction, managers require a strategy to learn how to use and develop financial models over time, by drawing from management science experience and financial theory; and thus ultimately improve their 'state of the art' (Holland, 1978, 1981). In addition, this strategy should encourage managers to codify their own financial decision-making expertise and to contrast it with conventional corporate finance theory.

The major elements of this strategy include the use of:

(1) Model design guidelines derived from the 'state of art' of corporate modelling;
(2) A local theory of financial decision-making;
(3) Guidelines from the general theory of business finance to guide the use of models.

Design Guidelines from the 'State of the Art'

Research on corporate modelling indicates that successful corporate models contain many common features and implementation characteristics (Grinyer and Wooller, 1975; Naylor and Jeffress, 1975; Power, 1975; Gershefski, 1969; Hall, 1973, 1975). Models considered most useful are those that:

(1) Are sponsored by top management;
(2) Form part of existing decision processes;
(3) Are simple data processing models;
(4) Can be used as research and learning tools by management;
(5) Respond quickly to environmental uncertainty;
(6) Enhance creative problem capacity;

(7) Are tailor-made for a company;
(8) Contain separate sub-models for investment, financing and dividend decisions, with the sub-models easily linked for data flow;
(9) Are thoroughly documented throughout their development and use.

A 'Local Theory' of Financial Decision-making

A local theory of financial decision-making includes detailed studies at company or industry level of:

(1) The unique nature of the investment decision and its cash flow patterns. This covers existing decision rules including 'rules of thumb'.
(2) Similar studies of the financing and dividend decisions, and the relationships between these areas.
(3) Management science techniques currently in use, and areas with likely applications.

This concept of a local theory of financial decision-making emerged during research by the author (Holland, 1978). During this research it was clear that financial decision-making was poorly documented within companies and industries. Existing documentation generally amounted to a statement of accounting principles and the investment appraisal method used. Financing and dividend decisions were not based upon an explicit statement of underlying principles. Clearly such decisions are made but the analysis involved, especially the trading-off of the interdependencies between the investment, financing and dividend decisions, do not generally appear to be explicit formalized procedures. The development of a local theory is designed to bridge this gap. Specifically, to ensure ease of communication this 'local' theory should use the financial decision-making terminology common to the industry concerned.

Guidelines from the General Theory of Business Finance

An important ingredient of this local theory would be an input from the general theory of finance which is simple and flexible enough to be used in a practical decision process to guide the use of financial submodels. For example, Sihler (1971) has attempted to systematize in easily understood fashion the insights provided by research in corporate finance by directly considering management needs. The result is a compendium of suggested procedures which if followed will produce sensible financial plans (Carleton, Dick and Downes, 1972). These procedures are:

(1) Assume projected capital requirements of the company;
(2) Tentatively settle the debt/equity question;

(3) Make the dividend growth analysis within the framework of the debt/equity choice;
(4) Investigate the impact of the last two steps on the capital costs, and the impact of the capital costs on the investment volume.

This approach has considerable merit because it focuses on the key financial decision areas and allows the manager to explore possible interrelationships which exist in his company's specific situation. McInnes and Carleton (1982) identified a similar sequence in the firms they investigated. The predominant logic in these firms was to proceed from a plan for operations, to a plan for new investment, and finally to a plan to finance these. There was some feedback of information through the sequence but generally there was considerable separation between the investment and financing decisions and little attempt was made to explore the joint set of opportunities and constraints. The above procedure recognizes this practice but also encourages managers to focus on the issues of interdependence between the major financial decisions. It therefore provides a direct, if simple, link from theory to practice, and it can be used to guide the way in which the financial sub-models are used in relation to each other.

The existing theory of corporate finance is, despite the practical limitations identified by McInnes and Carleton (1982), a major source of concepts for financial decision-making. The NPV rule applied to the capital budgeting and financing decision, the concept of efficient capital markets applied to financing decisions and financial reporting issues, and capital market theory employed in measuring the capital budgeting discount rate, are all examples of the richness of this theory source and its relevance to financial decisions in all corporations. Such theory is not just limited to the domestic, mainly US corporation. Its application to multinational firms, especially multicurrency issues, shows considerable promise in this rather complex area (Holland, 1986). This body of thought can therefore play a major part in structuring and criticizing a local theory of financial decision-making.

8.4 A Case Study of Model Development and Evolution

Introduction

In the following case study the use of the model design guidelines, local theory, and guidelines from business finance theory, are demonstrated in the development of a suite of models in an instalment credit financial intermediary (i.e. a 'finance house').

The author was involved in several such model-building exercises as part of a research project (Holland, 1978). The strategy for model development and evolution emerged from early model-building experiences and was then tested in the companies. This case study therefore reflects a typical experience in model building during the research.

(a) The Context of the Study

The company was a medium-sized finance house with hire purchase and similar instalment credit balances outstanding of approximately £6 million, and an annual turnover of approximately £7.5 million (turnover is the aggregate of new business financed, excluding finance charges).

The company was a subsidiary of a large financial corporation and had 15 branches in the UK. The branches were mostly located in the major regional centres and the company was moving towards nationwide coverage. Sources of finance were initially loans from the parent group, but arrangements existed between the company and the banks for deposits, and the public were invited to make deposits. Consideration was being given at the time to the raising of short and long-term debt in the London money markets. The senior manager of this company was an accountant and his company title was controller. He had responsibility for:

(1) Overall control of operations, through his head office, and through branch management;
(2) Policy-making for medium and long-term decisions (e.g. growth rate, composition of asset and liability portfolios).

This wide range of roles performed by one decision-maker was due to the firm being at an early state in its development. A subdivision of these roles was expected as the company grew. The manager had a strong interest in corporate modelling and some ideas on applications in the policy-making areas.

(b) Initial Problem Definition

Early discussions between the manager and researcher indicated that there was:

(1) Immediate need for a simple budgetary model to replace tedious manual calculations;
(2) Medium-to-long-term need for a model capacity to jointly manage the asset/liability portfolio.

The strategy proposed was as follows:

(1) Develop the simple budgetary model to satisfy the immediate need, and to gain some experience and insight into model building.

(2) At the same time, develop a framework to analyse asset/liability decision-making, i.e. an initial statement of local theory of investment/financing decision-making was required.
(3) The experience gained from the above was expected to point towards the kind of model capacity required for joint asset/liability decision-making.

The actual development of models occurred in four major stages:

Stage 1: Initial budgetary (accounting) models.
Stage 2: Adapted accounting model, and the initial asset (investment) portfolio model.
Stage 3: Final accounting model, the adapted asset model, and the initial liability (financing) portfolio model.
Stage 4: Establishment of links between the models.

These four stages are described below.

Stage 1

(a) Manual Budgetary Process

The existing budget, prior to the introduction of the budgetary model, was hand-calculated as follows:

(1) Branch managers prepared budgets for advances of new business. This was done one year ahead in quarters, and for the following two years on an annual basis, and budget estimates were single-point expected values.
(2) Branch values could be amended by head office.
(3) Head office prepared budgets for expenses both for head office and branches.
(4) Branch and head office figures were aggregated to develop a company budget.
(5) The income and cash flows expected as a result of these new business advances were laboriously hand-calculated using the accounting method and cash-flow calculation rules.

The final step involved a very tedious calculation, even with very limited budget data, e.g. three months' budget data containing four classes of instalment credit business. Thus the initial role of the computer model was to calculate quickly these income and cash flows for company profit and cash plans.

(b) Purpose of Initial Budgetary Model

The manager's view of the required uses of the budgetary model was as follows:

(1) To help make policy decisions, i.e. ask 'What if' questions, about such policy variables as: the growth rate of advances; pricing (per annum flat rates); asset mix; commission and handling costs and their effect on cash flow and income.
(2) Given decisions in these policy areas, to help to establish a budget or a set of flexible budgets which could subsequently form a basis for control and analysis of variance at company level.
(3) To amend new business targets for branches, and give branches guidelines for the setting of per annum flat rates (PAF).

A longer-term use envisaged was that as the branches grew into larger operations, the model could be used to develop branch budgets. This could be done either by head office or by the branches, using initial branch estimates amended where necessary by head office. To summarize, the manager saw the model as:

(1) A data-processing aid for part of his existing budgetary process.
(2) A tool for the investigation of policy variables.

(c) Structure of Initial Budgetary Model

Using the model design guidelines outlined earlier in this chapter the budgetary model was developed with the structure shown in Figure 8.1. The accounting logic was based on the conventional 'Rule of 78' employed in instalment credit revenue recognition. The model itself was written in the BASIC language and developed on a commercial time-sharing system. This language was chosen primarily because:

(1) It is widely available.
(2) Programs in BASIC can be easily transferred between commercial systems.
(3) It is easy to use, is an interactive language, and permits flexible input/output.

The budget model was successfully incorporated into the existing budgetary process with few problems. This success was not surprising, given that it merely automated a well-tried calculation procedure. However, after six months of frequent use the manager began to see major limitations in the model.

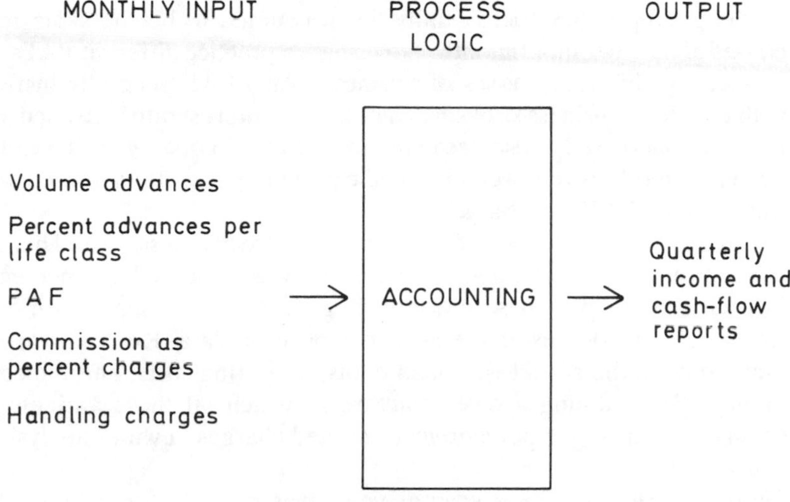

Figure 8.1 Budgetary model

Stage 2

(a) Budgetary Model Limitations

At this point, the manager and the author investigated the limitations of this budgetary model by assessing it against:

(1) The manager's expanding decision requirement;
(2) The initial statement of a local theory of investment and financing decision-making for finance houses;
(3) The theory of business finance;
(4) The set of design guidelines for financial modelling;

The result of these influences can be summarized as follows:

(1) The manager was aware that the model was based on the original manual calculations. These included many approximations and short cuts to reduce the calculation load. These were now seen as constraints on model usefulness. It was therefore thought possible to disaggregate key policy variables and look at the output in greater detail. Thus the use of the model had not only eliminated computational constraints but also relaxed their associated perceptual constraints, and the manager was beginning to investigate his problem situation in greater depth. Two specific variables were considered in more detail: the per annum flat rate (PAF) and the cost structure of instalment credit contracts.

The pricing policy had initially been assumed to be the same for all classes of data per input month. However, in practice different PAFs were applied for different classes of business. Thus PAF generally increased with the life of business to ensure that the true interest rate increased as the time risk increased. Also, certain categories of goods were considered riskier than others (e.g. second-hand cars were riskier than new cars) and thus a higher PAF was charged.

Costs previously developed in the model were commission and handling charges (acquisition charges). Commission was estimated as a percentage of total charges per class, and handling charges were input as monthly totals to be divided using the asset composition data. Key cost variables omitted from the model were bad debts, operating costs, and the cost of money. By assuming a cost structure in which all these variables are estimated as a simple percentage of earned charges, a wider analysis was deemed feasible.

(2) Output by quarters over several years was suitable for a longer-term outlook, but for shorter-term profit and cash planning, monthly figures were more suitable. In the long run an option in the model to allow various levels of output (period) aggregation was necessary.

(3) Further developments were also indicated in the collection and storage of input data for the model. Crude links could be initially established with the data processing and reporting system by inputting the unearned charges schedule from existing business into the model. This could be linked to new business calculations in the model to develop an updated unearned charges schedule. This in turn provides the basis for calculating earned charges taken from new and old business for a month. Finally, this data could be used with the cost structure to develop a budget.

Another change considered useful was the storage of several years of new business data. This was required to consider the accounting consequences of the longer-term investment decision.

(4) It was also considered useful to have the capacity to easily redefine the accounting method, and thus the ability to assess the 'best' method.

(b) Other Modelling Needs Perceived

The manager was also becoming increasingly aware of the inadequacies of the budgetary model as a tool for analysing the asset portfolio, especially with regard to the sole use of the accounting framework for investment appraisal and cash planning. Investment appraisal was also done on an aggregate portfolio profit basis. Further, cash output from the model was only in the form of contractual payments. Such contractual payments were an unlikely outcome given the number of contracts settled early.

The manager therefore felt that a separate asset portfolio model should be developed with a capacity for producing:

(1) A detailed analysis of the effect of variables such as arrears and early settlements, which disrupted contractual cash and income flows.
(2) An analysis over different segments of the portfolio, and over the whole portfolio, of return and of the margin over the cost of capital.
(3) Assessments of the risk/return characteristics of asset portfolios of varying composition.

These extra decision needs had been mentioned at the start of the research; they had now been emphasized by the limitations of the existing budgetary model and the influences of local and general business finance theory. They indicated the development of a separate asset portfolio cash-flow model, using a present-value cash-flow frame of analysis, suitably adapted to the unique nature of the decision to invest in instalment credit financial assets. The manager also became interested in the possible development of a financing model. Its role was seen as:

(1) Providing useful input information in the form of interest costs to the accounting model. The accounting model was at the time using subjectively determined estimates for the cost of money.
(2) Providing data to calculate the cost of capital for use with asset portfolio decision-making.
(3) Complementing the asset portfolio by providing comprehensive cash-flow data covering both asset and liability portfolios.
(4) Investigating long-term financing decisions.

Limited resources were available for model development and therefore the manager had to set priorities for the next stage of development. He made the following assessments of the urgency, relevance and feasibility of the identified requirements:

(1) All of the proposed adaptations to the accounting models were simple to implement and from the manager's position offered the most immediate return.
(2) The asset portfolio model shared many structural similarities, and much common input data, with the accounting model. It therefore seemed a straightforward model to flowchart and program. It was also a much-needed model for the manager. This was because he was relatively new to this business and he felt a strong need to understand the phenomena affecting asset cash flows. He therefore hoped to improve his cash-forecasting skills and his general management of the existing portfolio.

(3) The financing model was not considered an urgent priority because funds were at the time available from the parent banking group and were fairly predictable. However, it was expected that as the company grew it would borrow more funds from the conventional money markets and thus the need for a financing model would increase.

(c) The Adapted Accounting Model

Adaptation of the existing budgetary model to satisfy the new decision needs was a straightforward task. This was partially due to the minor nature of the programming changes, and also because of the segmental nature of the original design. This latter feature allowed easy addition of new segments to input, process and output logic. There was therefore little fundamental change in the structure of the model, but major changes occurred in its capacity to satisfy managerial decision needs. This can be demonstrated by the following applications of the adapted model:

(1) It was used to ask 'what if' questions concerning the following short-term profit planning issues:
   (a) Varying levels of business for the overall asset portfolio segments of the portfolios. For example, it was used to assess the effect of seasonality on profit and other output.
   (b) Changes in elements of the cost structure per class.
   (c) Changes in the pricing policy.
   (d) Changes in the product classes analyses, including: changes in transaction life classes; and changes in transaction value classes; changes in goods financed classes; and combinations of these changes.
   (e) Changes in estimates of early settlement refunds as a percentage of charges. This was a very simple approach to the prediction of the cash-flow effects of changes in this variable.
   (f) Any combination of the above changes, and their joint effects on any of the output variables.
(2) It was used in the medium (twelve months) to long term (three years) within the context of the strategic and financial planning cycle. Thus it was used as the accounting model in a longer-term planning exercise. The input options in the model were such that it was possible to proceed quickly through twelve months of input.
(3) It was used throughout the management hierarchy to produce company, regional and some branch budgets.

(d) Initial Asset Portfolio Model

Given the expanded investment decision needs and the limitations of the accounting model, a simple working version of an asset portfolio model was

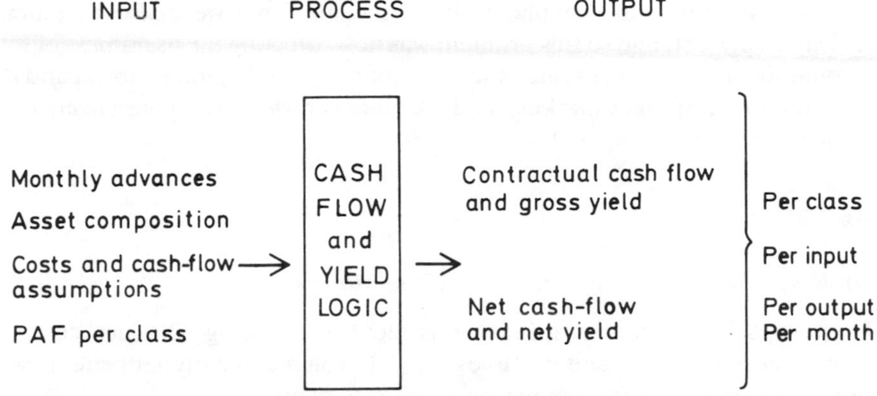

Figure 8.2 Asset portfolio model

built. This model had the basic structure shown in Figure 8.2. The model was also written in BASIC, using the same commercial time-sharing system. This ensured consistency and common standards for the existing models. This principle was also adopted for all subsequent models in the company.

Some problems were encountered in implementing this model because the manager was unfamiliar with the discounting logic at the heart of the model. The problems were circumvented by programming and implementing the model in simple, confidence-building stages. Thus, the model was firstly built to analyse the cash flow and yield (internal rate of return) of a single transaction. The model was then extended through many transaction classes, then many months of input data, and finally included the required cost cash-flow variables. From demonstration runs it was clear to the manager that this simple asset portfolio model needed the following improvements.

(1) The ability to work towards a target percentage composition of asset portfolio at the end of each year.
(2) The ability to assess the effects of: (a) changing many cost structure assumptions such as commission rates; (b) arrears and bad debts; (c) early settlements on cash flow and yields. This was seen as essential for short-term (one to six months) cash management, and for long-term cash projections.

Each of these improvements, with the exception of early settlements, was found to be feasible over a three-month period. However, the early-settlements variable proved to be intractable during this stage of model development. This considerably reduced the usefulness of the asset portfolio model because this variable was by then proving to be an important influence on cash-flow volatility. In a similar fashion, income flows were also becoming difficult to predict, and so this problem was now affecting the usefulness of the accounting model. At the same time, the company was beginning to expand its operations in the money markets, and the manager was developing a need for a financing model.

Stage 3

(a) Revised Accounting and Asset Portfolio Models

These models had common limitations identified in Stage 2 which centred around the early settlement variables, i.e.: (1) volume of early settlements per month per class; (2) rebate policy on early settlements.

The required output information was, (1) earned charges taken (after settlement) by the finance house per month; (2) charges rebated or refunded to customers per month.

The manager had always seen early settlements as a 'problem' in that although higher profits were produced in the period of settlement, contractually agreed income and cash flows were disrupted in a manner that was difficult to predict. This problem had recently become acute. He was aware that if he could estimate the effects of this variable, and given that he had some control over the volume of early settlements per month (through offering favourable rates), he would have an important control over income and liquidity.

Thus additional design specifications for the accounting and asset portfolio models were developed. These included the following:

(1) The generation of early settlements distribution per input month from historical records, or through the manager subjectively developing the data.
(2) Random sampling of these distributions in order to simulate the effect of this variable (i.e. risk analysis).

The specifications suggested:

(1) A long programming effort which would result in very large asset portfolio and accounting models requiring extensive input of data by the manager;
(2) Final models of dubious value because of time spent developing input data, and actually inputting it.

The manager did not want the model-building effort to develop into a large and expensive programming activity focused around one variable, and he therefore indicated that 'cut-down' versions would probably prove adequate.

Thus simpler risk-estimating procedures were adopted. These had the potential to develop into an extended risk analysis if needed, and proved fairly easy to program.

Other information output now seen as useful was the asset capital balances outstanding resulting from new business decisions over several periods. Given an investment decision, and the accounting method, the valuation of these asset balances was defined, and it proved fairly easy to adjust the accounting model for this output to balance-sheet calculations. Finally, it was required that all output data could be aggregated into monthly, quarterly, or annual values, and that monthly earned charges could be disaggregated to show the estimated monthly interest charges for tax calculations.

These changes in both models took over six months to implement. This was due to a problem of data collection for the early settlement estimation procedures. However, once this variable was included, albeit using a very crude form of risk analysis, the manager expressed considerable satisfaction with the models and considered them fairly complete for the existing decision needs.

(b) The Financing Model

The manager's interest in this model grew considerably during this period due to:

(1) The company's increased dependence on the money markets for funds.
(2) A higher than usual level of volatility in the money markets.

The author had also investigated the financing decision for the company as part of the development of a statement of local theory. From these two sources it was clear that a financing model was required to help in the following areas:

(1) Decisions relating to the financing of the capital requirements for each period;
(2) Projection of liabilities in the balance sheet;
(3) Liability maturity analysis;
(4) Liability mix analysis;
(5) Risk analysis of the liability portfolio;
(6) Updating of the source of funds budget;
(7) Development of data for calculation of liquidity ratios and cost of capital.

This was an extensive initial list of decision requirements and clearly involved much programming effort. The central logic of the program was expected to be the calculation of balances and interest charges for each liability type. This was seen to be relatively straightforward, and the major program-

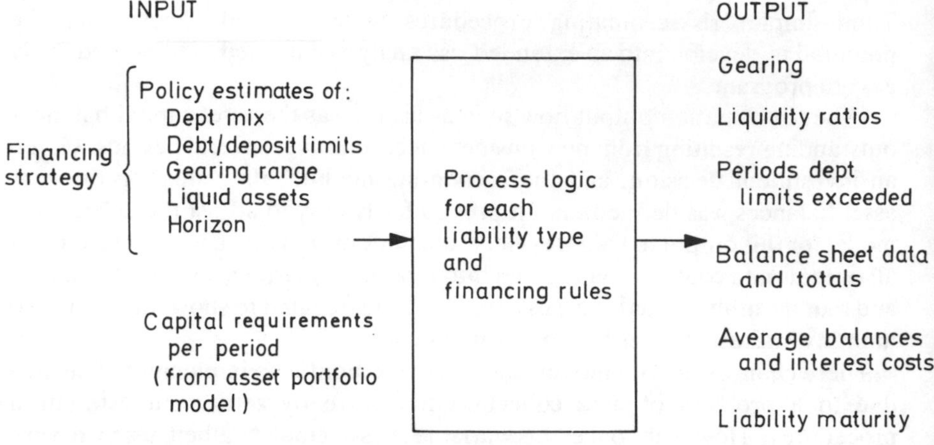

Figure 8.3 Financing model

ming effort was expected to be in designing flexible input and output software to cope with specific decision needs taken from the list above, or with groups of such needs.

The basic structure of the initial design of the financing model was as shown in Figure 8.3. Once again, the model was programmed in BASIC, and was implemented in a number of steps:

(1) Submodels were built for each liability type and these were validated using manual calculations from historical liabilities with known data.
(2) These submodels were aggregated into a portfolio model which could calculate balances and interest charges, for each liability, and for the whole portfolio.
(3) Further adjustments include many months of input and years of output data.
(4) At this point a variety of financing rules were built into the model with options open to the manager to choose sets of rules.
(5) Considerable effort was expended at all stages in adding flexible input and output software to the model.

This incremental approach to validation and implementation was essential in ensuring that the manager fully understood and had confidence in the wholly new model. Thus few problems were encountered in using this model during the financing decision process. Its major value proved to be in allowing the manager to understand the implications of various financing rules generally employed in the industry, and to devise suitable rules for his company. However, the model was considered to have a major limitation, in that the capital requirements data was manually transferred from the asset portfolio model. It was this limitation that led to the final stage of model development involving physical links between models.

Stage 4

(a) Liquidity Planning

The increased need to analyse the financing decision enhanced the manager's awareness of the range of issues which existed with respect to joint/asset liability decision-making. In particular, problems were emerging in assessing the risk of insolvency and in analysing the liquidities (maturities) of asset and liability portfolios. These issues suggested that the manager should consider in detail the joint effects of the investment and financing decisions. In Figure 8.4 the sources of liquidity from the asset and liability portfolio are identified and their influences on insolvency pinpointed.

In Figure 8.4, asset liquidity is divided into four major components:

(1) Liquid assets; these are the 'cushion' against insolvency.
(2) Block discounting, which with the liquidation values of segments of the asset portfolio, can be considered sources of liquidity.
    If a regular market exists for sale of segments of the portfolio under discount, either under duress (liquidation) or as a normal transaction (block discounting), then the company can rely on this to some degree as a source of concealed asset liquidity.
(3) Basic liquidity, which is the liquidity resulting from the investment decision of the firm, and its associated business risk (i.e. bad debts, arrears, dealer defaults, etc.).
(4) Control liquidity, which is the extra liquidity the firm can generate by making terms for early settlement more attractive, and is therefore a major source of concealed asset portfolio liquidity.

Liability liquidity is divided into three categories:

(1) Short notice repayables, such as Bank overdraft and acceptance credits.
(2) Contractual repayables, such as short-term deposits or long-term loans.
(3) Concealed liability liquidity, which consists of bank and acceptances lines of credits, and possible roll-overs of deposits. Also, most large finance houses have links with major financial institutions who will ultimately guarantee them funds.

Figure 8.4 indicates that joint asset and liability portfolio liquidity can be assessed if the asset and liability portfolio models are run in sequence. This

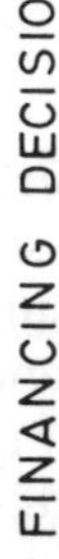

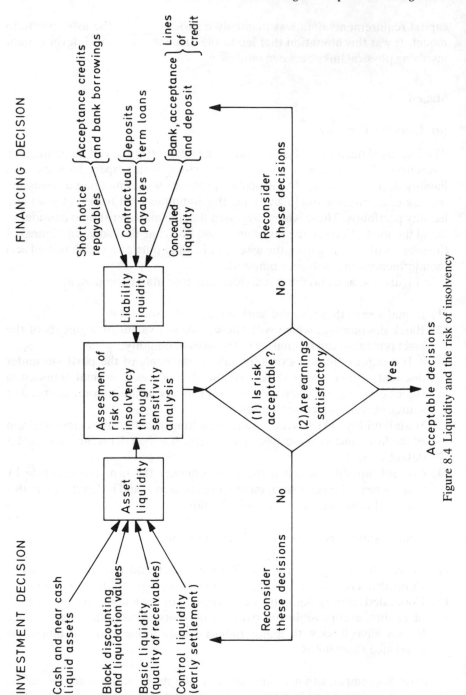

Figure 8.4 Liquidity and the risk of insolvency

proved to be a very easy adaptation of the models, and only involved the setting up of output files from one model to be used as an input file to the other.

The joint asset/liability models were then used to assess the risk of insolvency by sensitivity analysis of these liquidity components of the joint investment-financing plan. Various assumptions of uncertainty were employed. These were:

(1) Pessimistic outcomes for joint investment-financing plans. For example, arrears and bad debts were expected to be high, early settlements were expected to be late in the life of HP agreements and very uncertain. On the liability side, shrinkage in deposit markets was expected. Thus the manager was interested in finding values for gearing, debt structure, levels of liquid assets and asset composition which would stand up to these severe financial problems.
(2) Expected (or the most likely) cash-flow outcomes of joint investment-financing plans were simulated, and their risk of insolvency assessed. The level of liquid assets required to keep this risk at acceptable levels was compared with the pessimistic value developed above. This allowed the manager to assess the cost of his risk attitudes and therefore aid his choice of what was an appropriate level of liquid assets.

Given this understanding of the firm's insolvency risk, 'rule of thumb' liquidity ratios relevant to the firm were developed. These were used to aid operational decision-making and to influence lenders.

(b) Financial Planning

Having established and tested the physical link between the asset portfolio and liability portfolio for this one major decision need (i.e. liquidity planning), the models were now available for a whole range of joint uses.

These included:

(1) Variance analysis of the sources and use of funds budget.
(2) Long-term (up to five years) financial planning.
(3) Investigation of the interdependencies between the investment, financing and dividend decisions.

The financial planning and interdependencies issues required the development of a minor model to calculate the cost of capital for the company. Figure 8.5 summarizes the use of the models in financial planning.

(c) Further Development

The models had essentially reached a stage where they were recognizable *vis-à-vis* the theory of business finance. The next major development

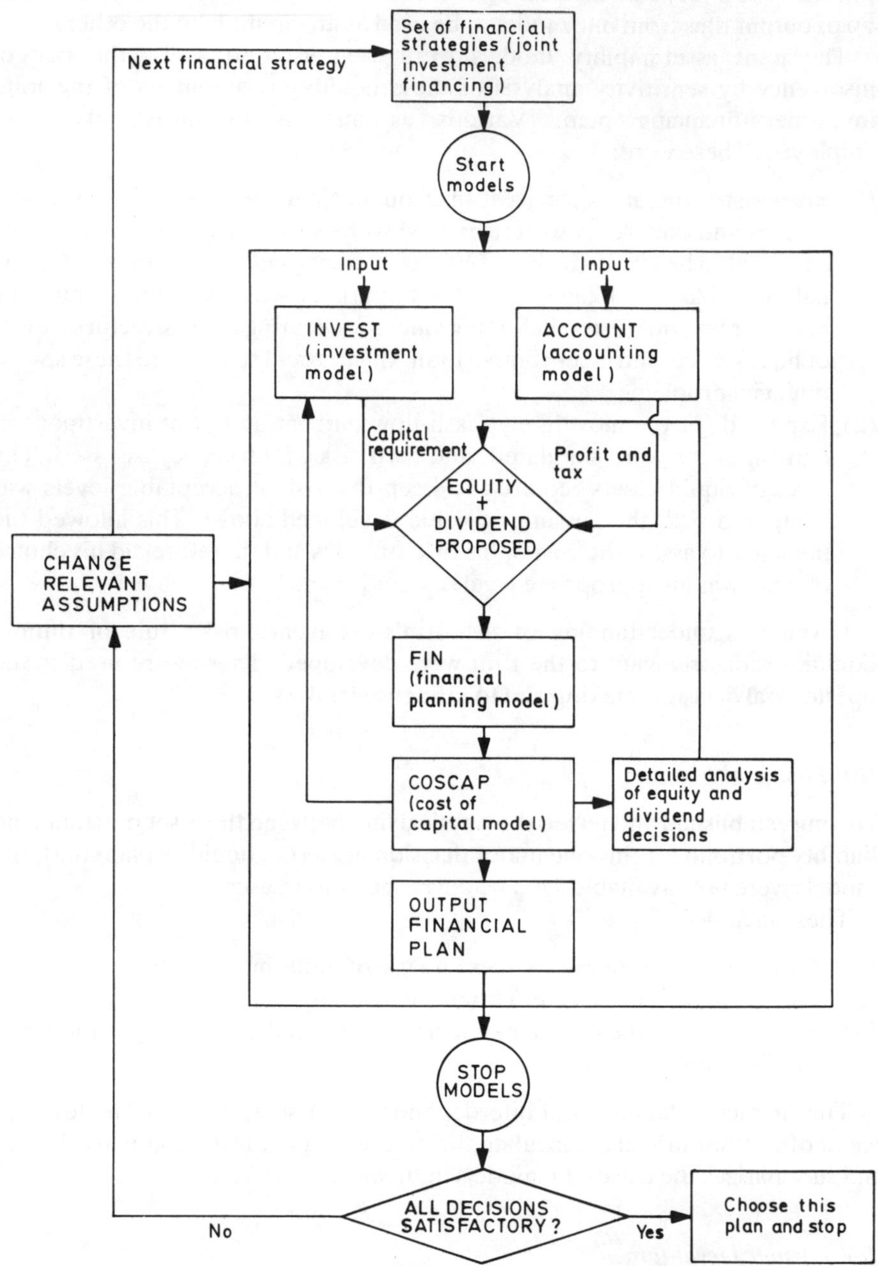

Figure 8.5 Use of models in financial planning

envisaged was to use the model to assess the impact of the investment, financing, and dividend decision on the value of the company. However, the development never materialized because the manager was more interested in developing 'satisfactory' (to him!) plans, and using these plans to argue for more long-term funds from the parent corporation.

Summary

The major steps in implementing the strategy in the case study were as follows:

(1) Initial statements were developed concerning relevant local theory and the accounting methods used in the budget.
(2) The first model to be built was the model which promised the most immediate impact and highest return for the manager. In this case it was the accounting model.
(3) The other financial models were based on the decision rules embodied in local theory, and the model design guidelines. These were built in order of managerial priority.
(4) The guiding procedure from the general theory of business finance was used to link the submodels in developing comprehensive financial plans, and investigating joint investment/financing issues.
(5) The local theory was expanded by documenting the use and effectiveness of the models.
(6) The models were continuously adapted from changes occurring in local theory.

This approach was initially sequential through steps (1)–(6). However, in the long run steps (1)–(4) interacted in a continuous manner, as the firm expanded its knowledge base.

8.5 Appraisal of the Methodology

The role of models and local theory mediating between theory and practice can be summarized diagrammatically as shown in Figure 8.6. Thus the 'local' theory, expressed in the language of the industry but influenced by general theory, provides an important communication medium between theory and practice. The models developed in the context of the local theory are guided and influenced by theory, and have potential as research tools. For example, a manager can blend existing rules of thumb with the guiding procedure as follows:

(1) Use the rules of thumb, based on a historical understanding of the interrelationships between the investment, financing and dividend decisions, to identify the 'scale' or size of these expected decisions.

(2) Use the submodels and linking framework to investigate many alternatives in much greater detail.

This approach is rational in that it is based on sound finance. Also, by speeding up the process, managers have the opportunity to learn how the decisions interact. They can therefore develop a 'feel' for the linked nature of these decisions, and hopefully extend both local and general theories of decision-making.

Hence, one is attempting to benefit from the theory of finance by trying to approach the simultaneous ideal in a practical interactive manner. This is also done in the context of a decision process in which the skills, judgements, biases and personal goals of the key actors are present. This allows the role of the financial planning models in the decision process and procedure to be made explicit. Such a perspective is a key ingredient in modelling to aid financial decision-making. It also creates the opportunity for an eventual feedback to theory from practical observations.

In this learning experience managers may develop linear programming and risk analysis models as aids for decision-making. The financial submodels, guided by simple theory, are therefore seen as a first step in developing a financial planning model, which may eventually include elements of stochastic processes and programming (e.g. stochastic cash generation models, or LP for financing decision with debt only).

Academics are in a key position in starting such a communication process between existing decision theory and practice. Academic studies of 'local' theories and their uses as a basis for financial model-building will provide useful stimuli for the managers concerned. More significantly, they will influence the long-term development of theoretical models for decision-making. In the author's view such models normally start from a theoretical base and build on this, rather than continuously interacting with practice. Thus, these two roles for academic model builders are necessary complements, with the former role now emerging in response to the problems identified in model building.

Another change of role may occur for the manager by moving from being predominantly involved in deterministic model building to additional involvement in local theory building and eventually general theory building.

Hence, this philosophy of modelling to learn, learning through modelling, and further modelling through experience, is a deliberate attempt to release managers from the constraints of abstract decision theory, both financial and mathematical, while eventually benefiting from these by selecting those tools of direct and proven use.

The author believes that this approach recognizes that the qualitative benefits of a modelling research effort will come from giving managers a capacity to research their decision behaviour. Also by making the investigation

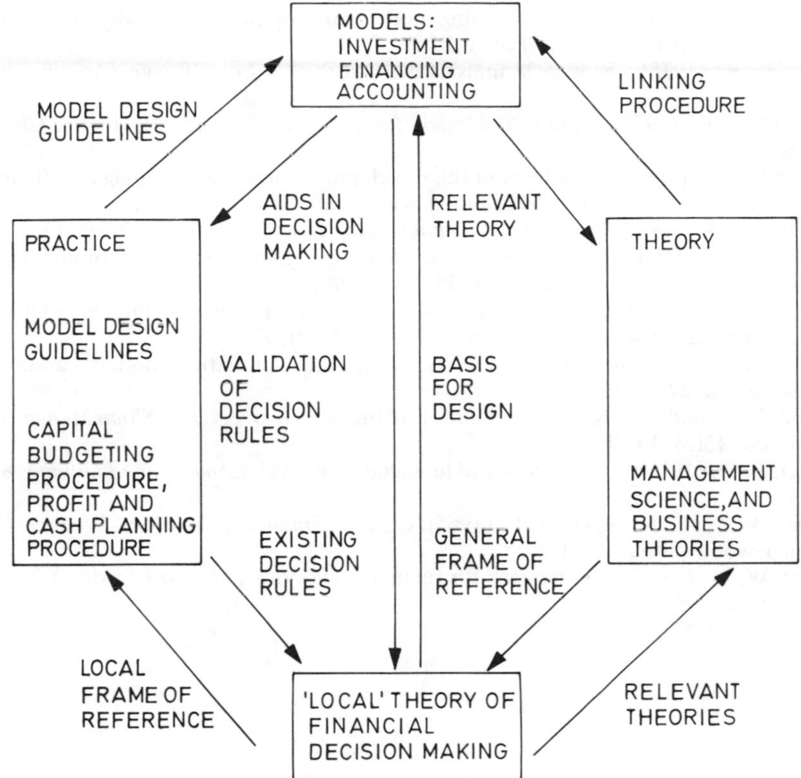

Figure 8.6 Theory and practice in financial planning

of decision-making as important as taking the decision, one hopes to improve the quality of the decision eventually taken.

References

Carleton, W. T. (1970). 'An analytical model for financial planning', *Journal of Finance*, **25**(2), 291–315.

Carleton, W. T., Dick, C. L. and Downes, D. H. (1972). *Converting Finance Theory into Practice*, Working Paper, Amos Tuck School, Dartmouth College, Massachusetts.

Cooley, P. and Copeland, R. (1975). 'Contrasting roles of financial theories and practice', *Business Horizons*, **18**(4), 25–31.

Gershefski, G. (1969). 'Building a corporate financial model', *Harvard Business Review*, **47**(4), 61–72.

Grinyer, P. H. and Wooller, J. (1974). 'Cash in on corporate planning', *Computer Management*, **9**(10), 31–4.

Grinyer, P. H. and Wooller, J. (1975). *Corporate Models Today*, Institute of Chartered Accountants in England and Wales, London.

Hall, W. K. (1973). 'Strategic planning models: are top managers really finding them useful', *Journal of Business Policy*, **32**(2), 33–42.
Hall, W. K. (1975). 'Why risk analysis isn't working', *Long Range Planning*, **8**(6), 25–9.
Holland, J. B. (1978). *Financial Models for Finance Houses*, PhD thesis, CNAA, London.
Holland, J. B. (1981). 'Problems in the development and use of managerial financial models', *Managerial and Decision Economics*, **2**(1), 40–8.
Holland, J. B. (1986). *International Financial Management*, Basil Blackwell, Oxford.
Myers, S. C. and Pogue, G. A. (1974). 'A programming approach to corporate financial management', *Journal of Finance*, **29**(2), 579–99.
McInnes, J. M. and Carleton, W. T. (1982). 'Theory, models, and implementation in financial management', *Management Science*, **28**(9), 957–78.
Naylor, T. H. and Jeffress, C. (1975). 'Corporate simulation models—a survey', *Simulation*, **24**(6), 171–6.
Pogue, G. A. and Lall, K. (1974). 'Corporate finance: an overview', *Sloan Management Review*, **15**(3), 19–38.
Power, P. D. (1975). 'Computers and financial planning', *Long Range Planning*, **8**(6), 53–9.
Robichek, A. A. and Myers, S. C. (1965). *Optimal Financing Decisions*, Prentice-Hall, Englewood Cliffs, New Jersey.
Sihler, W. M. (1971). 'Framework for financial decisions', *Harvard Business Review*, **49**(2), 123–35.

PART 3
MODELS IN ACTION

Finance Modelling in Corporate Management, 2nd Edition
Edited by J. W. Bryant

9

Budget Modelling at TAC Construction Materials

IAN CRAWFORD

9.1 Introduction

TAC Construction Materials plc is one of the largest companies in the Turner & Newall Group and one of the principal manufacturers of fibrous cement products in the UK. The main products include fibrous cement roofing and cladding material, pipes, flat sheets and fire protection materials. The company also produces certain electrical and mechanical products. TAC has been in existence since about 1930, though the beginnings can be traced back to about 1870, and it now operates six factories throughout England. In 1976 the company was split into five divisions:

Building Products (BP) Division
Pipes Division
Engineering Materials (EM) Division
Vicuclad Division
} Four trading divisions
Service Division (includes Finance and Personnel Departments)

A standard costing system has been in operation for a number of years. However, the budgetary control system commenced in 1969 and has evolved into a comprehensive system over the period since then. The process of preparing the annual budget follows a standard approach. This involves collecting data from a number of sources covering:

sales volumes (home and export);
selling prices;

selling-price increases;
standard costs or standard gross margins;
cost of all departmental budgets (about 60 in total).

Certain variances are also included in the budget since the standard costs are based on realistic standards at an authorized capacity level. However, a number of factors may affect production so an amount which recognizes that:

(1) the authorized hours will not be worked, and/or
(2) the standards will not be achieved (e.g. higher breakages and rejects, lower output rates, etc.)

is included.

9.2 Model Development

Until the early 1970s the company produced quarterly accounts and the budget was manually prepared. However, when Turner & Newall introduced monthly accounts throughout the Group it was decided to look at the possibility of computerizing the budget routine with the following potential advantages:

(1) Reducing manual calculations, especially now there was a monthly accounting base;
(2) Reducing the typing load for budget reporting;
(3) Providing facilities for sensitivity testing in financial planning.

In computerizing it had to be decided at what level to input data. The options were to start:

(1) At product level (about 10 000), at which level standard costs are produced,
(2) At product family level (about 200), where a family is a group containing a number of different sizes, thicknesses, etc. of products, or
(3) At product group level (about 20), each of which contains a number of product families.

The product family level was chosen, since all reports issued are at this level and it also kept the input data and model to a more manageable size.

The first model was based on the Prosper package and run on our own in-house ICL computer. The system was mainly developed by the Management Systems Department and because of changes in personnel and organizational structure proved difficult to run. Management Systems personnel had to carry out any changes and run the model.

In 1977 a Group computer was introduced and TAC removed their own ICL computer in the July before the budget had been prepared. It was therefore necessary to change to a different modelling system and the FCS package marketed by EPS Consultants was chosen because:

(1) It is specially written for budgeting and financial applications;
(2) It is easy to understand and write the logic;
(3) It can be operated by non-computer personnel;
(4) Modifications can be carried out by accountants;
(5) Data can be input by accountants;
(6) A hierarchy section had just been introduced which made it easier to define the relationship between various input levels;
(7) It was expected to be possible later to use FCS on the Group computer, although initial implementation was through Comshare bureau services.

In fact, point (7) above was well founded and when in 1979 the Group Computer Centre offered a timesharing service which included FCS, the model was transferred to the Group computer.

9.3 The Budget Model

The financial model that is now to be explained is the current FCS budgeting model. After describing the model, its use for control purposes and its benefits, associated developments will be discussed.

A basic premise of the model was that it should be simple enough to be operated by non-computer personnel both in terms of changing the logic and inputting data. However, certain advantages arose through using the Computer Department:

(1) Simplification of certain parts of the model;
(2) Introduction of easy-to-understand instructions for display when starting to run the model through a question-and-answer section.

The model will be considered in four parts: structure, input, operation and output.

Model Structure

(a) Overall Logic

In order to describe the model structure it is necessary briefly to outline the main features of the FCS modelling system. The key entities handled are called files and there are three types. All basic calculations performed by a model are defined in *logic files* in which the relationships between financial variables are stated. These contain the logic for all computations in the form of equations relating variables to one another. In many applications of financial modelling essentially similar calculations may have to be carried out for a range of activities and the results consolidated for reporting purposes: for example, a single model may apply to the costing of a number of products. This is where the second kind of file, the *hierarchy file*, is used. This describes the structure of the consolidation to be carried out, and permits repetitive model logic to be incorporated without having to be expressed in full every time it is required. The third and last file type is the *data file* which, as might be expected, simply contains the input values for calculation variables.

The TAC model was required to produce the following eight reports:

(1) Quarterly report showing turnover and gross profits by product family for each division, called the Gross Family Trading Account (GFTA).
(2) Monthly report showing sales volume, turnover and gross profits by product family for each division.
(3) Summary of quarterly turnover and gross profits by division.
(4) Monthly divisional profit statements.
(5) Quarterly divisional profit statements.
(6) Monthly company profit statement.
(7) Quarterly company profit statement.
(8) Summary trading account detailing on a quarterly basis the carriage, distribution, selling, research and administration budgets by department (these are the Non-manufacturing Expenses (NME)), and giving the company net trading profit.

The system that was developed consists of a number of interlinked files through which calculation and output are ordered in particular manner as shown in Figure 9.1. This structure makes it possible to ask 'what if' questions at various levels of consolidation and, through the use of files containing the results of intermediate computations, avoids the need for a complete re-evaluation of the entire system each time. Taking the above sequence of reports as a guide, the modelling system first calculates the GFTA for each division in turn (Reports (1) and (2) above), and then these results are consolidated into the company-wide picture given by Report (3). Next, divisional NME are calculated for each division by combining specific expenses for the division with a proportion of central company expenses. Reports (4) and (5) can then be generated and consolidation then produces Reports (6) and (7). Finally Report (8) is output, bringing together the NME and GFTA results into a summary trading account.

The file basis that is used contains five principal files for each trading division: both logic and data files for GFTA and NME calculation and a hierarchy file defining the divisional structure. Additional logic and data files relate to central

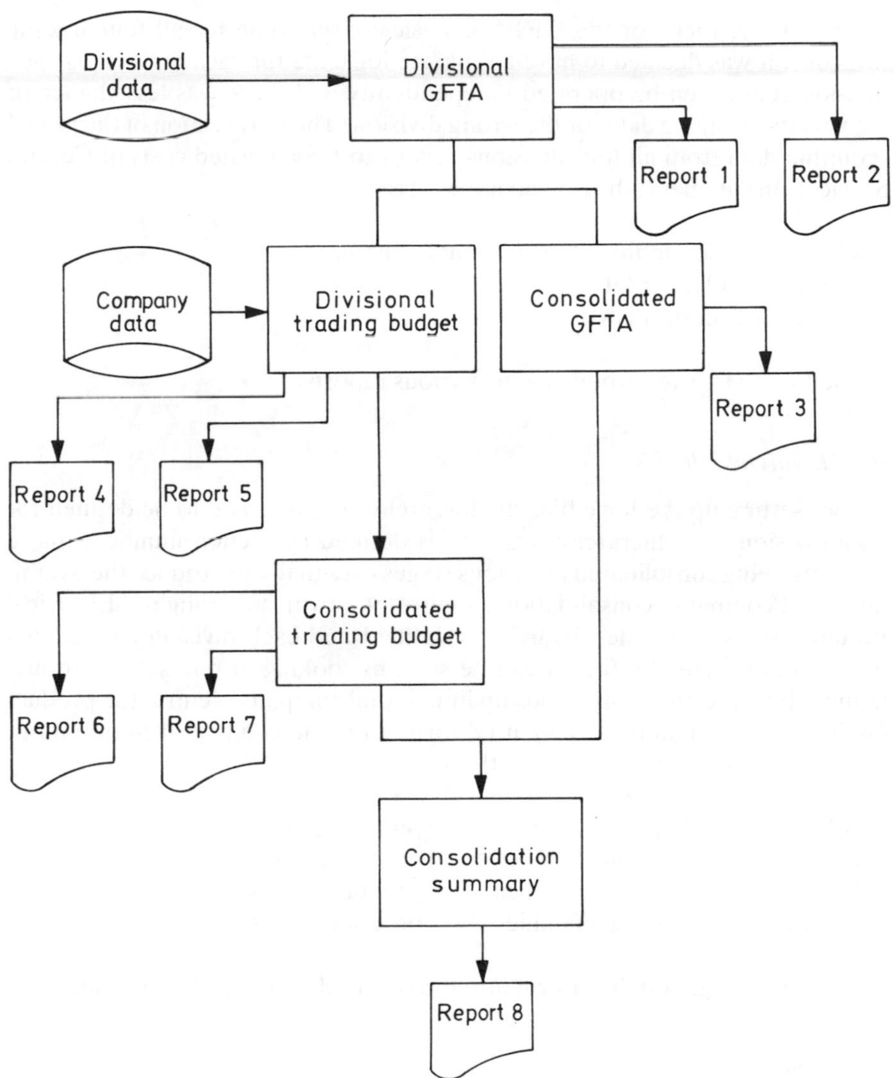

Figure 9.1 Overall logic of trading budget system

company expenses. The files are identified by a two-digit code. Thus the first digit denotes the division (BP = 1, Pipes = 2, E & M = 3, Vicuclad = 4) and the second digit the model (GFTA = 1, NME/Profit Statements = 2). For example, DATA 21 is the data file for the Pipes Division GFTA calculation, while RESULTS 42 holds the results of the NME calculations for Vicuclad Division. These codes are used in the diagrams describing the modelling system.

Though the logic for the GFTA is basically the same for all four trading divisions, it was decided to have a separate logic file for each division as each division could then be operated independently and there was less chance of incorrectly changing data for the wrong division. The only section of the model requiring data from all four divisions relates to the allocated costs of Central Services. In summary, the principal files are:

4 hierarchy files defining the divisional structures
4 logic/data files/for GFTA
5 logic/data files/for NME

in addition to files for producing the various reports.

(b) Hierarchy Files

Before setting up the logic files the hierarchy structure had to be defined for each division. The hierarchy structure is defined by section numbers, these numbers being consolidated at various stages eventually to produce the overall divisional/company consolidation. Figure 9.2 which highlights Electrical Products shows how the hierarchy is defined and each division has its own independent hierarchy file. It can be seen by looking at one set of product families how the hierarchy builds up into a total company picture, the product families' section numbers being used for both home and export information. The scale of the model is such that there are:

BP	49 product families	6 product groups
Pipes	24 product families	6 product groups
EM	43 product families	6 product groups
Vicuclad	5 product families	3 product groups

By applying the hierarchical structure the consolidations can be calculated.

(c) Logic Files

Once the hierarchies had been defined, the next stage was the build-up of the logic of the *GFTA model*. The principal calculations of the GFTA can be broken down into product family calculations and product group calculations. The product family calculations which are carried out for each section number are as follows. First, monthly volumes are calculated from the annual sales volume (in tonnes) multiplied by monthly seasonal factors. Once this monthly tonnage is available, the monthly turnover is readily calculated by multiplying by the selling price. The gross margin can then be found and hence the quarterly and annual totals. These margin calculations can be based either on

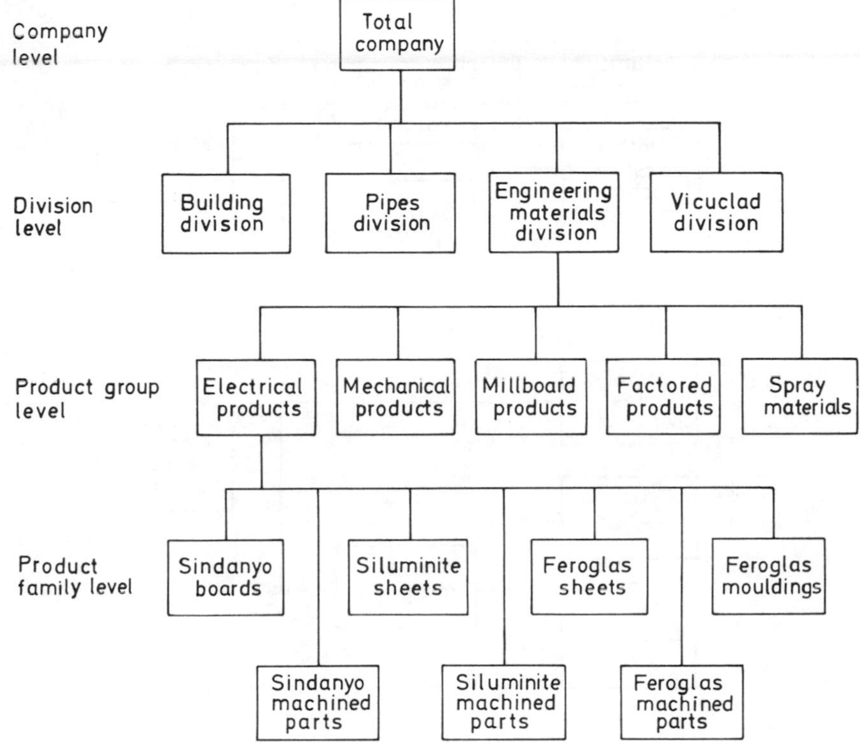

Figure 9.2 Electrical products within the hierarchy

the use of a specified gross margin percentage or else upon the difference between selling price and standard cost. The corresponding operations tree diagram is given in Figure 9.3. The model calculates the turnover and gross margins for each section number (home and export). After aggregation at product group level, certain variances are input and the model apportions these between home and export sales. The hierarchical commands are then applied and Reports (1)–(3) produced. Though part of the non-manufacturing costs, carriage rates (which may be related to either volume or turnover) and cash discounts as a percentage of turnover are calculated in this part of the model. These calculations are carried out at a product group level.

The *NME model* is not built up in the same hierarchical fashion as the GFTA and does not use section numbers. The logic is basically similar for each division except that each obviously covers different departments of the company. There are five logic files comprising four divisional files and one total company file, the latter handling expenses to be allocated. These produce not only details of non-manufacturing costs but also generate the profit statements. The first stage of evaluation involves the transfer of the results of the GFTA

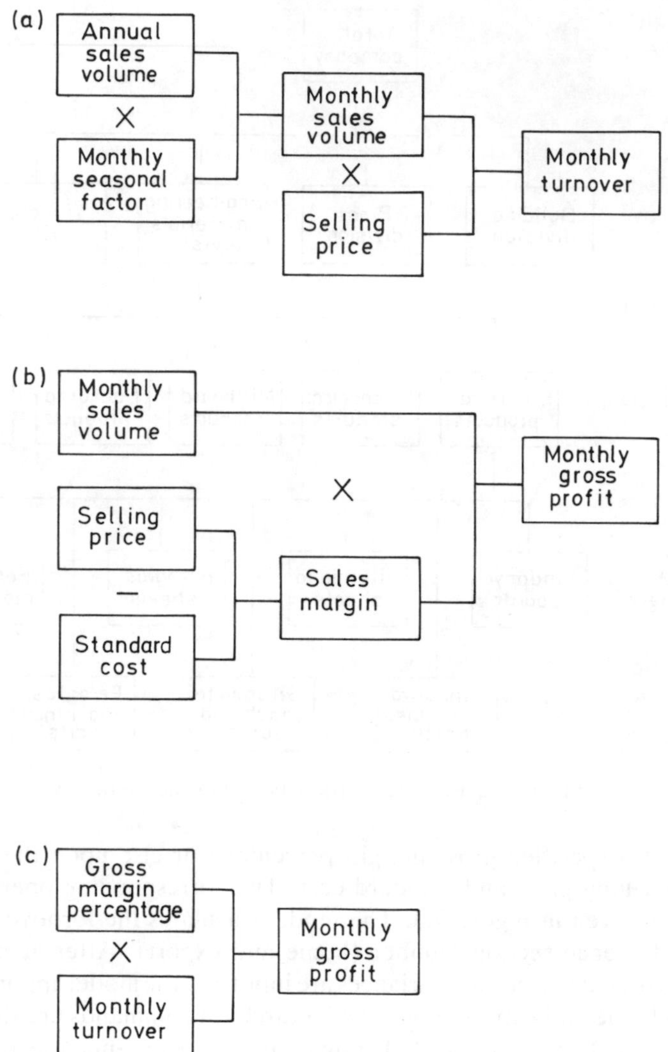

Figure 9.3 Logic of the GFTA model. (a) Calculation of turnover. (b) Gross profit calculation: sales margin basis. (c) Gross profit calculation: margin percentage basis

model and data from the company NME file to divisional files. This transfers the following information previously produced by the GFTA Logic:

(1) carriage and cash discounts.
(2) turnover and gross profit figures (to enable the profit statement to be produced).

Details of the central costs to be allocated are brought in from the NME file. Additionally for each division data are input covering departmental selling, research and distribution budgets. These data can be input either monthly or quarterly (in which case they are broken down into months on 5/4/4 basis). Once the proportion of central costs to be allocated to each division has been calculated these can be added to specific divisional NMEs. The logic for calculating the non-manufacturing costs for each division is simple and consists of adding a number of row numbers in the relevant file. Thus for example, for BP Division distribution costs, the four defined costs, Stockroom (row 20), Forwarding (row 21), Scottish Depot (row 22), South East depot (row 23), are added to give the Distribution Costs (= row 20 + 21 + 22 + 23). The results from the GFTA file and NME file are then brought together and the profit statement of Reports (4) and (5) produced. Again the logic for the profit statement is a simple addition or subtraction of rows.

The *Consolidation* logic file brings together the results from the four divisional NME models with central company data to produce a total company profit picture. The central data, which consists of information about central services departments and certain non-divisional trading items, is input for each area by quarters and allocated to the divisions on a percentage basis. Again the logic consists of simple additions and subtractions of data items. The total company profit statement is thus produced by bringing together the results from the four divisional NME files and adding the corresponding results for each item. This file is also used to produce the detailed report of non-manufacturing expenses.

Full details of the information transfers and reporting in the budget model as a whole are provided in Exhibit 9.1 in the Appendix to this chapter, where the generation of each individual report is shown in turn.

Model Input

Data forms were designed for the input to and creation of GFTA and NME files. Since the input forms were to be completed and input by non-computer personnel, it was decided to keep them simple. The GFTA input uses two forms, one for product family data and one for product group data. The NME data consist of departmental budgets for division and central services, and are entered via two further forms. All data input forms have a similar layout, being essentially in a matrix format: budget items make up the rows, while each column is a different time period, column 1 being reserved for annual data and columns 2–13 for any monthly figures. Specimen data forms are shown in Exhibit 9.2 in the Appendix. All data are entered directly at a VDU terminal.

Before any data can be input the information has to be collected from a number of sources throughout the company. Sales information is built up from the recommendations of the sales managers who use the knowledge of their representatives and economic forecasts supplied by Turner & Newall. Computerized forecasting techniques are not therefore used, the budgets being based on individuals' assessments. A number of different departments are involved in establishing factory costs covering factory, research, quality control, buying and accounts departments. Again the build-up is from personal forecasts based on relevant information. Departmental budgets are built up by individual managers. For both factory and departmental budgets, the aim is to get the managers to build up the budgets from an estimate of the resources that they require rather than to use previous year figures with a percentage added. Once data have been received and agreed by the managers they are approved by the appropriate director.

Model Operation

As mentioned previously an advantage of using computer personnel is that they are able to simplify certain aspects of the model. It is in the area of running the model that their expertise was most useful.

To operate the model a set of questions and answers has been set up through which the user interacts with the financial planning system. A typical sequence (or menu) might be as follows, where the user response is underlined:

Which Division BP (1) Pipes (2) EM (3) Vicuclad (4)?		<u>3</u>
Do you want to work with GFTA (1) or NME (2)?		<u>1</u>
Do you want to calculate (1) or print results(2)?		<u>1</u>
Do you want:		
the quarterly GFTA report for this division	(1)	
the monthly GFTA report for this division	(2)	
the summary of All Divisions GFTA	(3)	
to go on to NME	(N)	
to stop	(S)	
or to do another division?	(A)	<u>2</u>

It can be seen from the above instructions that individual sections of the model can be run independently. Following any changes to individual section number data, subsequent calculations can be limited to that section number if desired. Results are saved, in case any sensitivity runs are required, and the reports printed.

Model Output

The reports that are produced by the system (examples of which are shown in Exhibit 9.3 in the Appendix) have been so constructed that they are in the same format as the financial accounts issued on a monthly and quarterly basis. The intention has been to preserve the familiar and proven presentation formats, rather than to introduce any novel reports.

9.4 Use of Model in Planning Process

Planning in TAC is carried out during the autumn for the following financial year beginning in January. This includes the preparation of the trading budget which forms the basic company control document.

Once the budget has been agreed by the company directors it is summarized and submitted to Turner & Newall together with an outline position on the next year and a five-year capital expenditure projection. At Group level it is consolidated with the budgets of all other Group companies. If the consolidated plan does not meet Group requirements, unit companies will be told to review their budgets. The acceptability of the budgets is discussed at a planning meeting between the directors of each company and Turner & Newall Group personnel. When the budget has been accepted by Turner & Newall it not only becomes the basic control document for the year but indicates what decisions may have to be taken during the year, e.g.

(1) Capacity planning for machines with a link to stock control policy.
(2) Anticipated price increases and dates.
(3) Wage and salary awards that can be afforded.
(4) When looking at cash-flow aspects, what action needs to be taken on debtors or creditors to achieve cash requirements.
(5) Cost savings required if required profit is not being achieved.

A complete set of budget reports is issued to the directors while divisional managers receive a set of their own division's reports. Therefore each manager is in a position to see what he is expected to achieve in relation to the budget.

As already mentioned, the trading budget is the basic control document, and all accounts have a comparison of actual and budget. During the year monthly reports are produced explaining differences between actual and budget. Depending on the reasons for the differences and the trends in variances, decisions are taken as to what further action, if any, is necessary if the plan is to be achieved. However, no firm rules can be laid down as to the action to be taken, since it will necessarily depend on the circumstances.

During the planning cycle, once the initial data have been input they can quickly and easily be amended for any number of sensitivity runs. What sensitivity runs are usually undertaken? The key figures affecting the forecast are sales volume, selling prices and costs, and these are the items that are most frequently amended in sensitivity runs. Changes may be made because:

(1) Figures are considered too optimistic or pessimistic by the directors.

(2) Reassessments are made of the relationship between volume and selling prices.

Even before the forecasts are submitted to the directors, the divisions would probably carry out two or three sensitivity runs on sales volume and price.

As the company is a part of the Turner & Newall Group, it is not necessary to assess the effects of tax changes, since all taxation is dealt with at the head office.

The model has certainly made the preparation of the trading budget a more practicable exercise, especially in terms of altering the budget. Also as each division's logic and data are kept separate, changes in individual divisions can be made without affecting any other division's plans.

9.5 Associated Developments

The budget system as described above now runs routinely. Since it was first developed a number of other models have been written using the FCS time-sharing facility on the mainframe computer. These models, which now number over twenty, have been produced by Management Accounts personnel capitalizing on their experience of financial modelling gained from the budget model.

The portfolio of more recent models covers such applications as:

(1) Cash-flow and balance sheet projections.
(2) Trading division profitability.
(3) Profit profiles for individual factories.
(4) Investment appraisal.
(5) Standard cost and variance calculations.

These models are simple to operate and run. They are not linked directly to the trading budget model, but information on sales, profit and cost of sales is shared.

As an example, consider the cash-flow and balance sheet models. The data required to operate this consists of:

fixed assets covering opening balances, depreciation, disposals, capital expenditure, investments;
stock level as volume or percentage of sales;
debtor days for home and export;
days for trade creditors;
sundry debtors, creditors, provisions;
inter-company balances.

There is not a larger number of calculations, the principal ones being calculations of stock, debtors, and creditors, with the other items being input directly. Once the balance sheet has been produced the next stage is the cash-flow calculation, where further information is input concerning profit levels. Information from the balance-sheet file is transferred to the cash-flow file and by sorting the appropriate data a cash-flow statement can be produced. This model is run on the Group computer using the FCS package, and though the logic files are the same for each division, separate logic and data files are again maintained. For the total company position the four divisional files are brought together.

9.6 Conclusion

The purpose of this chapter has not been to explain the detailed operation of the budget model in use at TAC. What has been attempted is to show the importance of the model within TAC, and how it has been structured to meet the company's organization structure. The model is flexible enough to cope with organizational changes and is not too cumbersome to make it unwieldy to operate.

Appendix to Chapter 9

Exhibit 9.1 Model structure

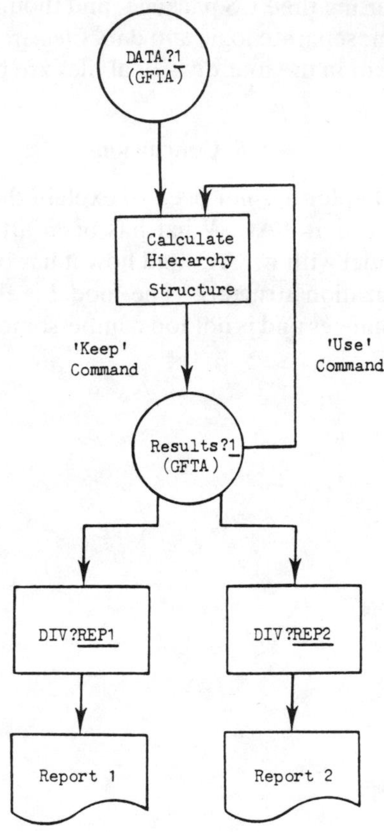

(a) Gross family trading account for each division (Reports 1 and 2)

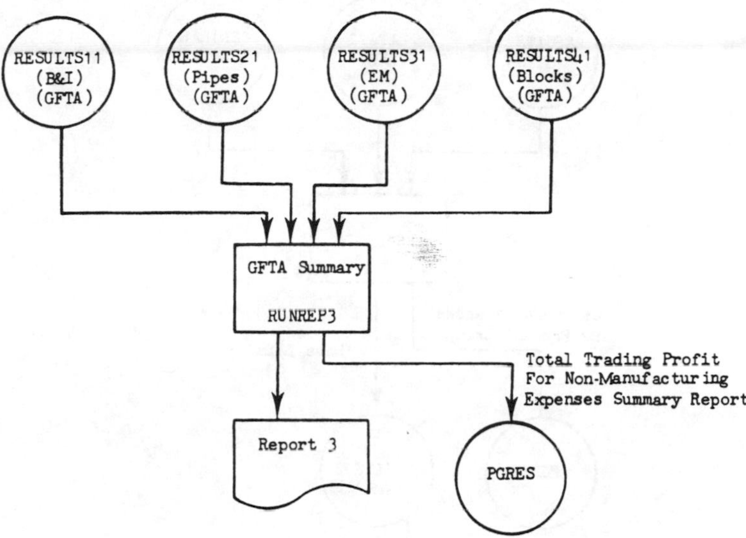

(b) Gross family trading account company summary (Report 3)

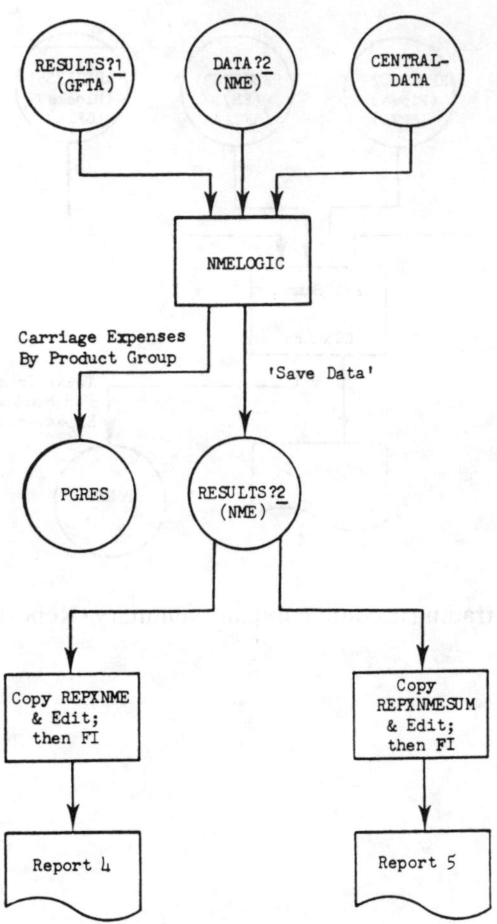

(c) Non-manufacturing expenses for each division (Reports 5 and 6)

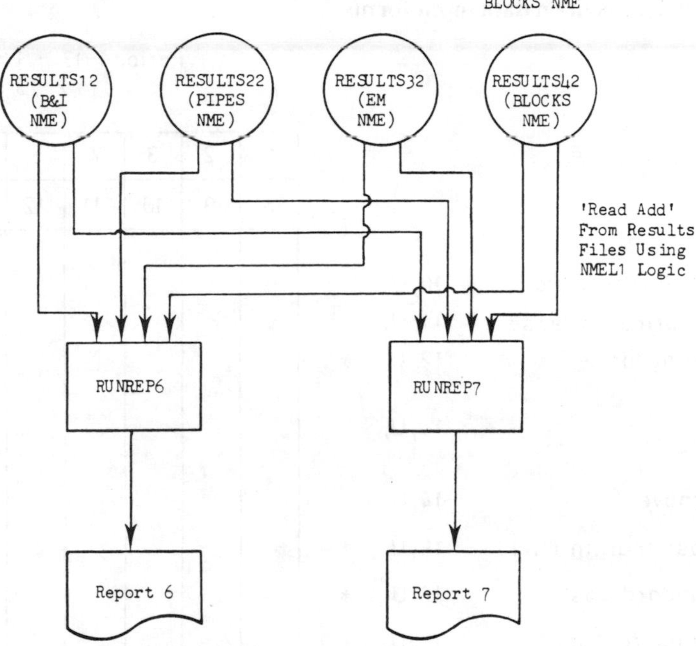

(d) Non-manufacturing company summary (Reports 6 and 7)

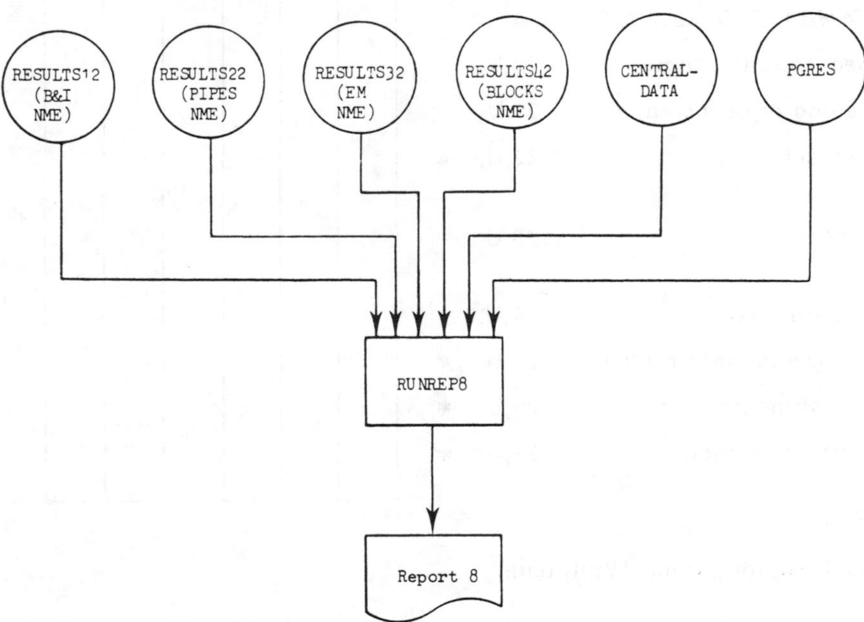

(e) Summary trading budget

Exhibit 9.2 Specimen data input forms

Period 1–13 1 = YEAR
2–13 = Months

			1	2	3	4	5	6	7
			8	9	10	11	12	13	
******SE*									
Seasonability factor	10, U,								
Selling-price increase	11, U,								
Old selling price	12, U,	*							
Tonnes	13, U,								
Old turnover	14, U,								
Old gross margin (%)	15, U,	*							
Old standard cost	16, U,	*							
Cost price factor	17, U,	*							
FAMILY DATA–EXPORT									
Seasonability factor	20, U,								
Selling price increase	21, U,								
Old selling price	22, U,	*							
Tonnes	23, U,								
Old turnover	24, U,								
Old gross margin (%)	25, U,	*							
Old standard cost	26, U,	*							
Cost price factor	27, U,	*							

END

(a) Form for product family data

		1	2	3	4	5	6	7
		8	9	10	11	12	13	
*SE								
Capacity variance	30,U,							
Price variance	31,U,							
Manufacturing variance	32,U,							
Stock revaluation	33,U,							
Carriage – home (%o or rate)	34,U,							
Carriage – export (%o or rate)	35,U,							
Cash discount (%o)	36,U,							

END

N.B. Carriage Rates — B & I, Pipes, Blocks } £/tonne (m^2)
EM %o of turnover

(b) Form for product group data

		1	2	3	4	5	6	7
		8	9	10	11	12	13	
Monthly or Quarterly								
Stockroom, packing & despatch	20,U,							
Forwarding	21,U,							
Quarterly only								
Marketing and admin.	30,U,							
Regional sales – N	31,U,							
Regional sales – S	32,U,							
Export sales	33,U,							
Export commissions	34,U,							
Commercial exps.	36,U,							
Publicity	38,U,							
Gen. selling pensions	39,U,							
Development	46,U,							
Interest	54,U,							
Monthly								
Non-trading items, divisional	55,U,							
Extraordinary items	56,U,							

END

(c) Form for non-manufacturing expenses

Exhibit 9.3 Specimen output reports

TAC CONSTRUCTION MATERIALS LIMITED

GFTA - HOME TRADE

	JAN	FEB	MAR	APRIL	MAY
MILLBOARD - MB600					
TONNES (H)	96	83	83	96	75
NEW PRICE(H)	373.75	373.75	373.75	373.75	373.75
NEW TURN (H)	35829	31156	31156	35329	28040
NEW GM (H)	3547	3084	3084	3547	2776
NEW GM% (H)	10	10	10	10	10
MILLBOARD - MB626					
TONNES (H)	3	2	2	3	2
NEW PRICE(H)	1158.05	1158.05	1158.05	1158.05	1158.05
NEW TURN (H)	3196	2779	2779	3196	2501
NEW GM (H)	761	661	661	761	595
NEW GM% (H)	24	24	24	24	24
MILLBOARD - MB121					
TONNES (H)	8	7	7	8	6
NEW PRICE(H)	571.55	571.55	571.55	571.55	571.55
NEW TURN (H)	4732	4115	4115	4732	3704
NEW GM (H)	1387	1206	1206	1387	1085
NEW GM% (H)	29	29	29	29	29
MILLBOARD - MB800					
TONNES (H)	49	42	42	49	38
NEW PRICE(H)	736.00	736.00	736.00	736.00	736.00
NEW TURN (H)	35752	31089	31089	35752	27980
NEW GM (H)	13407	11658	11658	13407	10492
NEW GM% (H)	37	37	37	37	37
MILLBOARD - BF89					
TONNES (H)	19	16	16	19	15
NEW PRICE(H)	1343.98	1343.98	134[illegible].98	1343.98	1343.98
NEW TURN (H)	25224	21934	2[illegible]34	25224	19740
NEW GM (H)	3531	3071	[illegible]071	3531	2764
NEW GM% (H)	14	14	14	14	14
MILLBOARD - OTHER					
TONNES (H)	-	-	-	-	-
NEW PRICE(H)	-	-	-	-	-
NEW TURN (H)	-	-	-	-	-
NEW GM (H)	-	-	-	-	-
NEW GM% (H)	-	-	-	-	-
FELTS PFR					
TONNES (H)	413	251	247	391	305
NEW PRICE(H)	425.88	425.88	425.88	447.17	447.17
NEW TURN (H)	176092	107030	105087	174694	136553
NEW GM (H)	28351	17232	16919	35105	27441
NEW GM% (H)	16	16	16	20	20
MILLBOARD & FELTS					
TONNES (H)	588	403	398	565	442
NEW PRICE(H)	-	-	-	-	-
NEW TURN (H)	280825	198103	196160	279428	218519
NEW GM (H)	50983	36912	36600	57738	45153
NEW GM% (H)	18	19	19	21	21

(a) Gross family trading account (Report 2)

							17123

JUN	JULY	AUG	SEPT	OCT	NOV	DEC	TOTAL
83	104	79	83	104	83	71	1042
373.75	373.75	373.75	373.75	373.75	373.75	373.75	373.75
31156	38945	29598	31156	38945	31156	26482	389447
3084	3856	2930	3084	3856	3084	2622	38555
	10	10	10	10	10	10	10
2	3	2	2	3	2	2	30
1158.05	1158.05	1158.05	1158.05	1158.05	1158.05	1158.05	1158.05
2779	3474	2640	2779	3474	2779	2362	34741
661	827	628	661	827	661	562	8268
24	24	24	24	24	24	24	24
7	9	7	7	9	7	6	90
571.55	571.55	571.55	571.55	571.55	571.55	571.55	571.55
4115	5144	3909	4115	5144	4115	3498	51439
1206	1507	1145	1206	1507	1206	1025	15072
29	29	29	29	29	29	29	29
42	53	40	42	53	42	36	528
736.00	736.00	736.00	736.00	736.00	736.00	736.00	736.00
31089	38861	29534	31089	38861	31089	26425	388608
11658	14573	11075	11658	14573	11658	9909	145728
37	37	37	37	37	37	37	37
16	20	16	16	20	16	14	204
1343.98	1343.98	1343.98	1343.98	1343.98	1343.98	1343.98	1343.98
21934	27417	20837	21934	27417	21934	18644	274171
3071	3838	2917	3071	3838	3071	2610	38384
14	14	14	14	14	14	14	14
-	-	-	-	-	-	-	-
-	-	-	-	-	-	-	-
-	-	-	-	-	-	-	-
-	-	-	-	-	-	-	-
-	-	-	-	-	-	-	-
300	367	225	235	299	324	152	3510
447.17	447.17	447.17	447.17	447.17	447.17	447.17	425.88
134356	164178	100767	105005	133571	144715	68120	1550166
26999	32992	20249	21101	26841	29081	13689	295997
20	20	20	20	20	20	20	19
-------	-------	-------	-------	-------	-------	-------	-------
452	557	369	386	488	475	281	5404
-	-	-	-	-	-	-	-
225428	278019	187286	196077	247412	235788	145531	2688571
46680	57593	38946	40781	51442	48761	30417	542006
21	21	21	21	21	21	21	20

TAC CONSTRUCTION MATERIALS LIMITED

GROSS FAMILY TRADING ACCOUNT (HOME)

	FIRST QUARTER			SECOND QUARTER		
	TURN	GROSS	PROF	TURN	GROSS	PROF
	£	£	%	£	£	%
MILLBOARD - MB600	98141	9716	9.9	95025	9407	9.9
MILLBOARD - MB626	8755	2084	23.8	8477	2018	23.8
MILLBOARD - MB121	12963	3798	29.3	12551	3678	29.3
MILLBOARD - MB800	97929	36723	37.5	94820	35558	37.5
MILLBOARD - BFB9	69091	9673	14.0	66898	9366	14.0
MILLBOARD - OTHER						
FELTS PFR	388209	62502	16.1	445603	89545	20.1
GROSS MARGIN	675088	124496	18.4	723375	149570	20.7
CAP VAR H						
PRI VAR H		14000	2.1		4000	.6
MAN VAR H		-12654	-1.9		-12252	-1.7
STK REV H		16000	2.4		14000	1.9
MILLBOARD & FELTS	675088	141842	21.0	72337	155318	21.5

(b) Gross family trading account (Report 1)

17:20:1

THIRD QUARTER TURN £	GROSS PROF £	%	FOURTH QUARTER TURN £	GROSS PROF £	%	ANNUAL TOTAL TURN £	GROSS PROF £	%
99698	9870	9.9	96583	9562	9.9	389447	38555	9.9
8894	2117	23.8	8616	2051	23.8	34741	8268	23.8
13169	3858	29.3	12757	3738	29.3	51439	15072	29.3
99484	37306	37.5	96375	36141	37.5	388608	145728	37.5
70188	9826	14.0	67995	9519	14.0	274171	38384	14.0
369949	74342	20.1	346406	69611	20.1	1550166	295997	19.1
661382	137320	20.8	628731	130621	20.8	2688571	542006	20.2
							18000	.7
	-9641	-1.5		-12453	-2.0		-47000	-1.7
	15000	2.3					45000	1.7
661382	142679	21.6	628731	118168	18.8	2688571	558006	20.8

TAC CONSTRUCTION MATERIALS LIMITED

SUMMARY TRADTNG ACCOUNT

QUARTERLY SUMMARY

	FIRST QUARTER	SECOND QUARTER
TURNOVER H	995743	1323187
TURNOVER EXP	-	-
TURNOVER TOTAL	995743	1323187
GROSS MARGIN H	271565	438449
GROSS MARGIN EXP	-	-
GROSS MARGIN TOTA	271565	438449
CAP VAR TOTAL	-	-
PRI VAR TOTAL	3000	6000
OTH VAR TOTAL	-53000	-17700
STOCK REV TOTAL	35200	35200
GPAV T	256765	461949
CARRIAGE	-166465	-214291
DISTRIBN	-27319	-26489
SELLING	-46388	-39359
SELLING - COMM/GE	-41684	-52030
SELLING - PUBLICI	-11000	-11000
DIV SERV - DEV	-5825	-5825
DIV SERV - TECH	-	-
ADMIN CENTRAL	-65745	-65093
PENSION FUNDING	-14566	-14566
TOTAL NON-MANUF O	-378992	-428653
NET MARGIN	-122227	33296
PROFIT/LOSS ITEMS	-12136	-4282
INTEREST CHARGES	-19000	-19000
NET PROFIT/LOSS	-153362	10014
EXTRAORDINARY ITE	-	-
NET PROFIT BEFORE	-153362	10014

(c) Divisional trading account (Report 5)

23:15:

THIRD QUARTER	FOURTH QUARTER	ANNUAL TOTAL
1825493	1719876	5864294
-	-	-
-	-	-
1825493	1719876	5864295
677755	710664	2098431
-	-	-
-	-	-
677755	710664	2098432
-	-	-
2000	-2000	9000
-11200	-13100	-95000
35600	-	106000
------	-	------
704155	695564	2118431
-316878	-283830	-981464
-27741	-26905	-108455
-39361	-39358	-164466
-64587	-61947	-220247
-11000	-11000	-44000
-5825	-5825	-23300
-	-	-
-65585	-65223	-261646
-14566	-14566	-58265
------	------	------
-545543	-508654	-1861840
-------	-------	--------
158612	186910	256591
-11217	-11177	-38812
-21000	-27000	-86000
------	------	------
126394	148733	131779
-	-	-
126394	148733	131779
------	------	------

TAC CONSTRUCTION MATERIALS LIMITED

SUMMARY TRADING ACCOUNT

	FIRST QUARTER	SECOND QUARTER
SELLING EXPENSES		
B&I DIVISION		
MARKETING	40640	40640
HOME SALES	171577	170238
EXPORT SALES	18540	18540
CONTRACTS & MATLS	41851	41849
SALES SERVICES	98116	98115
COMMERCIAL EXP	105000	105000
B & I DIVN	475724	474382
PIPES DIVISION		
MARKET/ADMIN	37132	35682
REG SALES - N	25001	25001
REG SALES - S	21291	21291
EXPORT SALES	10563	10613
EXPORT COMMISS	14063	14063
COMMERCIAL EXP	16113	16113
PIPES DIVN	124163	122763
EM DIVISION		
MARKETING	0	0
ENG MATLS - HOME	22787	22788
ENG MATLS - EXPOR	15885	16160
MILL, FELT & PAPE	4725	4725
MARINE PRODS	0	0
SALES SERVICE	16145	16145
COMMERCIAL EXP	26723	28223
EM DIVN	86265	88041
BLOCKS DIVISION		
ALFRETON SALES	25388	25388
HALTON SALES	21000	13971
COMMERCIAL EXP	15950	15950
BLOCKS DIVN	62338	55309
PUBLICITY	103000	103000
GENERAL SELLING E	302432	317488
TOTAL SELLING EXP	1153922	1160983
SERVICE AND ADMINISTRATION EXPENSES		
FINANCE/ADMIN		
BUYING	17190	17190
FIN ACCS	94492	91043
MAN ACCS	17477	17475
MAN SERV	38523	36523
COMPUTER OPERATIO	87133	87085
H.O. SERVICES	202055	201621
GENERAL SERVICES	154960	154960
PENSION FUNDING	153500	153500
SERV & ADMIN SUB-	765330	759397

(d) Part of summary trading account (Report 8). *Note:* This report was generated prior to a change in divisional structure and so does not correspond with the company hierarchy presented elsewhere

12/11/79 23:20:

THIRD QUARTER	FOURTH QUARTER	ANNUAL TOTAL	% TURNOVER
40640	40640	162560	.3
171265	172600	685680	1.3
17140	17140	71360	.1
41851	41849	167400	.3
98116	98103	392450	.7
105000	105000	420000	.8
474012	475332	1899450	3.5
32728	32868	138410	.3
24999	26299	101300	.2
21287	22287	86156	.2
10562	10702	42440	.1
14062	14062	56250	.1
16112	16112	64450	.1
119750	122330	489006	.9
0	0	0	.0
22787	22788	91150	.2
16160	16160	64365	.1
4725	4725	18900	.0
0	0	0	.0
16145	16145	64580	.1
26722	28222	109890	.2
86539	88040	348885	.6
25388	25388	101552	.2
13973	13970	62914	.1
15950	15950	63800	.1
55311	55308	228266	.4
103000	103000	412000	.8
357024	337179	1314124	2.4
1195636	1181189	4691731	8.6
17190	17190	68760	.1
91442	90443	367420	.7
17627	17965	70544	.1
39023	39023	153092	.3
85459	85460	345137	.6
196104	201990	801770	1.5
163480	154960	628360	1.2
153500	153500	614000	1.1
763825	760531	3049083	5.6

Financial Modelling in Corporate Management, 2nd Edition
Edited by J. W. Bryant

10

The Imperial Group Five-year Planning Model

STEPHEN LYUS

10.1 Introduction

Over the period 1970–81 the Operational Research Section of the Imperial Group had been very actively promoting the use of computers for financial modelling within the company. This activity centred around the use of ICL's modelling language, Prosper, on ICL mainframes within the Group. In-house training courses were run by the Section for a wide variety of different audiences, from computer appreciation for senior management to advanced techniques for afficionados. The Section was often used as the technical 'Help-desk' by users once they started writing their own models. A number of models were also commissioned from the Section by companies who either felt they did not want to be involved in the writing (and subsequent maintenance) of models, or who did not feel they would have the time to carry out the work. Over this period a number of versions of Prosper were evaluated and subsequently implemented if they were thought to provide worthwhile enhancements. At the end of this period the version being used was VDU Prosper +. This was an extremely sophisticated, albeit often complicated, financial modelling language with full-screen data entry facilities running on the mainframe computer.

Looking back over this period, the promotion of financial modelling had produced mixed results. The target audience was, almost without exception, the accountants within the subsidiary companies. Some of them went overboard in their commitment to financial modelling and in a short period of time could not work without writing and using models, others showed no interest at all, but the vast majority fell in between these extremes. Once this majority returned to their desks and their normal workload, a lot of the initial enthusiasm died away, and they said that they did not have time to develop the programs, that would, if they existed, reduce this workload. Or, if they did eventually make time available, found that they had by that time forgotten most of the commands, and were continually having to refer to the manual. Some groups recognized these problems, and created a small project team who locked themselves away until they had produced the system that was required. However, it is interesting to note that most of the 'successful' models were developed by lone enthusiasts in their own time. A number of them saw that gaining experience with computers was becoming important in their profession. Unfortunately, the 'success' of a number of these models did not survive their originators' departure. The three pricing models described in the previous edition of this book, and presented in summary form in the Appendix to this chapter are good illustrations of the variety of uses to which financial modelling had been put within Imperial at that time.

The advent of VDU Prosper, with input screens and control menus, was a big breakthrough for the OR Section as it meant that it became possible to transfer the responsibility for keying in the data and running the models to the end-user. These users did not need to know anything about Prosper, but only about the particular application. As they were usually the staff who were responsible for the manual method that had been computerized, this did not involve much training.

Late in 1981, with the advent of a new chairman, the section was asked to demonstrate the use of financial modelling at the Group level. As the London end of Group head office had no computing facilities, it was decided that a small 8-bit micro (a Superbrain) would be used, with APL as the modelling language (APL had begun to replace Fortran in the OR Section as the preferred language for OR-type modelling). The demonstration went well and the section was commissioned to work with the chief accountant's department to produce a one-year (Budget) model of the Group consolidated accounts. This was initially squeezed onto the Superbrain and was very well received. The ability to do more than the one or two 'What-Ifs' that the manual calculations allowed, opened up a whole new world of possibilities. It also complemented the 'Management by strategy' approach that was being implemented by the new chairman.

The purchase of two multi-user MicroAPL Spectrums (a specialist APL machine using the new 16-bit processor chip) for head office in July 1982, one for the Chief Executive's Information System (this is an internal information system designed for the directors and senior managers that is very easy to use, based on colour graphic terminals in their offices as well as on a large screen projection system in the boardroom. Some 2000 graphs and tables are instantly available at the push of a button, e.g. the latest monthly accounts) and the other for the chief accountant's department to do the routine consolidation of the monthly accounts, meant that a very powerful and sophisticated version of APL became available. The Budget model was very easily transported over to the new computer and work began almost immediately on a model with a three-year time horizon.

This meant an order of magnitude change in the complexity, mainly connected with time lags inherent in the calculation and payment of corporation tax. In January 1983, the model was expanded, again, to a five-year horizon, a much less traumatic change. The complexity was increased however, in April 1983, by the desire to input US data in dollars and have the model deal with the US tax regime, borrowing in the US, and exchange-rate conversion.

The model had become by then an integral part of the strategic planning process, and was at times in use twelve hours a day, and at weekends. The ability to investigate the numerous strategic options being considered, without being constrained by the time it takes to 'turn the handle' was exploited to the full.

Since mid-1983 the pace of development has slowed considerably, though not the usage. Further enhancements included the ability to acquire and/or dispose of companies. It was extensively used to explore the possibilities available before deciding to dispose of most of the Howard Johnson company in 1984, and before deciding to approach United Biscuits with a view to a merger late in 1985. The latest change to the model structure has effectively removed the limit on the number of years in the planning horizon.

Current Statistics

(1) There are currently available some 200 different scenarios which can be run again or used as the springboard for further analyses. Also, some 300 scenarios are available from previous, less refined, versions of the model logic. These are retained in case someone wants to re-examine old assumptions.
(2) Each run of the model requires about 35k of storage.
(3) 118 input variables are used, ranging from scalars to three -dimensional arrays.
(4) The data is entered via 49 different input screens.
(5) The model takes about one minute to calculate the five years of a plan, in an empty machine. It is a multi-user system, so it often takes longer than this. It will run in a 500k work-space.
(6) There are 25 different result tables available. A print of the whole set runs to 36 pages, though this is rarely selected.

10.2 Model Structure

The basic structure of the model can be conveniently split into two parts; the input, calculating procedures and reporting sections; and the background file administration modules. These are shown diagrammatically in Figures 10.1 and 10.2.

The Main Options

Input

All data is entered via uniquely defined data input screens, usually in the form of items (rows) by time (columns). One of the features in the software is the ability to execute a special procedure, uniquely defined for that input screen, by a single key depression. This is mainly used for recalculation of subtotals, but could be used for data validation. The user has the option to initiate a print of all the input screens (with non-zero data) or only a few specified ones. An example of one of these input screens is given in Figure 10.3.

There has always been a large number of input variables (118 at present). It became apparent, even in the early days of the model, that a facility to print-off a report of the differences between two input files would be exceedingly useful. It started life as a 'special', but is now one of the options on the main menu. The result is an exception report (i.e. only those tables where there is a difference), using the same format as that used to input the data on the screen.

Calculations

A large number of relatively small modules are used during the calculations, each of which takes care of a particular aspect of the accounts. The following list gives an idea of the range:

Depreciation
Lease rentals—capital and interest payments
Capital allowances—UK and US
Conversion of $ Balance Sheet
Interest charges—UK and US
UK tax—corporate, future and deferred
US tax—state and federal

Modularity is very important in this kind of work, as the rules for a particular aspect can change very quickly (e.g. overnight, as a result of the UK Budget statement). When the 'rules' are rewritten, it is usually a question of examining one easily identified module and changing it appropriately. At the worst, it can be simply thrown away, and a new module put in its place. APL is an ideal language for this type of structure.

The interest charges are calculated using coding that incorporates the solution of the usual set of simultaneous equations met in this sort of work. This

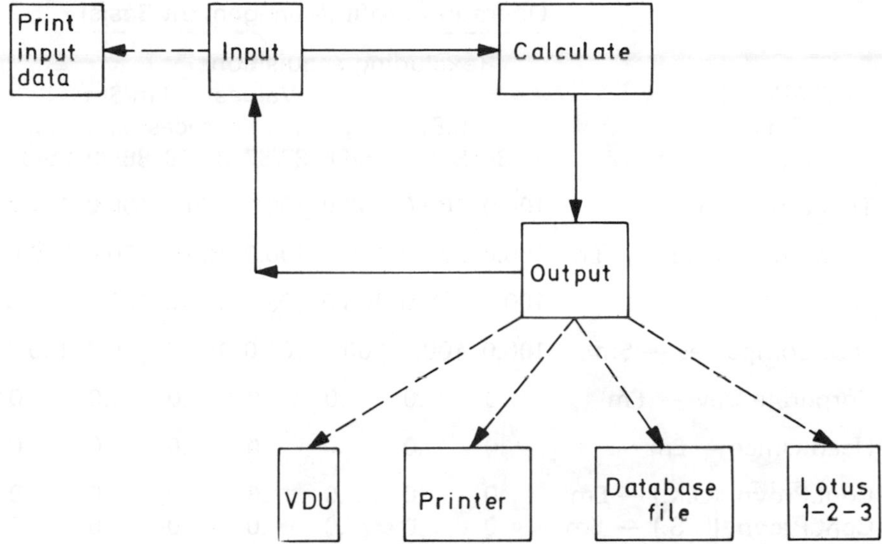

Figure 10.1 Model structure: main options

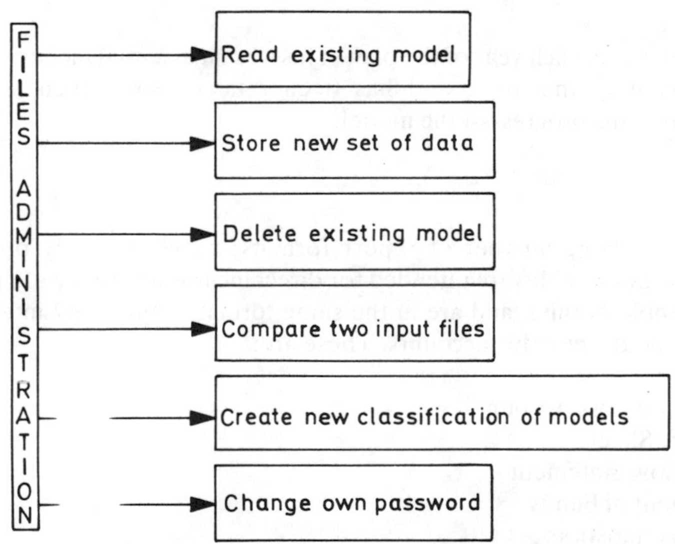

Figure 10.2 Model structure: file administration options

seemed preferable to forcing the computer to solve what is the same equation for each year of each model run. While a run is in progress it provides a running commentary of the particular tax cases (e.g. whether Imperial was paying mainstream corporation tax, or whether there was surplus ACT available) that

credit/(debit) (£m.)	Operating Profit (Management Basis) (excluding acquisitions)				Values — £m/$m		
		L.E.	..............Forecast..............				
	83/84	84/85	85/86	87/87	87/88	88/89	89/90
Tobacco — £m	100.0	100.0	100.0	100.0	100.0	100.0	100.0
Brewing & Leisure — £m	100.0	100.0	100.0	100.0	100.0	100.0	100.0
Food — £m	100.0	100.0	100.0	100.0	100.0	100.0	100.0
U.S. Companies — $m	100.0	100.0	100.0	100.0	100.0	100.0	100.0
Corporate Dev. — £m	.0	.0	.0	.0	.0	.0	.0
Head Office — £m	.0	.0	.0	.0	.0	.0	.0
Cont.Provn. (U.K.) — £m	.0	.0	.0	.0	.0	.0	.0
Cont.Provn. (U.S.) — $m	.0	.0	.0	.0	.0	.0	.0
Total — £m	400.0	400.0	400.0	400.0	400.0	400.0	400.0

Figure 10.3 A specimen input screen

have been met in each year of the plan. This was an essential facility during the development of the logic, and has been retained since then as a visual indication of the progress of the model.

Output

There are a large number of report formats, which are only produced if requested. Some tables are intended for direct inclusion in reports (Figure 10.4 is an example of this), and are in the same format as that used internally for reporting on the monthly accounts. These are:

Profit and Loss Account
Balance Sheet
Cash Flow Statement
Statement of Funds
Various statistics

while others are much more detailed 'working papers' that allow the accountants to reconcile the results of several runs:

Divisional Operating Profit Analysis
Divisional Cash Flow

Extraordinary Items
Interest Charges Analysis
Analysis of Capital Employed
Capital Expenditure Analysis
UK Tax Computation
Tax Paid Analysis
US Profit and Loss Account
US Balance Sheet
US Cash Flow
US Tax Computation
Balance Sheet Exchange Rate Movements

The following options are available at the output stage (Figure 10.5 is a copy of the main menu presented at this stage):

View any table on the VDU screen.
Send any table to the printer (high-speed matrix or quality daisy-wheel).
Send a subset of the results into a special database file (see Section 10.4 below).
Send most tables to an IBM PC (for 'importing' into Lotus 1-2-3 for further analysis (see Section 10.4 below).

File Administration Options

The file handling and general housekeeping routines are an important and often overlooked part of any system. It is important to make them as unobtrusive as possible in order to encourage the use of any computer system. Even these routines need to evolve over time according to the use being made of the system.

File handling

Only input data is routinely stored, with one component of the file for each different scenario. There is also an administrative component, holding the text used to describe each run, the date and time of creation, as well as the name of the creator.

In the early days, frequent major changes to the structure meant that no file became too large (100 runs was typical). However, recently this has become a problem, both in terms of an enormous list of model names being presented whenever the 'read-file' option was chosen, and, more seriously, the limit on physical storage on the hard disk was reached (6.5 megabytes for a logical disk surface).

The latest change has been to create a meta-file structure (i.e. a file of files).

Produced on: 3/APR/1986 14:24 1985 Strategic Plan

Group Consolidated Profits

£m.

		Actual	Latest Estimate	Plan				
		1984	1985	1986	1987	1988	1989	1990
[1]	Imperial Tobacco Ltd	100.0	100.0	100.0	100.0	100.0	100.0	100.0
[2]	Imperial Brewing & Leisure Ltd	100.0	100.0	100.0	100.0	100.0	100.0	100.0
[3]	Imperial Foods Ltd	100.0	100.0	100.0	100.0	100.0	100.0	100.0
[4]	Ground Round/Orangeroof of Canada	100.0	100.0	100.0	100.0	100.0	100.0	100.0
[5]	Corporate Development	0.0	0.0	0.0	0.0	0.0	0.0	0.0
[6]	Acquisitions	0.0	0.0	0.0	0.0	0.0	0.0	0.0
[7]		400.0	400.0	400.0	400.0	400.0	400.0	400.0
[8]	Group Central Charges & consolidation adjust.	0.0	0.0	0.0	0.0	0.0	0.0	0.0
[9]		400.0	400.0	400.0	400.0	400.0	400.0	400.0
[10]	Contingency adjustment	0.0	0.0	0.0	0.0	0.0	0.0	0.0
[11]	GROUP OPERATING PROFIT — (Management)	400.0	400.0	400.0	400.0	400.0	400.0	400.0
[12]	Less: trade loan income	0.0	0.0	0.0	0.0	0.0	0.0	0.0
[13]	GROUP OPERATING PROFIT — (Statutory)	400.0	400.0	400.0	400.0	400.0	400.0	400.0
[14]	Investment Income	0.0	0.0	0.0	0.0	0.0	0.0	0.0
[15]	Share of Profits of Associates	0.0	0.0	0.0	0.0	0.0	0.0	0.0
[16]	Interest payable (incl. finance leases)	0.0	0.0	0.0	0.0	0.0	0.0	0.0

[17] GROUP PROFIT BEFORE TAXATION	400.0	400.0	400.0	400.0	400.0	400.0	400.0
[18] Taxation	0.0	0.0	0.0	0.0	0.0	0.0	0.0
	----	----	----	----	----	----	----
[19] GROUP PROFIT AFTER TAXATION	400.0	400.0	400.0	400.0	400.0	400.0	400.0
[20] Minority interests	0.0	0.0	0.0	0.0	0.0	0.0	0.0
	----	----	----	----	----	----	----
[21]	400.0	400.0	400.0	400.0	400.0	400.0	400.0
[22] Extraordinary items	0.0	0.0	0.0	0.0	0.0	0.0	0.0
	----	----	----	----	----	----	----
[23] GROUP PROFIT ATTRIBUTABLE TO PARENT COMPANY	400.0	400.0	400.0	400.0	400.0	400.0	400.0
[24] Ordinary dividends	0.0	0.0	0.0	0.0	0.0	0.0	0.0
	----	----	----	----	----	----	----
[25] Profit retained	400.0	400.0	400.0	400.0	400.0	400.0	400.0
	====	====	====	====	====	====	====
Ratios:							
[26] Interest cover — times	0.0	0.0	0.0	0.0	0.0	0.0	0.0
[27] Dividend cover — times	0.0	0.0	0.0	0.0	0.0	0.0	0.0
[28] Earnings per share — pre-tax (pence)	0.0	0.0	0.0	0.0	0.0	0.0	0.0
[29] — post-tax (pence)	0.0	0.0	0.0	0.0	0.0	0.0	0.0
[30] Overall effective tax rate	0.0	0.0	0.0	0.0	0.0	0.0	0.0

– 3 –

Figure 10.4 A specimen report format

Main Output Options

1. Divisional Operating Profit
2. Group Profit before Tax
3. Group Consolidated Profits
4. Group Balance Sheets (Assets)
5. Group Balance Sheets (Financed by)
6. Group Cash Flow
7. Extraordinary Items
8. Group Funds Statement
9. Interest Charges Analysis

Print : 10. Hard Copy of the Main Results

Menu : 11. Output (Detailed) Options

Database : 12. Set up a File

IBM PC : 13. Transfer Output to an IBM PC

Return : 14. Main Option Menu

Figure 10.5 Output options menu

This allows much more flexibility, both in terms of the physical location of the files, and also in terms of the actual usage of the model (e.g. one file would be for all the runs connected with the United Biscuits merger, another with the 1985/1986 Budget).

Security

The figures used in the various runs (even the titles!) are obviously very sensitive. There is the usual multi-level passworded access to the model. However, an additional level is imposed, whereby the creator of an input file has to specify who can access (read only, or read/overwrite, or not at all) that file. Thus the user, when choosing his input file, only has available those files he is allowed to know about.

10.3 Important Model Characteristics

Evolutionary Development

The development was always undertaken in close contact with the accountants; in fact, most of the important code was written while actually sitting at the terminal with the accountant responsible for the model. In this way the modularity available to a writer in APL was used to the full. Functions were often tested in isolation with all possible (and impossible?) combinations of input. This was especially important when trying to model the UK tax structure. The ability, in APL, to stop the function wherever necessary, investigate variables, and then restart was also well used. This was most fruitful in areas where misunderstandings arose over the interpretation of the words used to specify a section of logic.

User Driven

The method used to develop the model led naturally to the accountant involved taking over the running of system. He was totally familiar with what was going on, and indeed the words used in the menu-driven dialogue are mainly his. Once it was accepted as working, three other accountants (including the Chief Accountant and his deputy) started to use it with no obvious difficulty. One of the reasons for the success of the model is that it is now 'owned' by that department.

Top-level Model

As mentioned above, the aim of the program is to model the Group consolidation process. It works in a 'middle-up' fashion, data being input at the Divisional level. This data arrives from the Divisions and has been produced by them from a consolidation of the Strategic Business Units (SBUs) that make up their Division. These figures are used as the base point, or submitted plan. Depending on how the consolidated results fit with the Board's aim for the future (e.g. earnings per share growth), modifications are made to a number of items, including profit and project expenditure projections. Commitment to the revised plan is then sought from the Divisions.

In terms of the complexity of the calculations, it is very definitely at the detailed, as opposed to the 'broad-brush', end of the spectrum. Some parts of the model allow for two modes of input (e.g. depreciation) so either 'accurate' calculations are carried out off-line and the results fed in, or additional data is provided to enable a special module to produce a good approximation. The trade-off between the volume of input data required to achieve an end result and the ease with which it can be derived from other sources is an important consideration.

10.4 Unique Features of the Model

There are a couple of facilities available to the user of this model that are likely to be unique to this kind of modelling. These are described below:

Database Link

Considerable use is made of the in-house relational database language in the work connected with Chief Executive's Information System. The idea of using the many facilities available for re-formatting results, producing graphs, and displaying comparisons between the results of different runs of the model seemed very attractive. The output format is by its nature less easy to specify as a fixed format that will cope with all the many reasons for a particular run of the model. A facility to store away a subset of the results of a run in a separate file, that could then be accessed as a database of different results, was made available as an experiment.

In practice, re-formatting, when required, has been undertaken using a word processor (at the moment it all has to be retyped, an electronic link has been tested but has not been considered worth the effort required to make it usable by non-technicians). The database was used in the early days for producing the graphs, but this is no longer the case for two main reasons. First, the volume of data necessary to draw a graph is usually very small. The time taken to exit from the five-year planning model, load the database and specify the graph format was too long when compared with typing in a few numbers into the general graph-drawing package that is available on the Spectrum. Secondly, the required layouts of the graphs were always unique, and usually differed in important ways from the settings easily available in the graphics part of the database. However, the exercise has not been a complete failure. Considerable use has been made of the facilities for certain special exercises. For example, in order to understand the implied synergy in an acquisition, runs can be made of Imperial on its own, Company 'X' on its own, and then Imperial plus Company 'X'. The database then easily allows the user to table the 'synergy' in the Balance Sheet, Profit and Loss or even the tax payments. Manually this would not only be very time consuming, but also error prone. This procedure has also been used to provide an estimate of each SBU's contribution to the Group profit before tax, the database being used to check that the sum of the results from the constituent parts of a Division is the same as that found using the original Divisional-level figures.

PC Link

All of the main reports can be sent to a PC. The PC is connected to the Spectrum as another peripheral (a printer!) and the Spectrum completely controls the transactions via one of the specialist communications packages available for the PC. On defining which tables are to be sent, the Spectrum mimics the typing of PC-DOS commands at the keyboard, and a file is created on the PC for each output table requested. The format of the file is such that it can be 'imported' into Lotus 1-2-3 (i.e. a PRN file). The complete table, including page and column headings as well as row titles is reproduced. This facility has not been heavily used as yet. Several alternatives are at present under review to make the process simpler and quicker, including having the PC as the Spectrum terminal with the communications package (it is also a terminal emulator) running concurrently with 1-2-3.

10.5 Conclusion

The model that has been described became an essential part of Imperial's strategic planning process. There are four main reasons for its widespread use:

(1) Right from the start, it received considerable backing at the highest level in the organization.
(2) An evolutionary approach was used in order to produce usable results very quickly. Having results appear so soon after starting meant that the initial momentum was not lost. There was no attempt to produce a complete system specification which would then be used to deliver a system many months afterwards.
(3) It quickly became integrated with the new strategic planning process and was flexible enough to change in response to new demands being placed upon it.
(4) Senior management very quickly came to trust the results produced by the model (with the obvious caveat that it was only an approximation of reality).

The power available from a computerized financial model cannot be oversold. As to the decision to write the model in APL as opposed to one of the specialist financial planning languages, there are no regrets at all. Neither the computer nor the language have constrained the many user requests for enhancements. If the decision were to be made today, the competition is undoubtedly a lot closer, but it would be a surprise if any can provide exactly what our users have available today.

Although only passing reference has been made to the use of graphs in this chapter, it is worth pointing out that the results of the model runs are often given to senior management and the Board using graphics rather than the more usual tables. It is often far easier to portray difficult messages using pictures rather than figures. A display of the 'strategic gap' between submitted plans and the desired outcome is one example of such a message (see Figure 10.6). Another is where a comparison is to be made between the last plan and the current one, where the in-built assumptions of the Retail Price Index are important. Here, a chart using bars for the forecast money values with an overlay of a line plot of the values at constant prices has been particularly useful. The future for financial modelling will see this graphics side exploited even more.

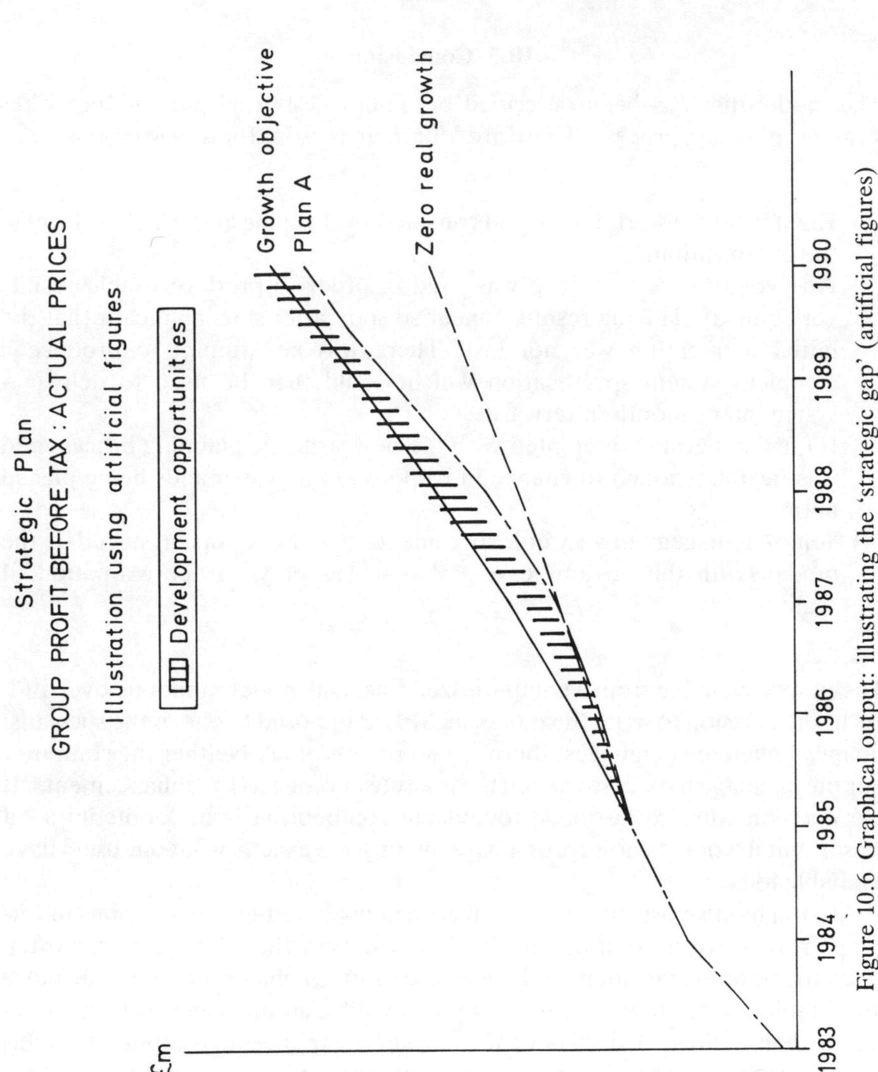

Figure 10.6 Graphical output: illustrating the 'strategic gap' (artificial figures)

Acknowledgements

The author wishes to thank Ian Henson and Peter Carrington for providing the substance, around which the model has been built. The views expressed in this account are those of the author and are not necessarily shared by Imperial Group.

Appendix to Chapter 10

This appendix briefly outlines three models developed by the Imperial Group to investigate pricing policy from an accounting viewpoint. These models, which typify the earlier phases of financial modelling work within the Group, fall into three distinct areas. First, models to investigate exchange rate fluctuations are described. Next, a model which was used to carry out extensive calculations in response to changes in excise duty is presented. Finally, a costing model which illustrates the importance of being able to react to commodity price changes is discussed. All three applications therefore are of models which allow management to deal more effectively and creatively when faced with changes in environmental variables.

Example 1: Imports Models

The performance of sterling in the international money markets is an important factor in determining the prices charged by UK companies. This section describes two examples from within the Imperial Group where the exchange rates of sterling are major determinants of a product's profitability.

Imperial Tobacco (Imports) Ltd, imports foreign cigars and cigarettes and operates a sales force to market them throughout the UK. This involves three currencies; the Dutch guilder, the Swiss franc and the Danish kroner. Apart from duty, the most important cost factor is the purchase price in the foreign currency, and a model has been developed to carry out the costing calculations.

Ashton Containers Ltd (the Imperial Group has since disposed of its interest in this company) manufacture corrugated packing cases. The materials used in the process come from various countries including USA, Norway, Sweden, Finland, Portugal and the UK. There are many combinations of component materials giving a very large number of final board grades, the costs of which are dependent on a few exchange rates.

The Imperial Tobacco model performs the detailed costs and gross profit calculations, by month, for each of the 26 major brands of cigar. The company total gross profit and turnover is also produced, as well as subtotals by cigar manufacturer. The whole process is covered in the model from, say, a change in the Dutch guilder rate to a change in the retail price at a UK outlet. The Imperial Imports model was originally designed for helping in the preparation of the annual budgets, and has been in use since 1974. However, it has also been extensively used within the year whenever changes in the UK selling price are being considered. There has, of course, to be more stability in the UK sterling price charged to the public than that reflected by the exchange rates which vary on a daily basis. It is usual to produce several sets of output based on different assumptions about future exchange rates.

In the Ashton Containers application there are two models. The first calculates the supplier price in sterling per hundred square metres of board, given carriage and other costs. The next model takes as input these supplier prices and calculates:

(1) The average price for a material, taking into account the various tonnages from different suppliers, and the corresponding exchange rates.
(2) A return on capital figure to be added to the material price.
(3) The cost of the component materials per hundred square metres.
(4) The final board grade cost, being the addition of the various elements required for that particular board.

The model was run on an *ad hoc* basis several times a year by the Accountants Department and was an important link in the costing process at Ashtons.

Example 2: Beer Costing Model

This application is concerned with producing the product standard costs by packaging type and size for all the different beer recipes brewed by Courage Ltd. The term 'product standard cost' means the material and duty cost of each beer in its final packaged form.

The cost of the beer must cover both the basic raw materials and also the various substances added. Since these additions are usually in liquid form, volume adjustments to the costs must be made. To this must then be added the cost of the various packaging materials. Losses arise (of a duty-paid product!) during the brewing process, mainly due to transfers between the various plants but also as a result of the processes themselves. Further losses occur at the packaging stage and again must be taken account of in costing.

The model was designed with four separate programs corresponding to the four regional operating companies, plus a consolidation program to provide a national picture.

Each operating company model has its own input of budgeted prices of raw materials and budgeted usage of those materials within defined brew sizes. The production departments provide the budgeted process losses, the types and sizes of packaging, and the gravities. The final important common input to all the models is the beer duty rate, provided by HM Customs and Excise. Each of the company programs then produces a detailed stage-by-stage report of the way that each standard cost is built-up. The standard costs are picked up by the consolidation program, and a summary is produced. However, the main rationale for this program is that some of the beers are produced at several locations to the same recipe, and so the national average cost of these over all locations weighted by budgeted throughput thereby can be found. The program provides these averages, as well as the consequent national averaging variances attributable to each operating company.

The model was produced to help in the production of the 1977/78 budget and has been used since then for this purpose. It has also been used for providing the costs which are used to value the finished goods and work-in-progress stocks at the financial year-end. Finally, it was occasionally used when major external suppliers significantly increased their prices.

Example 3: Foods Pricing Model

Smedley-HP Foods Ltd, produces a wide range of canned, bottled and frozen foods. Government price control legislation provided the impetus necessary to start using computer models to help decision-making. The problem posed was, given a total amount of price increases allowable under price-control legislation, how should this be allocated over products? This might not at first appear a very complicated process, but when trying to increase prices to the maximum amount allowed, while taking into account retailers' margins, competitors' prices and sales volumes, the number of combinations involved makes the process very laborious. Later the allocation of overhead costs to products and the basic raw material cost calculations were tackled.

The first, very simple, program took as input current and proposed future retail selling prices, and calculated the standard 1000-case rate based on a specified retailer's margin and the number of items in each case. The model calculated the amount of the increases based on the sales volumes for the following twelve months and also gave the gross profit percentages. In addition it produced four other tabulations showing the effect of variations in either direction in the future retail selling prices. Thus there were five print-outs for each group of products. If in the base case there had been an over-recovery, then the subsidiary print-outs were used to juggle the prices manually.

The overhead allocation program calculates overhead rates per case on a moving annual average basis. These rates are then increased to take into account recent price levels.

The construction of a raw material cost program was an ideal application for modelling as these costs were continually being recalculated, incorporating price, usage and recipe variations for latest estimate and standard costing. The program was built up in stages, according to the different product groups. It took, as input the ingredients, their costs and the raw material usages, and then calculated the raw material price costs.

Financial Modelling in Corporate Management, 2nd Edition
Edited by J. W. Bryant

11

Financial Planning Models for ICI

JOHN MACGREGOR AND PETER WHYTE

11.1 Introduction

Imperial Chemical Industries Limited (ICI) is one of the world's largest multinational chemical companies. Its turnover of £5368 million in 1979 included products as diverse as fertilizers and paints, plastics and explosives, dyestuffs and pharmaceuticals.

This case study concerns the Management Accounting Group of the Treasurer's Department situated at their head office in Millbank, London. The Management Accounting Group is mainly involved in collecting, consolidating and analysing financial and management information for presentation to the Main Board, relating to both achieved results, both monthly and quarterly, and forecasts, short and long term.

The collection of actual financial accounting data was already satisfied by a batch-orientated IBM system with some on-line capability. This received a large amount of telexed information from over 150 units world-wide each quarter, which was validated and consolidated to a Group total.

The management information required to aid analysis of these actual results and prepare forecasts was still being collected and processed by hand. It was to speed up the processing and allow more time for thinking that models were developed upon a computer bureau with the help of ICI's Central Management Services.

11.2 Early Applications using Bureau Services

The first application in 1977 was a straight 'number cruncher'. This was to speed up a comprehensive exchange effect calculation used to analyse the sales and profit variances shown by the £-sterling financial accounts into 'real' variances and those due to the conversion of results of overseas units at different exchange rates for each period under consideration. In order to achieve the result, data were required to be transferred from the in-house IBM collection system to the bureau via a terminal with floppy discs. This also served as a useful introduction to data management.

The next two applications were concerned with five-year cash forecasting. These were a unit's view—bottom up, and a central view—top down. The unit's view was essentially a collection of data from UK divisions and overseas units (about 70 in all) of their own cash forecasts which required to be converted into sterling and consolidated to territorial and group totals. This was assigned to a database-type language—COMPOSIT 77. The central view was a Group-level four-way split which was designed to allow a base case to be calculated and then changes applied to test sensitivities to various strategies. A 'report-writing' package was used for this—DATAFORM. These two systems were successful in achieving their own requirements but incompatible when it was decided that the computer should be able to take the difference between the two views and show the central adjustments required to amend the unit's view to the central view. A third package was employed to consolidate the unit's data to the same level as the central view—PLANMASTER. Finally, the loop was closed so that the central adjustments could be input into the unit's view making it equal to the central view in total but containing all the unit's details. The system therefore evolved over about 18 months (three planning cycles) as shown in Figure 11.1.

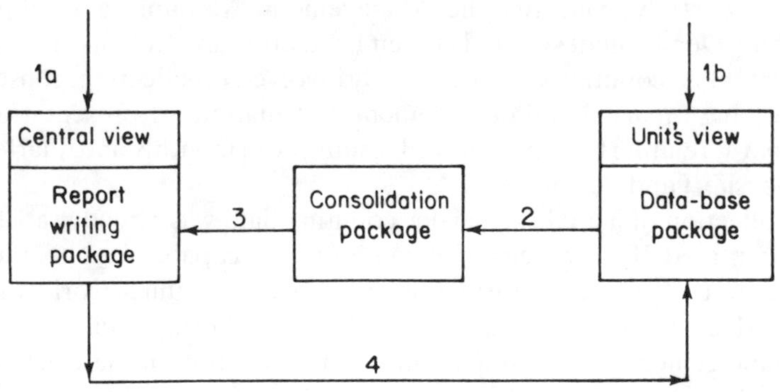

Figure 11.1 The five-year cash-forecasting system

Although operable, the above system had disadvantages:

(1) Three different packages had to be learned.
(2) Time was involved and expense incurred in transferring data between systems.
(3) Effort was needed to maintain the three systems separately but to remain compatible.

(4) The packages produced the numbers, but not in a form which could be directly incorporated in issued reports. Typing was therefore required for final results.

Rationalization was essential and the medium chosen, based on experience in one of the ICI divisions, was FCS–EPS (a brief description of the salient features of this widely-used system is provided in the Appendix to this chapter). Both systems were rewritten, the central and unit's views still as separate entities, but with the following features:

(1) Sections in the hierarchy of the unit's view were defined both for territorial output reports and to allow the comparison with the central-view analysis.
(2) Although not a true hierarchical model, the central-view data file was defined to compare directly, row for row, with the unit's view.
(3) Input of data into a matrix model allowed extensive on-line validation and correction by cross-checking and check totals rather than a separate batch program run as in a database system.
(4) Currency conversion, carrying forward of closing to opening balances and calculation of related exchange differences could be made automatic. (This feature saved much time in calculation and recalculation when data were updated.)
(5) Output reports were written in a form suitable for inclusion in published documents.

Development of the systems to this stage had considerable benefits to the department, but there were constraints. These were mainly related to costs. There is always the feeling of a continually ringing cash register at the other end when connected to a computer bureau, and a small data change in a large integrated system can necessitate a very expensive re-run. The question is also asked 'Is it worth running the system for this extra case? It may cost too much!' Similarly, with the above experience, a whole new vista of possible applications can be seen 'if only it didn't cost so much'.

On the purely logistical side, one or two terminals connected to a bureau via telephone are generally shared with other users and require checking availability, operating in that room with working papers and coping with bad lines/line noise (especially on final print-outs) when eventually running. It would be much more sensible to have a terminal on the desk which would allow immediate access without charging for every operation performed once the price for the facility had been paid.

11.3 In-house Model Development

From the previous bureau experience it had already been decided that FCS–EPS was the modelling system most suitable and when it became known that it was to be offered on a mini, enquiries were immediately commenced. These showed that to replace current bureau usage a configuration including three VDUs and utilizing the current teletype terminal for printing would be available at a price giving a payback period of two years. There was also at the time the possibility of using the software on an ICI Division machine which amounted to the same facilities as the bureau at half the bureau cost. The latter option was resisted as it was felt that greater benefits would accrue from a mini dedicated to the department, but as there was little experience of its hardware reliability or capacity it was agreed to rent the system for a trial period in order to evaluate performance.

The equipment was installed three months later, models readily transferred from the bureau and the cash forecast immediately embarked upon. In order to complete the installation in time for this to take place, a machine intended for EPS was diverted to ICI. This included a 600 lines per minute printer which was not in the original specification but remained 'temporarily'.

During the successful running of the two-month forecast cycle, it became apparent how useful it was to have immediate access to data through a VDU on the desk, especially for checking and referring quickly to data in detail or summary form, whereas a long time had previously been spent maintaining up-to-date manual records. Also, the facility acquired by the accountants in the department prompted more suggestions of routine collecting, consolidating and reporting of data which could be implemented. These could all be considered now as the marginal cost for each application was zero. The main areas covered were monthly sales and profits reporting to the Main Board and tax modelling which is a very complex matrix problem. Through all this time the line printer was becoming more an essential part of the system in order to obtain fast hard-copy reports and those which were too large for the VDU screen.

The developments thus far were certaintly cost effective compared with the previous bureau usage but were only using a small amount of the capacity of the machine available. The time was now ripe for the next step.

A major part of the department's effort was directed to analysis and presentation of the financial data collected quarterly on the IBM system. This consists of end-of-quarter balance sheet and cumulative profit and loss account information. The presentations required are mainly analyses showing the quarterly values derived from cumulatives from the previous and current years together with comment on and detail of the variances between these quarterly figures. Hence, although all the data were collected by computer, much time was expended in deriving and presenting results in the required format. This had not been computerized on the IBM system because the programming effort required to produce satisfactory prints in a lower-level language such as PL1 would be immense and the output difficult to change once completed. In addition to this, the current programming team were completely occupied with maintenance and development of the collection system. Conversely, once the data is entered into the FCS–EPS hierarchical system, extractions, quarterly values, variances and print-outs are relatively easy to produce. Accordingly it was decided to use FCS–EPS to carry out these analyses and to generate the required reports.

The first stage of this work was completed in six weeks with consultant programming aid. It included housekeeping routines, conversion of data from the IBM to the mini (a daily tape) and thirty reports suitable for direct inclusion in the published report. The modelling consultant was used merely as extra resource, given a fairly tight timetable. The vast majority of the ICI Millbank models are written by the management accountants in the Treasurer's Department and a management services programmer-analyst with no previous FCS–EPS experience.

Following the success of these early experiences, FCS–EPS has since been used at ICI in a wide variety of applications. Three of these are now briefly described in the remainder of this section.

Long-term Cash Forecast Models

The Central View

This system consists of a main cash-flow model which produces cash-flow statements, profit and loss account, balance sheet and statistics prints. Changes to the basic information may be applied to enable assessments of sensitivity to be made and arrive at a final agreed central forecast. Subsidiary models supply data concerning loan interest, dividends, tax, profit sharing and CCA information (see Figure 11.2).

The base-data file contains four sections of cash-flow data equivalent to the levels at which the forecast is being made. Rows are also provided for opening balances and journal entries which allow the cash-flow movements to be converted into profit and loss and balance sheet forecasts. Statistics such as capital gearing, interest cover and internal generation are then calculated. The model requests the base-file name and calculates and prints all or selected reports. The model also requests the name of a file of changes to be applied to the base. If this is supplied, changes to profit, capital expenditure, working capital, loans and dividends generate subsequent additional interest savings or payments together with tax implications. These may be displayed if required and added to the data input from the base file before printing.

The results of calculation can be passed on to a CCA model which adjusts values according to inflation data held on a separate file to enable full CCA profit and loss, balance sheet and ratio reports to be output.

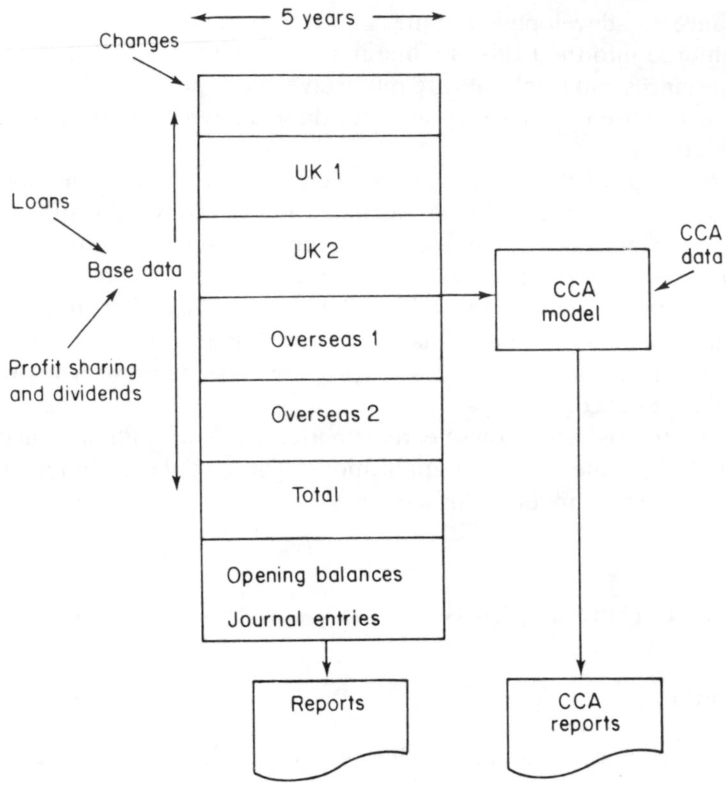

Figure 11.2 The long-term cash-forecast models

The Units' View

Forecast cash flow, sales, working capital and other sundry information is collected from units in local currency. This is then converted into sterling and consolidated according to the defined hierarchy (see Figure 11.3).

The input/validation model requests the section number (i.e. operating unit) to be updated on the original currency file and accepts input from the terminal. At the end of input validation, checks are carried out (e.g. 'movement in cash' row equals sum of individual rows; sales rows add up to total) and any errors are displayed. Corrections are accepted and the data re-checked. When all the data are valid, exchange rates from the control file are used to convert movements, opening and closing balances to sterling and calculate exchange effects. The sterling section is then written to a different file. Once all sections have been validated and converted, the HIERARCHY command is issued to calculate consolidated nodes up to a group total. Two extra hierarchy structures are calculated on the same file to give alternative

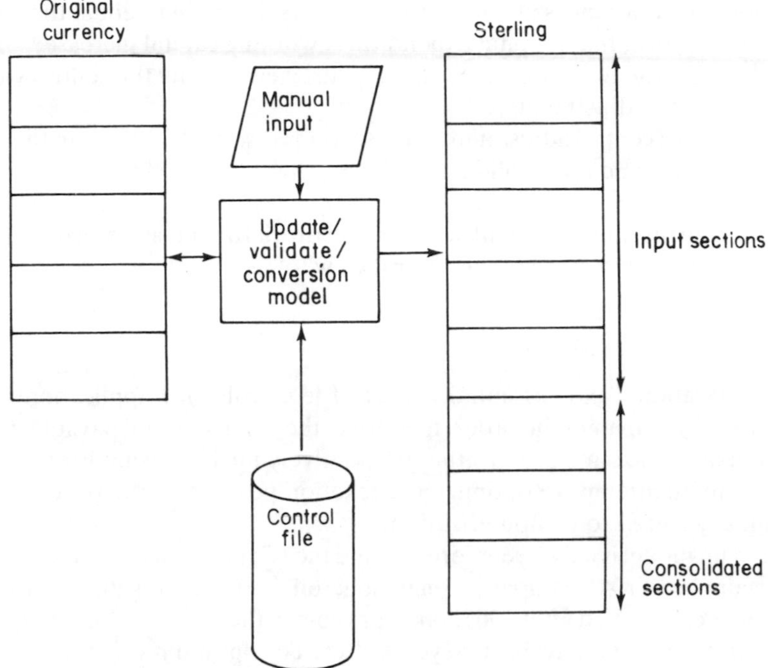

Figure 11.3 The unit's view

groupings of sections. All consolidated results are written back to the same sterling data file to enable displays of both input and calculated sections or full BYROW reports. Report models, generally of the BYROW nature, which access the sterling file to print in publishable form analyses of each cash-flow item or territorial cash flows for each year, are also run.

The Central Versus the Units' View

Forecasts submitted by units are statements of their individual profits and expenditure proposals. They must, however, agree in total with Group targets. Therefore it is necessary to compare the units' and central views.

The central view only requires cash-flow details, but at the four consolidated levels. In order to facilitate comparison, the units' view cash-flow rows are numbered identically to the central view and four of the consolidated sections are at the same level as the four central view forecasts. The stages required to bring the two forecasts into line are:

(1) create a central view base-data file from the units' view;
(2) difference the central and units' base files;

(3) apply the differences as changes to the units' base file to equal the central view of profit, fixed capital expenditure, working capital increase;
(4) difference the resulting 'centralized' units' view file and the central view to give central adjustments;
(5) input these central adjustments into sections reserved for them in the units' view system and reconsolidate.

Reports from the units' view will now show territorial details as given by units but centrally adjusted to come to the central view totals.

The Suite of ICI Tax Models

UK Corporation Tax is essentially a set of legal rules for application to the accounts of companies in order to derive the contribution payable to the government. Since in a group situation relatively intricate complications may result from an attempt to optimize the taxation position of the payer, it is an area ideally suited to computerization.

The main model is a five-year forecast and the ICI position is dealt with under four main headings: company, financing, oil and minor subsidiaries. For companies established after 1965, tax is payable in the year after the charge, for those before 1965 it is payable two years after. The optimum situation, which is determined by deterministic simulation, combines the following:

(a) full utilization of tax losses;
(b) full utilization of Group relief;
(c) Group relief taken in the order which leaves residual tax payable in pre-1965 companies.

The model is used for:

(1) Planning purposes—to calculate tax charge, and payments for five-year forecast. It enables sensitivities of changes in capital expenditure dividends, loans, etc. to be measured in their effect on tax charges and payments.
(2) Tax planning—illustrating where a future tax problem ought to receive attention, for example, covering overseas charges by overseas income.
(3) Actual results—first-year forecast combined with interim period (e.g. 6 months) figures to produce an interim tax charge which is used in the interim accounts.

While an integrated approach is the aim, which will enable transfers of data between models to take place within the minicomputer, currently there exist auxiliary models, the output from which is used as input in the main model. The models interrelate as shown in Figure 11.4.

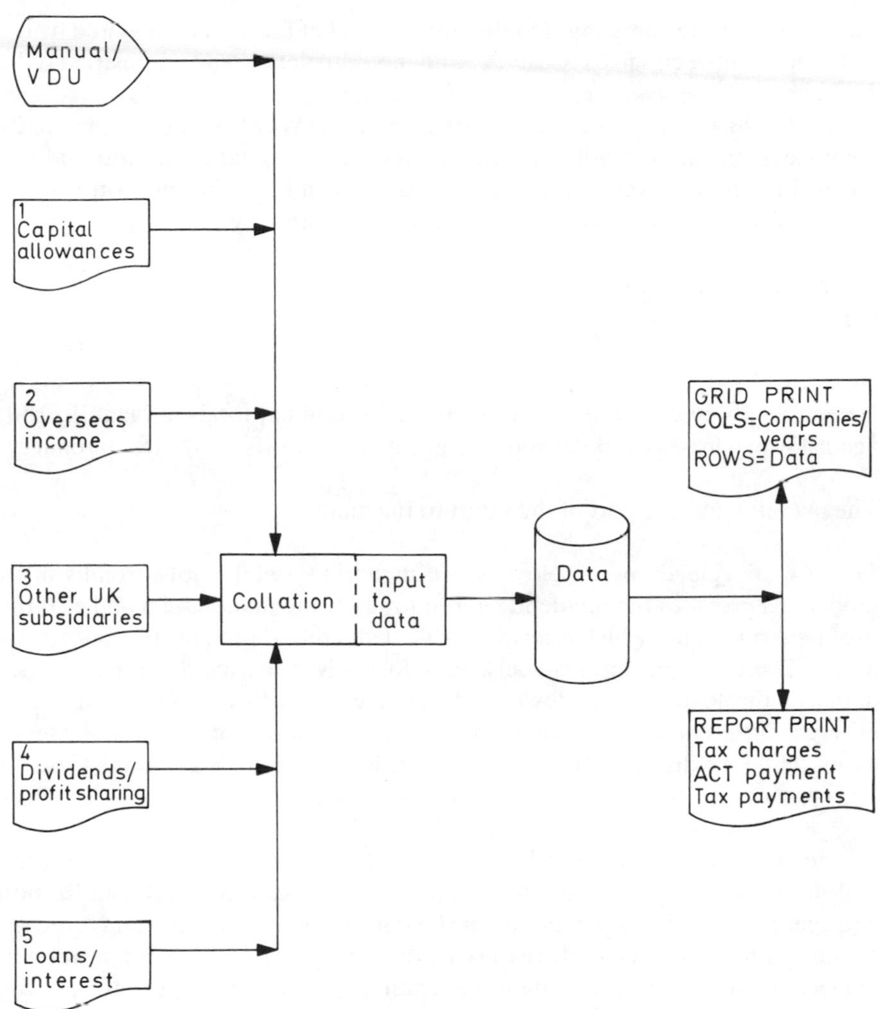

Figure 11.4 The five-year tax model

A brief description of each model follows:

Model 1. Capital allowances—takes capital expenditure by each unit split: buildings, plant, motor cars, research, plus written-down value brought forward, and calculates annual capital allowances. This is then used as input in the main model.

Model 2. Overseas income—takes net dividends received from overseas companies and separately grosses them up for underlying tax and withholding tax to give the gross Case V income and WHT which become part of the tax

calculation for the company. Double taxation relief (gross) is calculated by the difference between gross Case V and net dividend, and is restricted by reference to 52 per cent of gross Case V income.
Model 3. Other UK Subsidiaries—takes main items of tax calculations for 24 companies, including trading profit, depreciation, capital expenditure/allowances, interest received/paid, and calculates taxable profit and notional tax charge. The totals are aggregated into classes of company:

(a) 70–75 per cent owned
(b) 75 per cent owned
(c) over 75 per cent owned

Categories (b) and (c) are used to provide discrete net totals of taxable profit against which losses for the rest of the group may be offset by 'Group relief'.

The overall totals are part of the input to the main model.

Model 4. Dividend and employees profit sharing—whilst not formally a tax model this provides the dividend charge total for the main model and also the profit-sharing figure which is an allowable deduction for tax purposes.
Model 5. Loans and interest—also not formally a tax model; this provides detail of the loans drawn down and planned for with the relevant interest charges. Different rules are applicable in the main model for different classes of loans, while the discrete interest figures are important in determining Case III and charges.

The main model takes detail from the auxiliary models, plus data from the cash-forecast program in order to calculate the UK tax charge, ACT utilization and charge, and UK tax payments for the current year plus four years forecast. Minor routines also included are the calculation of stock relief, formalization of overseas income and the calculation of trading income for tax purposes.

Specific detail has been built in for the optimizing of group relief, the calculation of tax losses utilized and carried forward, the utilization of ACT by reference to dividends payable in the period and the write-off/credit of ACT by reference to dividends charged, and the payment of mainstream corporation tax after utilization of ACT and including ACT paid in the period, which happens to be by reference to dividends charged in the previous period.

A minor complication is the 'ring-fence' which operates in the oil business. This enables tax losses arising in oil (resulting possibly from excess capital allowances) to be offset against profits in the rest of the group, but losses from the rest of the group may not be offset against oil profits—however, they may be offset against 'non-ring-fenced' refining and dealing profits.

The interim accounts model provides the UK tax charge for the ICI results for interim (3 months, 6 months and 9 months) accounts. It takes the relevant proportion of certain items from the current year of the main model, for example, capital allowances, stock relief, overseas income, ACT charge/credit and applies these to the trading and interest flows of the interim period.

Attention is given to the interrelationship between the current-year forecast and the interim accounts charge to ensure that they are consistent in treatment of general items. For example, if the forecast is a taxable loss at trading level, then no tax losses brought forward may be utilized in the interim figures even though this may be a profitable result. The ACT charge/credit is a compensating figure.

The following dimensions give an idea of the size of models:

	Variables	Periods
(1) Capital allowances	2760	5
(2) Overseas income	920	10
(3) Subsidiaries	5712	6
(4) Dividends/profit sharing	103	6
(5) Loans	100	46
Main model	300	24
Interim accounts model	300	24

For model 1, there are 40 input rows + 144 calculated rows, for 15 sections, i.e. 2760 variables; for model 3 there are 32 input rows + 136 calculated rows, for 34 sections, i.e. 5712 variables.

The Capital allowance model has the following structure—rows are model variables, periods are time, and sections are ICI divisions. The overseas income model has a transposed structure—rows are time, periods are variables and the sections divisions. The other UK subsidiary model has the usual structure—variables, time and divisions, but uses extensively the FCS–EPS allocation facilities to allocate group items down the hierarchy, and the FCS–EPS facility to change model logic for sections, for example, input and consolidated sections. The various model logics use most of the advanced language facilities described earlier, for example, file handling, looping and indirect addressing.

While the models have been developed by four people over the last three years the main development has been in the last year for the main model, interim model and models 2 and 3. The smaller models 2 and 3 took a week to write in total spread over a three-month period. The main model has taken 2–3 months spread over a nine-month period, and the interim accounts model perhaps two weeks. All models include logic, job tracks and report specifications, any of which may be subject to amendment at short notice.

Future developments are seen in terms of further enhancement of current systems, for example the provision of more supporting detail, tax creditor, reconciliation for full deferral purposes, and the computerization of interrelationships between interim accounts and current-year tax models; automatic reading from auxiliary files into the main model; more detail of intra-merger flows of interest for information purposes; formalization of inputs for internal discussion of the resulting tax charge and payments; the updating of the tax model as legislation changes. This could also result from changes in group structure or large changes in data which necessitate an amendment to the logic in the model.

Quarterly Profit and Sales Report

Data are fed down to head office from the central computer on a tape suitable for FCS–EPS, loaded on to the minicomputer into a hierarchy model using a conversion table. For a six-week period during each quarter data arrive daily and are checked with the previous day's data to identify changes. The original data have been telexed from all over the world to the Centre and are 'cleaned-up' before transfer to head office.

The tape contains current-quarter cumulative data, and so, given previous cumulative data, each quarter may be derived by differencing. A current annual forecast is also supplied. All data are recorded in operating-unit detail, and using the hierarchical facilities of FCS–EPS, territorial and group totals are derived. The actual hierarchy comprises 390 input sections and 130 consolidated sections, giving 520 in total. Sales and profit data are kept on two separate data files. For sales, an input section comprises 140 rows for five time periods, while for profits an input section comprises 170 rows for five time periods. The previous year has been constructed in the same format. In total, this represents several hundred thousand data elements! Report specifications are used to output quarterly figures and variances for the current year and previous year as shown in the two examples given in Exhibit 11.1 in the Appendix to this chapter.

Inter-company transfers are easily treated by identifying them on separate rows in each section and inputting contra entries to ensure they cancel out at group level. The hierarchy is used to simply add up the data, and via VDU screens check any data item using section and cross-section displays.

The reports are fairly detailed—headings and selected text are dynamically created, depending on year and current quarter; the de-cumulating depends on current quarter; zeros in columns with no data are blanked out, in columns with data they must appear as dashes; column output positions are variable; variances differ by report and there are many other intricate requirements.

The models have been 'parameterized' to ensure that if, for example, in the current year, the input-section sizes or the number of sections change, then they need not be re-written. An important distinction has been made between the concept of applying logic rules to a data matrix to identify and obtain final numbers, and separate report specifications for the final reports. This helps to differentiate between the two processes of checking and producing the base data, and then reporting on it. Writing and maintaining the system is thus easy to understand and implement.

The consolidations themselves take several minutes to perform, but this again only serves to emphasize the different attitude created by modelling on an in-house mini. All marginal costs are zero, or very nearly so; if the consolidation takes a few minutes that is a fairly good excuse for popping out of the office for a cup of tea!

11.4 Conclusion

The Management Accounting Group of ICI Treasurer's Department have shown how the concept of financial modelling on a dedicated in-house minicomputer can be successfully implemented. The use of a computer bureau for the initial applications was expensive, correction of small data errors in a large integrated system involved expensive re-runs, sensitivity analysis was restricted by cost, model development not always encouraged. The in-house move was easily justified, the benefits were more than expected. A VDU on each accountant's desk gives immediate data checking and presentation, and a feeling of involvement. A major change was a new attitude to modelling, the marginal cost for each application was zero, the accountants creatively suggested new methods of routine collection, consolidation, analysis and reporting of data. The extent of the current applications has been earlier demonstrated—long-term cash-forecasting models, tax-planning models, quarterly profit and sales reporting, and corporate reports to the Board, direct from the computer print-out to the boardroom.

The above application has shown that non-technical data-processing staff can successfully operate a computer system supporting several users simultaneously; the only operating experience necessary is the ability to select and mount the correct generation magnetic tape.

Appendix to Chapter 11

The FCS–EPS System

FCS–EPS was written by EPS Consultants and first released in 1973. The system has been successfully applied to problems in the area of short-term planning, typically budgetary planning and control; to problems in the longer term, typically the 'five-year plan'; to problems of investment appraisal—new capital, new products, acquisition; and to such problems as manpower planning and even production scheduling.

The system may be divided into four major elements, as shown in Figure 11.5. The LOGIC is the definition of the relationship between variables in the

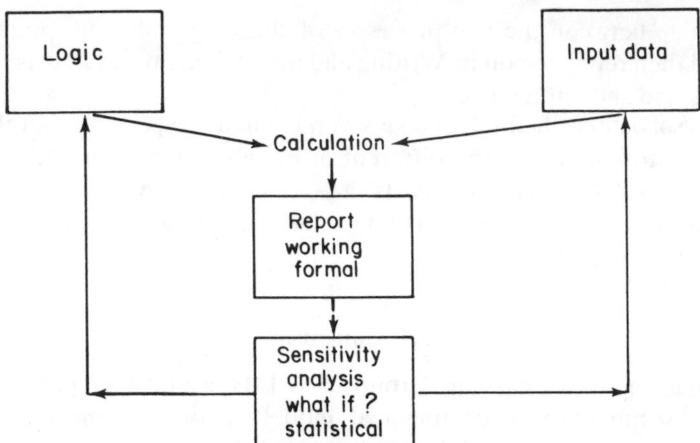

Figure 11.5 Elements of the FCS–EPS system

model; for example, revenue equals volume × price. Input data are the forecasts obtained for the variables; for example, volume will be 10 000 per month, price will be £10 until June, then £11.50. These two elements are brought together, and the calculations carried out according to the definitions in logic. Then various reports can be produced; working reports, formal reports and graphical output. Finally, sensitivity analysis may be performed in terms of changes to the data, changes to several input variables, several stepped changes to a single variable, or working to a target; for example, what sales growth is necessary to achieve a minimum target and DCF yield? Changes may also be made to the logic—for example, to evaluate the impact of removing a production constraint. Analysis of a more statistical nature may be employed.

A major factor contributing to the success of financial modelling systems, is the ease of use. Planners and accountants have been able to develop their own models, ranging from simple to complex. The often fruitless dialogue between planners and the data-processing department, to get even the simplest of models built, has been avoided. The people who know the model they want are able to construct it themselves. An example is given below of the model logic from one of the ICI models.

```
SYSTEM) LOGIC
+1Ø1'TRADING PROFIT'
+1Ø2'DEPRECIATION'
+1Ø3'CAPITAL ALLOWANCES'
+1Ø4'STOCK RELIEF'
+1Ø5'CASE I'='TRADING PROFIT' SUM 'STOCK RELIEF'
```

```
+111'INTEREST RECEIVED'
+112'OVERSEAS INCOME'
+113'INTEREST PAID'
+114'NON-TRADING ITEMS'=111+112−113
+121'TAXABLE PROFIT'=1Ø5+114
+125'TAX CHARGED'=121 AT 52.Ø
+END
SYSTEM⟩
```

FCS–EPS is command driven—the command LOGIC is used to enter the logic or model, CALCULATE calculates the input variables to give calculated variables according to the rules of the logic, LIST prompts for the columns and rows that are to be listed for a 'working paper' report. The commands are self-explanatory, again re-emphasizing the need for ease of use. An example is given below of the data that might be entered for the simple model already described, using, as one might expect, the DATA command.

```
SYSTEM⟩ DATA
*1Ø1,U,1ØØ,11Ø,13Ø,135
*1Ø2,U,5Ø,6Ø,65,65
*1Ø3,U,−8Ø,−85,−9Ø
*1Ø4,U,−2Ø,−25,−35,−45
*111,I,3Ø,5
*112,I,2Ø,5
*113,U,*45
*END
SYSTEM⟩
```

The logic and data are combined using the CALCULATE command, and a LIST of results produced.

```
SYSTEM⟩ CALCULATE
SYSTEM⟩ LIST
COLUMNS? 1–4
ROWS? 1Ø1–125
```

	1	2	3	4
1Ø1 TRADING PROFIT	1ØØ.ØØ	11Ø.ØØ	13Ø.ØØ	135.ØØ
1Ø2 DEPRECIATION	5Ø.ØØ	6Ø.ØØ	65.ØØ	65.ØØ
1Ø3 CAPITAL ALLOWANCE	−8Ø.ØØ	−85.ØØ	−85.ØØ	−9Ø.ØØ
1Ø4 STOCK RELIEF	−2Ø.ØØ	−25.ØØ	−35.ØØ	−45.ØØ
1Ø5 CASE I	5Ø.ØØ	6Ø.ØØ	75.ØØ	65.ØØ
111 INTEREST RECEIVED	3Ø.ØØ	35.ØØ	4Ø.ØØ	45.ØØ

```
112 OVERSEAS INCOME          20.00    25.00    30.00    35.00
113 INTEREST PAID            45.00    45.00    45.00    45.00
114 NON-TRADING ITEMS         5.00    15.00    25.00    35.00
121 TAXABLE PROFIT           55.00    75.00   100.00   100.00
125 TAX CHARGED              28.60    39.00    52.00    52.00

SYSTEM
```

A simple REPORT specification can be written, to provide a more formal report, again the report specifications being self-explanatory.

```
SYSTEM) HEADINGS
OPTION: NU
FIRST VALUE,PERIOD STEPS,OMITTING PERIODS? 1980
OPTION: EN
SYSTEM) TITLE
TITLE: TAX CALCULATION
SYSTEM) REPORT
SPECIFICATIONS
  10 SUPROW
  20 BRACKET
  30 ROWS 101–104 UDATA
  40 ROWS 105
  50 SKIP
  60 R111–113 U R114 U S
  70 U'='R121 U'='
  80 END

SYSTEM) DISPLAY
20:41:44 ON 08/07/80
```

TAX CALCULATION

	1980	1981	1982	1983
TRADING PROFIT	100	110	130	135
DEPRECIATION	50	60	65	65
CAPITAL ALLOWANCE	(80)	(85)	(85)	(90)
STOCK RELIEF	(20)	(25)	(35)	(45)
CASE I	50	60	75	65
INTEREST RECEIVED	30	35	40	45
OVERSEAS INCOME	20	25	30	35
INTEREST PAID	45	45	45	45

NON-TRADING ITEMS	5	15	25	35
TAXABLE PROFIT	55	75	1ØØ	1ØØ
SYSTEM)				

From this base data various sensitivity analyses can be carried out—single, stepped or targeted.

It is very important to realize that while a modelling system must be fundamentally designed on the basis of the criterion of ease of use, it must also have the ability to model complex problems. Complexity will obviously arise if the logic is itself complex, as will be seen in the description of the tax model. Complexity may also arise if the models are, for example, 'parameterized'—for example, given the parameter of 'current quarter of plan', the respective data files and period, the report headings and contents are accessed. The actual model should not change, given a change to the parameter-current plan period.

A comprehensive modelling system will possess such facilities as logical expression, conditional and unconditional jumps, redefinition of variables, facilities for interpolation and extrapolation, matrix handling and financial functions. Of major importance are: file-handling functions; facilities for directly and indirectly reading or writing data; terminal input/output of both numeric and string characters; issuing of commands in models; means of string comparison and concatenation; features for looping by variable or by period and for nesting loops; and the capability of indirectly as well as directly defining relationships between variables. Many of the models in ICI Treasurer's Department use these facilities; the models are complex, and mainly written not by professional data-processing people, but just by simple planners and accountants! It requires considerable training and experience, but this case study proves what can be done.

A major task facing ICI Treasurer's Department is the consolidation or aggregation of plans. FCS–EPS contains facilities to help the modeller deal with consolidation problems. The facilities are designed to allow complex multilevel consolidations, involving such problems as currency conversion, cost allocation and various inflation scenarios to be simply modelled. Figure 11.6(a) shows the common feature of these applications, the presence of a company tree of hierarchy. Three types of files are required during hierarchical consolidation. One file describes the hierarchy or tree, and contains the description of each section—product, division, company, etc. (see Figure 11.6(b)). The logic file is the logic which applies to each section (see Figure

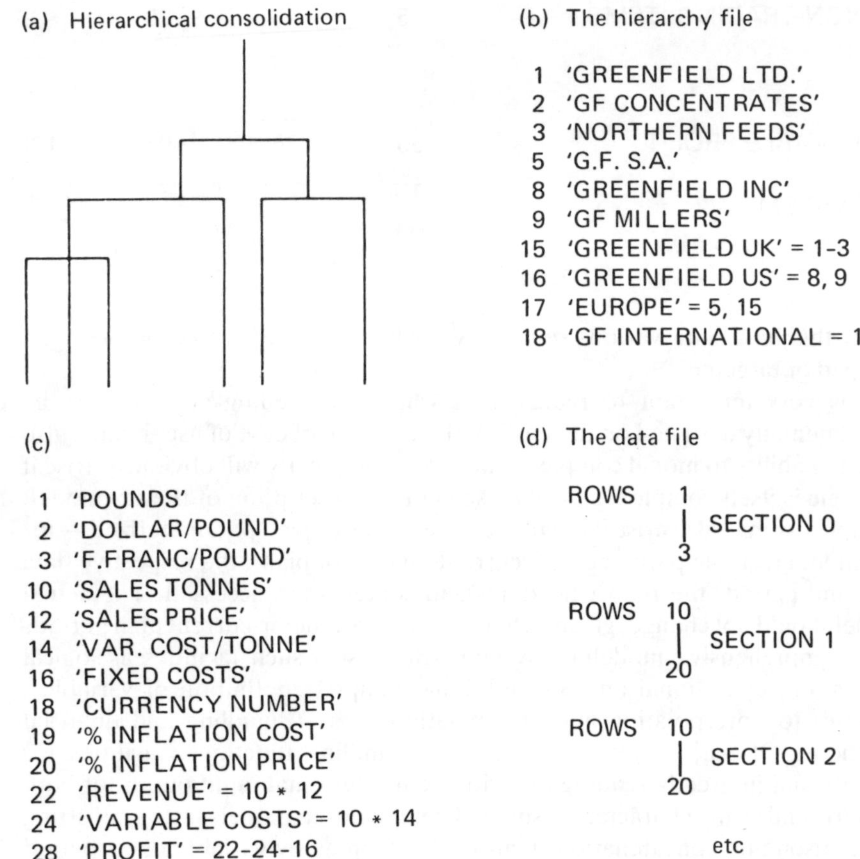
(a) Hierarchical consolidation
(b) The hierarchy file
1 'GREENFIELD LTD.'
2 'GF CONCENTRATES'
3 'NORTHERN FEEDS'
5 'G.F. S.A.'
8 'GREENFIELD INC'
9 'GF MILLERS'
15 'GREENFIELD UK' = 1-3
16 'GREENFIELD US' = 8, 9
17 'EUROPE' = 5, 15
18 'GF INTERNATIONAL = 16, 17
(c)
1 'POUNDS'
2 'DOLLAR/POUND'
3 'F.FRANC/POUND'
10 'SALES TONNES'
12 'SALES PRICE'
14 'VAR. COST/TONNE'
16 'FIXED COSTS'
18 'CURRENCY NUMBER'
19 '% INFLATION COST'
20 '% INFLATION PRICE'
22 'REVENUE' = 10 * 12
24 'VARIABLE COSTS' = 10 * 14
28 'PROFIT' = 22-24-16
(d) The data file
ROWS 1
3
SECTION 0
ROWS 10
20
SECTION 1
ROWS 10
20
SECTION 2
etc

Figure 11.6 The hierarchy structure

11.6(c)). Common rows contain data common to all sections, the input rows and calculated rows describe the logic of each section. The logic may vary from section to section, and from level to level in the hierarchy. The data file contains the common data and the data for each section or company. The data are in blocks of rows on the file known as 'sections'. Section zero is reserved for the common data; section 1 upwards contain data for each company (see Figure 11.6(d)). The structure of the hierarchy is defined, in terms of the hierarchy file, logic, and data files. The latter is also defined in terms of the zero section, and input rows and consolidated rows for each section. The complete hierarchy may be consolidated by issuing the one command HIERARCHY. Some of the hierarchies used in ICI Treasurer's Department contain several hundred base sections, with over 100 rows of input data for each section and ten or more columns of data. With such a large consolidation, it is important that the modelling system allows not only the rather brutal consolidation of all sections, but control over the various stages of consolidation: control in terms of being able to consolidate a section, using the information immediately below the section, to be able to input and analyse a particular section, and to be able to minimize the cost of recalculating the hierarchy after specified input sections have been changed or updated. These controls and more are specified using keywords with the command HIERARCHY, for example, HIERARCHY UPDATED 55.

The normal reporting facilities of the system can be used to look at the results of a consolidation. Any section may be displayed and, of great value, cross-section reports may be produced. A particular row or variable for a group of sections may be displayed in one report, and a particular column or period for a group of sections may be displayed in one report, see Figure 11.7.

```
SYSTEM> DISPLAY SECTION
SECTIONS? 1-3, 15

                    GREENFIELD LTD.
                         1            2            3
22 REVENUE          170000       207000       250000
28 PROFIT            17000        24650        32500

        SIMILAR REPORTS FOLLOW FOR SECTIONS 2, 3, AND 15

SYSTEM> DISPLAY SECTION COLUMN 3 TITLE
TITLE: EUROPEAN COMPANIES PLAN 1981
SECTIONS? 1-3, 5, 17

                    EUROPEAN COMPANIES PLAN 1981

                  GREENFIELD LTD   GF CONCEN.  GF NORTH  G.F. S.A   EUROPE
SALES TONNES                2500         800      4000      1500     8800
PROFIT                     32500      113000     54000     17647   217147
                           -----      ------     -----     -----   ------
PROFIT %
REVENUE                     13.0        35.3      12.9      11.1     18.9

SYSTEM> DISPLAY SECTION BYROW 28

                            1979

GREENFIELD U.K.             199500
GREENFIELD U.S              301667

GF INTERNATIONAL            518814
```

Figure 11.7 Hierarchical reports

Exhibit 11.1

SCHEDULE I

GROUP PROFIT AND LOSS ACCOUNT

1979 £m	1980 £m	Variation £m		1980 £m	1981 F/c £m	Variation £m
			SALES TO EXTERNAL CUSTOMERS (Schedule III)			
-	-	-	United Kingdom	-	-	-
-	-	-	Overseas	-	-	-
-	-	-		-	-	-
-	-	-	TRADING PROFIT (Schedule IV)	-	-	-
-	-	-	After charging depreciation	-	-	-
-	-	-	Exchange gain/loss on net current assets of overseas subsidiaries	-	-	-
-	-	-	Profit less losses from trade investments (Schedule VII)	-	-	-
-	-	-	Interest and financing costs less income	-	-	-
-	-	-	PROFIT BEFORE TAXATION AND GRANTS	-	-	-
-	-	-	Taxation less grants (Schedule VIII)	-	-	-
-	-	-	PROFIT AFTER TAXATION AND GRANTS	-	-	-
-	-	-	Applicable to minorities	-	-	-
-	-	-	PROFIT APPLICABLE TO PARENT COMPANY BEFORE EXTRAORDINARY ITEMS	-	-	-
-	-	-	Extraordinary items	-	-	-
-	-	-	PROFIT APPLICABLE TO PARENT COMPANY AFTER EXTRAORDINARY ITEMS	-	-	-
-	-	-	Less: Preference dividend	-	-	-
-	-	-	EARNINGS FOR ORDINARY STOCKHOLDERS	-	-	-
-	-	-	Less: Ordinary dividend	-	-	-
-	-	-	PROFIT RETAINED FOR THE YEAR	-	-	-

1979 £m	1980 £m	Variation £m		1980 £m	1981 F/c £m	Variation £m
-	-	-	By Parent Company	-	-	-
-	-	-	By Subsidiaries	-	-	-
-	-	-	In Principal Associated Companies	-	-	-
-	-	-		-	-	-

(a) Specimen Profit Report

GROUP EXTERNAL SALES IN THE UNITED KINGDOM

	1979					1980				
	QUARTERS				YEAR	QUARTERS				YEAR
	1st	2nd	3rd	4th		1st	2nd	3rd	4th	
	£m	£m	£m	£m	£m	£m	£m	£m	£m	£m
UNITED KINGDOM										
Business 1	-	-	-	-	-	-				
Business 2	-	-	-	-	-	-				
Business 3	-	-	-	-	-	-				
Business 4	-	-	-	-	-	-				
Business 5	-	-	-	-	-	-				
Business 6	-	-	-	-	-	-				
Business 7	-	-	-	-	-	-				
Business 8	-	-	-	-	-	-				
Business 9	-	-	-	-	-	-				
Business 10	-	-	-	-	-	-				
TOTAL UK	-	-	-	-	-	-				
OVERSEAS SUBSIDIARIES										
Australasia	-	-	-	-	-	-				
Canada	-	-	-	-	-	-				
Europe	-	-	-	-	-	-				
Indian sub-continent	-	-	-	-	-	-				
United States	-	-	-	-	-	-				
Other Territories	-	-	-	-	-	-				
TOTAL OVERSEAS	-	-	-	-	-	-				
GROUP TOTAL	-	-	-	-	-	-				

(b) Specimen Sales Report

Financial Modelling in Corporate Management, 2nd Edition
Edited by J. W. Bryant

12

Blue Circle's Investment-planning Models

JOHN DOLBEAR

12.1 Introduction

Blue Circle Industries plc is a British company which has developed into one of the largest manufacturers of cement in the world. It is organized into four operating groups together with a small corporate staff providing services to them. The historical genesis of the company is represented by Blue Circle Cement which operates 16 cement works in the UK. Blue Circle Enterprises represents the group's diversification mainly into the related fields of Building Materials Supply and Merchanting. Blue Circle Overseas (BCO) is a holding company for the group interests in foreign cement works and building material suppliers. Lastly, Blue Circle Technical provides Engineering, Chemical and Geological expertise to the rest of the group and on a consultancy basis to outside companies, besides carrying out basic research and new product developments.

This chapter will attempt to describe only one of the financial modelling activities currently being carried out within the group: one in which the author has been most closely involved.

The Overseas operating group has interests in Asia, Africa, America and Australasia. Typically the investment in these overseas companies is in the range of 30–60 per cent of their ordinary share capital. In addition to this capital, investment is also made in terms of management and technical experience. The group, however, rarely owns 100 per cent of an overseas company, unlike the classic American multinational corporation.

Cement is such a basic material in any developing economy that it is one of the first industries that any Government attempts to establish. Since it is such a low-value, heavy-weight product, the relatively high distribution costs favour production near the potential market. The capital-intensive nature of the processes by which cement is manufactured, however, necessitates careful evaluation of both the raw material and market potential. Whereas there may be many potential sources of capital (e.g. private individuals, government agencies, commercial banks and international development banks), there are few organizations to rival Blue Circle's access to both capital and technical and management expertise. The management of BCO is thus frequently faced with the need to evaluate various investment proposals, both for entirely new cement companies, as well as for expansion proposals from companies in which it already holds a stake.

Faced with this challenge (and problem), what has emerged is a family of long-term financial models, each describing one of the actual or potential manufacturing companies. The family resemblance between the models is great, since they all describe roughly similar manufacturing processes, while at the same time differences in taxation and financing reflect the individuality of each company. The models have helped in the choice between alternative proposals for each project, and whether or not this best proposal should be proceeded with. In those cases where the decision has been made to proceed, the models have been updated with subsequent actual data on costs incurred and the latest estimates of future costs and prices, etc. This is especially critical during the early construction phase of the project, when cost escalation or construction delays might necessitate renegotiation of the financing package.

12.2 Model Development

The question of how the models developed from one another can be tackled in two ways. Firstly, as a straightforward historical account of which model was built first, and second, and so on up to the present time. The alternative approach is, with the benefit of hindsight, to try and link the models together by their logical developmental relationship. We shall begin with the historical approach and then switch to the logical approach in order to avoid repetition and to provide insight into the structural relationship within the family of models.

The first model which was developed for BCO was of an existing company which was proposing to build an additional cement works. Thus although the profitability of the venture had to be judged on the incremental effects alone, the viability of the financial arrangements depended crucially on the cash flow that would be generated by the existing business, so this too had to be modelled. A whole series of runs was performed to assess the effects of alternative plant sizes, phasing of the project, uncertainty regarding the capital costs and uncertainty regarding the sales volume and price.

A rather similar model was then developed for a company proposing to expand one of its existing works. Although this problem was conceptually similar to the previous one, quite a lot of programming modifications were required in order to accommodate the rather different taxation rules and accounting practices.

The next problem tackled was the setting up of an entirely new company, which would build a new cement works on a green-field site. In many ways this represents a rather easier problem to analyse than the previous ones, in that the effects of the 'no go' decision are clearly defined. Closely allied to this problem was that of looking at the acquisition or partial acquisition of an existing cement company, where the investment involved was not only the initial purchase price but also the subsequent pumping in of new capital.

Logically then, we can regard the models as being divided into three levels of complexity. The simplest models represent new companies and acquisitions of existing companies. A second level of complexity involves the expansion of an existing works or the addition of new works. The third level of difficulty (which we have not previously mentioned) concerns the replacement of existing facilities. This last may either represent the replacement of old plant at a works by more modern equipment, a change of process or even the replacement of a whole works by a more favourably situated modern works. The additional difficulty is caused by the treatment of the written-off assets and any scrap value arising, as well as the conceptual problem of determining what were the incremental effects of the project.

Although, so far, we have been talking in terms of financial models of cement works, we also developed the model slightly to cover plants producing other building materials and companies providing technical services.

Another aspect, which did not affect the model as such, but did affect the analysis of the results, was the relationship between the company modelled and the Blue Circle Group. Most of the companies modelled were actual or potential members of the group. In some cases the analysis was carried out on behalf of BCO on a fee-paying basis; in other cases the costs were borne by the parent company. We have also had experience of carrying out financial modelling work on a consultancy contract for independent companies not connected with the Blue Circle Group.

12.3 Model Structure

Development Philosophy

The models evolved from one another historically as just described, so it was natural to develop the initial computer program in a similar way by the addition of options to handle the successive enhancements, each controlled by parameters set in the data file. When an old model was required to be rerun, the practice was adopted of updating its data file to conform with the latest version of the program. Then this run was repeated to ensure that no errors had been introduced by the latest programming changes. When this run had been verified, the actual model changes were coded and the new model run. This verification of each model was performed in addition to running each new version of the program with a test pack consisting of three diverse models. The test-pack models were changed with each development, so that at least one of the test models tested out the new facilities. The advantage of revising each model in this way was that only a single version of the program, test models and documentation had to be maintained in terms of computer disc files, tape back-ups, printed listings and typed manuals. This approach minimized the use of file storage space on the computer and eliminated the danger of running the right data with the wrong program.

Computer Language

The model was programmed in FORTRAN IV as this was the most suitable language available at that time on the company's IBM computer. Both time and cost militated against looking for alternative languages. The great advantage of FORTRAN is its universality, thus making the models written in it easily transferred to other machines. It is widely used by Operational Research personnel so it is relatively easy to support and it is very efficient in terms of machine usage once a program has been compiled and loaded.

Its disadvantages are that it is essentially a batch-oriented language and this reduces the rate at which changes can be implemented. However, given the necessity to check quite extensive models when changes had been implemented, the batch processing of them was not too serious a problem. The extensive reports were printed very rapidly on a line printer and these could then be compared with previous runs.

Model Outline

It is customary to set out financial statements with the various accounting items (e.g. cost or revenue) beneath each other down the page (i.e. each accounting item is represented by a row) and each accounting period (e.g. a year or month) is represented by a column representing the values of these items during that period. In calculating this basic matrix of information there are two alternative methods of proceeding: we can either perform all the calculations for a given period first before proceeding to the next period (calculation by column), or we can perform all the calculations for a given accounting item (e.g. capital expenditure) for all of the periods under consideration before proceeding to the next item (e.g. depreciation). Most financial planning packages operate on the latter (row) method by default, but with facilities built in so that, where necessary, one can specify that a subset of the rows is to be calculated period by period. Our model, however, was calculated period by period (the column method) in its entirety.

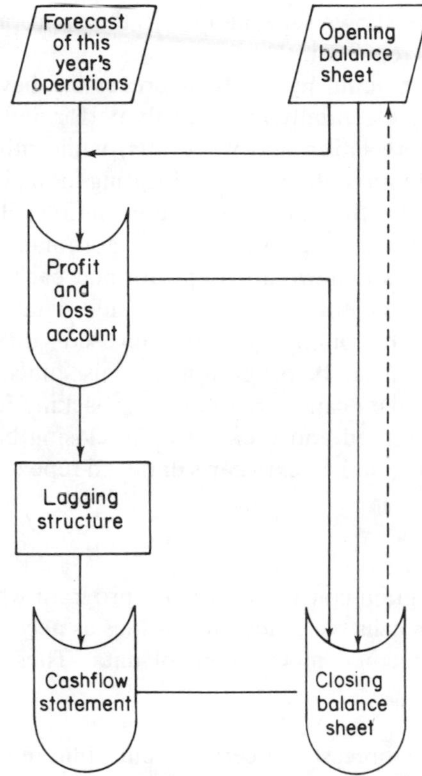

Figure 12.1 Flowchart of calculations performed each period

Referring to the simplified flowchart of the model in Figure 12.1 we see that starting with the opening balance sheet figures, we use forecasts of costs, capital expenditure, sales and other variables to build up the profit and loss account of the company in its first year of modelled operation. A lagging structure is then applied to such items as dividends, taxation, creditors and debtors to arrive at the cash-flow statement of the company for its first year. Then, using the opening balance sheet together with the profit and loss account and cash-flow statement, we can calculate the closing balance sheet for the company at the end of its first year. Our closing balance sheet for year 1, of course, becomes our opening balance sheet for the second year. The calculation subroutine can then be called again to obtain all the second-year results. And so the model proceeds from year to year until our specified horizon is reached. Then the various reports which have been requested can be printed out from the results which have been stored each year. Where the horizon specified is sufficiently far ahead for the number of columns not to fit on a sheet of computer printout, the program automatically splits the report so that the later years are shown separately with the appropriate titles, headings and item descriptions repeated.

Both the row and column methods of processing have their advantages. Some calculations are essentially more easily performed by the row method (e.g. straight-line depreciation and write-offs) while others are more easily performed by the column method (e.g. allocating intangible assets to various fixed-asset categories for the purposes of depreciation). The column method, modelling as it does the passage of time, is a more natural method in that it reflects the calculations that would be performed each period if the actual figures turned out to be identical to the estimated figures used in the model. Another advantage of the column method when used with say, monthly models over five years, is that it can be programmed to use much less main computer memory. Each year's data can be read in from backing files, the calculations performed, reports printed and then only the closing balance sheet figures retained before reading in the next year's data and repeating the cycle.

Subroutine Structure

The FORTRAN program consists of a main program which reads in certain control data and then calls the other subroutines as necessary to carry out the particular options specified in this control data. These subroutines are as follows:

INPUT reads in the forecasts for certain items, plus information from which other forecast items can be calculated.
INPRINT prints selected items of the input data.
CALC is the major subroutine which calculates the model for a particular period.

Most of the remaining subroutines define a particular optional report. They all call subroutine HEAD which prints the necessary headings at the top of the page.

CSHFL prints the cash-flow statement which is probably the single most important report.
SHEET prints the balance sheet report.
PROFIT prints the profit and loss account.
NOTES prints some notes to the accounts which elaborate some of the items which have been reported in the balance sheet and profit and loss account.
ALLOW prints details of the tax allowance calculations to enable the modeller to check that these are being performed correctly.
DEPREC prints details of the depreciation calculations for each of the asset categories.

CHARGE prints details of the financial charges incurred on the various debenture and loan stocks.

RATIO calculates and prints the various common financial ratios.

DCF eliminates the financing for the company, calls CALC to recalculate the model, and then calls IRR.

IRR calculates and prints the internal rate of return of the net cash-flow of the company.

BCKDCF iterates backwards to find what percentage change in the contribution is required to achieve a specified target internal rate of return. Each iteration calls DCF in order to calculate the model and the internal rate of return. In practice somewhere between three and ten iterations were found to be necessary to obtain the desired target internal rate of return to within a tolerance of 0.1 per cent.

Output Reports

The reports produced by the model may be divided into two categories: those whose use was limited to testing the model and data, and those which were used by management to evaluate whether the specified scheme represented a sufficiently profitable and viable investment proposal.

Dealing first with the debugging and validation reports, since a large amount of data had first to be assembled on paper and then typed into the computer, there was obviously scope for straightforward data errors. Some tests were performed on the input data to check for self-consistency. Some data were printed out to allow a visual check and some totals printed could be checked against manually calculated totals. Far more important, however, was to ensure that the calculations were being performed correctly and that, as new facilities were added, the original facilities were still working correctly. The most complex calculations concerned:

(1) The financial depreciation for the various fixed asset categories;
(2) The tax allowances (or fiscal depreciation) for the various fixed asset categories;
(3) The draw down, repayment and interest charges of the various categories of loans and debentures.

Each of these topics was therefore the subject of a separate report which enabled the validity of the model logic to be checked by the model builders. These three reports also enabled the validity of the models to be demonstrated to various accountants from external organizations, who came into contact with them from time to time. A fourth report, The Notes to the Balance Sheet, elaborated some of the figures on the balance sheet and demonstrated how items from the profit and loss account had modified the previous year's balance sheet figure to arrive at the present year's balance sheet figure.

Turning now to the reports which were of ultimate use to the financial management of these various projects, the single most important report was probably the cash-flow forecast. This illustrates the build-up of the net cash flow from its various sources and applications and finally arrives at the cash balance of the company at the end of each year. Probably the next most important report is the profit and loss account. This illustrates the contribution that can be expected from the various activities of the company and how this figure is diminished by various fixed costs, taxes and dividends to leave the retained profit in the bottom line. The balance sheet illustrates the position of the company at the end of each year. It is probably of more use to financial managers in the form of the financial ratios. Here, various balance sheet figures are expressed as percentages of each other and various profit and loss items are also expressed as percentages of balance sheet items. The financial ratio report also contains the single most important statistic, the internal rate of return of the project. This measures the attractiveness of the project as a whole, independently of how it is financed. (The ordinary shareholders can usually gear up their expected return by replacing some of the equity capital by fixed-interest loans. They pay for this greater expected return, however, by incurring greater risk, as the interest on loans is a fixed cost, whereas the additional equity capital would have shared the risk of having its dividends cut in hard times.)

Model Facilities

In contrast with the majority of models of this type, our emphasis was on fiscal and financial aspects rather than on the operating details. This reflects the areas of greatest uncertainty. While the process and operating details are relatively well defined and consistent from one proposal to another, the fiscal and financial aspects can vary widely from one country to another. Any proposal which had widely different operating details would have probably been ruled out on technical grounds at an earlier stage of the evaluation process. This emphasis on tax and depreciation was reflected in the number of different fixed-asset categories that could be modelled (10) and the number of intangible asset categories (10). Each of these categories could have their own depreciation rate, initial and annual tax allowance rates and method of writing down. In addition, there was provision for various forms of tax holiday, turnover tax and multirate corporation tax. As far as depreciation was concerned, this could be delayed for several years after the capital expenditure had been incurred until the plant actually started production. During this preproduction period, finance charges would be capitalized if required. When production began, preproduction finance charges together with the other intangible assets could begin to be depreciated at the average rate at which the fixed assets were being depreciated or at some specified rate. When production began with the new plant, it was sometimes necessary to scrap old plant, write off some fixed assets, take the final allowance or possibly face a balancing charge. On the other hand, in some cases, facilities were needed to revalue periodically the fixed assets, in order to conform to current cost-accounting practices.

As far as financing the project was concerned, provision was made for ordinary share capital and preference capital which could be drawn down as necessary. Provision was made for a share premium account to accommodate ordinary shares sold at above par and a capital redemption reserve fund, to be set up when preference capital was retired. Up to twelve long-term loans or debentures could be specified, each with their own interest rate and repayment schedule. An annual rate of commitment fees could also be specified to run from any point in time up to the draw-down of the loan. The loans could be acquired or redeemed part way through a year if necessary. Short-term borrowings on overdraft were allowed to cover any cash deficit. Later in the life of the project, when a cash surplus had been achieved, this could be deemed to earn interest at a specified rate. In addition investment income could also be generated from subsidiary companies and trade investments. Provision was made for dividend payments as well as financial charges. Accumulated preference dividends were the first call on after-tax profits and then ordinary dividends. Management and technical fees as well as profit participation by the work force are also catered for in the model.

12.4 Use of the Model

The model has been put to a number of uses over the life of each project. In summary, the initial emphasis during the project appraisal is on profitability, whereas later the emphasis switches to liquidity. Below we describe some of the uses made of the model during the evaluation process. Naturally, no actual project is ever used in all these ways, nor is the sequence of events ever as straightforward. In practice, there are steps backwards to previous stages of the analysis, as new factors come to light, and perhaps, because of lack of time, jumps forward to later stages of analysis.

Profitability

The initial runs of the model are often used to examine the implications of alternative plant sizes, alternative processes or alternative capital expenditure phasing. They have even been used to evaluate alternative locations for a works. At this stage the model is an integral part of the dialogue between the engineers and technical personnel responsible for the technical evaluation and initial plant costings, and the project managers and accountants responsible for the financial evaluation. The single most important figure in choosing between alternative possibilities is the discounted cash flow internal rate of return, but the profit/turnover ratio and return on capital employed are also examined. Other constraints such as the current ratio and quick ratio are relatively easily accommodated by adjusting the debtors, creditors and stocks.

Since relatively few numbers need to be changed to evaluate each alternative, the results can be obtained within a matter of about an hour, and so many more alternatives can now be examined than was possible using manual calculations. The computer model also produces a full evaluation of each alternative, whereas previous manual methods had to concentrate on obtaining only the most critical figures and ratios.

When one or two of the most promising schemes have been identified they may be subjected to sensitivity analysis. This merely means assessing the effects on the schemes of changes in some of the most crucial and uncertain variables—e.g. the volume of sales, the price of fuel, the capital cost of the new plant. In practice, sensitivity analysis is unlikely to differentiate between proposals, but rather give some feeling for the risk inherent in them. Many of the forecast factors are by no means independent, but on the other hand it is very difficult to specify what their relationship is. Therefore, it has not been found possible to perform a comprehensive risk analysis using the model. Rather, the factors are varied independently, although it is known for instance that the sales price of cement is very dependent on its production costs. One method of approach to this problem is to perform a so-called backwards iteration procedure. For any given scenario of, say, pessimistically high capital costs, the model can be set to calculate what the company needs to achieve by way of contribution per unit production volume. Then, assuming a particular production cost, we can calculate the required selling price that would have to be achieved in order to meet the company's target discounted cash flow rate of return. Basically, the program guesses a particular level of contribution and works forward to the internal rate of return that this produces. If this is not within a certain tolerated margin of the required internal rate of return, the program goes backwards and makes another better estimate of the necessary level of contribution. This loop is then repeated until the required internal rate of return has been achieved and the necessary level of contribution has been calculated.

Liquidity

While the engineers and technologists have been refining their plant plans and cost estimates, the accountants and financial managers have been seeking out possible sources of finance. Many diverse institutions and organizations may be involved: banks (both local and international, commercial and intergovernment), governments (national, regional and local, both directly and indirectly via state holding companies and development boards), companies (both local and international) and private individuals (usually local). Additionally, a common source of finance is the manufacturer of the process plant or his government who will usually loan a certain proportion of the capital cost in order to capture the export order. Not only will the sources be diverse, but the legal form of the loan will also be varied—e.g. debenture stocks of various types and seniority, term loans, foreign currency loans, mortgage bonds, etc. Despite these profound differences, the model treats them all identically (although some adjustment in the nominal interest rate may be made outside the model to compensate for currency appreciation of loans denominated in a non-local currency).

When such a financial package is fed into the model, the usual first result is a number of years when there is a surplus of cash and a number of years of deficit. The model is extremely useful at this stage, as very rapidly the acquisition and redemptions of the various loans can be adjusted and the model rerun. After, say, four or five runs a reasonable package emerges, or at least the shortfall in finance is quantified and banks and other institutions, can be approached with a relatively well-defined requirement. The financial institutions will be interested not only in the timing of the loan repayments and in the net cash flow of the project, but also in such ratios as the debt/equity ratio and the debt/service ratio, as these give them an idea of the level of risk to which their loans are exposed.

Over a period of many months, many financial packages will be modelled as the negotiations with various backers firm up, as the cost estimates are revised, and as interest and currency rates fluctuate. Even when negotiations are concluded and contracts signed, there may still be the need to update and revise the model, as actual capital costs become known and can be substituted for the most likely estimates. Indeed revised estimates of the vital items, such as selling price and production start-up data, may need to be incorporated and the model rerun in order to assess the impact of the latest information.

Many models never reach the stage of being updated as the proposal is rejected and the plant never erected. This in no way means that the modelling effort has been abortive. Indeed it is just as important to highlight projects which are not satisfactory as it is to help in the assessment and planning of ones which are. Of course many other considerations have to be taken into account besides those coped with by the model: considerations of political, economic, and currency instability, considerations of global diversification and competitors' reactions to name but a few. Although they influence variables within the model (such as sales volume), they merit very profound study of themselves.

One of the advantages of using a computerized model is that, when costs are revised and the model needs to be rerun, not only is relatively little effort involved (as few numbers need changing), but also the method of appraisal will be consistent with that previously adopted (possibly many months previously, possibly by a different financial manager). Indeed, not only does the model impose a consistent frame of reference for the same project, but also provides it for different projects, even when the analysis is probably being carried out by different parts of the organization.

Accountancy and Operational Research

The model was initially designed as a co-operative effort between accountants and operational research analysts, the accountants being responsible for the definition of the required output, accounting conventions and methods of calculations, and the operational research analysts being responsible for turning these requirements and rules into a working computer system.

This system was not designed for use by the accountants directly. It was always envisaged that the two professions would work together on any particular project appraisal, with the operational research analyst interpreting the accountant's requirements within the available facilities of the model and, if necessary, extending these to cope with any vital new requirement. This close collaboration had several effects:

(1) It meant that any new model facility could be extremely rapidly incorporated in a working model;
(2) There was little incentive to produce a user-friendly system; rather the data input formats were designed to be used by someone with quite a lot of computer experience (e.g. fixed format fields);
(3) A very efficient system was produced in terms of computer utilization. Little file space was required to store each model. Only a few seconds central processor unit time and a region size of less than 200K bytes was required to run a typical model on an IBM 370/158 at a cost of only a few pounds.

12.5 Conclusions

This family of financial models has reached maturity. Only very minor programming changes have been made in recent years. One possible opportunity for developing the model lies in extending the model backwards to help in some of the cost estimation that has to be performed to calculate the various capital expenditure amounts. A great deal of effort has to be put into obtaining reasonably accurate estimates and it is felt that automating this could well be cost effective. However, at the moment this possibility is not under active investigation and development resources have been transferred to other financial modelling applications.

This is not to say that the models have stopped being used. Far from it! Besides continuing to update already existing models as cost estimates and situations change, new models of new investment proposals are still being built, but essentially within the existing framework. It has been found that putting together aspects of the already existing models has been sufficient to cover the problems raised by new proposals. No doubt the models are far from perfect, and with extra time, effort and cost they could be improved, but the question that must always be asked is 'Is the extra accuracy worth the extra cost?' Our collective answer has been 'No'. We realize the danger of trying to 'shoehorn' a problem into an already existing model, but equally we realize the danger of suboptimizing by incurring a greater cost in analysis than we can expect to save as a result.

Appendix to Chapter 12

Exhibit 12.1 Specimen Output Reports

ST1B0007 C O R P O R A T E F I N A N C I A L M O D E L J.DOLBEAR, OR GROUP, BLUE CIRCLE IND

14/ 4/80 SAMPLE MODEL. NEW KILN STUDY CASHFLOW STATEMENT

DURING YEAR	1981 (£'000)	1982 (£'000)	1983 (£'000)	1984 (£'000)	1985 (£'000)	1986 (£'000)	1987 (£'000)	1988 (£'000)	1989 (£'000)
TRADING PROFIT	7021	21284	23457	34008	34547	34066	34587	34439	34290
INVESTMENT INCOME	1309	1300	1300	1300	1300	1300	1300	1300	1300
DEPRECIATION	4394	10598	13050	15085	14546	15027	14506	14654	14803
FINANCE CHARGES	0	9954	7496	6098	4908	3766	2587	1535	1154
	------	------	------	------	------	------	------	------	------
	12724	23228	30311	44295	45485	46627	47806	48858	49239
TAXATION	4511	0	0	0	12138	14461	15282	16085	16797
DIVIDEND	1940	2160	2970	2970	2970	2970	2970	2970	2970
	------	------	------	------	------	------	------	------	------
GROSS CASHFLOW	6273	21068	27341	41325	30377	29196	29554	29803	29472
	------	------	------	------	------	------	------	------	------
NEW EQUITY CAPITAL	0	5000	5500	0	0	0	0	0	0
INCREASE IN SHARE PREMIUM	0	0	-5500	0	0	0	0	0	0
NEW PREFERENCE CAPITAL	0	0	-5500	0	0	0	0	0	0
ACQUIRE 1 ST. DEBENTURES	0	10000	0	0	0	0	0	0	0
REDEEM 1 ST. DEBENTURES	0	0	2150	2150	3150	3150	3150	3150	3150
ACQUIRE ACC INT ON 1ST DBNT	1405	1755	600	600	0	0	0	0	0
REDEEM ACC INT ON 1ST DBNT	0	0	491	491	646	646	646	646	646

ACQUIRE DEBENTURE	8000	0	0	0	0	0	0	0	0
REDEEM DEBENTURE	0	0	0	1500	0	0	500	500	500
ACQUIRE VARIOUS BANK LOANS	0	43100	0	0	0	0	0	0	0
REDEEM VARIOUS BANK LOANS	0	0	0	13420	7420	7420	7420	7420	0
ACQUIRE SUPPLIER CREDIT	6782	0	0	0	0	0	0	0	0
REDEEM SUPPLIER CREDIT	0	0	3183	3183	3183	3183	3183	0	0
ACQUIRE BUYER CREDIT	0	10000	0	0	0	0	0	0	0
REDEEM BUYER CREDIT	0	0	0	2000	2000	2000	2000	2000	0
TOTAL INCREASE OF CAPITAL	16187	69855	-10724	-22144	-16399	-16399	-16899	-13716	-4296
BUILDINGS AT NEW WORKS	1253	6052	3009	303	0	0	0	0	0
PLANT AT EXISTING WORKS	4347	3000	3000	4000	4000	4000	4000	4000	4000
PLANT AT NEW WORKS	48108	23294	12370	7075	3500	3500	3500	3500	3500
PREPROD FIN CHARGES	3768	0	0	-3768	0	0	0	0	0
COMMITMENT FEES	55	55	0	-110	0	0	0	0	0
WORKING CAPITAL NET INCREASE	2646	5008	1455	1772	0	0	2000	0	0
INCREASE IN TRADE INVESTMENT	477	-500	-500	0	0	0	0	0	0
NET CASHFLOW	-38194	54014	-2717	9909	6478	5297	3155	8587	17676
OPENING BALANCE	-13404	-51598	2416	-301	9608	16086	21383	24538	33125
CLOSING BALANCE	-51598	2416	-301	9608	16086	21383	24538	33125	50801

(a) Cash-flow statement

ST1B0007 C O R P O R A T E F I N A N C I A L M O D E L J.DOLBEAR, OR GROUP, BLUE CIRCLE IND

14/ 4/80 SAMPLE MODEL NEW KILN STUDY BALANCE SHEET

AT END OF YEAR	1980 (£'000)	1981 (£'000)	1982 (£'000)	1983 (£'000)	1984 (£'000)	1985 (£'000)	1986 (£'000)	1987 (£'000)	1988 (£'000)	1989 (£'000)
ORDINARY CAPITAL	25000	25000	30000	35500	35500	35500	35500	35500	35500	35500
RESERVES	19759	25929	35589	44380	58482	71990	85338	99583	114020	128305
PREFERENCE CAPITAL	5500	5500	5500	0	0	0	0	0	0	0
	------	------	------	------	------	------	------	------	------	------
TOTAL SHAREHOLDERS CAPITAL	50259	56429	71089	79880	93982	107490	120838	135083	149520	163805
DEBENTURES & LOANS	32733	48920	107951	85807	70008	53609	36710	22994	18698	9902
	------	------	------	------	------	------	------	------	------	------
	82992	105349	179040	165687	163990	161099	157548	158077	168218	173707
	------	------	------	------	------	------	------	------	------	------

CURRENT ASSETS										
STOCKS	12335	15500	15500	15500	16000	16000	16000	16000	16000	16000
DEBTORS	2969	3500	3500	3500	4000	4000	4000	6000	6000	6000
CASH	1174	0	2416	0	9608	16086	21383	24538	33125	50801
	------	------	------	------	------	------	------	------	------	------
	16478	19000	21416	19000	29608	36086	41383	46538	55125	72801
CURRENT LIABILITIES										
CREDITORS	10547	11597	6589	5134	4362	4362	4362	4362	4362	4362
BANK OVERDRAFT	14578	51598	0	301	0	0	0	0	0	0
LOAN REPAYMENTS	0	0	5824	22744	16399	16399	16899	13716	4296	8796
TAXATION	4511	0	0	0	12138	14461	15282	16085	16797	17181
DIVIDEND	1940	2160	2970	2970	2970	2970	2970	2970	2970	2970
	------	------	------	------	------	------	------	------	------	------
	31576	65355	15383	31149	35869	38192	39513	37133	28425	33309
WORKING CAPITAL	-15098	-46355	6033	-12149	-6261	-2106	1870	9405	26700	39492
WORK IN PROGRESS	47421	96782	30536	41776	0	0	0	0	0	0
FIXED ASSETS	49546	49499	137493	131582	169651	162605	155078	148072	140918	133615
PREPROD FIN CHARGES	0	3768	3768	3768	0	0	0	0	0	0
COMMITMENT FEES	0	55	110	110	0	0	0	0	0	0
TRADE INVESTMENTS	1123	1600	1100	600	600	600	600	600	600	600
	------	------	------	------	------	------	------	------	------	------
	82992	105349	179040	165687	163990	161099	157548	158077	168218	173707
	------	------	------	------	------	------	------	------	------	------

(b) Balance sheet

ST1B0007 CORPORATE FINANCIAL MODEL J.DOLBEAR, OR GROUP, BLUE CIRCLE IND

14/ 4/80 SAMPLE MODEL. NEW KILN STUDY PROFIT AND LOSS ACCOUNT

FOR YEAR	1981 (£'000)	1982 (£'000)	1983 (£'000)	1984 (£'000)	1985 (£'000)	1986 (£'000)	1987 (£'000)	1988 (£'000)	1989 (£'000)
NEW WORKS									
SALES VOLUME ('000 TONNES)	93	575	700	1050	1050	1050	1050	1050	1050
TURNOVER	3820	28750	35000	52500	52500	52500	52500	52500	52500
VARIABLE COSTS	1209	7475	9100	13650	13650	13650	13650	13650	13650
FIXED COSTS EX. DEPRECIATION	817	5151	5151	5400	5400	5400	5400	5400	5400
EXCESS OF INCOME OVER EXPEND	1794	16124	20749	33450	33450	33450	33450	33450	33450
OLD WORKS									
SALES VOLUME ('000 TONNES)	740	750	750	750	750	750	750	750	750
TURNOVER	30592	37500	37500	37500	37500	37500	37500	37500	37500
VARIABLE COSTS	8880	9000	9000	9000	9000	9000	9000	9000	9000
FIXED COSTS EX. DEPRECIATION	10157	10157	10157	10157	10157	10157	10157	10157	10157
EXCESS OF INCOME OVER EXPEND	11555	18343	18343	18343	18343	18343	18343	18343	18343

COMPANY TOTAL									
SALES VOLUME ('000 TONNES)	833	1325	1450	1800	1800	1800	1800	1800	1800
TURNOVER	34412	66250	72500	90000	90000	90000	90000	90000	90000
VARIABLE COSTS	10089	16475	18100	22650	22650	22650	22650	22650	22650
FIXED COSTS EX. DEPRECIATION	10974	15308	15308	15557	15557	15557	15557	15557	15557
HEAD OFFICE FIXED COSTS	1934	2585	2585	2700	2700	2700	2700	2700	2700
EXCESS OF INCOME OVER EXPEND	11415	31882	36507	49093	49093	49093	49093	49093	49093
DEPRECIATION	4394	10598	13050	15085	14546	15027	14506	14654	14803
INVESTMENT INCOME	1309	1300	1300	1300	1300	1300	1300	1300	1300
FINANCE CHARGES	0	9954	7496	6098	4908	3766	2587	1535	1154
EARNINGS BEFORE TAX	8330	12630	17261	29210	30939	31600	33300	34204	34436
TAXATION	0	0	0	12138	14461	15282	16085	16797	17181
PROFIT AFTER TAX	8330	12630	17261	17072	16478	16318	17215	17407	17255
PREFERENCE DIVIDEND	660	907	0	0	0	0	0	0	0
ORDINARY DIVIDEND	1500	2063	2970	2970	2970	2970	2970	2970	2970
RETAINED PROFITS	6170	9660	8791	14102	13508	13348	14245	14437	14285

(c) Profit and loss account

ST1B0007 C O R P O R A T E F I N A N C I A L M O D E L J.DOLBEAR, OR GROUP, BLUE CIRCLE IND

14/ 4/80 SAMPLE MODEL. NEW KILN STUDY NOTES ON BALANCE SHEET

AT END OF YEAR	1981 (£'000)	1982 (£'000)	1983 (£'000)	1984 (£'000)	1985 (£'000)	1986 (£'000)	1987 (£'000)	1988 (£'000)	1989 (£'000)
INVESTMENT INCOME:									
OTHER INVESTMENTS	1309	1300	1300	1300	1300	1300	1300	1300	1300
	------	------	------	------	------	------	------	------	------
	1309	1300	1300	1300	1300	1300	1300	1300	1300
	------	------	------	------	------	------	------	------	------
RESERVES:									
BALANCE BROUGHT FORWARD	19759	25929	35589	44380	58482	71990	85338	99583	114020
RETAINED EARNINGS	6170	9660	8791	14102	13508	13348	14245	14437	14285
INCREASE IN SHARE PREMIUM	0	0	-5500	0	0	0	0	0	0
INCR. IN CAPITAL REDMPT RESV	0	0	5500	0	0	0	0	0	0
	------	------	------	------	------	------	------	------	------
	25929	35589	44380	58482	71990	85338	99583	114020	128305

FIXED ASSETS:									
GROSS BOOK VALUE B/F	98399	152107	184453	202832	214210	221710	229210	236710	244210
CAPITAL EXPENDITURE	53708	32346	18379	11378	7500	7500	7500	7500	7500
	------	------	------	------	------	------	------	------	------
GROSS BOOK VALUE C/F	152107	184453	202832	214210	221710	229210	236710	244210	251710
CUMULATIVE DEPRECIATION	5826	16424	29474	44559	59105	74132	88638	103292	118095
NET BOOK VALUE	49499	137493	131582	169651	162605	155078	148072	140918	133615
ASSETS FULLY DEPRECIATED	0	0	0	2000	8579	11579	17597	21597	25597
TAXATION:									
EARNINGS BEFORE TAX	8330	12630	17261	29210	30939	31600	33300	34204	34436
DEPRECIATION	4394	10598	13050	15085	14546	15027	14506	14654	14803
	------	------	------	------	------	------	------	------	------
	12724	23228	30311	44295	45485	46627	47806	48858	49239
ALLOWANCES FOR THIS PERIOD	32145	19620	16895	14922	13346	12664	12058	11528	11057
ALLOWANCES B/F	0	19421	15813	2397	0	0	0	0	0
TAXABLE EARNINGS	0	0	0	26976	32139	33963	35748	37330	38182
TAX AT 40.0%	0	0	0	2	2	2	2	.2	2
TAX AT 45.0%	0	0	0	12136	14459	15280	16083	16795	17179
	------	------	------	------	------	------	------	------	------
	0	0	0	12138	14461	15282	16085	16797	17181

(d) Notes on balance sheet

ST1B0007 C O R P O R A T E   F I N A N C I A L   M O D E L   J.DOLBEAR, OR GROUP, BLUE CIRCLE IND

14/ 4/80 SAMPLE MODEL. NEW KILN STUDY   FINANCIAL INDICES

YEAR	1981 (£'000)	1982 (£'000)	1983 (£'000)	1984 (£'000)	1985 (£'000)	1986 (£'000)	1987 (£'000)	1988 (£'000)	1989 (£'000)
DEBT EQUITY RATIO	87%	152%	107%	74%	50%	30%	17%	13%	6%
CURRENT RATIO	29%	139%	61%	83%	94%	105%	125%	194%	219%
QUICK RATIO	5%	38%	11%	38%	53%	64%	82%	138%	171%
OPERATING PROFIT / TURNOVER	33%	48%	50%	55%	55%	55%	55%	55%	55%
YIELD	2.9%	3.1%	3.7%	3.2%	2.8%	2.5%	2.2%	2.0%	1.8%
RETURN ON SHAREHOLDERS FUNDS	15%	18%	22%	18%	15%	14%	13%	12%	11%
RETURN ON CAPITAL EMPLOYED	6.7%	11.9%	14.2%	20.7%	21.4%	21.6%	21.9%	20.5%	19.7%
DEBT SERVICE RATIO	0.0%	210.3%	125.0%	179.8%	176.6%	176.2%	218.9%	640.1%	346.7%

INTERNAL RATE OF RETURN = 33.80%

INTERNAL RATE OF RETURN OF 20.0 % IS OBTAINED BY MULTIPLYING CONTRIBUTION BY 0.7109

END OF RUN

(e) Financial indices

Financial Modelling in Corporate Management, 2nd Edition
Edited by J. W. Bryant

13

Financial Models for Industrial Development Strategy

LEO BRESSMAN, JAMES BROWNE AND JOHN DROBNY

13.1 Introduction

The Port Authority of New York and New Jersey is a self-supporting corporate agency. It was created as the Port of New York Authority in 1921 under the terms of a bi-state treaty, and given responsibility to plan, develop, and operate terminal, transportation and other facilities of commerce, and to improve and protect the commerce of the bi-state Port without burden to the taxpayer. In 1972, the Authority's name was changed to identify more accurately its status as a bi-state agency of New York and New Jersey.

The Port Authority is responsible for operation of six interstate tunnels and bridges, the regional system of three airports and two heliports, seven marine terminals, three bus terminals, a truck terminal, the World Trade Center and a network of six Trade Development offices. In addition, the Port Authority Trans-Hudson Corporation (PATH), a subsidiary of the Port Authority, has responsibility for operation of the PATH rapid transit system, which links Newark, Jersey City and Hoboken with lower and mid-Manhattan. In total, these facilities represent an investment of close to $4 billion.

In 1978, bi-state legislation was passed to enable the Port Authority to move into a new area of endeavour-industrial development. The passage of the legislation capped two years of preliminary planning. This planning included evaluation of the economic feasibility of several inner city industrial parks, each of which was coupled with a resource recovery facility.

The Port Authority's traditional approach to evaluating the economic feasibility of a new project has been to weight annual net revenues (gross revenues less operating and maintenance expenses) expected to be generated by the project, against debt service (equal annual payments based on capital costs) that would be incurred by the project. This computation is based on single-point or 'most-likely' estimates for each of the key factors—e.g., revenues, capital costs, inflation rate. It is usually carried out for a single year, either a typical year or the first full year of operation. Implicit in this approach is the assumption that the cost and revenue flows will be relatively stable once full operation is achieved.

In a world where cost inflation rates often exceed revenue escalation, the traditional approach does not take into account some of the risks involved. Analysis based on a single 'typical' year assumes an environment in which, after a construction period, revenues and costs are stable and predictable. While this type of analysis might be acceptable for a tunnel or bridge financially supported by toll revenues, it is inappropriate for a project such as an industrial park in which cash flows are expected to vary significantly by year. Moreover, because the general area of industrial development was a new one for the Port Authority, and because there were so many uncertainties and complexities associated with developing and operating inner-city industrial parks, it was decided that the traditional approach to evaluating economic feasibility would not provide decision-makers with adequate information on the project's risks and potential returns. It was felt that what was needed was an approach that would account for the variabilities inherent in the most relevant factors, resulting in an evaluation of risk and identification of conditions yielding each possible level of return.

The objective of such a method is to provide the decision-maker with a clear picture of the relative risk (i.e. the range of possible outcomes and the probable odds of financial success or failure in light of uncertain foreknowledge). Port Authority top management also wanted to know which of the many assumptions about the future were most critical and just how much the expected financial results would be affected by changes in those key assumptions.

It seemed clear that some sort of computer simulation would be necessary. Although the technique of computer simulation had never been used at the Port Authority for financial analysis, simulation had been used regularly in operational analysis (e.g. evaluating PATH rapid transit train schedules (Browne, 1966), planning airport passenger and baggage flow at Kennedy Airport (Browne, Lui and Nanda, 1972), designing the World Trade Center elevator system (Browne and Kelly, 1968)), and was well accepted by Port Authority management. To meet the need for a more complete financial analysis, therefore, a study team, comprising staff from the Management Services, Planning and Development, and Finance Departments, developed a financial simulation model to obtain the expected return and the dispersion about this expected return for an investment proposal under given assumptions. This model was used specifically for performing risk and sensitivity analyses on one of the proposed industrial park complexes. While similar approaches have been used in the private sector (Hertz, 1964), this model represents, as far as we know, one of the first uses of such an approach to evaluation of the expected financial returns on investment in the public sector. Such analyses are especially important in organizations which, like the Port Authority, are fully self-supporting and do not have access to tax revenues for financial support.

In carrying out the overall project's financial simulation, it became clear that the resource recovery plant was of great importance in the project economics and that critical decisions had to be made on the design of the resource-recovery facilities. These decisions involved trade-offs between capital and operating costs. Because of the emphasis on decisions to be made, i.e. controllable variables, a deterministic model was used to evaluate the resource recovery facility, whereas a probabilistic model was used in the previous overall project evaluation.

The resource recovery facility would require a capital investment in excess of $100 million and site preparation for the total industrial park area might require an investment of approximately $50 million. In addition to these Port Authority expenditures, investments by industrial park tenants would bring the total to more than $500 million.

Because two distinct simulation methodologies were used, the following sections include a discussion of both. The next section addresses the probabilistic approach to the industrial park application (Bressman *et al.*, 1978), while the deterministic modelling approach of the resource recovery model is presented (Bressman, Browne and Drobny, 1980) in the following section.

13.2 Industrial Park Model

In general, the methodology used for the probabilistic model was to assign values to each of a set of critical (basic) variables in accordance with assigned probabilities, and then to calculate annual revenue and cost flows over the project's life based on these values. The yearly cash-flow data were then integrated to obtain three measures of overall financial impact. This process was repeated a number of times to provide the basis for risk and sensitivity analyses.

The development process for the model involved four components:

(1) selection of basic dynamic variables;
(2) Monte Carlo simulation;
(3) revenue/cost generator;
(4) measures of financial impact.

The following sections describe these components in some detail and outline how they were applied to the Port Authority's industrial development project.

Selection of Basic Dynamic Variables (BDVs)

The first step in building the model was to select input variables (BDVs) based on two criteria:

(a) they were expected to significantly affect the outcome of the project; and
(b) they were subject to a significant degree of uncertainty.

For the industrial park project, the following eight BDVs were chosen by a multidisciplinary study team:

(1) *Marketability schedule*—the number of years to market the industrial park to full capacity.
(2) *Resource recovery construction duration*—the number of years to construct the resource recovery plant.
(3) *Revenue inflation rate*—the annual rate at which the industrial park's revenues escalate.
(4) *Cost inflation rate*—the annual rate at which the park's capital and operating costs escalate.
(5) *Resource recovery total construction cost*—the uninflated capital cost for constructing the resource recovery plant.
(6) *Ground rent/ft²*—the annual ground rent to be charged to tenants of the industrial park.
(7) *Tipping fee*—the amount in dollars per ton that the municipality agrees to pay the Port Authority for disposal of its garbage.
(8) *Tenant power ratio*—the proportion of power produced by the resource-recovery plant to be sold by the Port Authority to tenants of the industrial park. Any remaining power would be sold to the local utility.

These eight variables were judged by the study team as the most critical out of fifty variables identified in the formulae for calculating annual revenues and costs.

Monte Carlo Simulation

After the BDVs were selected, an uncertainty profile (probability distribution) was developed for each. Because of the subjective nature of this task, the uncertainty profiles were developed jointly by team members possessing expertise in financial, engineering and marketing areas. For the eight BDVs involved in our application, both normal (skewed and unskewed) and discrete

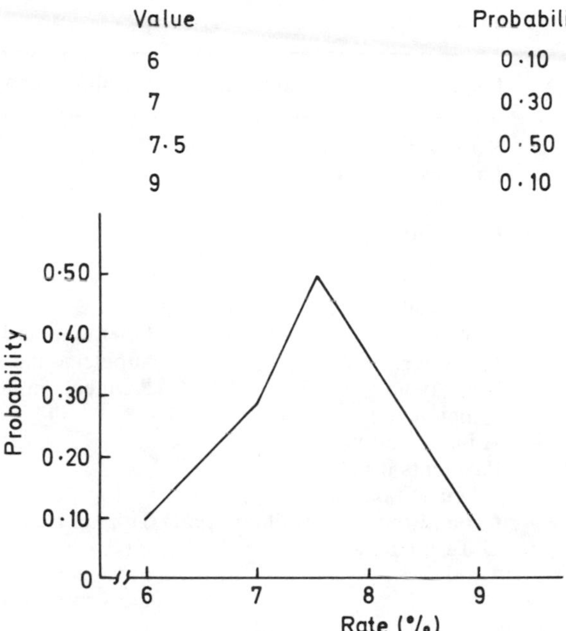

Figure 13.1 Revenue inflation rate–uncertainty profile. *Note:* The distribution shown is hypothetical

distributions were permitted. Figure 13.1 is an example of an uncertainty profile for 'revenue inflation rate', one of the project's BDVs.

Once the probability distributions were assigned, a Monte Carlo simulation was performed. For each run, individual values for each of the BDVs were selected independently, based on their individual probability distributions and random combinations of these BDV values were obtained, simulating possible future situations. For the Port Authority's industrial development project, 200 combinations were simulated to ensure a statistically valid sample. (In order to obtain an error no greater than ±0.05 in the revenue/cost ratio—one of the measures of financial impact defined in a subsequent section—with a 95 per cent confidence level, it was necessary to simulate 200 combinations.)

Revenue/Cost Generator

Once the desired number of BDV combinations were obtained, they were input, one set at a time, into the revenue/cost generator (R/C generator) program, which calculated the annual cash flows of the project over its thirty-year life. Based on the values of the BDVs, formulae contained within the R/C generator calculated yearly revenues and costs associated with the

Table 13.1 Revenue and cost centres

	Land	Buildings	Resource recovery
Capital costs	Stabilization Utilities Paving Landscaping Contingency Engineering Appraisal	Construction	Construction
Operating and maintenance costs	Selling Insurance Security and maintenance Administration Payments in lieu of taxes	None*	Operating and maintenance Supplemental fuel† Payments in lieu of taxes
Revenues	Ground rent Government aid	Building rent	Tipping fees Fuel sales Ferrous metal sales Government aid

*It is assumed that tenants will be responsible for all operating and maintenance costs related to the buildings.
†It is assumed that power will be purchased from the local utility and provided to the tenants at a reduced cost until the resource-recovery plant is operational.

construction and operation of the industrial park complex. Table 13.1 contains a list of the revenues and costs generated.

Each of these revenues and costs were generated by appropriate formulae stored in the R/C generator program. Many were dependent on one or more of the BDV values selected. As an example, land selling costs (in thousands of dollars) were calculated as follows. (Please note that the numerical values stated below are hypothetical.)

For years 1 and 2:
$\text{cost}_1 = 500$
$\text{cost}_2 = 450$
For years 3 to X:

$$\text{cost}_i = \left(\text{cost}_{i-1} - \frac{450 - 300}{X - 2}\right) Y_i,$$

where X is the first year of full occupancy (one of the BDVs) and Y_i is the appropriate cost inflation factor (another of the BDVs) for Year i.

For years $(X + 1)$ to 30:
$\text{cost}_i = 50Y_i.$

After formulae such as the above were used to calculate all of the costs and revenues listed in Table 13.1, the R/C generator produced output consisting of many sets of combined annual revenues and costs over the thirty years of the project's life.

Measures of Financial Impact

The next task was to calculate annual financial measures for each set of cash flows (revenues and costs), generated in the previous step, which allowed runs of the model to be compared easily. This task required that some criteria of financial success or failure be defined. Three measures were chosen:

(1) *Present-valued revenue/cost ratio (R/C ratio)*—This measure was obtained by discounting all revenues and costs to present value, using the projected cost of capital as the discount rate. The ratio was then calculated by dividing the cumulative present value of thirty years of net revenues (revenues minus operating costs) by the cumulative present value of capital costs.
(2) *Internal rate of return (IRR)*—The discount rate at which the cumulative present value of revenues equalled the cumulative present value of total costs (capital and operating).
(3) *Time-valued payback year (TVP year)*—The first year in which the cumulative present value of revenues equals the cumulative present value of total costs (i.e. the time at which the capital funds invested would be recovered through net revenue flows).

Risk Analysis

Figure 13.2 contains a flowchart which shows how the simulation was used to perform the risk analysis. After the 200 iterations were completed and the corresponding measures of financial impact calculated, frequency distributions and risk profiles were plotted for each of the measures. The expected (average) return of the project, and the dispersion (variability) about this expected return were then determined. The risk profiles (probability distributions) provided management with the probability that the investment would provide a return greater or less than a certain amount.

Figure 13.3 is a frequency distribution for the range of outcome values of the IRR of the project. (Please note that while the format used is the same, the numerical values presented here are purely hypothetical.) As shown in the illustration, the range of IRR values generated by the model approximates a skewed Normal distribution around a mean of 15.15 per cent, with a standard deviation of 3.824 per cent.

The likelihoods of either achieving or bettering specified IRRs were determined from the risk profiles like Figure 13.4. The risk profile shows about

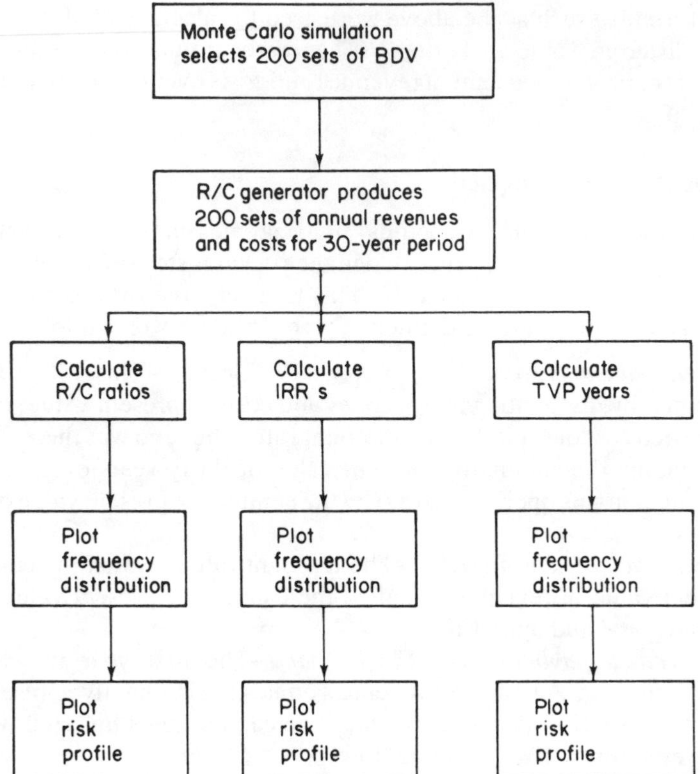

Figure 13.2 Industrial park risk analysis application—flowchart

a 96 per cent chance of achieving or bettering an IRR of 8.25 per cent (a projected cost of capital), and about a 50 per cent chance of achieving or bettering an IRR of 15.25 per cent. (These values are also hypothetical.)

Sensitivity Analysis

In addition to plotting and analysing the results of the iterations, sensitivity-analyses were performed to determine which BDVs were most critical to the project's financial outcome. The sensitivity analyses were performed by iterating the R/C generator over the range of values for a single BDV, while holding the other BDVs constant at their mean values. The measures of financial impact were then calculated for each iteration and compared to determine the extent to which the individual variable would affect the results.

The statistical range of the resulting set of R/C ratios was used as a measure of the relative impact of the variable on the project's outcome. In addition to

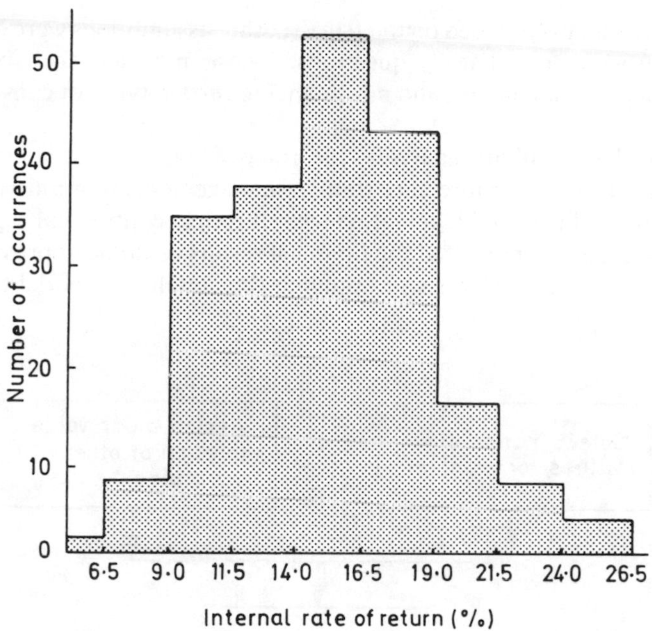

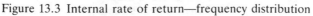

Figure 13.3 Internal rate of return—frequency distribution

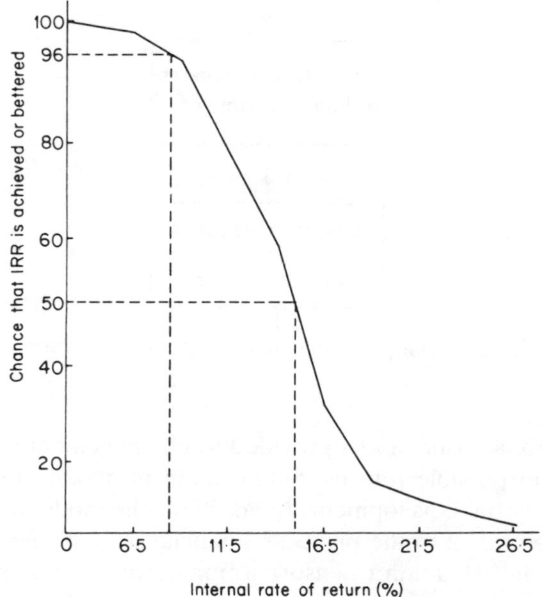

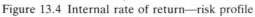

Figure 13.4 Internal rate of return—risk profile

the sensitivity analyses based on the BDVs, other assumptions were changed to provide answers to 'what if' questions. These included such changes as eliminating government aid, and not financing certain types of construction in the park.

Through the sensitivity analyses, the relative importance of the different BDVs was determined. More importantly, management attention was directed toward those which could be influenced through contractual agreements, controls or negotiations so that the financial results could be improved. Figure 13.5 flowcharts the mechanics of applying the simulation model to perform sensitivity analyses.

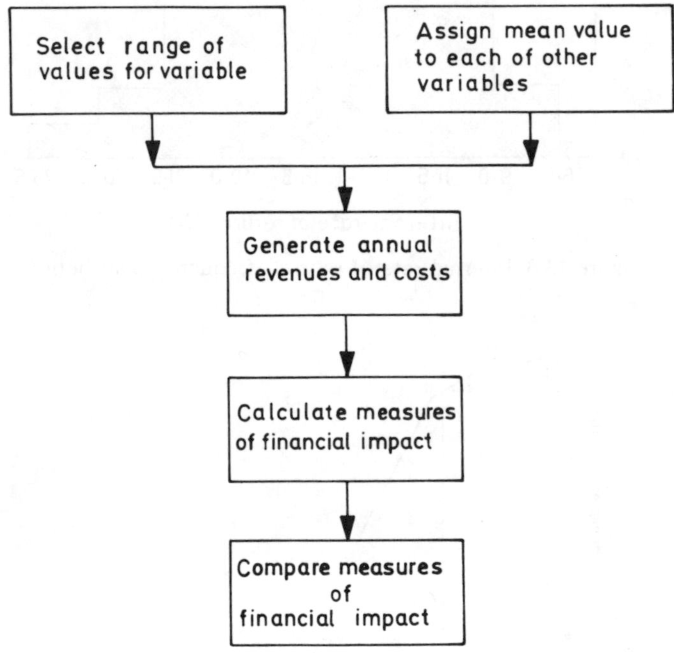

Figure 13.5 Industrial park sensitivity analysis application—flowchart

The initial probabilistic model provided top management with information on the risks and possible returns, aiding them in making the GO/NO GO decision on industrial development. In addition, the model highlighted those areas that were critical to the project's financial success. These areas would require further investigation to ensure a financially feasible project. One of these areas was the resource recovery component of the industrial park project.

13.3 Resource Recovery Model

The resource recovery deterministic model was designed to simulate three resource recovery technology options: Mass Burning, RDF 'A', which consists of producing refuse derived fuel (RDF) strictly for sale, and RDF 'B' in which some (up to 100 per cent) of the RDF produced is burned at the site. The model was designed to analyse a plant built and operated in either New York or New Jersey.

Input The input parameters required to drive the model fall into two categories: primary and secondary. Primary input must be entered interactively at the terminal every time the model is run. Once the model is loaded and executed, it will begin prompting for the primary input. Figure 13.6 contains a sample run sheet showing this prompting sequence. The first question asks the user to select one of the three technology options. Once this selection is made, the user is prompted for the number of tons of solid waste to be processed daily and the number of days per year that the plant will be operational.

After specification of the primary variables, a file consisting of secondary variables relating to the chosen technology is read into the model. There are approximately 200 secondary variables covering all areas including efficiency parameters for boilers and turbines, sale prices for steam and electricity during peak and off-peak hours, sale prices for recovered materials, operations and maintenance costs, inflation factors and capital costs for various components. The values that are read into the model for each of these variables are the *most-likely* estimates compiled by experts in the engineering, financial and marketing areas. Once these variables are read into the model, the user is given the opportunity to change any combination of variables interactively to reflect the scenario or design alternative that is being analysed.

After changes have been made in the secondary variable file, the user is prompted to select a turbine configuration (automatic extraction, condensing and/or non-condensing) and to select the number and size of turbines desired for the run. Once these design variables have been entered, the input stage is complete and the simulation begins.

Logic Figure 13.7 contains a flowchart of the simulation logic performed by the model. The model itself consists of mathematical formulae which generate annual revenues and costs associated with the construction and operation of a resource recovery plant. The formulae generate these annual cash flows over a thirty-year period, based on the values that are input for the primary and secondary variables. These cash flows are then reduced to several overall financial measures and ratios and then assembled into a report.

```
RRFS13 07/24/80 11:29:21
WELCOME TO THE RESOURCE RECOVERY FINANCIAL SIMULATOR–VERSION 1
ENTER THE PROCESS YOU WISH TO CONSIDER:
1––MASS BURN
2––RDF A
3––RDF B
?
1
ENTER THE NUMBER OF TONS OF MSW PER DAY:
IN THE FORMAT:    MUNICIPALITY, PRIVATE
?
2000, 1500
ENTER THE NUMBER OF MSW COLLECTION DAYS PER YEAR:
?
365
ENTER THE NUMBER OF OPERATING DAYS PER YEAR:
?
302
DO YOU WANT A LISTING OF THE MOST-LIKELY VALUES FOR THE VARIABLES? Y/N
?
N
HOW MANY VARIABLES DO YOU WISH TO CHANGE? (IF NONE ENTER 0)
?
1
ENTER:    VARIABLE #, NEW VALUE
?
17,.5
WARNING:    YOUR CAPITAL COSTS SHOULD REFLECT A PLANT CAPACITY
OF                  5324.125                TONS/DAY
DO YOU WISH TO ALTER YOUR CAPITAL COSTS –– Y/N
?
N
ENTER THE TURBINE CONFIGURATION YOU WISH TO CONSIDER:
1–––AUTOMATIC EXTRACTION
2–––CONDENSING AND NON-CONDENSING
?
1
YOUR PEAK KWH DEMAND/HR IS:            59000
ENTER THE # OF AUTO EXTRACT. TURBINES
YOU WANT IN OPERATION AND THE MW RATING
IN THE FORMAT:    # OF TURBINES, MW RATING
?
2,30
```

Figure 13.6 Resource recovery sample run sheet

One of the more complex parts of the model involves the mass burning formulae dealing with energy generation and sale. In this section, the model uses heat balance equations and turbine performance factors to calculate the quantities of process steam, heating steam, and electricity produced, given all the input parameters specified. The model then determines the revenue flow resulting from the sale of these types of energy. This module is critical since it deals with the design of the cost-intensive components of the plant.

Output Once the simulation is performed and the cash flows generated, a financial report is produced containing the following:

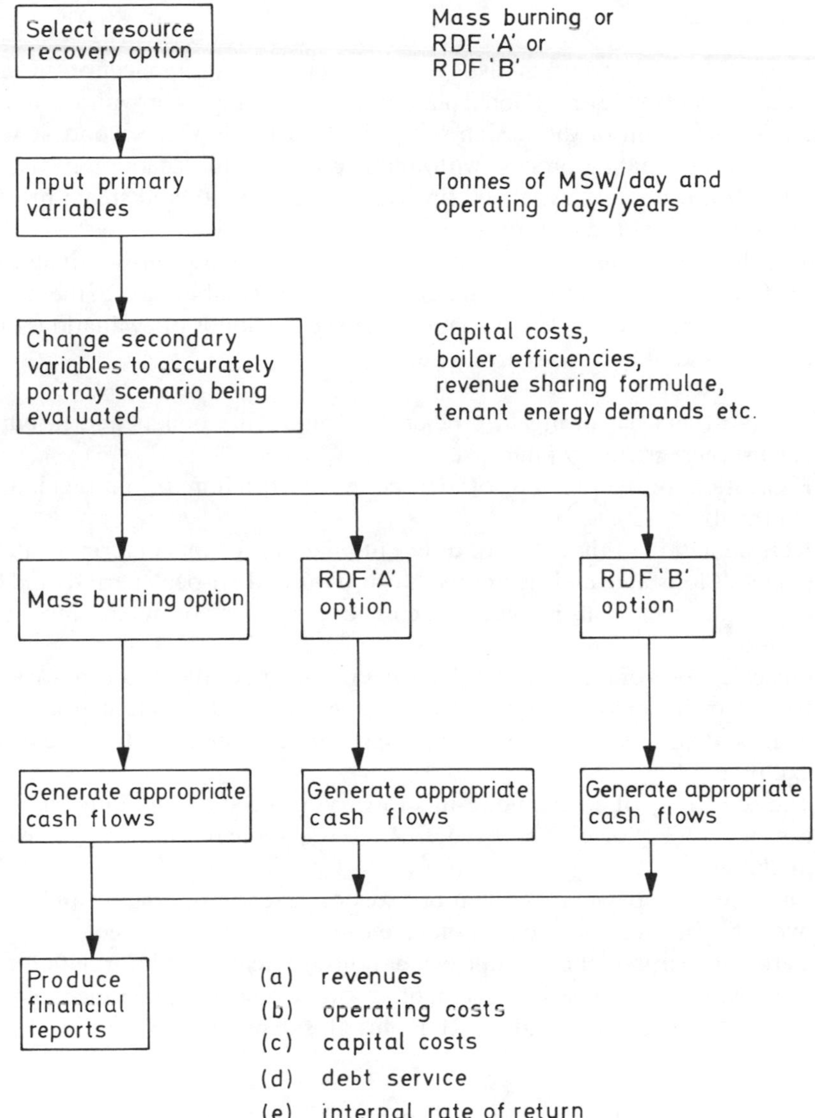

Figure 13.7 Resource recovery financial simulation—logic flowchart

(1) The primary variables used for this run;
(2) A record of the changes made to the secondary most-likely file;
(3) Annual cash flows;
(4) Financial measures including debt service coverage and IRR.

Applications

The resource recovery deterministic model had two major applications. First, it served as an aid in the operational planning of the facility by providing a quick economic evaluation of the design strategies and trade-offs. Second, it was used for the negotiating process with municipalities, utilities and tenants, to help establish economic variables, tipping fees, electricity and steam prices, and prices for recovered materials.

While the deterministic model provides the user with a print-out of all two hundred stored values and allows the user to alter any combination of them, the following list will give an idea of some of the specific kinds of evaluations and 'what if' analyses that can be carried out.

(1) Trade-off analysis of higher-efficiency, high-quality boilers and turbines against their greater capital costs.
(2) Evaluation of the effects of delays in construction or in regulatory approvals.
(3) Determination of the effect of different mixes of tenants in terms of their demands for steam and electricity during peak and off-peak periods and by day of the week. This involves the costs of generating or purchasing these utilities.
(4) Once the costs of these utilities have been estimated, the effects of various cost-recovery methods and the economic effects of different prices for peak and off-peak process steam, heating steam and electricity can be explored.
(5) The sensitivity of economic results to varying inflation and interest rates can be gauged for different types of lease agreement and cost-recovery methods.
(6) The effects of payments in lieu of taxes or revenue sharing formulae on overall debt coverage and economic feasibility can be evaluated.
(7) Through a variety of economic evaluations, critical input information can be provided for the basic decision on resource recovery plant technology—mass burning, total RDF or RDF plus on-site process generation.

13.4 Appraisal of the Simulation Approach

When there are a number of variables that can significantly affect the financial results, it is unrealistic and incomplete to analyse results based on a single projection of most likely results. If there are eight important variables, each with three possible values, there are over 6000 ($3^8 = 6561$) possible outcomes. It does not seem reasonable to base all of one's planning on one possible outcome, any more than one would bet on the assumption that seven will come up on a roll of two dice. The fact that this is the most likely outcome should not be the end of the analysis, but the beginning. How likely is it? What are the other possible outcomes? What are their financial implications and how likely are they? Just as it is necessary to consider all possible outcomes in betting situations to determine if a wager is fair or favourable, the range of possible financial results and their likelihoods should be evaluated to determine whether an investment provides a fair or favourable return. It is important to be aware of the possible outcomes, understand how they can arise, and develop plans to cope with both favourable and unfavourable contingencies. If necessary, one may restructure the project or investment or devise means to identify undesirable conditions and cut possible losses by taking action. In the analysis of projected financial results for the industrial park, it became clear, for example, that low tipping fees led to very poor financial results. Therefore, a minimal level of tipping fee was necessary to ensure a financially viable project.

The use of computer simulation made it possible to evaluate a large number of possible future situations and to analyse their expected results in terms of discounted cash flow and rate of return on investment. By incorporating the known relationships in a computer program, calculations that would be impractical to carry out manually are produced at great speed and with accuracy. It provides a means for easily determining the sensitivity of results to changes in each of the variables. Furthermore, results are automatically summarized and presented in a form designed for the management user.

In the resource recovery application, the use of the computer provided flexibility in selecting assumptions about both management decisions and outside factors. The complete financial analysis was redone automatically and quickly for any combination of decisions and variables specified. Thus, the use of the model facilitates the handling of a complete set of analyses rather than the few limited cases that could be processed manually.

The benefits of modelling and simulation of financial results are by no means limited to the particular objectives, measures and projects that were discussed here. The industrial development project methodology is a straightforward application of a widely used approach. It is essentially the application of Monte Carlo simulation and expected values to discounted cash flow and rate of return analysis. The heart of the model was based on the conventional relationships used to estimate cash flow. The method is potentially applicable to any project or investment involving uncertainties that can significantly affect financial results. In addition to providing information on possible outcomes at the time investments are made, simulation can be used to re-evaluate investments when expectations change.

The resource recovery application was less conventional in its use of a deterministic model. This type of model was more appropriate because the emphasis was on decisions, i.e. choices, rather than uncontrollable variations. Balances and trade-offs involved in key plant design choices were evaluated in a trial-and-error process that also allowed for variations in about two hundred other variables affecting the outcome. Unlike the industrial park application in which many of the basic formulae and relationships were known at the outset from the previous 'most likely' financial projection, the resource recovery model required learning and research on the technologies involved and the development of both engineering and economic models to estimate results. This required a larger study team, incorporating members from the Engineering and Risk Management units. It also required a literature search and a series of visits to operating source recovery facilities and meetings with equipment manufacturers to obtain the necessary information to develop the model. Similarly, the validation of this model required more reviews to ensure that all aspects of this new endeavour were modelled accurately.

The use of simulation models for complex, but deterministic, operational or financial analyses is often overlooked because the Monte Carlo capability is so well known and easily implemented. It is often desirable, however, to avoid the random variations in results that accompany a Monte Carlo simulation. In an operational simulation of the World Trade Center elevator system, for example, the Monte Carlo demand generation program was run separately from the deterministic model that simulated elevator movements and evaluated system performance (waiting times by floor and direction) (Browne and Kelly, 1968). Thus, any changes in results were attributable directly to differences in the elevator control system logic or in the floor assignments. A deterministic simulation often provides the only practical way to model a complex operation accurately and obtain comparative estimates of service levels based on given assumptions on design and staffing. The deterministic approach shows directly the effects of decisions without the confounding effects of other variables. Of course, any deterministic simulation can be converted to a Monte Carlo one by 'feeding' it input through a random-number generator to provide probabilistic analyses if this is desired.

In general, either type of simulation enables one to analyse a complex situation without making the simplifying assumptions often required in an analytical model. In simulation, the model is specially designed to correspond to the nature of the situation and the specific needs of the decision maker.

Simulation provides much greater flexibility to the model builder, calculation costs are continually decreasing as computers become faster, and the methodology is both easier to understand and better suited to meet any specific information requirements of the manager. For these reasons, analytical models, valuable as they may be for obtaining approximate solutions and as aids in conceptualizing certain problems, will be used less as time goes on. The methods and ways of thinking of pre-computer days will gradually be replaced by simulation, a methodology that takes advantage of the new computer capabilities that are now available. Simulation provides a powerful new way of dealing with the world, analysing quantitative relationships and obtaining information on which to base decisions.

This contrasts with many analytical models which require one to compromise on assumptions to fit the problem to a pre-conceived model for which a solution method is readily available.

13.5 Conclusions

The main benefits of the models consist of an increased capability for more complete analysis and the availability of specific information on the sensitivity of results to key decisions and variables.

These financial simulation models represent the first attempts in the Port Authority to make explicit (i.e. quantify) the risk associated with a major capital investment proposal. The essential difference between the simulation method and the Port Authority's conventional approach to financial analysis is the fact that with the former, many combinations of values of the key variables are evaluated to determine the full range of possible outcomes. For project analyses like the one described, in which no single measure of return is typical or fully indicative of the total project's future prospects, and in which there are many uncertain elements, the simulation approach is superior to the conventional method. In addition to providing the decision-maker with important information on the risks and potential returns of a specific project, it also generates insight that is valuable in determining appropriate courses of action for the implementation phase of the project. This is made possible by the sensitivity analysis and evaluation of alternative scenarios to determine the combinations of conditions most favourable to the project's outcome.

The application of financial simulation methodology was widely accepted by both planners and decision-makers, who continue to use the approach for other proposed projects. It is not practical to estimate the monetary values of benefits derived from the models since they were used as part of the planning process and there is no way to accurately evaluate the alternative decisions and results that might have occurred if they had not been used. It is clear, however, that these studies have fostered a significant change in the way the Port Authority views and evaluates projects. Both the Finance Department and the new Office of Strategic Planning now plan to use risk and sensitivity analysis to evaluate the economics of individual project proposals and the methodology is presently being applied to evaluating a department's long-range (ten-year) forecast.

13.6 Postscript

The studies outlined in this chapter were conducted almost ten years ago. The continuing relevance of this material to today's environment, may be judged in terms of three major features: context, method and technology. The authors feel that in these terms the material maintains its applicability in today's times.

First, the types of situations where simulation modelling would be an appropriate tool still exist today. In fact, recent volatility of the financial markets (interest rates, costs of capital), wildly fluctuating real estate, construction and labour costs, and increasing market uncertainties, clearly make it more difficult to forecast intuitively the profitability of a proposed capital project. In addition, new technologies, coupled with innovative financing options have multiplied the number of scenarios and alternatives to evaluate. These developments make simulation modelling an attractive tool to assist in the evaluation process.

Secondly, the theory and methodology used in the models highlighted in the discussion above are still valid today. The use of probability distributions to represent the uncertainties of input variables is certainly sound provided that the data used to construct the distributions are credible. The use of Monte Carlo simulation for sampling is also a widely accepted modelling technique. Finally, the output measures used in the financial models (Net Present Value, Internal Rate of Return, Payback Year), are still commonly accepted financial measures of profitability.

The only major component of change since the original account was written is the vehicle used to execute the modelling process. At the time the original work was conducted, the models were developed on a large time-sharing computer system. A large part of the code was developed in Fortran using Fortran statements as well as Fortran statistical subroutines. In today's environment, with the advent of personal computers, the modelling systems could easily be developed at far less cost in terms of CPU resources, and could probably be developed a lot quicker. There are many financial modelling packages available for personal computers that would greatly facilitate the development of the models. This would free the model developers from the burden of coding so they could spend more time on model definition and on collecting more accurate input data to drive the model, therefore yielding more realistic results.

References and Bibliography

Baumol, W. J. (1972). *Economic Theory and Operations Analysis*, Prentice-Hall, Englewood Cliffs, New Jersey.

Bressman, L. H., Browne, J. J., Nanninga, C. L. and Weintrob, B. (1978). 'Financial simulation model: assessing project risk at the Port Authority', *Proceedings of 1978 Winter Simulation Conference*, Miami, December 1978.

Bressman, L. H., Browne, J. J. and Drobny, J. (1980). 'A financial simulation model for a resource recovery plant' paper presented at Joint National Meeting of the Institute of Management Science & Operations Research Society of America, Washington, DC, May 1980.

Browne, J. J. (1966). 'Simulation of public transportation operations', *Proceedings of First Annual Conference on Simulation in Business and Public Health*, New York, March 1966.

Browne, J. J. and Kelly, J. (1968). 'Simulation of elevator system for the world's tallest buildings', *Transportation Science*, February.

Browne, J. J., Lui, R. and Nanda, R. (1972). 'Simulation of passenger arrivals at airports', *Industrial Engineering*, March.

DeGarmo, E. P. and Canada, J. R. (1973). *Engineering Economy*, Macmillan, New York.

Helfert, E. A. (1972). *Techniques of Financial Analysis*, Richard D. Irwin, Homewood, Illinois.

Hertz, D. B. (1964). 'Risk analysis in capital investment', *Harvard Business Review*, **42**(1), 95–116.

Hertz, D. B. (1968). 'Investment policies that pay off', *Harvard Business Review*, **46**(1), 96–108.

Newendorp, P. D. (1975). *Decision Analysis for Petroleum Exploration*, Petroleum Publishing, Tulsa, Oklahoma.

Van Horne, J. C. (1974). *Financial Management and Policy*, Prentice-Hall, Englewood Cliffs, New Jersey.

Van Horne, J. C. (1977). *Fundamentals of Financial Management*, Prentice-Hall, Englewood Cliffs, New Jersey.

PART 4
MODEL TEMPLATES

Financial Modelling in Corporate Management, 2nd Edition
Edited by J. W. Bryant

14

A Computerized Financial Planning Model for Health Maintenance Organizations

JOHN COLEMAN AND FRANK KAMINSKY

14.1 Introduction

The American health care system is massive. In 1984 it was ranked as the second largest industry in the USA, employing 7.9 million people, and it was also one of the fastest growing (faster even than the computer industry, with a increase of 87 per cent in the number of workers between 1970 and 1984). Health care American-style is also very expensive, costing $387.4 billion (10.6 per cent of GNP) in 1984, and recent estimates show that the USA is now spending annually more than $1500 per person; if the cost increases, by public and private spenders alike, continue to go unchecked, the annual bill for the nation's health will exceed $1000 billion by the turn of the century.

Health care in the USA is delivered by a wide spectrum of providers and institutions and, although there is some informal connection, they are not linked together in any systematic way. Services are provided in a variety of outpatient and inpatient care settings: the former includes the doctor's office, group practice clinics, hospital outpatient clinics, neighbourhood health centres, free-standing surgery centres and community health clinics; the latter, short- and long-stay hospitals, nursing homes and other facilities such as those for the mentally retarded and emotionally disturbed. The balance of this provision between state or local governments, non-profit, and profit-making organizations, varies from sector to sector. However, because of the way health care is financed by the government and private health insurance plans, high priority is assigned to acute care, with a noticeable lack of attention to prevention and continuing primary (early detection and routine care) provision.

Even though large sums are provided by public funds, a large part of the US health care system is controlled by the private sector and in 1986 private businesses are expected to pay about one-quarter of the nation's health care bill. Because of high annual increases (recently of about 11–12 per cent annually) in expenditures, both the public and private sectors have been prompted to make major changes in the way health care is financed in the future (Klett, 1986). The public sector has instituted major changes and benefits, with more cost sharing with the recipients of their programs, and use prospectively net fixed payments for covered services, while in 1974 the Medicare programme shifted its payments from approved costs to fixed payment amounts based upon the diagnosis and condition of the patient when admitted to the hospitals. The health care system in the USA is now undergoing those drastic economic and social changes that normally accompany deregulation.

14.2 Health-maintenance Organizations (HMOs)

During the late 1960s and early 1970s, Federal policymakers became increasingly concerned about ways to curb the chronic inflation of medical expenditures and about methods to guarantee consumers a better return for the increased cost of health care. Numerous controls evolved, many of which were designed to change the financial and organization structure of the delivery system. One initiative to curb spiralling costs and to reduce the inefficiencies in the delivery system was increased Federal support to create organized systems of health care that would provide a comprehensive range of health-maintenance and treatment services to voluntarily enrolled populations in exchange for fixed and prepaid periodic payments. Such an organization, called a Health Maintenance Organization (HMO), received national attention in early 1971 as President Nixon sought the support of Congress because, in his words:

> HMOs simultaneously attack many of the problems comprising the health-care crisis. They emphasize prevention and early care: they provide incentives for holding down costs and for increasing the productivity of resources: they offer opportunities for improving the quality of care; they provide a means of improving the geographic distribution of care; and by mobilizing private capital and management talent, they reduce the need for federal funds and direct controls. ... Because HMO revenues are fixed, their incentives are to keep patients well, for they benefit from patient well-days, not sickness. Their entire cost structure is geared to preventing illness and, failing that, to promoting prompt recovery

through the least costly services consistent with maintaining quality. (US Department of Health, Education and Welfare, 1971)

While such organizations can have different sponsors and take on various organization patterns, all of them are designed to integrate, in a balanced structure, the following basic ingredients:

(1) A group of *consumers* who desire pre-paid comprehensive medical care;
(2) A qualified group of *providers* suited to pre-paid medical practice;
(3) *A comprehensive set of medical and health-care services* that meet the needs of its consumers and are within the capacity of the providers to provide;
(4) A *medical facility or group of facilities or offices* in which to provide the necessary services;
(5) An *administrative organization* to plan, coordinate, manage and control the plan's resources;
(6) *Financial resources* for initial and continuous operation.

The generic term HMO is new but the concept has existed for more than fifty years in the form of pre-paid group practice.

In 1971 there were 33 HMO prototypes in the USA serving an estimated population of 3.6 million. Motivated by Congressional and administration support HMOs have emerged rapidly since that time, so that their number had increased to 183 by the end of 1974, and 236 by mid-1980. After investing nearly $400 million dollars in the HMO industry the Federal government discontinued its financial interest in 1981 as the private sector support was such that it began to invest billions of dollars to open HMOs throughout the country: in mid-1985 there were 393 HMOs with an enrolment of almost 19 million, while experts predict that by 1990 there will be 750 HMOs in operation with a total of 40 million enrollees (Traska, 1986).

The explosive growth of the HMO industry is supported by major businesses and labour organizations, because HMOs have the ability to provide comprehensive medical services at reasonable costs, while maintaining desired levels of care and service quality. It has been argued (Luft, 1981) that HMOs are less expensive because of their low hospital utilization rates and use of surgical procedures and the provision of more ambulatory care. The evidence continues to mount in support of HMOs as a viable economic alternative to fee-for-service medicine and as a result huge sums of capital are being pledged to start more HMOs.

The once frail HMO industry now has a bright future. While the opposition from hospitals and the medical profession hindered development at the start, most of the early problems were caused by lack of planning technology and management skills. This lack of expertise resulted in many failures: for example, between October 1974 and May 1975 more than a dozen HMOs went out of business due to financial reverses, while dozens more closed between then and 1980. Postmortems on failures and fiscal examinations of some now in danger suggest that most of the problems stem from a lack of experienced planners and managers, and a lack of planning methodologies specifically designed for HMOs.

Planning an economically viable HMO is by no means simple and the resources involved can be considerable (typically \$1–2 million to start a new HMO, with \$2–4 million needed to offset the operating deficits that accumulate before membership revenues finally exceed costs). The task of bringing together the essential ingredients of the existing health-care delivery system to create an HMO is technically complex and therefore should embody a systems-planning approach and an orderly systematic planning process. Several guides have been developed to bring an HMO to life and four major phases can be identified: feasibility study, planning, initial development, and implementation/operation. The design of an HMO requires that during this process the planning group study and evaluate, among other things, the medical and economic consequences of alternative benefit-package designs, marketing strategies, organization formats, service-use patterns and operating policies and procedures. The process which involves thousands of hours of analysis at each step, is an iterative one, with the group proceeding from one design to the next, hoping to find that one 'best' design that is economically feasible while, at the same time, meeting a number of design criteria initially set to guide the planning and decision-making processes.

The ultimate test of a soundly planned HMO is its ability to achieve quickly an enrolment level producing revenues that exceed costs and to maintain this position for each succeeding year of operation. Experience has shown that that this phenomenon does not happen immediately and that expert financial planning and management skills must be used to keep the HMO financially solvent, particularly during its formative years when it is most vulnerable.

HMO financial planning is concerned with estimating, in advance, the financial requirements and fiscal consequences of the enterprise once it has decided what is to be done. It involves an explicit economic evaluation of alternative courses of action and the selection of the 'best' acceptable alternative for implementation once planners have made policy decisions concerning how the plan is to be managed, what health-care services it will provide and so forth.

An overview of the HMO financial planning process is shown in Figure 14.1. This simplified activity chart shows that the financial needs and requirements of an HMO are outcome measures for a given set of policy decisions and assumptions relating to:

(1) *What* health services are to be covered;
(2) *Who* will be eligible to receive them;

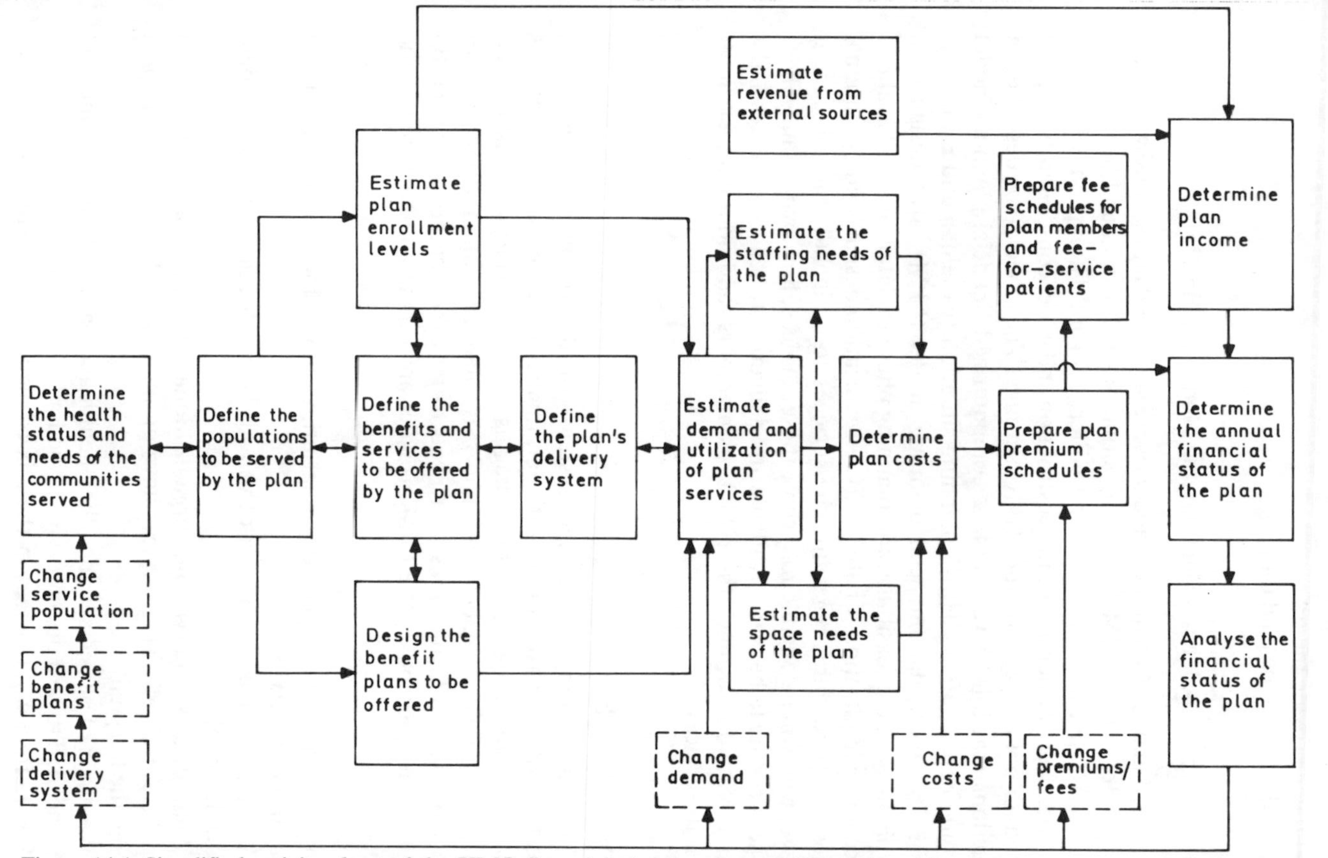

Figure 14.1 Simplified activity chart of the HMO financial planning process (Reproduced by permission of the publisher from *Ambulatory Care Systems, Volume IV, Designing Medical Services for Health Maintenance Organizations*, by John R. Coleman and Frank C. Kaminsky: Lexington, Mass.: Lexington Books, D. C. Heath and Company, Copyright 1977, D. C. Heath and Company)

(3) *Where*, *when*, and *how* they are to be provided;
(4) *Who* will provide them;
(5) *How* they are to be paid for.

14.3 Financial Planning Models for HMOs

During 1973 and 1974 computer models were suggested and several were later developed for specific HMO planning situations (Moustafa and Sears, 1974; Greene and Grimes, 1974; Hersch and Miller, 1974 and Thompson, 1974). The first models were rather simple in construction and were, consequently, neither adopted for nor adapted to other HMO settings. The model to be described in the sections that follow was the first computerized financial planning model that could be used in any HMO planning situation (Coleman and Kaminsky, 1977a). This particular financial planning model (FPM)—was designed to assist planners in the feasibility and planning phase to determine and evaluate the economic implications of alternative organization designs and operational policies and procedures regarding the services to be included in the benefit package, who will be eligible to receive these services, how, when, and where these services are to be made available and delivered by health resources in the community, and how much the HMO, its members, and non-members must pay for its services.

An Overview of the FPM

The FPM is a computer-assisted system for determining the economic implications of alternative organizational, financial and operational strategies and policies before the HMO actually begins operation. The model can be used as a simulator and is designed to provide HMO planners with rapid answers to a number of 'what if?' questions that need to be asked before a final HMO configuration is accepted. The FPM provides answers to a number of specific design questions:

(1) What will be the expected annual utilization of the plan's medical and health-care services?
(2) What is the financial impact of various hospitalization rates on the plan and hospital?
(3) What effects will various organizational structures and operational policies for delivering services have on the financial security of the plan and the hospital?
(4) What mix of physicians and allied health and paramedical personnel will be needed to be a direct service provider?
(5) What effect will changes in the mix of medical and health-care services have on yearly costs and revenues?

(6) What external funding should the plan secure during its formative years in order to meet its financial obligations?
(7) What are the effects of the plan's size, and the premium and fee-for-service schedules on annual cash flow and financial security?
(8) What co-payment and capitation fee schedules and membership levels are needed to break even within the first five years of operation?
(9) What physical resources must be made available each year to provide the services on a direct-service basis?
(10) What will be the effect of changes in the socio-economic and demographic characteristics of the subscribing population?
(11) What organizational structure and operational policies will result in low initial operation costs, low indebtedness, early break-even?
(12) What are the annual proforma cost and revenue schedules for each HMO configuration to be evaluated?

General Structure of the Model

Figure 14.2 illustrates the general structure of the model. The FPM consists of eight components or 'program modules', an edit/control program, and seven planning models: service population, demand/utilization, staff, space, cost, revenue and financial analysis. The FPM, the assumptions and the data bases used in its design and all of the modules are completely described in two volumes (Coleman and Kaminsky, 1977b, 1977c).

Input and Output

Input to the FPM consists of two data bases. One is built into the planning model (the HMO DATA FILE) and the other one is provided by the HMO planning group.

The HMO DATA FILE consists of two basic sets of data. The first consists of socio-economic and demographic data for urban and rural areas in various census regions of the country. The second contains service use rates for the different inpatient and outpatient health services a qualifying HMO may provide. Included in this file are inpatient care admission rates, physician and dentist visit rates, and the distribution of hospital admissions and physician visits by medical specialty and visit site. The utilization rates, which are by sex and age group, were obtained from a sample of operating HMOs located throughout the country. Although the HMO DATA FILE is built into the FPM, planners can modify the utilization data if some of these data do not satisfy regional or local conditions.

THE USER DATA FILE, which is also provided by the planning group, is essentially a data base defining the HMO under consideration. This data base contains 21 different sets of design data. Each set is used to indicate the design

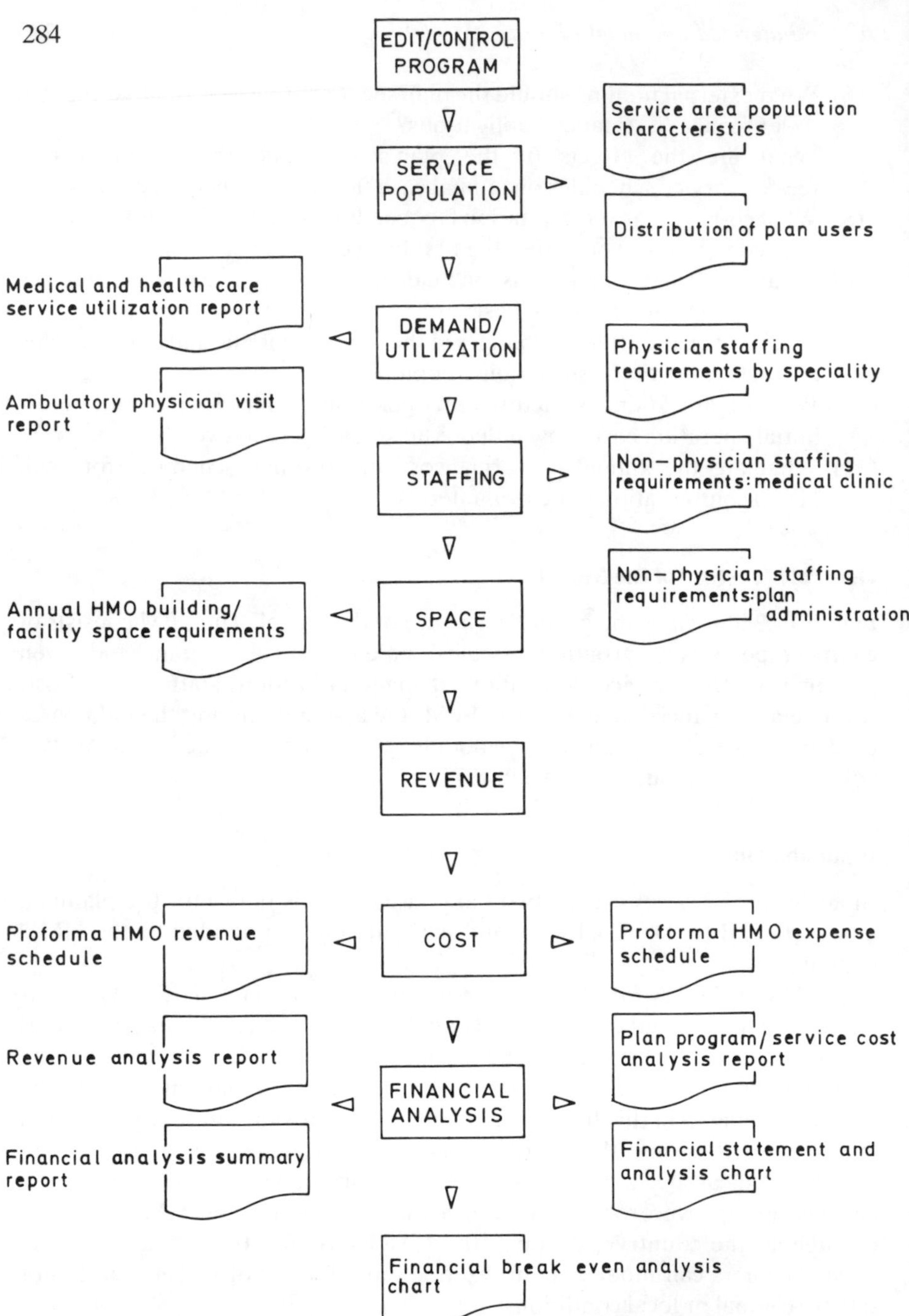

Figure 14.2 Systems diagram of the FPM (Reproduced by permission of the publisher from *Ambulatory Care Systems, Volume IV, Designing Medical Services for Health Maintenance Organizations*, by John R. Coleman and Frank C. Kaminsky: Lexington, Mass.: Lexington Books, D. C. Heath and Company, Copyright 1977, D. C. Heath and Company)

option to be made by the planners or to specify values of certain design variables and operating variables used to describe the beneficiary population, the benefit packages, monthly premiums, facility and delivery options, hospital and medical-service use rates, compensation schedules, fee schedules, fringe-benefit rates, labour turnover rates, loan and investment data, economic conditions, and organizational and operational strategies and policies. These data are provided for each of the first five years of HMO operation (Exhibit 14.1 in the Appendix lists the contents of the 21 data sets).

These inputs are operated upon by seven FPM modules. The transformation functions for the input data of each module were built with the experience data provided by many first-, second-, and third-generation HMOs.

Output from the FPM consists of 15 planning reports that contain annual and five-year summary information on:

(1) Demographics of the beneficiary population;
(2) Projected use of health and medical services by programme and physician speciality;
(3) Physician staffing requirements by speciality;
(4) Non-physician staffing requirements by programme or organization unit;
(5) Facility space needs by programme;
(6) Proforma revenue schedule by source and programme;
(7) Proforma expense schedule by programme;
(8) Cash flow and financial needs of the plan.

Details of output reports are given in the Appendix. (Exhibit 14.2 lists the different reports and their contents. Exhibit 14.3 gives illustrative examples of some of the reports for a particular HMO configuration under study.)

Sensitivity Analyses

The FPM has been designed with the flexibility of a simulator. For example, financial managers can study the economic behaviour of the HMO when certain operating and design variables remain fixed while others are allowed to vary. Ten such sensitivity analyses have been incorporated into the model.

(1) Days of hospital care per 1000 enrolled members;
(2) Monthly premiums for individual, family, Medicare, and Medicaid plans;
(3) Annual increases in the monthly premiums for plan members;
(4) Ratio of family-to-individual premium prices;
(5) Annual increases in service fees and charges for fee-to-service patients;
(6) Annual salary increases for HMO staff personnel;
(7) Annual staff turnover rates for HMO personnel;

(8) Annual cost inflation rates for hospital care;
(9) Annual cost inflation rates for medical and physician care services;
(10) Annual cost inflation rates for dental care services.

Whenever sensitivity analyses are to be conducted, the FPM will use a 'low', 'high', and 'incremental' value provided as input by the user. For example, if the user wants to study the financial impact of different hospital days per year per 1000 members, it can be stipulated that the FPM vary the hospital days per year per 1000 members from say, 400 to 600, in increments of 50 days.

The sensitivity options listed above are but a few of the many that can be computed. Additional analyses can be performed by repeatedly running the FPM under different values for the input variable to be examined. By using the model as a simulator a large number of designs can be evaluated by the planning group in a short period of time at a reasonable cost.

Examples of the FPM in Typical Planning Situations

A typical HMO planning situation requires planners to examine a number of feasible designs within a reasonable time and at a reasonable cost. This section illustrates how the FPM can be used to select the 'best' HMO configuration once an initial design has been selected for study. Although a large number of combinations of design and operating variables need to be studied in a real planning situation, only a few have been selected here to illustrate the model's usefulness and versatility. The operating variables for the HMO planning case which follows were chosen from a number of variables studied in an active planning situation. The ones chosen are those having the greatest impact on the financial security of an HMO and therefore would be likely candidates for sensitivity studies in other planning situations.

(a) Sensitivity of Hospitalization Rates

The deteriorating effects of hospital rates on the annual financial position of the HMO is illustrated by the family of cash-flow curves given in Figure 14.3. For this particular design, the monthly premiums for the first year were established at \$48 for the individual plan and \$120 for the family plan. As shown, the HMO did not have a favourable annual cash flow until the hospital days per 1000 members was started at 625 days per 1000 members and could be reduced each year by 25. If the HMO experiences 625–525 days per 1000 members, it finally reaches break-even in the 38th month of operation, and would have to borrow almost \$2.3 million to offset previous losses. When the hospital days per 1000 members starts out at 725 and is reduced annually by 25 to reach 625 in the fifth year, the HMO could not reach break-even until the 49th month of operation and would need to borrow \$3.5 million.

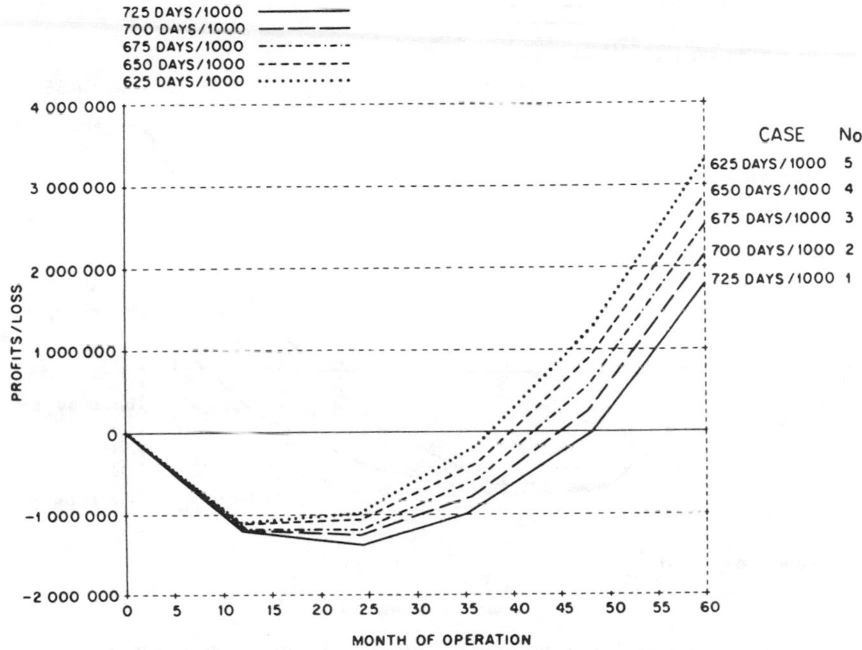

Figure 14.3 HMO group model: varying hospital days per 1000 members

The change in the HMO's financial position after five years of operations is from a cumulative loss of $1.7 million when it is at 725, to a gain of $2.2 million at 625. The impact of excessive hospital days on the cash flow of the HMO is quite obvious.

(b) Sensitivity of Annual Premium Increases

Figure 14.4 illustrates the financial impact on the HMO when the monthly premiums are increased annually at a rate of 8, 9, 10 and 12 per cent, and hospital costs and medical inflation are at 12 and 10 per cent respectively. For three of the cases (8, 9, 10), the HMO finds itself in a position with cumulative losses ranging from $4 to 7 million by the end of the fifth year. If the premiums are increased at 10 per cent annually, the HMO reaches break-even in the 53rd month with an enrolment slightly less than 31 000 members. The amount of capital to be borrowed is $3.9 million. When the premiums are increased each year by 12 per cent, the HMO reaches break-even in the 41st month with an enrolment of just over 24 000 members. While the HMO still has to borrow $2.8 million to meet operating deficits, at the end of the fifth year it will have a net gain of $248 502.

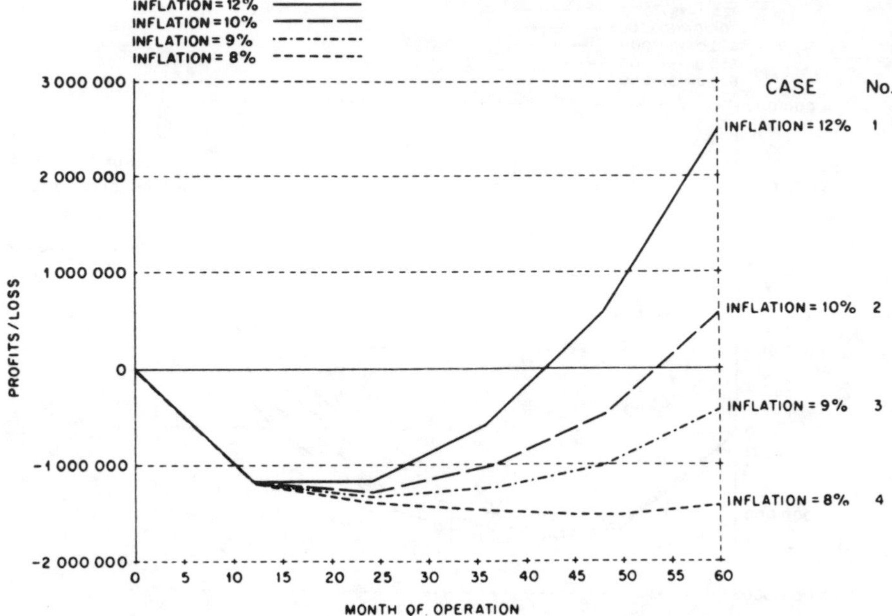

Figure 14.4 HMO group model: varying rates of premium inflation

It is obvious from the graph that there are definite financial trade-offs for pricing decisions—namely, the stretch out of the break-even and pay-back periods in return for lower annual rates of premium increases.

(c) Sensitivity of Hospital and Medical Cost Inflation

The annual rate of inflation assumed in the original design was 12 per cent for hospital care and 10 per cent for medical care. Figure 14.5 shows the cash-flow curves for various rates of inflation. For case 1, the HMO reaches break-even in the 41st month with an enrolment of 24 180. The amount of capital borrowed is $2.8 million. If medical-care costs increase by 3 per cent over the assumed rate of 10 per cent, the break-even enrolment becomes 25 893 and the time of break-even is pushed back to the 45th month. Cumulative losses for the five-year period total 0.8 million and an additional $175 194 needs to be borrowed.

Cases 3 and 4 have even more negative effects than case 2. For case 3 the break-even enrolment becomes 27 607 and the time is extended to the 48th month. Total cumulative losses are 1.5 million for the period with increased capital borrowing of $303 134. Obviously, case 4 is the worst. Cumulative losses become $2.7 million and break-even does not occur until the 51st month.

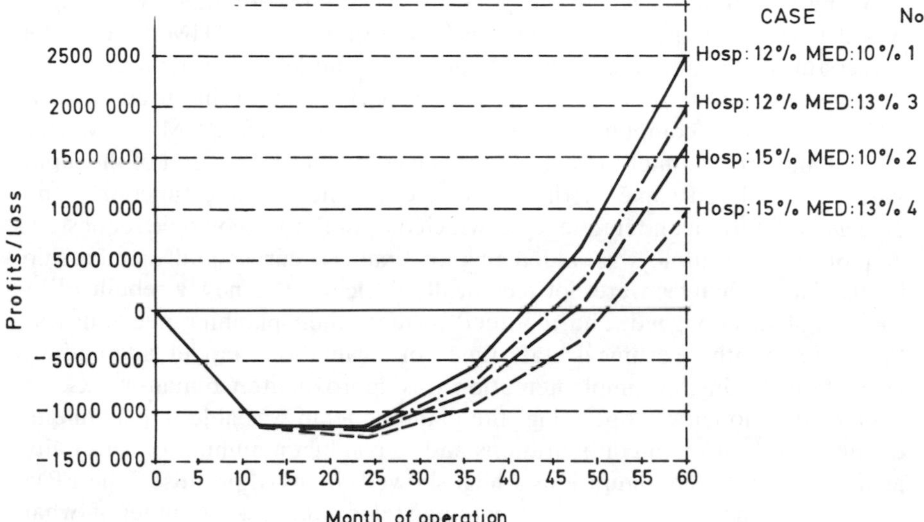

Figure 14.5 HMO group model: varying rates of hospital and medical services inflation

The effect of higher hospital and medical cost inflation rates over the projected rates illustrates the need for strong cost-containment initiatives by the HMO.

14.4 Implementation of the FPM in Different HMO Planning Settings

The FPM has been implemented successfully and used by several HMO planning groups. In some instances it was modified and adapted to their specific planning needs and used by an HMO design team to select the best configuration from among many alternative choices that appeared to be feasible. In other instances it was used as a design reference for developing an in-house financial model for feasibility planning or financial planning and control for an HMO in operation. Three case examples of how the model was used and its impact on the HMO planning process are presented below. All three cases are for HMOs sponsored or operated by Blue Cross/Blue Shield.

Case example 1 One of the first adaptations of the FPM was by a Blue Cross/Blue Shield (BC/BS) plan that was in the early stages of an HMO feasibility study jointly funded by the plan, industry, and the federal government. An examination of the FPM by systems analysts and the HMO technical and planning staff members indicated that the model could easily be adapted to satisfy their planning needs in the feasibility, and possibly also in the planning and initial development phases of HMO development, assuming it was concluded at the end of the feasibility study that an HMO would be successful in the community under study. The model, once debugged, was modified to operate on a commercial time-sharing system that used an IBM 370/158 as its host computer. By using a remote terminal and CMS, a systems analyst and programmer increased the range of values for several of the input variables modified some of the staffing, cost, and revenue functions, and changed the format and frequency at which output reports could be requested. A plotting subroutine was added to plot financial curves and membership levels. These changes were not technically difficult. The newly rebuilt FPM was installed, debugged, and modified to meet their planning needs in less than one month. Technical staff time for evaluation, model adaptation, evaluation, testing and implementation was approximately 6 man-weeks.

Once the model was operating, the planning team was able to examine in detail several different configurations and to conduct a number of sensitivity analyses on those configurations which showed the most promise. The FPM was installed in such a way that the planning team could ask a number of 'what if?' questions and have the financial impact analyses just minutes later. By using six, and in some cases only three, executive commands the planning team could analyse the financial consequences of their choice. As the planning team became more involved with the model, they began to make refinements, so more economic studies could be done with its assistance.

The average cost per configuration under study ranged from \$20 to \$30. While it is difficult to estimate the amount of personnel time and cost saved by using the model, its real value and contribution to the design effort became evident during the final three weeks of the feasibility study when many final choices were made and several sensitivity studies had to be done to determine their economic impact on the HMO, a task which would have been difficult to do without a computer model.

After the design team selected a configuration the FPM was revised again, this time to generate quarterly and monthly planning reports.

Case example 2 A second user or adapter of the FPM was a BC/BS plan that had already conducted six HMO feasibility studies and was the sponsor of five HMOs as a regular line of business. In this particular case, the HMO planning and development department was initiating its seventh HMO feasibility study and wanted to design and construct a planning model now that they had undergone the pains of manually designing the others and now had several planning and operational data bases that could be more appropriately used by a computerized financial planning model.

Placing the FPM up on the plan's Honeywell 6000 computer was the responsibility of the systems people assigned to work with the HMO planning staff by the Systems Department. Initial installation of the FPM was delayed because of system-compatibility problems. However, these and other technical problems were overcome by outside consultation with the original designers of the model and by technical assistance provided by other users.

After final debugging and testing, the model was examined closely to determine if it could be used to meet their short- and long-term planning needs. After their evaluation, minor as well as major program changes were undertaken to construct a model that best suited their planning needs, as well as the needs of several plan operated and sponsored HMOs. Major changes dealt with modifying the time frame of the FPM so it could be used to project month-to-month operations in the first couple of years of operation. Minor changes dealt with modifying the range of values for input variables, modifying some of the functions in the submodels, and adding some special subroutines for additional reports.

The FPM in this particular setting was used primarily as a design reference. While many of the original functions and component models were used frequently to verify some of the planning already completed, others were not because of time and cost factors and because some of the analyses were too far down the planning stream.

Although the level of integration of the FPM with their HMO planning process was not high, its impact on the design of new financial planning models was. The logical construction of the FPM greatly influenced the design of a mini-financial planning model just completed for their operating HMOs. In addition the BC/BS plan used several submodels of the FPM to generate monthly planning and operational reports for the first two years of HMO operation. Similar to the FPM these new models were capable of performing several sensitivity analyses. Over time the new FPM was adapted for use in a real-time on-line environment.

Case example 3 The third primary user of the FPM in an HMO feasbility study was a BC/BS plan that had just completed an initial feasibility study and there were sufficient indicators that an HMO would be accepted by the community. Time for debugging, for initial testing, and for understanding the model's assumptions, construction and input and output features was spread over a two-month period for members of the HMO planning staff and data-processing personnel assigned to the project. Total manpower expended, including the time to modify some of the input routines and to change several of the staffing, cost and revenue and financial functions, was eight man-weeks. The modified FPM was installed on an IBM 370/158 computer. It was operated using batch processing, with the HMO planners specifying the numbers and types of analyses to be made and data-processing personnel preparing the input cards and the FPM for use. The morning after the requests were made, the planning group was able to review the economic consequences of their decisions. Repeated use of the FPM allowed the HMO design team to look at a large number of designs in a relatively short period of time, helped them to identify the types and amounts of data that must be assembled and analyzed in the later stages of HMO development, and sensitized them to the many interrelating factors that come into play and need to be analyzed when creating an HMO. Adaptation, implementation, and repeated use of the FPM helped the HMO design team to adhere to a logical and systematic approach to HMO design and development planning.

Once the plan chose to go with a staff model HMO, the FPM was used to gauge the financial consequence of making several organization and delivery system choices before a final design was selected.

Case examples summary It is clear from the above case examples that the FPM has contributed to the state-of-the-art of financial modelling of HMOs by not only being adapted and successfully used in different HMO planning settings, but also by influencing the design and construction of another generation of models. While the FPM is the most generalized HMO financial planning model thus far constructed, its use in different planning settings can only be successful when:

(1) The HMO design team clearly understands the assumptions and logical construction of the FPM and its component submodels;
(2) The HMO design team understand the limitations, exclusions, and capabilities of the FPM;
(3) The HMO design team has the technical capability to change the FPM to meet its specific planning needs;
(4) The HMO design team will only use the FPM after it has been properly tested to determine its validity and utility.

14.5 Summary and Conclusions

Financially viable HMOs do not just happen, they have to be planned, replanned, and replanned again and again. HMO financial planning is a never-ending, complex process that consumes enormous amounts of time and resources. Sound financial planning requires that HMO planners and administrators recognize the financial implications of their decisions in all stages of the HMO, particularly during the design and early operational stages because many of the decisions are irreversible, and incorrect and hasty ones often result in financial catastrophes.

No computerized financial planning model can guarantee the short- or long-term financial success of an HMO. However, such models can help HMO planners to understand the complex interrelationships that exist in an HMO.

Hopefully, the original FPM and the newer ones that it nurtured can help the more than 100 HMOs now being designed and developed each year to become and remain economically viable alternatives to the traditional fee-for-service medical care system.

References

Coleman, J. R. and Kaminsky, F. C. (1977a). 'A financial planning model for evaluating the economic viability of health maintenance organizations', *Inquiry*, **14**(2), 176–88.

Coleman, J. R. and Kaminsky, F. C. (1977b). *Designing Medical Services For Health Maintenance Organizations, Vol. IV, Ambulatory Care Systems*, Lexington Books, D. C. Heath, Lexington, MA.

Coleman, J. R. and Kaminsky, F. C. (1977c). *Financial Design and Administration of Health Maintenance Organizations, Vol. V, Ambulatory Care Systems*, Lexington Books, D. C. Heath, Lexington, MA.

Greene, L. A. and Grimes, R. M. (1974). 'A simulation of the financial requirements of a pre-paid health care delivery system; examination of case studies in health facilities planning, *Proceedings of a Forum held at Washington, D.C., 3–4 December, 1973*. National Cooperative Services Center for Hospital Management Engineering, Richmond, Virginia.

Hersch, G. and Miller, S. (1974). 'Evaluating HMO policies with a computer simulation model', *Med. Care*, **12**(8), 668–81.

Klett, S. V. (1986) 'Corporate America opens the door to managed care', *Medical World News*, 13 January, 1986, 52–68.

Luft, H. S. (1981). *Health Maintenance Organizations: Dimension of Performance*, Wiley, New York.

Moustafa, A. T. and Sears, D. W. (1974). 'Feasibility of simulation of health maintenance organization', *Inquiry*, **11**(3), 143–50.

Thompson, D. A. (1974). 'Financial planning for an HMO', *Health Serv. Res.*, Spring 1974, 68–73.

Traska, M. R. (1986). 'HMOs: a shake-up (and shakeout) on the horizon', *Hospitals*, **60**(3), 40–43, 45.

US Department of Health, Education and Welfare (1971). *Towards a Comprehensive Health Policy for the 1970's. A White Paper*, Washington, DC, US Government Printing Office, May 1971, 31–2.

Appendix to Chapter 14

Exhibit 14.1 *Description of the user data file* (Reproduced by permission of the publisher, from *Ambulatory Care Systems, Volume V, Designing Medical Services for Health Maintenance Organizations*, by John R. Coleman and Frank C. Kaminsky: Lexington, Mass.: Lexington Books, D. C. Heath and Company, Copyright 1977, D. C. Heath and Company)

User data set	Contents
(1) Geographic, residential and community definition	The census region and types of communities served by the HMO including the fluoridation or nonfluoridation of community water supplies.
(2) Annual prepaid and fee-for-service patient populations	The number of individual, family, Medicare, Medicaid and fee-for-service patients to be served during each of the five years.
(3) Annual enrolment levels for supplemental health services	The number of plan members who have elected supplemental benefits during each of the five years.
(4) HMO organizational form benefit program and service options	The type and scope of service benefits to be provided by the HMO.
(5) Definition of HMO services and program delivery options	The delivery system options chosen to provide for the delivery of service benefits selected by the HMO.
(6) HMO building and medical facility occupancy options	The medical building and facility occupancy options for the medical and administrative components of the HMO.
(7) Service capacity of medical buildings and plan facilities	The service capacity of medical buildings and facilities to be constructed by the HMO during the first five years of plan operation.

Exhibit 14.1

User data set	Contents
(8) Plan member utilization rates for inpatient rates for inpatient care services	The birth rate per 1000 women of childbearing age, lengths of stay in inpatient care facilities, and the hospital days of care per 1000 members.
(9) Monthly premiums for 'basic' and 'supplemental' health benefit plans	The initial monthly premiums for individual, family, Medicare, and Medicaid plan members and for all supplemental benefit plans offered by the HMO.
(10) Annual percentage price increases in plan premiums	The annual increase in premium prices for 'basic' and 'supplemental' benefit plans.
(11) Co-payment fee schedule for HMO plan members	The point-of-service charges for services rendered to plan members.
(12) Other plan member service fees and annual increases in co-payment fees	Other fees for services rendered to members and the annual increases in co-pay,ent fees.
(13) Service fee schedules for fee-for-service patients (14)	The fees charged nonplan members for services rendered by the HMO.
(15) Monthly SSA cost reimbursement for Medicare	The average monthly cost reimbursement from SSA for Medicare members.
(16) External revenues	External income to the HMO from such sources as grants, gifts, endowments, and so forth.
(17) Service provider compensation options and schedules	The contractual costs tp the HMO for contracting with health service groups within the community to provide health services to plan members. These costs are on a capitation and/or unit of service (fee-for-service) basis.

(18)	Compensation schedules for HMO staff physician and non-physicians	The annual base salary for physicians and nonphysicians employed directly by the HMO including those in administration.
(19)	Fringe benefit, salary increase, and manpower turnover rates for HMO staff members	The annual percentage rates of salary increases for HMO employees. Also included are the percentage rates for fringe benefits, and the annual turnover rates for physicians and non-physicians.
(20)	Hospital and medical care services cost inflation rates	Annual rates of cost inflation for hospitalization and medical care services including physician, dental, optical, and pharmaceutical services.
(21)	HMO loan and plan investment income data	Annual interest rates and payment records for capital borrowed from The Department of Health, Education and Welfare and/or commercial banks to meet operating deficits and for the construction of buildings. Annual interest rates for funds (loans and/or profits) deposited in the bank.

Exhibit 14.2 *Description of the HMO planning reports generated by the FPM* (Reproduced by permission of the publisher, from *Ambulatory Care Systems, Volume V, Designing Medical Services for Health Maintenance Organizations,* by John R. Coleman and Frank C. Kaminsky: Lexington, Mass.: Lexington Books, D. C. Heath and Company, Copyright 1977, D. C. Heath and Company)

Planning report	Description
(1) Service area population characteristics	Age–sex distribution and socioeconomic data for persons living in the service area of the HMO.
(2) Distribution of plan users report	Age–sex distribution of plan members and fee-for-service patients who will use plan services during the year.
(3) Medical and health care service utilization report	Expected utilization of inpatient and outpatient services for the first five years of plan operation.
(4) Ambulatory physician visit report	Expected number of annual ambulatory visits to physicians by medical speciality.
(5) Physician staffing requirements by speciality	Annual staffing patterns for primary and speciality care physicians for each of the first five years of plan operation.
(6) Non-physician staffing requirements—medical clinic	The yearly staffing patterns for the medical clinic including nurses, laboratory technicians, administrative staff, and dental, pharmacy, home care, and mental health services.
(7) Non-physician staffing requirements—plan administration	The yearly staffing pattern for the administrative component of the HMO.

(8)	Annual HMO building facility space requirements	The yearly space needs of fourteen organizational components of the HMO.
(9)	Proforma HMO revenue schedule	Estimated yearly income to the HMO from plan operation and external sources including income from borrowed capital and profits if any.
(10)	Revenue analysis report	Detailed revenue data by source for the five-year planning period.
(11)	Proforma HMO expense schedule	The annual estimated costs of plan operations, including the cost of borrowing capital to meet projected losses during the first five years of plan operation.
(12)	Plan program/service cost analysis report	Detailed costs of HMO operations for the year of plan operation. This report is prepared on a yearly basis.
(13)	Financial analysis summary report	The financial position of the HMO at the end of each year including when and how much capital must be borrowed and the annual levels of outstanding debt.
(14)	Financial statement and analysis chart	The enrolment and financial position of the HMO during each year of plan operation including a graph of revenue vs. cost for the first five years.
(15)	Financial break-even analysis chart	A graph indicating the time when the HMO's income balances costs and the number of plan members and fee-for-service patients using the HMO when this occurs.

Exhibit 14.3 Specimen output reports

Exhibit 14.3(a) Sample FPM utilization report
IIMO group model
Pre-paid medical plan
Medical and health-care utilization report
Summary

Medical and health-care service	Service unit	Year 1	Year 2	Year 3	Year 4	Year 5
Physician services		16 323	43 394	71 068	94 156	114 818
Home	(visits)	81	216	355	470	574
Inpatient	(visits)	2 203	5 858	9 594	12 711	15 500
Office/clinic	(visits)	14 037	37 318	61 118	80 974	98 743
Hospitalization						
Short-term care						
Non-maternity cases	(number)	370	1 008	1 604	2 039	2 377
Length of stay	(days)	7.2	7.2	7.2	7.2	7.2
Non-maternity-days	(days)	2 663	7 255	11 551	14 683	17 116
Maternity/births	(number)	71	204	338	448	550
Length of stay	(days)	4.2	4.2	4.2	4.2	4.2
Maternity-days	(days)	298	857	1 420	1 882	2 310
Surgical cases	(number)	166	453	721	917	1 069
Long-term care						
Admissions	(number)	6	19	32	42	42
Length of stay	(days)	26.0	26.0	26.0	26.0	26.0
Patient days	(days)	156	494	832	1 092	1 352

Psychiatric care						
Admissions	(number)	12	38	61	83	103
Length of stay	(days)	23.0	23.0	23.0	23.0	23.0
Patient days	(days)	276	874	1 403	1 909	2 369
OP mental health	(visits)	861	2 294	3 757	4 978	6 071
Laboratory services						
Outpatient	(tests)	19 537	51 894	84 969	112 571	137 264
Pharmacy services	(prescriptions)	25 266	67 225	110 117	145 901	177 923
Injections	(number)	1 824	4 851	7 945	10 526	12 836
Physical therapy						
Outpatient	(visits)	146	389	637	844	1 029
Radiology services						
Outpatient	(exams)	2 931	7 785	12 745	16 885	20 589
Dental services						
Hygienist	(visits)	1 210	2 975	4 626	5 927	7 116
Dentist	(visits)					
Optical services						
Refractions	(number)	888	2 361	3 866	5 122	6 246
Prescriptions	(number)	532	1 416	2 319	3 073	3 747
VNA home-care visits	(visits)	255	687	1 123	1 487	1 815

Exhibit 14.3(b) Sample FPM physician staffing requirements report
HMO group model
Pre-paid medical plan
Physician staffing requirements by speciality

Medical speciality	Provide option	Year 1	Year 2	Year 3	Year 4	Year 5
GP/internists	Staff	2.00	5.05	8.26	10.95	13.35
Paediatrics	Staff	1.00	1.93	3.17	4.20	5.12
Obstetrics/gynaecology	Staff	0.50	1.23	2.02	2.68	3.26
General surgery	Staff	0.50	0.97	1.59	2.10	2.57
Ophthalmologists	FFS	0.09	0.25	0.42	0.56	0.68
Ear/nose/throat ENT	FFS	0.12	0.33	0.55	0.73	0.89
Orthopaedics	FFS	0.16	0.43	0.70	0.93	1.14
Dermatology	FFS	0.12	0.33	0.55	0.73	0.89
Allergy	FFS	0.06	0.16	0.27	0.36	0.44
Psychiatry	FFS	0.16	0.43	0.70	0.93	1.14
Urology	FFS	0.09	0.25	0.41	0.55	0.67
Radiology	FFS	0.17	0.46	0.75	1.00	1.22
Anaesthesiology	FFS	0.13	0.34	0.56	0.75	0.91
Pathology	FFS	0.07	0.19	0.31	0.42	0.51
Other	FFS	0.06	0.16	0.26	0.35	0.42
Total—psychiatry excluded		5.07	12.08	19.82	26.31	33.07
Staff—psychiatry excluded		4.00	9.18	15.04	19.93	24.30

Exhibit 14.3(c) Sample FPM financial analysis summary report
HMO group model
Prepaid medical plan
Financial analysis summary report

Plan revenue–expenses–balance ($)	Year 1	Year 2	Year 3	Year 4	Year 5
Total plan revenue					
Plan operations:	$2 022 402	$6 273 311	$11 614 434	$17 276 586	$23 647 675
Borrowed capital:	$1 137 230	$1 162 542	$573 381	$00	$00
Interest income:	$43 131	$44 091	$21 746	$19 092	$122 361
Total:	$3 202 763	$7 479 944	$12 209 561	$17 295 678	$23 770 036
Total plan expenses					
Plan operations:	$3 159 632	$7 435 853	$12 187 815	$16 668 228	$21 134 378
New loan principal:	$127 456	$130 293	$64 262	$00	$00
New loan interest:	$90 978	$93 003	$45 870	$00	$00
Total:	$3 378 066	$7 659 149	$12 297 947	$16 668 228	$21 134 378
Annual plan balance	($175 303)	($179 205)	($88 386)	$627 450	$2 635 658
Loan interest and principal					
Interest paid—new loans:	$00	$00	$00	$00	$00
Interest paid—other loans:	$90 978	$264 763	$462 983	$632 912	$772 285
Principal paid—new loans:	$00	$00	$00	$00	$00
Principal paid—other loans:	$127 456	$395 402	$749 047	$1 130 982	$1 543 473
Total:	$218 434	$660 166	$1 212 030	$1 763 895	$2 315 759
Capital borrowed to date					
New loans:	$00	$00	$00	$00	$00
Banks and other loans:	$1 137 230	$2 299 772	$2 873 153	$2 873 153	$2 873 153
Total:	$1 137 230	$2 299 772	$2 873 153	$2 873 153	$2 873 153

Financial Modelling in Corporate Management, 2nd Edition
Edited by J. W. Bryant

15

A Computer Model for Aiding Product-line Decisions*

BARBARA JACKSON AND BENSON SHAPIRO

15.1 Introduction

Product-line decisions form the basis of marketing strategy. Too often, however, product managers make such decisions without giving proper consideration to their broad strategic implications. They do not systematically consider the conflicting goals of marketing managers, who tend to prefer broad product lines, and of manufacturing managers, who like narrow cost-efficient product lines. Managers too frequently make these decisions on a tactical basis. Determining the most appropriate product-line lengths and characteristics can be accomplished in a more systematic way with a computer model. The actual process of constructing the model can begin to clarify the product-line decisions, and once the model is completed and working, the sales and profit implications of different product-line decisions become readily apparent. In this chapter the basic approach product managers can take to put together an industrial product-line computer model is outlined. A paper company product line is used to illustrate how one model was assembled, but this example represents an approach that can be tailored to different businesses.

15.2 Product-line Policy

The Problem

Among the products made by a large paper manufacturer is a line of index

*Reprinted by permission of the *Harvard Business Review*. 'New way to make product line decisions' by Barbara B. Jackson and Benson P. Shapiro (May–June 1979), Copyright © 1979 by the President and Fellows of Harvard College; all rights reserved.

paper, which is a stiff stock used to make menus, index cards, and promotional flyers. Each day the company's product manager faces questions about adding and deleting items in the line.

Should we add a new pale green colour to our offerings of index paper? Or should we instead extend the weight range of index offerings and begin to market a heavier grade? Should we do both and evolve into a full-line supplier? Or should we cut back some of the existing items in the company's index line and concentrate resources on a more limited range of offerings?

Such mundane questions form the practical day-to-day basis of product policy. (Product policy can be defined as the management of a company's product and service offerings.) The decisions made on such questions can be viewed as basic building blocks of marketing strategy. Too often, however, these basic decisions are made without any real consideration of their strategic implications. Thus strategies simply evolve to support initial tactical decisions.

One problem with these decisions is that marketing and manufacturing managers frequently disagree about the appropriate number of items to include in a particular product line. Marketers want a broad product line. Manufacturing managers stress a short product line with long production runs and reduced set-up costs and machine changeovers. The decision on line length is important in both financial and organizational terms.

A line longer than needed, on the one hand, faces high costs from increased inventory, production changeovers, and additional order processing and transportation. An overly long line also creates confusion in marketing to distributors, sales people and customers.

An overly short line, on the other hand, results in different cost problems. Potential losses include sales, competitive position and economies of scale. Distributors and sales people may reduce their marketing effort.

The financial impacts of either type of mistake are clear. The organizational impacts arise because the costs of the two types of mistake are felt most heavily by separate parts of the organization. A mistake in either direction can create costly problems in different company areas. The costs of the overly short line fall most directly on the marketing area. Conversely, costs associated with a line that is too long hit hardest in the manufacturing area.

Determining the appropriate product-line length is only part of the problem. The other part is determining a sensible set of characteristics for each item in the line. Each must be positioned appropriately with regard to other items in the line, customers' needs, competitive offerings, and the company's own manufacturing process and marketing strategy.

A Computerized Approach

A more systematic approach to managing product lines is possible. It involves using a computer model that can be put together through a joint effort between the product manager and a computer programmer. The reader should note here that what we are really suggesting is an approach rather than a single, general model. Thus product managers can tailor models to their own product lines.

The actual process of beginning to assemble a computer model forces managers to think more deeply than is customary about their product offerings and those of their competitors. Managers can be led to ask important questions about their product-line items, including such hard or unpleasant questions as those concerning competition and cannibalization, which involves a company's new items stealing sales from its existing items.

Also, if they are to explore fully the implications of product-line changes, managers must extensively manipulate numbers involving such issues as competition, cannibalization, and manufacturing. In searching for the best positioning of a product line's items, managers should manipulate the numbers for a variety of possible configurations. Most managers simply do not have the time to perform lengthy calculations for each of many possible decisions about items. A computerized aid can mechanize the numerical analysis so that the manager can spend time on judgemental matters rather than on computation.

Thus the two primary aims of a computerized model for product-line planning are to help the manager through a carefully constructed process for considering product-line changes and to handle the many calculations needed to evaluate the profit impact of such changes. To overcome the shortcomings of existing approaches, the model should have the following characteristics:

(1) It should consider the costs involved in manufacturing and distributing operations along with the impact of changes on the sales of other product-line items.
(2) It should enable marketing managers to vary their sales estimates easily and to gain a feel for the sensitivity of how variations will affect forecasted profits.
(3) It should help managers visualize their company's product offerings in terms of customers' needs and competitive offerings.
(4) It should be relatively easy to use even though the data requirements will necessarily be considerable. (In fact, as we shall discuss later, data collection is by far the most difficult part of the process. Data requirements should thus be made as reasonable as possible. The outputs of the model should be given in terms that the managers understand and consider important—in, for instance, gross margins and net profit.)
(5) It should be simple enough to make the issues clear, yet complex enough to capture the essence of the real-world problem.

15.3 The Product-line Model

Product Mapping

As a first step in constructing a computer model, a product manager should make use of the product-space, or product-map, concept. A product map identifies a small set of relevant dimensions for defining and comparing one company's product line with those of competitors. (The basic concept of placing products in a product space has existed since the late 1950s. It was developed by Wroe Alderson, Hans Brem, Lee Preston, Volney Stefflre, Norman Barnett, Richard Johnson and others.)

Table 15.1 A product map (product space)

	White	Buff	Canary	Red
90 weight			■○	
110 weight	△	■△		
140 weight	■○	■○△	○	○
155 weight		■△	■	■

■ The user company makes this product.
○ Competitor A makes this product.
△ Competitor B makes this product.

Table 15.1 is a heavily disguised diagram of the index paper offerings of a large paper company from which we first developed the ideas for this chapter. For our index example, the relevant criteria have been identified as weight and colour. By convention, items are offered in 90, 110, 140, and 155 basis weights. (Basis weights are measures of thickness.) Colours for our disguised version of the actual market are white, buff, canary and red. On the map, we use different symbols for each competitor to show what combinations of weight and colour each competitor offers. Thus, as indicated in Table 15.1, our company has seven items in its product line. Competitor A offers five items, while Competitor B offers four.

Diagrams like this enable managers to visualize their own and competing companies' positions in the market place. For example, a diagram may help to emphasize that one competitor specializes in one part of the space, that another sticks to a different segment, and that yet another aims for overall coverage.

Product spaces are useful in describing other industrial lines as well. In small electrical motors, one might find that the most important product dimensions are torque and horsepower. In a space for electric drill bits, cutting power and life of the bit might be characterized as the two most relevant dimensions.

Such product maps can be incorporated into computerized models as a powerful way of describing product-line markets. Users can then experiment with changes in the individual items within the space. Selecting two dimensions seems to make the best use of the managers ability to assimilate data because few people can think in more than two dimensions.

Many managers feel initially that *their* products and markets are far too complex to be summarized in only two dimensions. Ultimately they discover that two basic dimensions will usually suffice if the criteria are carefully chosen. It may be, for example, that while an electric motor can be specified in up to 20 or more dimensions, some of the criteria, such as base plate size, are defined by others, such as horsepower and torque. Often industry tradition or standards specify these relationships. To simplify the situation further, products are typically offered at only certain specified points in the range of the relevant dimensions. Thus attention can often be limited to relatively few points along a dimension that at first appears to be continuous.

Model Design

How can the product map be used to construct a workable computer model? Primarily it can be done by assembling the most relevant data and relationships among them for the model. Not surprisingly, that is easier said than done. Data collection especially is a tedious and time-consuming task.

The kinds of data required can be illustrated by reference to the product map in Table 15.1, which shows the offerings of the user company and its two competitors. Existing sales for each item and each competitor are built into the model. In practice, of course, many such figures are only estimates. The paper products are assumed to be commodities for which one price per product prevails industrywide. The prices for the items currently being offered are built into the model, as is information on manufacturing capacity, materials and labour costs, batch sizes, and output rates. The model also starts with a rough estimate of the total manufacturing capacity for each competitor.

In a process industry of the type being considered, changing from one item to another in the production sequence involves both time and materials costs. The time cost is obvious. The materials cost is incurred because scrap material is produced as the machine is changed from one item to another. In changing from pink to green paper, the machine goes through a phase during which a mixed colour of little value is produced. Consequently, the index paper model must consider the order in which items are made and the time required to make changes in such features as paper weight and colour. The model also needs the value of each unit of scrap produced during changeover, which is approximately equal to the value of the pulp in the scrap.

Finally, cost estimates per dollar of sales of the raw materials, the work in process and the finished goods inventories are required. When the user varies the number of items offered during the computer model's operation, the model assumes that finished goods inventories per dollar of sales vary but that the work in process and raw materials inventories per dollar of sales do not change.

The initial set of data is entered into the computer by a computer programmer. Once that task is completed, a manager communicates with the computer through a VDU. The user types requests for analyses and responds to questions posed by the computer.

Illustrative Use of the Model

For the index paper model, which we call PROFIT (for Product Offering Interactive Technique), the program begins by providing an income statement for the product line (as illustrated in Exhibit 15.1 in the Appendix). The model then asks (Exhibit 15.2) the manager what to do next. It offers the options of adding and dropping items, of inflating and deflating either unit sales or price levels across the industry, of changing individual item sales and changing price values, and of simply requesting assorted information about the product space.

Expansion or contraction of industry sales and prices is an important tool for such a cyclical industry as the paper industry because such expansion or contraction enables the product manager to understand the impact of industry changes on the existing product line; also, the changes enable the product manager to test the impact of industry-wide swings on possible changed versions of the paper company's product line.

It is often useful in models such as this one for the computer to ask brief, almost cryptic questions. A user who does not understand the questions responds with a question mark to request more information. Once users become accustomed to the program, they respond to the short questions rather than wait for the extended explanations. Initially the model offers the user a collection of options, and in the example the user requests a description of the product space. The model then asks which information the user wants and provides a list of what is available. In this list, the term *estimates* appears repeatedly. The model uses smoothing techniques to estimate the prices, direct costs, or other quantities for items on which it does not have complete information. (It provides smoothed estimates only when it has data on nearby actual items in the space.) The user is always asked for approval before a smoothed figure is used. The model does not impose these values. The values do, however, prompt the user. (Exhibit 15.2 continues with examples of the user's requests for other descriptions of the product space—competitive offerings and sales as well as market shares.)

A user might next ask (see Exhibit 15.3) to increase unit sales for all products by some amount (such industry-wide expansions are particularly important in the paper industry) and then to produce a financial summary. Within seconds, the model provides the original case, the new results, and dollar and percentage variances.

Subsequently the user might ask to restore the original case and then to add a new product. Here (Exhibit 15.4) the user must approve the smoothed values for price and other quantities and must also specify where the new item will be placed in the production sequence (so that changeover costs can be calculated). The dialogue thus encourages its marketing users to consider the manufacturing implications of their decisions. Then, making sure that the user considers primary demand, sales taken from competitors, cannibalization from existing items in the line, and any other changes, the model leads the user through a series of questions about sales of the new item.

The model thus imposes a discipline on the manager's judgement about the item addition. Throughout the process, the computer tabulates how much the user has identified in new item sales and checks to see that all such sales come from an identified source. It also alerts the user to errors, such as transferring sales from an item that is not produced. (The Exhibit ends with the user's request for a financial report summarizing the results of the production addition. The user can see that revenues have risen 7 per cent, that inventory costs have gone up 9.9 per cent, and that scrap costs have increased 7.9 per cent. The net pretax earnings gain is 7.5 per cent. Exhibit 15.5 shows a similar sequence in which the user drops an item from the line and is led through a careful series of questions for allocating the previous sales of that item.)

Such computerized aids allows the user to experiment with product line changes in a matter of minutes. An hour or two at the terminal with carefully thoughtout analyses should result in a substantial increase in a product manager's understanding of the likely results of product-line changes and also of the effect of such changes on revenues, changeover costs and earnings.

Implementation

Notice in the foregoing examples what the model does and does not do. It *does* impose a discipline on the planning process. But the model *does not* exercise judgement itself. The judgements come from the user, who is presumably a knowledgeable product manager. The model organizes those judgements and, in seconds, explores their profit implications, which it then presents to the user in output reports.

The model just described is specific to a particular product line. Some of the assumptions made in the previously described model would be highly inappropriate for other types of businesses, particularly those not involving continuous production processes. Even the sequence of questions asked by the model should be tailored to an individual product manager's needs and views.

For example, the index paper product manager mentioned earlier was a firm believer in the importance of being a full-line supplier. Accordingly, the first version of the model included a question asking about overall changes in sales levels when individual items were added or dropped. The manager was required to give a specific factor to quantify the sales effects (something he did not find very easy to do). A product manager for a second company was equally adamant about saying that there was no such thing as the 'full-line house effect'. Consequently, the question was omitted from the second version of the model. More generally, if managers are required to make difficult quantitative judgements, the least the model can do is to leave the managers free to formulate their judgements in whatever ways they find most natural.

We chose our design approach because we believe that the relationships among items in an industrial product space are simply not yet understood well enough to allow a formal statistical (or other) model of the demand relationships. We made our choice of a simulation model without any attempt to have the model optimize the product offerings on its own for similar reasons. We think that computerized aids such as the one described here impose considerably more structure and careful analysis on product-line decisions than is usually the rule in industrial product-planning situations. We do not think it possible at this time to build more formal statistically based models that choose decisions or forecast sales.

15.4 Conclusions

It would be inappropriate to conclude this discussion without at least some consideration of specific steps that can be taken to implement such a model. Three basic steps are required:

(1) A model must be designed. The basic design must be done by the manager, not by the computer programmer. This task involves identifying the appropriate dimensions for the product space and deciding which aspects of the manufacturing process are critical enough to be included in evaluating possible product-line changes. Even more difficult is the task of deciding which aspects of the manufacturing process and market place are less crucial and can be simplified or ignored with relative safety. (Most managers seem to begin the process believing that *all* the details are critical.) The design step also involves decisions about how the model can request information from managers in ways most likely to elicit sound judgements.

The product manager should then work with a good programmer to complete the details of the model design. Together they must flesh out the specification of just how the program should calculate sales, costs, and other measurements. The manager and programmer must also decide what the program's output reports will be and design the dialogue through which the user and the program will communicate. These input and output design decisions are extremely important; in practice they often receive little attention, and computer programs are consequently unwieldy and difficult to use. Thus the programs may wind up not being used as often as they should be.

(2) A strongly user-oriented computer program for accepting inputs from the

user and for performing the relevant calculations must be written. Managers seem to be most concerned about this step, but in practice we find it the easiest of the three. Once the program has been designed properly, the actual coding (or writing the program) is relatively straightforward.

(3) A data collection step, which involves gathering all of the sales, production and financial data needed is necessary. As has been noted, the process is painfully tedious. Some of the numbers are known only roughly. In such cases, estimates must be used.

Even more of a problem is the fact that many companies do not routinely collect and maintain data in forms that are useful for evaluating product-line changes. One can argue that the collection process is most useful for such companies because it can help identify issues and inconsistencies that might not otherwise be addressed. It also facilitates communication between marketing and manufacturing areas.

Making the best product-line decisions involves developing a deep understanding of the strategic impact of tactical decisions about product-line items. Computerized aids of the sort described in this chapter provide the necessary rigorous structure along with a fast calculating aid that removes much tiresome 'dogwork'.

Such an approach appears to be most useful in two types of situations.

The one involves companies that make frequent item changes, such as producers of nuts and bolts, grinding wheels and paper. For such companies, a computerized aid helps make a frequent tedious task less onerous and more careful.

In the other type of situation, such models can have substantial impact on product lines with very few items and infrequent changes, such as lines of manufacturers of heavy equipment or jet aircraft engines. Each decision has great impact and must be carefully analysed from many points of view.

Thus a computerized aid provides a means of quickly testing many possible options, of identifying the most feasible options, and of then devoting additional resources only to those options that meet the initial criteria.

Appendix to Chapter 15

In all the following exhibits, user input within the dialogues has been underlined, and explanatory comments which do not form part of the user–computer 'conversation' are given in smaller type

Exhibit 15.1 Initial model outputs

```
.RUN PROFIT

REVENUE:                   4001.
COST OF GOODS:             2144.
-------------------------------
GROSS MARGIN:              1857.
SCRAP CREDIT:               153.
SCRAP COST:                 420.
FIXED COST:                 200.
CARRYING COST:               72.
-------------------------------
EARNINGS BEFORE TAX:       1319.

OUR UTILIZATION (HOURS):   76.81%
COMPETITORS' UTILIZATIONS (UNITS):
                   82.50%  87.50%
```

Exhibit 15.2 Product space description

```
OPTION? ?
AVAILABLE OPTIONS:
 A    ADD AN ITEM
 D    DROP AN ITEM
 F    RUN FINANCIAL PROJECTIONS
 PS   DESCRIBE PRODUCT SPACE
 IU   INFLATE OR DEFLATE INDUSTRY UNIT SALES
 IP   INFLATE OR DEFLATE ALL PRICES
 S    CHANGE INDIVIDUAL SALES FIGURES
 PR   CHANGE INDIVIDUAL PRICES
 PC   PROGRAM-SUGGESTED CHANGES
 $  STOP

OPTION? PS ◄──── Request for description of the product space
WHICH INFORMATION? ?
AVAILABLE INFORMATION:
 PS   PRODUCT SPACE
 S    SALES
 D    INDUSTRY UNIT DEMAND
 P    PRICES
 P*   PRICES AND ESTIMATES
 O    OUTPUTS/HOUR
 O*   OUTPUTS/HOUR AND ESTIMATES
 C    DIRECT COSTS
 C*   DIRECT COSTS AND ESTIMATES
 B    BATCH SIZES
 MS   OUR MARKET SHARES
 GM   GROSS MARGINS
 G*   GROSS MARGINS AND ESTIMATES
 $  NO FURTHER DESCRIPTION
WHICH INFORMATION? PS ◄──── Request for information about which competitors offer which items
WHICH COMPETITOR (Ø=US)? Ø
 ROWS GIVE     WEIGHT:     9Ø   11Ø 14Ø 155
 COLS GIVE      COLOUR:WHT BUF YEL RED
 .   .   *   . ◄
 .   *   .   . ◄──── Our company
 *   *   .   . ◄
 .   *   *   *

WHICH INFORMATION? PS
WHICH COMPETITOR (Ø=US)? 1
 ROWS GIVE     WEIGHT:     9Ø   11Ø 14Ø 155
 COLS GIVE      COLOUR:WHT BUF YEL RED
 .   .   *   .
               ◄
 .   .   .   .
               ◄──── Competitor A
 *   *   *   *
               ◄
 .   .   .   .

WHICH INFORMATION? S
WHICH COMPETITOR (Ø=US)? 1
 ROWS GIVE     WEIGHT:     9Ø   11Ø 14Ø 155
 COLS GIVE      COLOUR:WHT BUF YEL RED
****** ******   1ØØ.  ******
    Ø.      Ø. ****** ******
  4ØØ.    55Ø.   35Ø.    25Ø.     ◄──── Competitor A's sales
******      Ø.     Ø.      Ø.

WHICH INFORMATION? MS
 ROWS GIVE     WEIGHT:     9Ø   11Ø 14Ø 155
 COLS GIVE      COLOUR:WHT BUF YEL RED
*****  *****  6Ø.ØØ  *****    ◄
 Ø.ØØ  57.14  *****  *****    ◄──── Our market shares
42.86  34.48   Ø.ØØ   Ø.ØØ    ◄
*****  6Ø.ØØ  *****  *****

WHICH INFORMATION? $
```

Competitor A's sales (******means no company offers the item; 0. means other companies sell the item, but Competitor A does not)

Exhibit 15.3 Industry sales inflation

```
OPTION? IU
FACTOR? ?
GIVE FACTOR BY WHICH TO INFLATE OR DEFLATE INDUSTRY  UNIT SALES -
 AS A DECIMAL (FOR EXAMPLE, 1.05)
FACTOR? 1.08 <------------------------------------ Unit sales will be raised 8%
OPTION? F <--------------------------------------- Request for financial results

                         THIS CASE    BASE CASE    VARIANCE    VAR %
REVENUE:                   4321.        4001.         320.       8.0
COST OF GOODS:             2315.        2144.         171.       8.0
-----------------------------------------------------------
GROSS MARGIN:              2006.        1857.         149.       8.0
SCRAP CREDIT:               164.         153.          11.       7.4
SCRAP COST:                 451.         420.          31.       7.4
FIXED COST:                 200.         200.           0.       0.0
CARRYING COST:               78.          72.           6.       8.0

-----------------------------------------------------------
EARNINGS BEFORE TAX:       1442.        1319.         123.       9.3

OUR UTILIZATION (HOURS):  82.87%
COMPETITORS' UTILIZATIONS (UNITS):    89.10%  94.50%
```

Exhibit 15.4 Adding an item

```
OPTION? ?
AVAILABLE OPTIONS:
 A    ADD AN ITEM
 D    DROP AN ITEM
 F    RUN FINANCIAL PROJECTIONS
 PS   DESCRIBE PRODUCT SPACE
 IU   INFLATE OR DEFLATE INDUSTRY UNIT SALES
 IP   INFLATE OR DEFLATE ALL PRICES
 S    CHANGE INDIVIDUAL SALES FIGURES
 PR   CHANGE INDIVIDUAL PRICES
 PC   PROGRAM-SUGGESTED CHANGES
 B    SAVE CURRENT POSITION AS BASE CASE
 R    RESTORE LATEST BASE CASE
 $   STOP

OPTION? R <--------------------------------------- The user restores the original base case
PREVIOUS BASE CASE MADE CURRENT

OPTION? F <--------------------------------------- Original financial results

REVENUE:                   4001.
COST OF GOODS:             2144.
-----------------------------
GROSS MARGIN:              1857.
SCRAP CREDIT:               153.
SCRAP COST:                 420.
FIXED COST:                 200.
CARRYING COST:               72.
-----------------------------
EARNINGS BEFORE TAX:       1319.

OUR UTILIZATION (HOURS):  76.81%
COMPETITORS' UTILIZATIONS (UNITS):    82.50%  87.50%
```

```
OPTION? A
   WEIGHT INDEX,       COLOUR INDEX: 3,3 ◄──── A 140-weight canary paper will be added
PRICE=  2.14     OUTPUT/HR= 18.00      DIRECT COST=  0.91
                                       Model's estimates are accepted by the user
OK? Y ◄────
BATCH SIZE? 20
WHAT IS PRECEDING ITEM IN PRODUCTION SEQUENCE? 4,3
COMPETITOR,  UNIT SALES ◄
    1            350.  ◄──── Summary of the current situation for the new item
  TOTAL          350.  ◄
OUR SALES OF NEW ITEM? 200
OPTION FOR OTHER SALES CHANGES? ?
AVAILABLE OPTIONS:
 I  INDIVIDUALLY ENTERED SALES CHANGES
 P  PROMPTED SALES CHANGES
 D  DESCRIBE CURRENT SALES FURTHER BEFORE PROCEEDING
 E  END CHANGES

                             Model will lead the user with a series of questions
OPTION FOR OTHER SALES CHANGES? P ◄────
OF OUR     200. IN SALES, HOW MUCH (TOTAL)  COMES FROM COMPETITORS? 50
OF THE     150. REMAINING, HOW MUCH IS NEW PRIMARY  DEMAND? 75
    75. IS CANNIBALIZATION.
LIST TRANSFERS FROM OTHERS OF THE SAME     WEIGHT:
TRANSFER: ?
GIVE        COLOUR INDEX AND UNIT SALES TRANSFERRED
OR TYPE $ TO INDICATE NO MORE TRANSFERS TO SAME     WEIGHT
TRANSFER: 1,20 ◄────
TRANSFER: 2,35        20 units come from weight 3, colour 1 (140-weight white)
TRANSFER: $
LIST TRANSFERS FROM OTHERS OF SAME      COLOUR:
TRANSFER: 2,15
CHANGE UNACCEPTABLE - WE DO NOT MAKE ITEM  2, 3     ◄      Model catches an error
GIVE       WEIGHT INDEX AND UNIT SALES TRANSFERRED  ◄────
OR TYPE $ TO INDICATE NO MORE TRANSFERS TO SAME      COLOUR ◄
TRANSFER: 4,15
TRANSFER: $
    5. REMAINS: ◄──── The user has not yet accounted for all sales of the new item
TRANSFER: ?
SPECIFY TRANSFER BY GIVING     WEIGHT INDEX,     COLOUR INDEX AND CHANGE
OR TYPE $ TO  REQUEST DESCRIPTION FIRST
TRANSFER: 4,2,5
ANY OVERALL CHANGE IN OUR BUSINESS? N
ANY FURTHER INDIVIDUAL CHANGES? N
                                     The user requests the financial results
OPTION? F ◄────

                         THIS CASE     BASE CASE      VARIANCE    VAR %
REVENUE:                   4280.         4001.          279.        7.0
COST OF GOODS:             2284.         2144.          140.        6.5
-----------------------------------------------------------------
GROSS MARGIN:              1996.         1857.          139.        7.5
SCRAP CREDIT:               165.          153.           12.        7.8
SCRAP COST:                 453.          420.           33.        7.9
FIXED COST:                 200.          200.            0.        0.0
CARRYING COST:               79.           72.            7.        9.9

-----------------------------------------------------------------
EARNINGS BEFORE TAX:       1429.         1319.          110.        8.3

OUR UTILIZATION (HOURS):  82.96%
COMPETITORS' UTILIZATIONS (UNITS):   80.00%  87.50%
```

Exhibit 15.5 Dropping an item

The 140-weight buff will be dropped

```
OPTION? D
    WEIGHT INDEX,      COLOUR INDEX: 3,2
COMPETITOR,  UNIT SALES
    0             465.
    1             550.
    2             400.
  TOTAL          1415.
```

The current situation for 140-weight buff

```
OPTION FOR SALES CHANGES? P
OF OUR    465. IN SALES, HOW MUCH GOES TO COMPETITORS (TOTAL)? 300
GIVE RATIOS FOR DIVIDING THE SALES AMONG  COMPETITORS:
COMP 1: 2
COMP 2: 1
OF THE    165. REMAINING, HOW MUCH IS LOST TO  THE INDUSTRY? 75
    90. TRANSFERS TO OTHERS OF OUR OWN ITEMS:
LIST TRANSFERS TO OTHERS OF SAME     WEIGHT:
TRANSFER: 1,25
TRANSFER: 5
LIST TRANSFERS TO OTHERS OF THE SAME      COLOUR:
TRANSFER: 2,35
TRANSFER: 4,30
ANY OVERALL CHANGE IN OUR BUSINESS? N
ANY FURTHER INDIVIDUAL CHANGES? N
```

The user accounts for all of our sales of the item

```
OPTION? F
```

The financial implications

```
                         THIS CASE    BASE CASE     VARIANCE    VAR %
REVENUE:                     3530.        4001.        -471.    -11.8
COST OF GOODS:               1859.        2144.        -284.    -13.3
-------------------------------------------------------------
GROSS MARGIN:                1671.        1857.        -187.    -10.0
SCRAP CREDIT:                 132.         153.         -21.    -13.5
SCRAP COST:                   361.         420.         -58.    -13.9
FIXED COST:                   200.         200.           0.      0.0
CARRYING COST:                 64.          72.          -8.    -11.8

-------------------------------------------------------------
EARNINGS BEFORE TAX:         1178.        1319.        -140.    -10.6

OUR UTILIZATION (HOURS):   67.56%
COMPETITORS' UTILIZATIONS (UNITS):    90.00%  95.83%
```

Financial Modelling in Corporate Management, 2nd Edition
Edited by J. W. Bryant

16

The Use of Computers in Cash Management for the Small Company*

TONY RANDS AND BOB VAUSE

16.1 Introduction

Monitoring the movement of cash and controlling the cash flow is currently one of the key problems facing management in the smaller company, and the increased numbers of company liquidations over the last few years seem to indicate a failure to achieve this minimum requirement for business survival by many firms. However profitable a company may appear in its profit and loss account, if it fails to concentrate sufficient attention on cash flow management it can put its continued growth, and indeed survival, at considerable risk. The only certain means of ensuring survival in today's business climate is to maintain sufficient cash flow and liquid balances to cover payments to creditors. A company must always be able to pay its bills when they fall due. It is a lack of liquid cash funds that causes bankruptcy, not a low or negative profitability. For this reason the profit shown in the company's profit and loss account has long been seen as only one indicator of corporate success and management performance. The cash-flow statement is now seen by most managers as equally important as the profit and loss account, and the key indicator of the company's potential for growth or survival.

Unfortunately many small company managers concentrate their efforts solely in the generation of sales revenues and associated costs, and use profit as the main indicator of their business's success or failure. They pay little attention to cash-flow forecasting and control as, mistakenly, they believe this

*Revised with permission of the publisher from C. A. Rands, R. Vause and K. G. Pemberton, 'Using Computers in Small Company Cash Management', *Accounting and Business Research*; (16), Autumn 1974.

is a complex and difficult task. Indeed, for most small companies, the only time when any real effort is put into cash-flow forecasting is when the bank manager requests a cash budget to back up a request for loan or overdraft facilities being made by the company. Typically, once this exercise has been completed, the cash budget is relegated to the bottom drawer of the manager's desk and forgotten while he concentrates once more on generating sales.

The first sign of cash difficulties for a company is often that there is insufficient cash in the bank to pay a supplier. Management's response to this situation is often arbitrary and unplanned, consisting of an attempt to speed up the collection of cash from customers or applying to the bank for a short-term facility using the debtors expected to pay in the coming period as security. This solution is only, at best, a short-term palliative, and does little to get to the root causes of the company's difficulties. For a more exhaustive approach to the problem a series of questions must be considered:

(1) How was the cash crisis discovered?
(2) Did one particular decision precipitate the situation?
(3) What steps should be taken to remedy the situation?
(4) Could the crisis have been discovered earlier?
(5) How can similar situations be avoided in the future?

In recent years considerable advances have taken place in analytical techniques applicable to cash-flow control which can assist management to answer these questions. In parallel with these techniques there has been an even more rapid development in computer hardware and software, so that today for a few hundred pounds management can acquire for their company the computational power to analyse large and complex problems in a manner which a few years ago was, due to high capital costs, only open to the very large organizations.

It is the purpose of this chapter to consider how computer models of cash flow can provide ready and effective assistance to the management of the small company, to control cash flow, to predict potential cash-flow problems, and to provide assistance in determining what steps to take to remedy the situation.

16.2 Cash-flow Problems and Models

The cash flow of a company, and the residual cash balances at the end of each period, are the result of quite complicated movements in turning money into materials and services which are sold. The cash eventually received can once more be used to circulate within the company to generate further cash flows and profit, and to cover payments of taxation or dividends as well as to re-invest in capital assets necessary for the growth of the company.

At the simplest level, companies can develop a cash budget providing details of the cash movements expected within the coming period. This is achieved by translating the sales, production and other budgets into real cash-flow terms: when is the company going to have to pay cash out? This can be shown as:

	Month 1	*Month 2...*	*Total*
Opening cash balance	100	200	100
Cash inflow (sales)	300	400	700
Total cash available	400	600	800
Cash outflow (expenses)	200	400	600
(capital)	–	100	100
Closing cash balance	200	100	100

This is an example of a cash budget that many small companies will have supplied to their bank managers to assist in their loan or overdraft requests. It provides details of the manner in which the operations of the company, producing and selling goods, as well as investing in capital items (new machines or vans, for example) are going to be shown in the cash flow and balances for the coming period. The cash budget can show when money will be required to finance operations and when this, together with any interest, can be repaid.

This form of cash-flow forecasting or budgeting is quite simple. The difficulties management face in real life are normally due to a number of complementary factors such as time delays between the purchase of goods or raw materials and their sale and the eventual receipt of cash from the customers, seasonalities in trading which may cause large overdraft requirements at particular times each year, and the payment of lump sums (Corporation Tax and VAT, for example) during the year. Many of these factors impinge on each other in a complex manner, making it difficult for the small company manager to predict effectively cash movements and balances even a short time ahead. It is this that explains why many small company managers rely heavily on just knowing what their current cash position is, and making a series of day-to-day decisions relating to cash control under the mistaken assumption that in this way they are really in control of the company's cash flow. This approach, as many managers have learnt, can be a quick path to disaster.

The main difficulty facing managers trying to forecast cash flow is to allow for the interaction between the various factors which dictate cash movements within the firm, and it is towards assisting this process that most of the analytical techniques developed in recent years have been directed. The application of cash-flow modelling techniques allows the manager to build a model that represents the main structural elements in the company and the way in which they interact (for example, sales order patterns, sales deliveries, cash receipts from customers, etc.); by completing a series of calculations within the model, and receiving predictions from it in terms of cash flows for areas of specific concern, the manager is effectively simulating the operations of the company without having to await the actual events taking place. This provides the advantage of allowing a manager to feed into the model a series of possible alternative choices of action open to the company, together with likely outcomes to see, well ahead of the event, the expected impact upon the company's cash flow. The model anticipates the likely future impact of management action or policies and allows time for them to be assessed in order that the best alternative may be discovered.

Often a particular area of difficulty arises because many of the variables involved in the company's cash flow are subject to random fluctuations, and act to disguise the true cash-flow pattern developing. This means that in order to develop a truly useful cash-flow model, it must be possible to incorporate a facility to enable the manager to identify quickly whether adverse trends are developing. This can be achieved by isolating the trends from the random movements in cash that inevitably occur within any company. The adoption of a system of control charts, similar to those used in quality control, can assist in this process. Control lines can be drawn within which the cash flow is expected to fall. Should the actual cash flow move outside the range of the control lines, then this may act as a stimulus to the manager to question whether there is an adverse trend developing.

Inherent in many methods involving forecasting cash flows is the problem that the manager can only develop a single best estimate of the firm's likely cash flow, and is not offered the facility to develop effective control lines for any possible variations from this resulting from random fluctuations in cash movements. Thus these models may inform the manager what the overall cash flow is likely to be, but make it difficult for him to decide when corrective action should be initiated, or when no action should be taken. These models tend to have more application in cash-flow forecasting and planning rather than in day-to-day cash-flow control.

Often the reason why cash-flow models only allow the prediction of expected or most likely cash-flow outcomes, and do not indicate possible variations in cash flow, is that calculating such variations is often complex and time consuming when related to the small company. For just this reason it is a distinct advantage if cash-flow modelling can be accomplished with the use of computers, as these can be used to perform the rather tedious calculations necessary to determine likely cash-flow variations. Until quite recently the cost involved in using computer facilities, and the complexity and cost of cash-flow modelling designed for computer operation, has outweighed, for the small firm, any possible advantages which might occur.

Within the last few years this situation has changed quite dramatically. Firstly, computers have been reduced in both size and cost, so that today a machine will easily fit in the desk space previously occupied by a typewriter, and at minimal cost can offer the same computational capacity as machines of ten or so years ago requiring a special building to house them, with a cost of several million pounds. In addition, developments in modelling techniques allow models to be built that only require basic readily available company data, and which may be programmed simply by a manager with little experience in computer technology or programming.

This chapter continues with a description of the manner in which such a simple computer-modelling exercise can be effected to meet the needs of the small company.

16.3 A Computer Modelling Method for Cash-flow Management

The computer model described here has been developed at the Oxford Management Centre. It is suited to the needs of small companies because it is relatively easy to build the model and program the computer, while the information required is only basic data that any properly managed small company should have available.

Standard Program Blocks

A major difficulty in the development of a computer model of cash flow is to ensure that the model can represent the actual flows of cash, materials and services in the company. As each company is to a large extent unique in the kinds of services it offers and the relationships between the different cash-flow elements, this means no single standard cash-flow model may be used for all small companies. Instead, each company requires an individual model to be constructed for it alone, building the basic elements of cash-flows in the same way as they interact within the real company.

Building different elements together has always been one of the major difficulties with traditional computer programming, but developments in software now allow the various elements to be brought together simply and easily. A key feature of the model developed at Oxford, therefore, is that it contains blocks of computer programs which represent standard cash-flow operations. All a manager has to do is to bring together these blocks following the same structural relationship as exists in his company. In the Oxford model, he may do this directly from his cash-flow statements, in the way that is described below.

Each standard block of computer program that corresponds to a cash-flow operation is recognized by an identifying code. In modelling the system, it is only necessary to refer to the identifier, and the computer will place the cash-flow program corresponding to it in any position relative to other program blocks that is dictated by the manager. The modelling system contains a number of different program blocks that correspond to different elements of cash flows. Examples of these are shown, together with their identifying codes, in Table 16.1.

Table 16.1 Some examples of cash-flow operations and program block identifiers

Cash-flow operation	Identifying code of program block	Symbols in cash-flow diagrams
Running balance	B	[B]
Delay	D	(D)
Net VAT owed	V	[V]
Forecast	F	(F)
VAT rate	R	(R)

Constructing a Simple Cash-flow Model

To illustrate how a model may be constructed using this method, a simple example of a company shipping goods ex-stock and receiving cash at some time later from its debtors will be used. The first stage is to develop a flow diagram of the cash movements using appropriate symbols. This is given in Figure 16.1(a), where it can be seen that a forecast of the goods shipped is used, with a delay between this and the receipt of cash. The balance between the goods shipped and the receipt of cash gives the outstanding debtors; this is achieved by keeping a running balance between goods delivered and cash received later for those goods.

If the problem were slightly different, and the manager concerned could forecast sales orders received but not deliveries because of internal delays within the stock-handling system, then Figure 16.1(a) could be modified easily to give Figure 16.1(b).

In order that a flow diagram may be programmed into the computer each separate block must be identified by a number, and these have been added to Figure 16.1(b). The flow diagram is converted into a computer program by using a table that specifies the block number from which each cash-flow element receives its inputs. In this table, each line refers to a different cash flow block, and the layout of each line follows a format which tells the computer where inputs come from. The format for each line is:

Block number title	*Block type*	*Source of Input 1*	*Source of Input 2*	*Source of Input 3*

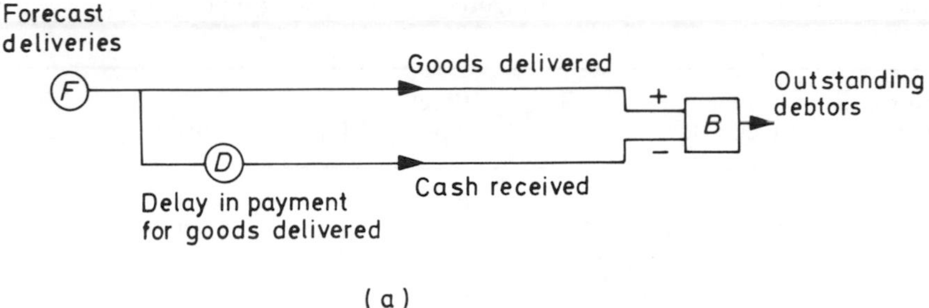

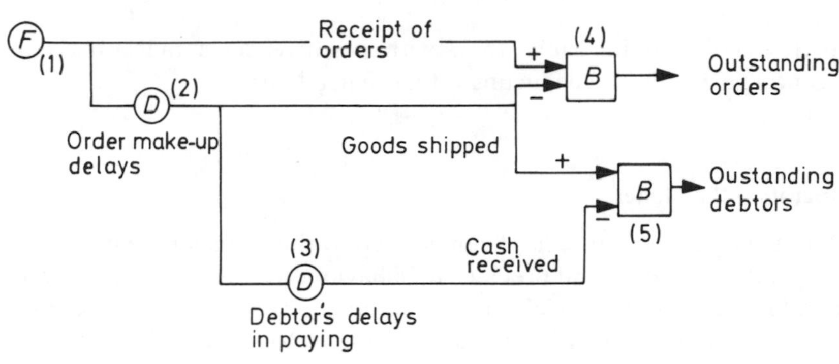

Figure 16.1 Flow diagrams for debtor's model. (a) Original model, (b) modified model

Following this format means, for instance, that the line for the delay in making up orders for shipment in Figure 16.1(b) would appear in the computer program as:

Block number title	*Block type*	*Source of Input 1*	*Source of Input 2*	*Source of Input 3*
2	D	1	0	0

The zeros under Inputs 2 and 3 indicate that the delay has only one input.

Using this table format means that a computer program corresponding to the flow diagram of Figure 16.1(b) may be written quickly and simply by a manager once the method of writing the table format has been learned. Moreover, it is easy to change the model structure by merely changing the flow diagram, and making appropriate corrections to the table. The complete program for Figure

Table 16.2 Computer program for Figure 16.1(b) showing inputs to each cash-flow element

Block number	Block title	Block type	Input 1	Input 2	Input 3
1	Order forecast	F	0	0	0
2	Order delay	D	1	0	0
3	Debtor payment delay	D	2	0	0
4	Order balance	B	1	−2	0
5	Debtors balance	B	2	−3	0

16.1(b) is shown in Table 16.2, with negative signs indicating that the balancing elements are deducting rather than adding.

Operating the Model

Once the model structure has been defined by the manager, he is in a position to operate the model and predict the behaviour of areas of special interest to him. In order that the model may be operated, it is necessary for the computer to be fed with certain basic data, such as values for expected orders received, the nature of the delay patterns, opening values for running balances such as outstanding debtors and others. Once the model is developed, the manager may specify what outputs he requires and these may be printed either numerically or graphically.

The manner in which a typical cash model would assist a manager is shown in Figure 16.2. There are a number of inputs to the model, namely the manager's forecasts of the external environment, e.g. the receipts of sales orders, and

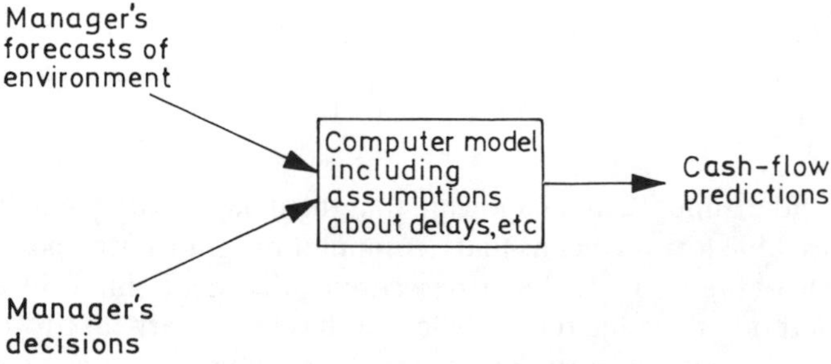

Figure 16.2 Operation of the model

decisions the manager expect to make. These decisions could be one area where the manager may want the model to help him determine strategies, such as the most viable manufacturing policy given seasonalities in demand. Built into the model are the relationships between cash-flow elements that have already been described, as well as the values of these elements, such as opening cash balances and the length of delays. Outputs from the model may be predictions of net cash balances, or other factors that will help the manager to investigate the cash-flow impact of his policies.

16.4 An Example of the Application of the Method

The Company

In order to show how the computer modelling method may be used, its application to a small electronics company will be described. This company manufactured electronic equipment which was marketed through a chain of distributors into the retail network. The company's operations were essentially the assembly of equipment from purchased-in components, and the supply ex-stock of equipment against orders received from distributors.

The basic data from which a cash-flow model was developed is shown in Table 16.3. This shows the movements of cash into materials, labour, and other variables, for the year previous to the cash exercise. It can be seen that the data contained in Table 16.3 is no more than the fundamental necessary to monitor the cash flow of the company. It can also be seen that the company uses some of its own conventions of accounting, e.g. that materials and overheads creditors are kept together.

Flow Diagram

The first stage in building a model for the firm was to develop a flow diagram that represented the cash movements within the company. Clearly there is a flow of materials into the company based on orders placed at suppliers, and there is a flow of products leaving the company based on orders received from customers. These materials generate a cash outflow and a cash inflow that has to be balanced against the outflows of cash into labour and overheads. An initial flow diagram related to this application is shown in Figure 16.3(a). It can be seen that this has been built using the structure of Figure 16.1(b) to represent both the outflow of materials as products and inflows as components for assembly. Additionally other factors have been added, such as outflows of cash for wages and salaries, overheads, VAT and Corporation Tax.

Table 16.3 Basic data for cash-flow model

Orders received	Jan 18 000	Feb 31 000	Mar 32 000	Apr 35 645	May 36 000	June 22 610	July 16 735	Aug 55 875	Sept 11 200	Oct 7 200	Nov 33 260	Dec 42 050
A Sales delivered	19 344	21 943	19 415	23 002	27 625	25 030	18 015	29 553	24 246	17 180	29 233	41 164
C Mats. bought	5 450	10 101	8 653	17 919	6 903	7 963	5 402	10 057	9 456	5 456	7 619	12 219
Labour:												
Weekly	6 088	6 744	8 096	7 009	7 652	9 810	6 822	10 236	7 241	4 970	9 726	9 720
Monthly	2 500	2 465	2 465	2 700	2 710	2 830	2 446	2 560	2 856	2 693	2 444	2 363
C O/H incurred	4 500	2 800	7 100	4 344	4 281	4 122	6 076	6 011	7 531	2 620	2 685	4 955
B Debtors	71 000	70 818	60 609	62 328	73 727	73 862	69 709	68 934	73 312	59 596	57 928	77 473
D Creditors (Mats + O/H)	30 294	25 990	23 726	40 280	37 487	39 747	37 463	40 858	46 049	36 901	23 031	35 479
Bank (OD)	13 980	110 000	110 533	113 821	122 748	115 508	122 573	112 379	120 390	114 095	112 748	107 359
WIP	38 000	48 000	62 500	75 620	84 240	82 595	81 315	107 860	95 030	85 220	89 470	90 530
Creditors + O/H payments	10 764	7 224	12 635	15 160	16 509	8 952	15 781	13 340	10 707	17 065	7 474	31 481

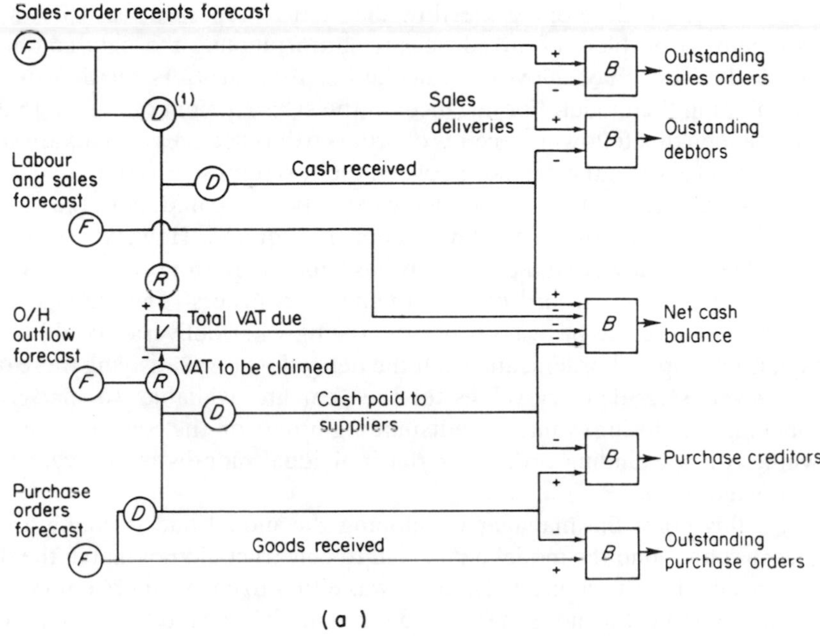

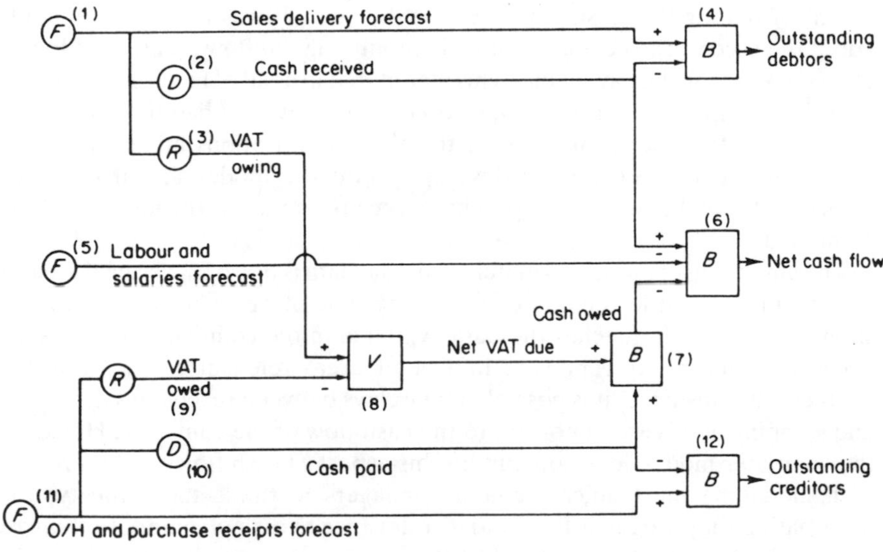

Figure 16.3 Flow diagram for cash-flow model. (a) Initial flow diagram, (b) amended flow diagram

However, in developing the flow diagram to represent cash flows in the company, a problem occurred because unfortunately the data contained in Table 16.3 does not allow the calculation of parameters relating to certain variables in the model. For instance, in the sales element of Figure 16.3(a), it can be seen that following receipts of orders from customers, goods are shipped out at a later time, the balance between the two representing outstanding sales orders. In order for the value of delay (1) to be calculated, both the past order receipts *and* levels of outstanding orders are required. However, examination of Table 16.3 shows that the company has kept records for orders received from customers, but no record of outstanding sales orders. The managers in the company therefore have no way of knowing what deliveries could be made against receipts of orders, and what the delay time is in satisfying these orders. However, sales-delivery values for the year are available, so that given an opening (or closing) value for outstanding orders on the company, remaining values of outstanding orders for the individual months of the year may be deducted.

At this point the manager developing the model had to make a choice, because he found the model he wanted to construct did not match the data he had available. The choice to be made was either to collect more data so that he might construct the model he wanted, or to modify the model he wanted in line with the data available. In this case the company did not keep a running balance of outstanding customer's orders, and moreover did not at that time have any means of finding the closing balance for the year. It was therefore forced to adopt the second choice above, namely modifying the flow diagram of Figure 16.3(a) to suit the data available. This meant that instead of feeding in forecasts of order receipts from customers, a forecast of deliveries had to be made (in other words the sales achieved). With other modifications made, the initial flow diagram of the company developed into the model shown in Figure 16.3(b). It can be seen that purchase receipts and overheads have been combined.

The amending of models to match available data is one of the crucial areas in cash planning, and in the modelling of any type of problem. Figure 16.3(b) shows a model that matches the data available in the company, but does not necessarily accurately represent important areas relevant to the cash-flow problem. For instance, it is possible that delays between receiving sales orders and shipping goods are important to the cash flow of the company. However, the computer model does not contain this aspect of cash flow, and therefore, cash modelling must quickly enable managers to think about the type of information they are recording, and its relevance to cash planning. In this case it may have been to the advantage of the company to record outstanding sales orders, and thereby be able to assess the effects of delays in satisfying these orders, by incorporating them in the computer model.

Programming and Operation of the Model

The computer program related to the flow diagram of Figure 16.3(b) can now be written in the tabular form that has been previously described. The program itself is shown in Table 16.4.

Table 16.4 Computer program for cash-flow model

Block number	Block title	Block type	Input 1	Input 2	Input 3
1	Sales delivery forecast	F	0	0	0
2	Debtors payment delay	D	1	0	0
3	VAT on receipts	R	1	0	0
4	Debtors balance	B	1	−2	0
5	Labour forecast	F	0	0	0
6	Net cash balance	B	2	−5	−7
7	Cash owed	B	8	10	0
8	Net VAT owing	V	3	−9	0
9	Purchase VAT rate	R	11	0	0
10	Payment delay	D	11	0	0
11	O/H forecast	F	0	0	0
12	Creditors balance	B	11	−10	0

The first stage in model evaluation is for the computer to calculate the values of delays in the cash-flow system corresponding to Blocks 2 and 10. The delay represented by rows A and B of Table 16.3 is 2.62 months with a variation having a standard deviation of 0.234 months. This is the debtors' delay, which corresponds to Block 2. The amount of credit taken by the company (Block 10) is calculated from rows C and D of Table 16.3, which give a mean delay of 2.88 months with a variation having a standard deviation of 0.186 months.

To operate the model, these values for delays were used for the period to be investigated, as it was assumed that payment patterns would not be changing quickly. Forecasts, and decisions likely to be taken in the company, were then fed into the model a typical set being given in Table 16.5. This shows the sales deliveries the manager expects to be made, given the orders already on hand and the priorities quoted to customers. At the same time the manager has included the materials he expects to receive, given the orders placed on suppliers and the additional orders placed to satisfy orders on hand.

Table 16.5 Forecasts used by cash-flow model

	January	February	March	April
Sales deliveries anticipated	28 600	33 000	38 500	38 500
Mats. received	9 900	11 000	11 000	12 100
Labour: Weekly	9 300	9 600	10 000	10 500
Monthly	2 600	2 600	2 400	2 900
O/H	7 000	7 000	7 000	7 000

Table 16.5 also contains the manager's estimate of the labour costs required to meet these planned delivery patterns.

Typical outputs from the model for these inputs are shown in Figures 16.4 and 16.5. Figure 16.4 shows the expected cumulative receipts of cash predicted by the model and includes the cumulative deliveries planned by the company. Here, therefore, the vertical distance between the lines represents the debtors of the company, the initial distance corresponding to the opening debtors at the end of December (i.e. £77 473). It can be seen in Figure 16.4 that the computer has predicted the region in which the actual cumulative cash received is likely to fall, and has therefore given an indication of the possible variations in cash received over the months January to April. Figure 16.5 meanwhile shows the cash inflow expected in any single month, and also contains control lines which indicated the maximum and minimum likely cash inflow in a single month. It can be seen that the general level of uncertainty on cash inflows in individual months (shown in Figure 16.5) is proportionately greater than the uncertainty on the cumulative inflows over several months (shown in Figure 16.4). The use of cumulative values is explained in a number of statistical textbooks and will not be explained here.

The computer will print outputs from any of the blocks specified in the program shown in Table 16.4. In this instance the management were interested in the cash outflows to pay creditors as well as the overall net cash flow and so the cumulative cash outflows likely to be incurred to creditors, as well as the individual expected cash outflow for each month were also plotted as well as the expected net cash flows in the company over the period of time covered by the forecast.

16.5 The Value of a Model

Models used as part of management decision-making can help managers in a number of ways, and this is particularly true in the case of cash-flow models. The most obvious use for a model is to predict likely outcomes, given events that managers believe will take place as in the example just described. However, models may effectively be used to help managers identify where

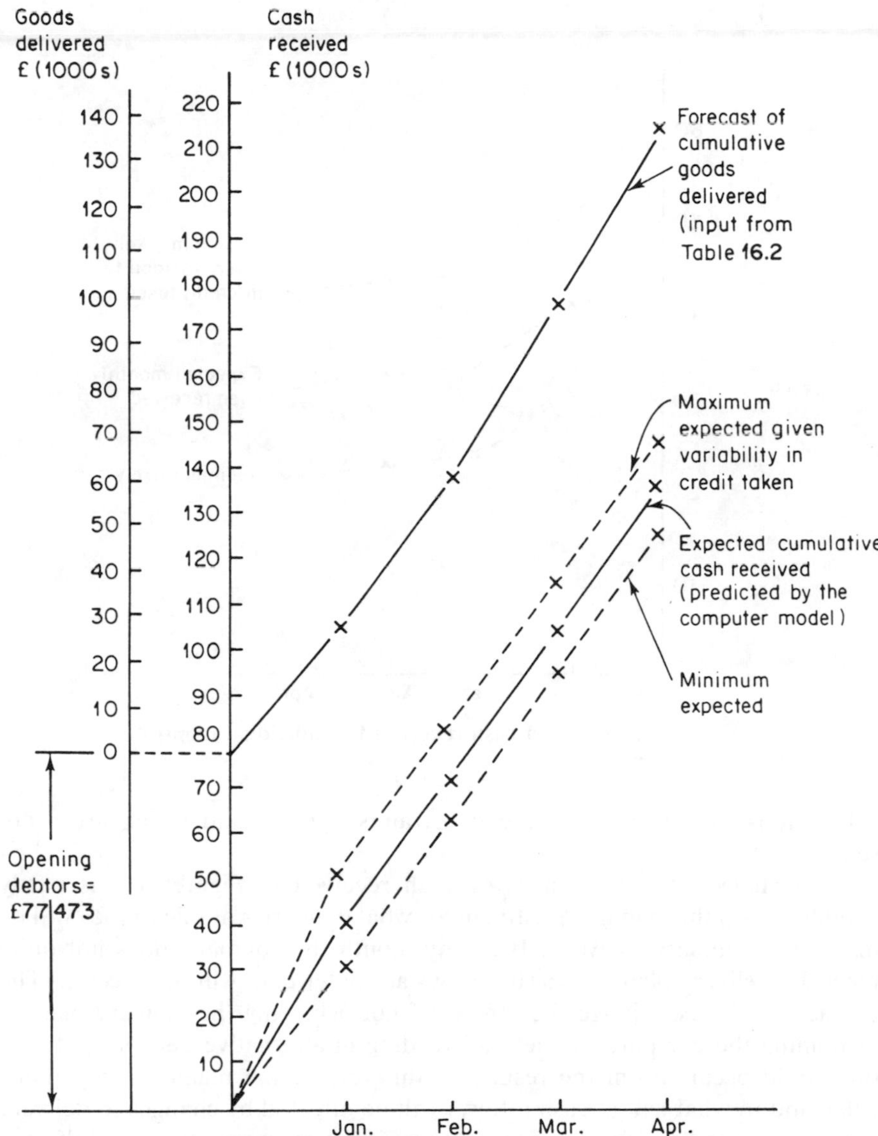

Figure 16.4 Cumulative forecast of cash received

specific constraints in their businesses lie, and where major sensitive areas are likely to be. These two aspects of modelling are most important where cash planning is concerned, as the identification of constraints and sensitivities are essential to obtain control over cash flows. Here the ability to use computers to operate the models is an advantage, as these can quickly do the necessary

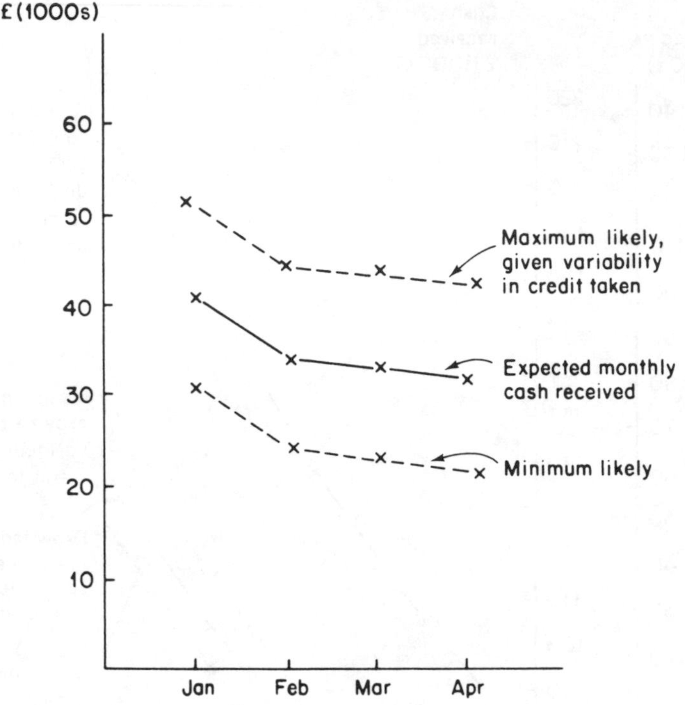

Figure 16.5 Forecast cash received for individual months

calculations to determine where constraints operate and which areas are sensitive.

For instance, the graph line for cash received in Figure 16.4 is partly conditional on the manager's estimate of what deliveries of sales goods will be made from January to April. If in any month the company does not quite meet the delivery plan, the cash inflows at a later date will be affected. The manager may easily judge the effects of not achieving the delivery plan by re-running the computer model and feeding in alternative delivery patterns that could occur. From the results of this return, the manager may judge when and to what extent cash inflows will be affected by changes in delivery patterns. It can be seen that, for instance, if the company does not fulfil the January sales delivery target, this will make no difference to cash inflows until March, because cash receipts for January and February will come from goods already delivered in October, November and December. The computer model will indicate to what extent cash receipts beyond March are likely to be influenced by a failure to meet January's deliveries target, and the manager can judge how important maintaining deliveries is in the control of the total net cash flow.

The ability of computer models to allow managers to calculate quickly the effects of alternative decisions or events on future outcomes means they may prove useful in helping managers formulate policies. This is particularly valuable whenever seasonal variations in business occur. For instance, the cash model described has been used by the managers of a company manufacturing goods with a marked seasonal trade to determine an acceptable manufacturing policy, given that during sales troughs continued production to meet the next peak generally caused large overdrafts to occur, with high interest charges. The managers could have performed the calculations manually, but this would have been very time consuming and tedious, which in fact meant the calculations were never done. However, with a computer model, the effects of alternative manufacturing could be calculated quickly so the managers could judge which policies were likely to be the most successful.

16.6 Conclusions

This chapter has covered the broad application of modelling techniques using computer or microcomputer hardware and software to problems of monitoring and control in the cash flow of the smaller firm and discusses one type of model. Given the current state of the art in these areas and further likely developments in computers, the small firm should be encouraged to assess seriously the introduction of some form of mechanized assistance within this area of planning. There are additional advantages too, in that although the hardware may immediately assist in cash-flow forecasting and control, it may also offer the potential of a wider range of future applications within the overall operation and control of the business. By undertaking the initial efforts of understanding and applying computer modelling to cash planning, management may be able to create a ready-made tool for further applications within their companies.

of the company of simulation models to allow managers to calculate quickly the effects of alternative decisions or events on future outcomes means they are an essential and helpful aid to corporate policy. This is particularly valuable where consideration of alternatives, e.g. the consideration of each alternative [illegible] the [illegible] but this would have [illegible] [illegible] [illegible] [illegible] [illegible] calculations were never done. However, with a computer model, the effects of alternative [illegible] [illegible] [illegible] [illegible] so the managers [illegible] [illegible] which [illegible] [illegible] [illegible].

[illegible] Conclusions

The chapter has covered the [illegible] of [illegible] [illegible] [illegible] [illegible] [illegible] [illegible] [illegible] [illegible] [illegible] [illegible] [illegible] [illegible] and control [illegible] the small firm should be [illegible] companies.

Financial Modelling in Corporate Management, 2nd Edition
Edited by J. W. Bryant

17

The Loan/Deposit Forecasting Model

JAE SHIM, S. V. LE AND CHERESSE SMOOT

17.1 Introduction

Banks in the United States have been controlled by a strong system of regulation since 1933. Government control over the banking industry was designed to provide soundness and stability to the industry. Beginning in the 1970s, the industry and regulators began studying the concept of deregulation. In 1980, the Depository Institutions Deregulation and Monetary Control Act was passed. This Act has been the primary force in deregulating the banking industry. In addition, other restrictions relating to the offering of financial services were amended with the Garn-St. German Act in 1982.

The pressures on the banking system and the emerging structure of the financial services industry have resulted from basic economic and competitive forces, such as an increased volatility in interest rates, greater customer sophistication, technological change and increased competition among different types of institutions. The most devastating change was inflation. The financial industry was not prepared for the double-digit inflation that occurred in the 1970s. As a result, high and volatile interest rates had an adverse effect on the banking structure. As open market rates climbed past deposit rate ceilings mandated under Regulation Q, depository institutions experienced disintermediation as deposits flowed out of these institutions. With the phasing out of Regulation Q for larger CDs in 1973, this pressure from large depositors eased. It was replaced by pressure from smaller depositors, causing a major structural change in the composition of bank liabilities. This change resulted in a general shift of funds from instruments that carried below-market rates to instruments that earned a market-determined rate. Another major result of the volatile interest rates was the substantially adverse impact upon the financial strength of the thrift institutions which were burdened with a large amount of low-yielding fixed-rate mortgage.

The situation in banking today is one in which fundamental external forces such as greater interest volatility, rapid technology change, deregulation of Reg. Q, increased competition and increased cash management sophistications have contributed to a change in the deposit mix. The higher cost of funds and the volatility of deposits have prompted bankers to reformulate their approach to asset/liability management.

Faced with growing competitive pressures and expanding opportunities, commercial banks' need for strategic planning has become critical and a formal asset/liability management system has become a necessity.

The objective of this chapter is to outline a loan/deposit forecasting model, utilizing Lotus 1-2-3, which is intended for asset/liability management. This model can be utilized for simulation purpose and can be applied to answer a variety of 'what-if' questions for bankers.

17.2 The Loan/Deposit Model

Objectives

The objective of a formal asset/liability management programme is to formulate a strategic plan which would yield the highest return to the shareholders with the minimum of risk. A key component in such a strategic plan is the ability to simulate various scenarios and to determine the potential risk associated with various loan or deposit policies. The formulated Loan/Deposit Forecasting Model has the following features:

(1) Forecasting asset/liability balances for the next year to determine the relationship between growth and the net interest margin.
(2) Changing the deposit mix and loan mix to determine the impact of a marketing campaign on the net interest margin.
(3) Developing interest rate mix to determine the impact of interest rate volatility on the net interest margin.

Structure

The Loan/Deposit Forecasting Model consists of the following items: (1) the current and projected balance sheet: the asset and liability matrices, (2) the interest rate matrix, and (3) the income statement: net interest margin calculations.

Asset and Liability Matrices

The asset and liability matrices can be constructed utilizing the current and historical data, the percentage of each asset and liability account as a percentage of total assets, and the historical and peer group trends. Various scenarios of projected asset and liability mix can be constructed for simulation purposes.

Interest Rate Matrix

The projections of various interest categories is dependent upon the interest rate matrix. Although actual interest rates are difficult to predict, the yield spread between various interest rates remains fairly stable over time. Therefore, a review of historical trends in interest rates should indicate the spread relationships between the various asset/liability categories. The interest rate matrix can be constructed utilizing yield spread information and interest rates projected by various economists such as Data Resources Inc. (DRI) or Chase Econometrics.

Template

The Loan/Deposit model has been developed and implemented within the programming environment provided by the Lotus 1-2-3 system. The detailed form of the model will not be described here; instead, the way in which it appears to a user is outlined, and some specimen output presented.

The model is menu driven: that is, the user moves through the program by making choices in response to sets of options (menus) shown on the VDU screen. A hierarchy of menus is available for display to the user; in the present case, there are four levels of menu present. The menu structure for the model is shown in Table 17.1. (The fourth level of menu has been omitted for simplicity; this is accessed through the selection of PRINT under the MIX menu where asterisked.) Initially, the user is shown the Main Menu, and has to select between the six options shown (i.e. ASSET, INTEREST, RATES, PRINT, SETUP, QUIT). A response to any of these leads to the presentation of the corresponding Secondary Menu (shown in the second column of Table 17.1). A further response either causes some action to be taken (e.g. the calculation or output of a report), or else leads to another level within the menu hierarchy (e.g. back up to the Main Menu, or down to a Tertiary Menu). Thus a response of ASSET to the Main Menu, produces the Secondary Menu containing FORECAST, MIX and QUIT; selection here of MIX produces the Tertiary Menu containing PRINT, CHANGE, ACTUAL and QUIT; a choice now of PRINT leads to the generation of a report of the chosen loan/deposit mix, and then re-presents the same Tertiary Menu as before; a response this time of QUIT throws up the original Main Menu once more; and so on. The user has simply to proceed as directed by the screen.

It may be noted from the menu structure that the system is capable of generating a variety of output reports. The most important of these are:

(1) Balance Sheet: the asset/liabilities matrix giving a monthly breakdown under various conditions (e.g. 10 per cent annual growth; to give total assets \$100 000 at year end)

(2) Interest Income and Expense Report: the application of the interest rate matrix and loan/deposit mix under chosen conditions (e.g. Prime rate 15 per cent, Actual loan mix; Prime rate 10 per cent, Projected loan mix)

Table 17.1 Menu structure of loan/deposit model

Main Menu	Secondary Menu	Tertiary Menu
ASSET	FORECAST f/c total asset growth for year	AMOUNT f/c year end total asset balance
		PERCENT f/c total asset annual growth rate
		QUIT return to main menu
	MIX f/c deposit/loan mix	PRINT print loan/deposit mix (*)
		CHANGE f/c loan/deposit mix
		ACTUAL send loan/deposit mix to actual
		QUIT return to main menu
	QUIT return to main menu	
INTEREST	DISPLAY show year end total net interest	
	QUIT return to main menu	
RATES	PRIME enter forecasted prime rate	
	SETUP setup interest rate matrix	
	QUIT return to main menu	
PRINT	REPORTS print various reports	RATES print interest rate matrix
		ASSET print balance sheet
		INTEREST print interest I & E report
		QUIT return to print menu
	SETUP setup printer for output	
	QUIT return to main menu	
SETUP	CURRENT input current balance sheet	
	NAME input name of bank	
	YEAR enter year to be forecasted	
	QUIT return to main menu	
EXIT	QUIT leave main menu	
	EXIT leave forecasting program	NO return to main menu
		YES confirm exit from program

Additionally, the data values held (the interest rate matrix, loan mix, etc.) can be printed out. Some specimen output reports are shown in Exhibit 17.1 in the Appendix to this chapter.

Application

The forecasting model is designed to help a bank plan a course of action which will yield the highest return with a minimum risk.

The first application for the model is to determine the amount of interest rate risk. Applying different interest rate forecasts (an increase or decrease in the prime rate forecast) to the projected assets and liabilities will help management determine the amount of interest rate risk they have in their proposed plan. The second application is to determine how promotional programmes will affect the interest margin. For example, paying a premium on Money Market Deposit Accounts (MMDA) to increase balances so that the bank can reduce the balances in Time Certificates of Deposits (TCD). The steps to be followed for simulation are as follows:

Step 1: Forecast new MMDA rate (increase)
Forecast new TCD rate (decrease)
Step 2: Forecast maximum mix change expected
Step 3: Forecast minimum mix change expected
Step 4: Review results

This application can be applied to both deposit or loan promotions.

Of course, the third application is to forecast market risk should the consumer alter his deposit or loan needs or if the competition institutes a new promotional programme which will affect the bank.

17.3 Conclusion

Increased competition, deregulation and increased consumer demands have forced the banking industry to develop a formal asset/liability management system such as the model called The Loan/Deposit Forecasting Model introduced in this chapter. The type of the model can easily be built within the framework of the Lotus 1-2-3 Spreadsheet Program. The main characteristic of such a model is its ability to perform 'what-if' scenarios to determine the potential risk to a bank should it adopt various loan or deposit policies. The model can be easily modified to tailor to the specific needs of an individual bank.

Appendix to Chapter 17

In Exhibit 17.1 below, sample output reports obtained based upon various 'what-if' scenarios are presented. (For a copy of the model system diskette, write to Professor Jae K. Shim, School of Business, California State University Long Beach, 1250 Bellflower Blvd, Long Beach, CA 90840 USA.)

Exhibit 17.1

(a) Balance Sheet: 10 per cent p.a. growth in total assets

ANYTIME BANK
FORECAST FOR 1985
01-Dec-84

	BUDGET JANUARY	BUDGET FEBRUARY	BUDGET MARCH	BUDGET APRIL	BUDGET MAY
*** A S S E T S ***					
CASH/CASH ITEMS	$371	$374	$377	$380	$383
DUE FROM BANKS - DEMAND	$2,521	$2,542	$2,563	$2,583	$2,604
TOTAL SECURITIES	$1,513	$1,525	$1,538	$1,550	$1,563
DUE FROM BANKS - TIME	$303	$305	$308	$310	$313
FED FUNDS SOLD	$4,817	$4,857	$4,896	$4,936	$4,976
COMMERCIAL LOANS	$22,183	$22,367	$22,550	$22,733	$22,917
REAL ESTATE LOANS	$6,958	$7,015	$7,073	$7,130	$7,188
INSTALMENT LOANS	$6,857	$6,913	$6,970	$7,027	$7,083
XTRA MONEY	$151	$153	$154	$155	$156
LEASES	$378	$381	$384	$388	$391
OTHER LOANS	$35	$36	$36	$36	$36
LESS UNDISBURSED	$101	$102	$103	$103	$104
TOTAL LOANS	$36,461	$36,763	$37,064	$37,365	$37,667
RES FOR LOAN LOSSES	$365	$368	$371	$374	$377
NET LOANS	$36,096	$36,395	$36,693	$36,991	$37,290
BANK PREMISES	$2,954	$2,979	$3,003	$3,028	$3,052
OTHER REAL ESTATE OWNED	$504	$508	$513	$517	$521
OTHER ASSETS	$1,260	$1,271	$1,281	$1,292	$1,302
TOTAL ASSETS	$50,339	$50,755	$51,171	$51,587	$52,003
*** L I A B I L I T I E S ***					
DEMAND	$14,369	$14,488	$14,606	$14,725	$14,844
NOW ACCOUNTS	$908	$915	$923	$930	$938
SUPER NOW ACCOUNTS	$2,521	$2,542	$2,563	$2,583	$2,604
MONEY MARKET DEPOSIT ACCOUNTS	$11,092	$11,183	$11,275	$11,367	$11,458
TOTAL INT/DDA	$14,520	$14,640	$14,760	$14,880	$15,000
SAVINGS	$1,815	$1,830	$1,845	$1,860	$1,875
TCD	$13,108	$13,217	$13,325	$13,433	$13,542
PUBLIC FUNDS	$1,412	$1,423	$1,435	$1,447	$1,458
TOTAL TIME	$16,335	$16,470	$16,605	$16,740	$16,875
TOTAL DEPOSITS	$45,224	$45,598	$45,971	$46,345	$46,719
FED FUNDS PURCHASED	$353	$356	$359	$362	$365
OTHER BORROWED FUNDS	$55	$56	$56	$57	$57
OTHER LIABILITIES	$1,008	$1,017	$1,025	$1,033	$1,042
TOTAL LIABILITIES	$46,640	$47,026	$47,411	$47,797	$48,182
*** C A P I T A L ***					
CAPITAL NOTE	$420	$420	$420	$420	$420
***SHAREHOLDER'S EQUITY					
ADDITION TO CAPITAL STOCK	$500	$500	$500	$500	$500
CAPITAL STOCK	$1,533	$1,533	$1,533	$1,533	$1,533
RETAINED EARNINGS	$1,246	$1,276	$1,307	$1,337	$1,368
TOTAL EQUITY CAPITAL	$3,279	$3,309	$3,340	$3,370	$3,401
TOTAL CAPITAL/NOTE	$3,699	$3,729	$3,760	$3,790	$3,821
TOTAL LIAB/CAPITAL	$50,339	$50,755	$51,171	$51,587	$52,003

BUDGET JUNE	BUDGET JULY	BUDGET AUGUST	BUDGET SEPTEMBER	BUDGET OCTOBER	BUDGET NOVEMBER	BUDGET DECEMBER	DECEMBER 1984
$386	$389	$393	$396	$399	$402	$405	$368
$2,625	$2,646	$2,667	$2,688	$2,708	$2,729	$2,750	$2,500
$1,575	$1,588	$1,600	$1,613	$1,625	$1,638	$1,650	$1,500
$315	$318	$320	$323	$325	$328	$330	$300
$5,016	$5,056	$5,095	$5,135	$5,175	$5,215	$5,255	$4,777
$23,100	$23,283	$23,467	$23,650	$23,833	$24,017	$24,200	$22,000
$7,245	$7,303	$7,360	$7,418	$7,475	$7,533	$7,590	$6,900
$7,140	$7,197	$7,253	$7,310	$7,367	$7,423	$7,480	$6,800
$158	$159	$160	$161	$163	$164	$165	$150
$394	$397	$400	$403	$406	$409	$413	$375
$37	$37	$37	$38	$38	$38	$39	$35
$105	$106	$107	$108	$108	$109	$110	$100
$37,968	$38,269	$38,571	$38,872	$39,173	$39,475	$39,776	$36,160
$380	$383	$386	$389	$392	$395	$398	$362
$37,588	$37,886	$38,185	$38,483	$38,781	$39,079	$39,378	$35,798
$3,077	$3,101	$3,125	$3,150	$3,174	$3,199	$3,223	$2,930
$525	$529	$533	$538	$542	$546	$550	$500
$1,313	$1,323	$1,333	$1,344	$1,354	$1,365	$1,375	$1,250
$52,419	$52,835	$53,251	$53,667	$54,083	$54,499	$54,915	$49,923
$14,963	$15,081	$15,200	$15,319	$15,438	$15,556	$15,675	$14,250
$945	$953	$960	$968	$975	$983	$990	$900
$2,625	$2,646	$2,667	$2,688	$2,708	$2,729	$2,750	$2,500
$11,550	$11,642	$11,733	$11,825	$11,917	$12,008	$12,100	$11,000
$15,120	$15,240	$15,360	$15,480	$15,600	$15,720	$15,840	$14,400
$1,890	$1,905	$1,920	$1,935	$1,950	$1,965	$1,980	$1,800
$13,650	$13,758	$13,867	$13,975	$14,083	$14,192	$14,300	$13,000
$1,470	$1,482	$1,493	$1,505	$1,517	$1,528	$1,540	$1,400
$17,010	$17,145	$17,280	$17,415	$17,550	$17,685	$17,820	$16,200
$47,093	$47,466	$47,840	$48,214	$48,588	$48,961	$49,335	$44,850
$368	$370	$373	$376	$379	$382	$385	$350
$58	$58	$59	$59	$60	$60	$61	$55
$1,050	$1,058	$1,067	$1,075	$1,083	$1,092	$1,100	$1,000
$48,568	$48,953	$49,339	$49,724	$50,110	$50,495	$50,881	$46,255
$420	$420	$420	$420	$420	$420	$420	$420
$500	$500	$500	$500	$500	$500	$500	$500
$1,533	$1,533	$1,533	$1,533	$1,533	$1,533	$1,533	$1,533
$1,398	$1,429	$1,460	$1,490	$1,521	$1,551	$1,582	$1,215
$3,431	$3,462	$3,493	$3,523	$3,554	$3,584	$3,615	$3,248
$3,851	$3,882	$3,913	$3,943	$3,974	$4,004	$4,035	$3,668
$52,419	$52,835	$53,251	$53,667	$54,083	$54,499	$54,915	$49,923

(b) Interest Income and Expense: prime rate 10 per cent, 'actual' mix

ANYTIME BANK
FORECAST FOR 1985
01-DEC-84

*** N E T I N T E R E S T M A R G I N ***	BUDGET JANUARY	BUDGET FEBRUARY	BUDGET MARCH	BUDGET APRIL	BUDGET MAY
*** I N T E R E S T I N C O M E ***					
INTEREST ON SECURITIES	$14,688	$13,905	$18,017	$18,607	$15,779
INTEREST ON FED FUNDS SOLD	$35,355	$34,496	$46,002	$47,596	$49,533
COMMERCIAL LOAN INTEREST	$126,543	$237,410	$304,960	$315,528	$334,274
REAL ESTATE LOAN INTEREST	$39,688	$74,460	$95,647	$98,961	$104,841
INSTALLMENT LOAN INTEREST	$39,113	$73,381	$94,260	$97,527	$103,321
LEASE CONTRACTS	$2,243	$4,209	$5,391	$5,578	$5,917
XTRA INTEREST	$1,242	$2,331	$2,772	$2,868	$3,156
LOAN FEES	$10,000	$10,000	$10,000	$10,000	$10,000
DOCUMENTATION FEES	$7,000	$7,000	$7,000	$8,000	$8,000
OTHER LOAN FEES	$2,500	$2,500	$2,500	$2,500	$2,500
TOTAL LOAN INTEREST/FEES	$228,330	$411,291	$522,530	$540,962	$572,008
TOTAL INTEREST INCOME	$278,373	$459,693	$586,549	$607,164	$637,320
*** I N T E R E S T E X P E N S E ***					
INTEREST ON NOW	$2,278	$4,273	$5,083	$5,259	$5,786
INTEREST ON MMC	$8,053	$15,108	$17,969	$18,592	$20,454
INTEREST ON MMI	$37,963	$71,223	$96,006	$99,333	$102,854
INTEREST ON SAVINGS	$4,556	$8,547	$7,287	$5,158	$8,911
INTEREST ON TCD	$50,847	$95,396	$126,810	$131,204	$136,749
INTEREST PUBLIC FUNDS	$5,476	$10,273	$13,656	$14,130	$14,727
TOTAL COST OF DEPOSITS	$109,172	$204,820	$266,811	$273,675	$289,479
INTEREST ON FED FUNDS PUR	$0	$2,374	$3,188	$3,299	$3,422
INTEREST ON BORROWED FUNDS	$266	$499	$649	$672	$707
INTEREST ON CAPITAL NOTE	$1,873	$3,383	$4,102	$3,970	$3,924
TOTAL INTEREST EXPENSE	$111,310	$211,076	$274,751	$281,616	$297,532
* * * NET INTEREST MARGIN * * *	$167,063	$248,617	$311,798	$325,548	$339,788

==

==

BUDGET JUNE	BUDGET JULY	BUDGET AUGUST	BUDGET SEPTEMBER	BUDGET OCTOBER	BUDGET NOVEMBER	BUDGET DECEMBER	BUDGET YTD
$16,197	$17,696	$18,654	$20,034	$23,999	$25,465	$27,485	$230,526
$50,846	$55,550	$58,559	$62,986	$75,646	$80,354	$86,729	$683,651
$343,141	$374,883	$395,187	$417,554	$486,081	$509,294	$549,698	$4,394,553
$107,621	$117,577	$123,945	$130,960	$152,453	$159,733	$172,405	$1,378,291
$106,062	$115,873	$122,149	$129,062	$150,243	$157,418	$169,907	$1,358,316
$6,074	$6,636	$6,995	$7,381	$8,571	$8,971	$9,682	$77,647
$3,239	$3,539	$3,731	$3,796	$4,114	$4,167	$4,498	$39,454
$10,000	$10,000	$10,000	$10,000	$10,000	$10,000	$10,000	$120,000
$8,000	$9,000	$9,000	$9,000	$10,000	$10,000	$10,000	$102,000
$2,500	$2,500	$2,500	$2,500	$2,500	$2,500	$2,500	$30,000
$586,637	$640,008	$673,508	$710,253	$823,962	$862,082	$928,690	$7,500,261
$653,680	$713,253	$750,720	$793,273	$923,607	$967,901	$1,042,904	$8,414,438
$5,939	$6,488	$6,840	$6,959	$7,543	$7,639	$8,245	$72,332
$20,996	$22,939	$24,181	$24,603	$26,666	$27,008	$29,151	$255,719
$105,582	$115,349	$121,596	$131,452	$159,233	$169,765	$183,233	$1,393,588
$11,878	$12,977	$13,680	$13,918	$15,085	$15,279	$16,491	$133,766
$140,376	$153,361	$161,668	$173,629	$207,994	$220,694	$238,203	$1,836,930
$15,117	$16,516	$17,410	$18,699	$22,399	$23,767	$25,653	$197,823
$299,888	$327,629	$345,375	$369,261	$438,920	$464,152	$500,975	$3,890,158
$3,513	$3,837	$4,045	$4,365	$5,272	$5,614	$6,059	$44,988
$726	$793	$836	$889	$1,048	$1,103	$1,191	$9,379
$3,797	$3,924	$3,924	$3,970	$4,459	$4,488	$4,637	$46,450
$307,924	$336,184	$354,180	$378,486	$449,699	$475,356	$512,862	$3,990,975
$345,757	$377,070	$396,540	$414,788	$473,908	$492,545	$530,042	$4,423,463

(c) 'Actual' loan/deposit mix

ANYTIME BANK
FORECAST FOR 1985
01-Dec-84

*** L O A N M I X ***	ACTUAL MIX
COMMERCIAL LOANS	60.84%
REAL ESTATE LOANS	19.08%
INSTALMENT LOANS	18.81%
XTRA MONEY	0.41%
LEASES	1.04%
OTHER LOANS	0.10%
LESS UNDISBURSED LOANS	0.28%
TOTAL LOANS	100.00%

*** D E P O S I T M I X ***	
DEMAND DEPOSITS	31.77%
NOW ACCOUNTS	2.01%
SUPER NOW ACCOUNTS	5.57%
MONEY MARKET DEPOSIT ACCOUNT	24.53%
TOTAL INTEREST/DDA	32.11%
SAVINGS DEPOSITS	4.01%
TIME CERTIFICATES	28.99%
PUBLIC FUNDS	3.12%
TOTAL TIME	36.12%
TOTAL DEPOSITS	100.00%

(d) Interest rate matrix: prime rate 10 per cent

ANYTIME BANK
FORECAST FOR 1985
01-Dec-84

*** R A T E S ***	JANUARY	FEBRUARY	MARCH	APRIL	MAY
PRIME RATE	10.00%	10.00%	10.00%	10.00%	10.00%
COMMERCIAL LOANS-PROJECTED	12.50%	12.50%	12.50%	12.50%	12.50%
REAL ESTATE LOANS-PROJECTED	12.50%	12.50%	12.50%	12.50%	12.50%
INSTALMENT LOANS-PROJECTED	12.50%	12.50%	12.50%	12.50%	12.50%
LEASES-PROJECTED	13.00%	13.00%	13.00%	13.00%	13.00%
XTRA MONEY	18.00%	18.00%	18.00%	18.00%	18.00%
SECURITIES-PROJECTED	8.50%	8.50%	8.50%	8.50%	8.50%
TCD DUE FROM INSTITUTIONS	10.00%	10.00%	10.00%	10.00%	10.00%
FED FUNDS SOLD	8.25%	8.25%	8.25%	8.25%	8.25%
FED FUNDS PURCHASED	7.75%	7.75%	7.75%	7.75%	7.75%
SAVINGS & NOW	5.50%	5.50%	5.50%	5.50%	5.50%
SUPER NOW	7.00%	7.00%	7.00%	7.00%	7.00%
MONEY MARKET DEPOSIT ACCOUNT	7.50%	7.50%	7.50%	7.50%	7.50%
CERTIFICATES-PROJECTED	8.50%	8.50%	8.50%	8.50%	8.50%
PUBLIC FUNDS-PROJECTED	8.50%	8.50%	8.50%	8.50%	8.50%
OTHER BORROWINGS	12.00%	12.00%	12.00%	12.00%	12.00%
CAPITAL NOTE	10.50%	10.50%	10.50%	10.50%	10.50%

JUNE	JULY	AUGUST	SEPTEMBER	OCTOBER	NOVEMBER	DECEMBER
10.00%	10.00%	10.00%	10.00%	10.00%	10.00%	10.00%
12.50%	12.50%	12.50%	12.50%	12.50%	12.50%	12.50%
12.50%	12.50%	12.50%	12.50%	12.50%	12.50%	12.50%
12.50%	12.50%	12.50%	12.50%	12.50%	12.50%	12.50%
13.00%	13.00%	13.00%	13.00%	13.00%	13.00%	13.00%
18.00%	18.00%	18.00%	18.00%	18.00%	18.00%	18.00%
8.50%	8.50%	8.50%	8.50%	8.50%	8.50%	8.50%
10.00%	10.00%	10.00%	10.00%	10.00%	10.00%	10.00%
8.25%	8.25%	8.25%	8.25%	8.25%	8.25%	8.25%
7.75%	7.75%	7.75%	7.75%	7.75%	7.75%	7.75%
5.50%	5.50%	5.50%	5.50%	5.50%	5.50%	5.50%
7.00%	7.00%	7.00%	7.00%	7.00%	7.00%	7.00%
7.50%	7.50%	7.50%	7.50%	7.50%	7.50%	7.50%
8.50%	8.50%	8.50%	8.50%	8.50%	8.50%	8.50%
8.50%	8.50%	8.50%	8.50%	8.50%	8.50%	8.50%
12.00%	12.00%	12.00%	12.00%	12.00%	12.00%	12.00%
10.50%	10.50%	10.50%	10.50%	10.50%	10.50%	10.50%

PART 5

OPPORTUNITIES FOR MODELLING

Financial Modelling in Corporate Management, 2nd Edition
Edited by J. W. Bryant

18

Modelling Dividend Growth in Financial Planning*

JOHN GRINYER AND ALASDAIR LONIE

18.1 Introduction

More than a decade ago the idea of using dividend growth as a planning variable was presented by Grinyer (1973) and independently, and with different emphasis, by Chambers (1972). Subsequent developments in the economic environment on the one hand and in the substantive literature on the other seem to have confirmed the appropriateness of Grinyer's original model. This chapter analyses these issues and justifies and outlines that model.

It has long been evident to the finance directors of companies that the level of dividend payments is of paramount importance in financial planning. Although few academic specialists in finance would have cared to dispute the truth of this statement during the past fifteen years, the academic explanation of the role of dividends in the financial decision-making process has altered out of all recognition during that period. When stripped to its essentials and shorn of its mathematical abstractions the explanation provided by the recent literature should appear to company executives to be realistic, which was not always so. In fairness, the theoretical analysis is still not wholly adequate, but it is getting better and gaining in credibility as one journal issue follows another.

The modern theoretical approach to financial management freely acknowledges that firms operate in imperfect markets in an environment of endemic uncertainty, that they may experience portfolio disequilibrium, cash-flow difficulties and financial distress and that they may suffer from intermittent

*Reprinted with permission from J. R. Grinyer, 'Financial Planning Models Incorporating Dividend Growth Elements', *Accounting and Business Research*, No. 10, Spring 1973.

capital rationing. But perhaps most important of all for the present argument is its interpretation of dividends as a method by which a management communicates important messages about the future prospects of a firm to the capital markets, which is based on the perception that management insiders have access to exclusive information about the firm's operations and about the prospective yield on any planned capital projects. As investors are usually outsiders, they are compelled to rely on published information. Yet managers recognize that the expectations held by equity investors concerning a firm's prospects will influence the market price of its equity with inevitable consequences for both the security of management and the ease with which it can raise new finance. The dividend payout therefore has a special role to play in transmitting information from management which reduces the uncertainty with which outsider expectations are held and facilitates any necessary revision of those expectations. It is clear that many modern theorists give dividend policy the important place in financial planning that it has long held in practice.

18.2 Objectives of Financial Management

The development of financial management analysis into an academically respectable body of doctrine owes an enormous debt to neoclassical economics. But there has been a price to pay for this great advance in theoretical and empirical sophistication. The bedrock of neoclassical propositions based on perfect market assumptions has created disenchantment not only among busy corporate finance practitioners but also among many academic teachers of financial management. A good deal of this disillusionment may be removed by the recent admission by certain of the most distinguished contributors to the neoclassical paradigm in finance that, instead of simply grafting modifications on to perfect market models, real world imperfections and uncertainties must henceforth be numbered among the basic postulates in any model worthy of our attention. Because of the prior published position and of the eminence of the authors, the articles by Myers (1984) and Miller and Rock (1985) are of particular significance in signalling the start of this change in the standard theoretical approach to the relationship between the managers of firms and their shareholders and creditors.

Myers's most arresting argument about dividends is that a theory of managers' financing priorities and preference for a gradual adaptation to target dividend payout ratios known as the 'pecking order hypothesis' (Donaldson, 1961, 1969) has recently acquired academic respectability through the acceptance of the reality of asymmetric information which recognizes that managers have a better appreciation than shareholders of the economic prospects of their enterprise. One can reason that, when this unexceptionable proposition about asymmetrical information is combined with the equally acceptable perception that the interests of the managers and the shareholders of a firm do not automatically coincide (Donaldson, 1963; Grinyer, 1986), then it is clear that there are good prima facie grounds for abandoning the argument that the principal objective of management is to maximize the wealth of the shareholders of the firm (MSW). Indeed, desertion of MSW enables us to make sense of the well-documented practice of adhering to a relatively stable dividend payout policy in different constellations of economic circumstances that underlies the 'pecking order' hypothesis. Many distinguished theorists have admitted that observed dividend policies appeared to conflict with MSW. Thus Nickell (1978) noted that, in terms of his optimizing model of company investment and financing behaviour, a stable payout policy appeared to be insufficiently flexible, sub-optimal and puzzling; although he perceived that the solution might lie in the role of dividends as a form of market signal, the state of the art failed to provide him with a persuasive explanation.

The special significance of the paper by Miller and Rock is that Miller was, along with Modigliani, a chief architect of the proposition that the dividend payout ratio was wholly irrelevant to the market value of the firm. As is well known, the 1961 Miller–Modigliani article was the starting point of virtually all subsequent analyses on dividend policy, regardless of their eventual conclusion. It is therefore remarkable that Miller now proposes that the standard financial assumption that underlay his earlier work, that outside investors and inside managers have access to identical information about the firm's current earnings and future opportunities, be replaced by the 'more plausible one' that managers know more than outsiders about the true position of the firm's current earnings. It follows that the signalling property of the dividends paid (the 'announcement effect') becomes a basic element in a public company's financial planning model, instead of a qualification to it. The selection by managers of a unique, MSW based, optimal portfolio of investment projects is no longer inevitable in this scenario.

It can be argued that managers need not attempt to maximize shareholder wealth because, so long as they achieve a rate of profit which compares satisfactorily with the returns of other firms in the same industry, there is no medium of communication capable of transmitting to shareholders the message that managers are failing to pursue the MSW objective (Albin, 1974). One can claim that in such circumstances managers would not seek to maximize the net worth of the firm. Indeed, as long ago as 1963 Donaldson suggested four areas in which managers' interests might conflict with those of shareholders:

(1) Managers' primary interest in financial performance is in the anticipated cash flow from any given operation. Healthy cash flows provide management with freedom to manoeuvre and independence from external interference by lenders and other parties. Management's

concern to preserve minimum standards of liquidity (which necessarily rise in conditions of increasing uncertainty) may conflict with shareholders' interest in capital market values.

(2) Second, as Grinyer (1986) has recently emphasized, managers are exposed to the total risk of the firm in contrast with well-diversified shareholders who are concerned only with market risk. Therefore, although they should have a much surer perception of the prospective stream of net cash flows from any project under consideration than any outsiders, managers can be expected to apply a discount rate which will usually exceed that which reflects shareholders' interests by amounts which vary according to the degree of unique firm risk associated with individual projects. This consideration will be significant if, as is commonly true, unique risk is a major component of total risk.
(3) In addition, although it is well known that efficiently diversified shareholders do not require firms to diversify in order to reduce risk, many managers do diversify their firm's products and markets by acquisition to diminish the total risk of the firm, frequently at the cost of reducing company profitability.
(4) Finally, shareholders might be expected to exhibit a preference for financing by relatively low cost long-term debt. In contrast, the bulk of company capital expenditure in the UK and in other industrialized countries is financed from retained earnings in accordance with long-standing management preferences, thought to reflect managers' strong desire for operational independence.

From the above, it can be concluded that managers operate in an environment which imposes on them effective constraints by reference to:

(1) Cash flows;
(2) Capital market perceptions which are influenced by dividend strategy and by accounting profits;
(3) Levels of tolerable total risk.

These constraints are all reflected in the dividend decision.

18.3 Dividend Policy and its Information Content

Lintner's behavioural model of dividend behaviour which was published in 1956 (Lintner, 1956) has had a remarkably enduring influence on most subsequent dividend analysis. On the basis of his fieldwork with a diverse group of 28 companies he noted that managers concentrated on the change in the existing rate rather than the level of the newly established rate. He added,

> It was equally clear that these elements of inertia and conservatism—and the belief on the part of many managements that stockholders prefer a reasonably stable rate and that the market puts a premium on stability or *gradual growth in rate* [our emphasis]—were strong enough that most managements sought to avoid making changes in their dividend rates that might have to be reversed within a year or so. This conservatism and effort to avoid erratic changes in rates very generally resulted in the development of reasonably consistent patterns of behavior in dividend decisions. The principal device used to achieve this consistent pattern was a practice or policy of changing dividends in any given year by only part of the amounts which were indicated by changes in current financial figures. Further partial adjustments in dividend rates were then made in subsequent years if still warranted. This policy of progressive, continuing 'partial adaptation' tends to stabilize dividend distributions and provides a consistency in the pattern of dividend action which helps to minimize adverse stockholder reactions. At the same time it enables management to live more comfortably with its unavoidable uncertainties regarding future developments.

Lintner's basis hypothesis was, as Tarshis (1956) was swift to remark, so simple that its very simplicity suggests some inherent flaw and Darling (1957) was almost equally swift to note that when expectations and liquidity positions appeared to be undergoing rapid change Lintner's model lost much of its predictive power. These criticisms are worth bearing in mind when we consider the possible relevance of Lintner's analysis to financial planning exercises in the very different context of the 1980s. For Lintner was aware that severe credit stringency might have been expected to disrupt the behaviour pattern described by his model but simply found that in the period of prosperity and stable business conditions covered by his study companies with a well-defined payout policy (they represented about two-thirds of his sample) were generally able to anticipate and cope with liquidity tightness without embarrassment. A recent survey of US management opinions (Baker, Farrelly and Edelman, 1985) revealed an impressive measure of support among the present generation of US managers, for the two fundamental Lintner findings. Thus they thought that a firm should avoid making changes in dividend rates that might have to be reversed in a year or so and should strive to maintain an uninterrupted record of dividend payments and that a firm should have a target payout ratio and periodically adjust the payout towards the target. Interestingly the key proposition that a change in the existing dividend payment is more important than the actual amount of dividends was not strongly endorsed.

Three points are worth emphasizing about a target dividend strategy. First, as Lintner found, most managers consider that such a policy is desirable in a stable financial environment as the linchpin of financial planning. We think that their policy is sound under stability but also that it should sensibly be extended to an unstable environment. In a climate of economic uncertainty the framework of financial planning should be sufficiently robust to withstand exogenous shocks from government policy or from other external sources, such as sharp adjustments in oil or other commodity prices. This implies that firms' liquidity policies should be formulated with enough foresight or flexibility to enable the maintenance of a stable growth strategy, regardless of random shocks. Second, given the adoption of a target payout ratio, dividends should approximate to the normalized stream in earnings and serve as a proxy for the financial growth of the firm. Third, dividends provide important signals to the capital markets and one could expect that a history of conformity to a dividend convention lends greater significance to any departure from it. Therefore the well-known reluctance of firms to reduce the dividend rate typically results in a stronger market reaction to a cut than to an equivalent increase (Woolridge and Ghosh, 1985).

There is a long-running and well documented dispute among empirical researchers over whether dividends add to the information provided by published statistics on company earnings. As is so often the case there are cogent technical reasons why this debate cannot be conclusively resolved one way or the other (Taylor, 1979; Riding, 1984). Our view is that information on both dividends and earnings is important in any proper evaluation of company prospects. Given disagreements among empirical researchers about whether or not dividends can convey new information, it is worth reviewing the fairly compelling intuitive arguments in favour of the proposition that dividends do contain useful information for investors. First, in the absence of significant transactions costs, dividends have no obvious *raison d'être* in a tax regime that discriminates in favour of retentions, so that the existence of positive dividend payout policies in such regimes implies a perception of an information content in dividends. Second, a company policy of paying a regular dividend in changing economic conditions implies that managers are prepared to accept what are commonly called 'dissipative costs' which reduce the company's potential for cash generation (Bhattacharya, 1979). For example, in circumstances of severe financial pressure, the firm may suffer penalties such as the transaction costs of selling marketable securities (which could mean a capital loss); the organizational and selling costs of divestment of physical assets; the opportunity cost of postponing capital projects with positive estimated net present values; the cost of keeping buffer stocks of liquid assets which earn interest below the company rate of discount; or, if the buffer proves to be inadequate, the rising marginal cost and associated financial risk of borrowing. In other words, managers may be prepared to pay a high price to retain their room to manoeuvre and their associated capacity to stick to their established dividend strategy in an uncertain and imperfect economic climate, and such behaviour is unintelligible unless dividends have a proper function. Although such 'dissipative costs' are most evident for a company suffering from capital rationing, the opportunity cost of adhering to an established payout ratio buttressed by significant liquid asset holdings could be at least as significant for a rapidly growing company faced by a menu of high and positive net present value projects. A third and more familiar adjunct is that, given the natural reluctance of managers to supply outsiders with firm forecasts of future performance, the dividend announcement may be the best forecasting indicator available to investors. A higher dividend payout rate provides a rough and ready but nevertheless valuable measure of managers' belief in their firm's anticipated stream of earnings when their behaviour corresponds to the Lintner model; for it places an additional and continuing financial burden on the firm, which is likely to be tolerable in the long term only if the improved flow of profits signalled by the change actually materializes. For this reason a rise in the dividend rate is more likely to inspire market confidence than the most sanguine declaration by the company chairman. Moreover, as dividend policy represents a deliberate action by managers to bring dividends more into line with the long-run pattern of earnings, a change in the dividend rate provides information about managers' perceptions concerning the sustainability of increases in published earnings, which they (but not necessarily outsiders) may perceive as essentially temporary in nature. Fourthly, dividends are cash payments and should therefore be linked to expectations about the long-term cash flows of the firm, rather than exclusively to annual profit figures that include accruals and valuations.

To argue in this fashion may appear to exaggerate the status of the dividend declaration, since earnings are, after all, the dominant influence on the dividend rate and any change in this rate tends to follow any sustained shift in the earnings trend line only after a lag (Lintner, 1956). But both indicators should be considered, not least because earnings establish the context in which the dividend announcement must be evaluated. As a recent study (Kane, Lee and Marcus, 1984) has demonstrated, the dividend statement may have a significant role to play in confirming (or perhaps in the case of aberrant figures, correcting) the impression conveyed by profit figures, even though the dividend announcement may appear to be a mere acknowledgement of evidence already published. This 'corroboration effect', which implies an interaction between earnings and dividend information, may be significant whether or not the dividend rate alters. Indeed, the 'informational content' of dividends was presented in precisely this light by Miller and Modigliani (1961), though they were at pains to emphasize that the real source of any subsequent change in market prices was the altered earnings prospects of the firm so that dividends were simply a channel of communication. Where our modern perspective differs from that of this classic analysis is that today's academic specialists have come to accept that managers possess superior insight into their firms' operations and that they are, within limits, in control of the magnitude and the timing of any change in the rate of dividend. They are also in command of the release of press information planned to reinforce or, conceivably, to offset the impact of the dividend announcement on the investor's view of the future prospects of their firm.

18.4 Dividend Growth Models

Obviously a firm will only survive if it generates sufficient cash to cover all costs, including interest. In addition, it must maintain sufficient liquidity to provide necessary flexibility and, on the above arguments, it must satisfy outsiders by paying adequate dividends and presenting acceptable figures of earnings. It therefore seems likely that the significant elements which should be modelled in the financial analysis of each alternative plan considered by management are:

(1) Future cash flows generated;
(2) Net present values;
(3) The pattern of accounting profit generated;
(4) Rates of compound growth of dividends possible;
(5) Rankings of alternatives by reference to key variables.

During the early 1970s one of the authors constructed several computer simulation models to test the feasibility of providing the information outlined above (Grinyer, 1973). These models simulated the outcomes of adopting different investment alternatives under two dividends policies, the first of which assumed that maximum dividends would be paid each year (i.e. that there would be no attempt to smooth the dividend stream over time), and the second of which assumed that the dividend stream would be smoothed to achieve the maximum compound rate of dividend growth over a specified period.

For both policies the models calculated:

(1) The net present value per share of after-tax dividend figures, derived after the imposition of constraints for cash availability and profit cover;
(2) The figures of annual profit which would arise, given the dividend policy and assumptions of the rate of return possible on re-invested funds, during the planning period;
(3) The figures of annual cash balances, after payment of dividends, during the planning period.

Maximum rates of compound growth of dividends, possible under each alternative, were calculated in the smoothed dividend run and were used, where appropriate, to provide ranking signals.

Comparison of the net present value figures, mentioned in (1) above, for a single investment alternative provided a measure of the anticipated loss to long-term shareholders from pursuing a policy of compound growth of dividends over the period specified for the model.

Basic Model

The first basic model combined the projected profit and cash flows associated with the existing business of a firm with the estimated flows from alternative investments and with the estimated cash flows associated with alternative financing plans. All of the information outlined above was calculated and printed for each alternative investment and financing combination, including the status quo. The model did not take explicit account of the financial risk implicit in gearing, but it did calculate the present values of dividends under a range of rates—thus making possible both a measure of sensitivity analysis concerning interest rates and the exogenous addition of risk premiums by the analyst if he wished to adjust discount rates for gearing.

Table 18.1 shows test input to the model. Three mutually exclusive projects were considered. Project 1 was a dummy project, indicating a situation of rejection of other alternatives; Project 2 represented diversification into a new product area by purchasing a factory and building the new business 'from scratch'; and Project 3 represented the purchase of a subsidiary. The model was run in 1970 and incorporated the UK tax regime of that year. The results for one combination of project and finance are shown in Table 18.2 and Table 18.3 shows the summary of present values and growth rates for all combinations considered. Detailed assumptions of the model are not discussed here as each firm would in any event wish to model its own environment and therefore to incorporate its own taxation, financial and accounting assumptions in its decision models. It is interesting to observe from the summary (Table 18.3) that Project 2 combined with finance alternative 3, which is the option with the highest present value of the dividend streams (at 10 per cent it is £2.27 for the smoothed stream) has a growth rate of only 3 per cent. In contrast, the option with the highest growth potential is Project 3 with finance alternative 2, which has a potential dividend growth rate of 8 per cent, but at 10 per cent a present value of only £1.96. Obviously a decision-maker would wish to consider the detailed figures. The example clearly indicates that dividend growth and NPV can give different signals because they model different characteristics of the data; management would have to use its judgement when such conflicts of evidence occur.

Uncertainty, Financial Interdependencies and Capital Rationing

Uncertainty influences management behaviour in three main ways: first, as we have seen, it causes them to seek levels of liquidity in excess of levels which a

Table 18.1

Project alternatives:	1	Dummy (= rejection of other alternatives)
	2	Factory purchase
	3	Subsidiary purchase
Finance alternatives:	1	No further finance raised
	2	All equity capital raised
	3	All debt finance raised (repayable in last year of evaluation)

Number of years in evaluation: 15

Project forecasts:

Project flow (£'000)	Project alternative 1	2	3
Capital Expenditure			
Year 1	Nil	300	1000
Year 2	Nil	200	Nil
Thereafter	Nil	Nil	Nil
Revenue			
Year 1	Nil	Nil	400
Year 2	Nil	Nil	300
Year 3	Nil	50	300
Year 4	Nil	100	300
Year 5	Nil	200	200
Year 6	Nil	300	200
Year 7	Nil	400	200
Years 8–15	Nil	500	200
Depreciation			
Year 1	Nil	Nil	30
Year 2	Nil	Nil	30
Years 3–15	Nil	40	30
Terminal value			
Year 15 (end)	Nil	1000	500

Existing business forecast flows (£'000):

Revenue	Years 1–15	1000
Depreciation	Years 1–15	200
Terminal value	Year 15 (end)	3000

Other cash flows (not connected with existing business, projects or related finance) (£'000):

Year 1	100
Years 2–4	Nil
Year 5	500
Thereafter	Nil
Existing capital	£2 000 000
Existing shares issued	2 000 000
Last divided declared (gross)	£400 000
Corporation tax payable (Year 1)	£320 000
Corporation tax rate 45%	
Rate of interest for short-term lending	20%
Minimum dividend cover required	1.0
Details of finance alternatives:	
Alternative 2	Finance capital cash flow £1000 per £1000 required, all receivable in Year 1 500 additional ordinary shares issued per £1000 of capital raised £1000 additional capital not-taxable on distribution per £1000 of capital raised
Alternative 3	Finance capital cash flow £1000 per £1000 required, all receivable in Year 1 Cash outflow of £1000 per £1000 of capital raised, in Year 15 Debt interest of £100 per annum per £1000 of capital raised

Table 18.2 Basic model output: results for one project/finance combination
Project 3 and Finance 3

Year	Unsmoothed dividends			Smoothed dividends		
	Profit	Dividends	Cash balance	Profit	Dividends	Cash balance
1	483 500	284 056	314 682	483 500	251 450	370 182
2	518 115	304 393	573 003	510 860	269 051	379 322
3	574 030	337 243	848 752	566 395	287 885	501 717
4	631 863	371 219	1 126 070	630 977	308 037	639 743
5	662 368	389 141	1 881 028	678 260	329 600	1 264 118
6	745 413	437 930	2 178 974	771 691	352 672	1 108 858
7	778 187	457 185	2 435 790	826 286	377 359	1 237 394
8	806 437	473 782	2 688 903	889 706	403 774	1 434 686
9	834 279	490 139	2 941 683	958 661	432 038	1 646 655
10	862 085	506 475	3 194 433	1 033 082	462 281	1 875 453
11	889 888	522 809	3 447 181	1 078 265	494 640	1 963 902
12	917 690	539 143	3 699 928	1 141 461	529 265	2 153 908
13	945 492	555 477	3 952 675	1 209 200	566 314	2 345 606
14	973 294	571 810	4 205 423	1 276 526	605 956	2 527 302

Present value of dividends at 0.10 rate Unsmoothed 2.1534 Smoothed 2.1847
Present value of dividends at 0.11 rate Unsmoothed 1.9823 Smoothed 1.9958
Present value of dividends at 0.12 rate Unsmoothed 1.8298 Smoothed 1.8284
Present value of dividends at 0.13 rate Unsmoothed 1.6936 Smoothed 1.6799
Present value of dividends at 0.14 rate Unsmoothed 1.5717 Smoothed 1.5477
Present value of dividends at 0.15 rate Unsmoothed 1.4622 Smoothed 1.4298
Maximum rate of compound dividend growth = 0.07

Table 18.3 Basic model output: summary statistics

Project no.	Finance no.	Discount rate	PV unsmoothed dividends	PV smoothed dividends	Max. compound div. growth rate
1	1	0.10	1.9118	1.9223	0.0600
1	1	0.11	1.7578	1.7627	0.0600
1	1	0.12	1.6208	1.6210	0.0600
1	1	0.13	1.4986	1.4948	0.0600
1	1	0.14	1.3893	1.3823	0.0600
1	1	0.15	1.2914	1.2817	0.0600
1	2	0.10	1.9118	1.9223	0.0600
1	2	0.11	1.7578	1.7627	0.0600
1	2	0.12	1.6208	1.6210	0.0600
1	2	0.13	1.4986	1.4948	0.0600
1	2	0.14	1.3893	1.3823	0.0600
1	2	0.15	1.2914	1.2817	0.0600
1	3	0.10	1.9118	1.9223	0.0600
1	3	0.11	1.7578	1.7627	0.0600
1	3	0.12	1.6208	1.6210	0.0600
1	3	0.13	1.4986	1.4948	0.0600
1	3	0.14	1.3893	1.3823	0.0600
1	3	0.15	1.2914	1.2817	0.0600
2	1	0.10	2.2172	2.2217	0.0400
2	1	0.11	2.0320	2.0168	0.0400
2	1	0.12	1.8673	1.8362	0.0400
2	1	0.13	1.7205	1.6768	0.0400
2	1	0.14	1.5893	1.5358	0.0400
2	1	0.15	1.4719	1.4108	0.0400
2	2	0.10	2.1398	2.1470	0.0700
2	2	0.11	1.9602	1.9629	0.0700
2	2	0.12	1.8013	1.7997	0.0700
2	2	0.13	1.6597	1.6547	0.0700
2	2	0.14	1.5331	1.5257	0.0700
2	2	0.15	1.4199	1.4105	0.0700
2	3	0.10	2.2619	2.2705	0.0300
2	3	0.11	2.0736	2.0560	0.0300
2	3	0.12	1.9060	1.8674	0.0300
2	3	0.13	1.7566	1.7011	0.0300
2	3	0.14	1.6231	1.5544	0.0300
2	3	0.15	1.5035	1.4245	0.0300
3	2	0.10	1.9425	1.9617	0.0800
3	2	0.11	1.7864	1.8053	0.0800
3	2	0.12	1.6474	1.6659	0.0800
3	2	0.13	1.5233	1.5413	0.0800
3	2	0.14	1.4124	1.4296	0.0800
3	2	0.15	1.3130	1.3294	0.0800
3	3	0.10	2.1534	2.1847	0.0700
3	3	0.11	1.9823	1.9958	0.0700
3	3	0.12	1.8298	1.8284	0.0700
3	3	0.13	1.6936	1.6799	0.0700
3	3	0.14	1.5717	1.5477	0.0700
3	3	0.15	1.4622	1.4298	0.0700

dispassionate and well-informed observer would consider necessary for wealth maximization; second, as Rosenhead, Elton and Gupta (1972) have noted, it may lead managers to seek robustness and stability in setting their targets instead of adopting a fast-shifting strategy in pursuit of an elusive optimum outcome; third, it may generate interdependencies among financial variables which do not exist in models of perfect certainty (Jalilvand and Harris, 1984). Although conventional wisdom suggests otherwise, in a significant minority of cases, this interdependence may mean that a firm's dividend decision will influence its investment (Dhrymes and Kurz, 1967; Anderson, 1983; Partington, 1985). This implies the existence of capital rationing.

Such capital rational occurs only in conditions of uncertainty and market imperfection and is normally portrayed in textbooks as a market aberation, requiring a modification of the procedure developed for the selection of an optimal investment. However, an analysis of the consequences of capital rationing is of special interest for two reasons. First, the capital budgeting constraints are part of the working experience of most businessmen. Modern investigations (Gitman and Forrester, 1977; Gitman and Mercurio, 1982) have revealed that managers in the majority of firms surveyed claim to have experienced capital rationing severe enough to cause the rejection of otherwise viable projects. Second, the conventional presentation of rationing as a simple restriction on the supply of funds by lenders does less than justice to the concert of forces which may operate to constrain the firm in a credit squeeze (Lonie, 1978). Of particular relevance to the argument of this chapter is the fact that, when we postulate sustained dividend growth, the dividend payout acts as a fulcrum in a rationing scenario.

For expositional convenience it may be useful to present a version of the firm's sources and uses of funds at time t as

$$\Delta A_t = \Delta SLB_t + \Delta TCT_t + \Delta LB_t + \Delta LD_t - \Delta LA_t + \Delta SH_t + (E_t - \mathrm{Div}_t)$$

where Δ = the change in the variable from time $t - 1$ to time t;
SLB = borrowing on bank overdraft
TCT = trade credit taken and other creditors
LB = bank term borrowing
LD = debentures
LA = liquid assets (cash, marketable securities, trade credit given)
SH = ordinary and preference shares
E = net profit after taxes and payments to preference shareholders
Div = cash dividends to equity shareholders
A = the firm's assets where A is defined as total assets minus liquid assets.

Changes in A represent the total financing requirement of the firm which can only be supplied through the sources indicated.

Assume a tightening of credit with higher interest rates, raising the level of uncertainty about future sales and profits. The increase in borrowing costs immediately diminishes company profits (ΔE_t), a deduction which was very significant for many UK compaies in 1973–4 and 1979–80. The firm's liquid assets (ΔLA_t) may come under pressure simultaneously on several fronts. Cash-flow interdependence will increase as the firm's ability to pay its suppliers' bills comes to depend more directly on prompt payment by its creditors. If it is in a weak bargaining position *vis-à-vis* its customers, the firm may be compelled to extend their credit period, increasing ΔLA_t but slowing the inflow of funds into the firm's cash balances. Should the firm be unfortunate enough to find itself in a similarly weak position relative to its suppliers, it may be coerced by larger concerns into paying its bills more promptly than before, reducing ΔTCT_t. Moreover, in the new regime of higher interest and correspondingly lower bond prices, the firm can only replenish its depleted cash balances by selling off financial assets by incurring the current high interest rate which will appear in the guise of a capital loss. In the more uncertain market conditions, bank lenders will tend to curtail their outstanding loans and to discriminate against their riskier clients; the maturity of overdrafts (ΔSLB_t) that had been renewed without question in a period of buoyant economic activity may suddenly become effective for the firm; its eligibility for a term loan (ΔLB_t) may be temporarily withdrawn.

The squeeze on the firm's liquidity position will be felt all the more acutely because, in the riskier economic environment in which the firm now operates, its demand for liquidity will inevitably have risen; and the size of an unanticipated demand for cash that may cause financial embarrassment will have become smaller (Roe, 1973). No relief may be possible through recourse to the capital market, because the firm will be strongly advised by its merchant bankers against issuing either shares or debentures (ΔSH_t, ΔLD_t) in adverse market conditions. The upshot is that in a situation of severe credit stringency virtually all the sources of funds of a financially vulnerable firm will tend to dry up. In our scenario the distressed company has been cut off from every acceptable escape route, leaving only the thorny path of a cut in the dividend payout.

A firm in this situation will find that its actual balance sheet position is very different from its desired one. However, unless it has been able to increase its net cash flow from sales to compensate for declining balance sheet liquidity from other sources, then the firm may find itself temporarily trapped in a portfolio imbalance combined with an unpleasing liability structure and experience a certain amount of financial distress. In these circumstances plainly any attempt to maintain a predetermined level of dividend payout would curtail planned investment. In other words, in this admittedly fairly extreme (though, regrettably, in the 1980s far from unknown) situation the independence of the investment decision from the dividend decision suggested by the majority of empirical studies in the UK and the USA cannot logically be sustained. It is, however, a scenario which is outwith the experience of the large well-established firms which dominate the samples of most investigations. Such firms tend to be prime customers of commercial banks and enjoy a measure of bargaining strength that often enables them to become net trade credit takers during a credit squeeze from whose worst effects they are normally cushioned by their overall balance sheet strength.

If the above perceptions are valid, capital rationing is a very real and not infrequent experience for a large number of companies. For this reason a second simulation model was constructed for use when considering projects that materially altered the cash and accounting profit flows of a firm which was in a capital rationing situation. It combined the cash and profit flows of each of a limited number of investment projects to obtain such flows for each possible combination of the considered projects. Flows for each combination were then aggregated with the projected cash and profit figures arising from the existing business and with cash receipts from sources external to the company. The output listed earlier and illustrated in Table 18.2 was then printed for each possible combination of projects.

An example of the use of the model is provided by a run that considered five independent projects which, with the inclusion of Project 1 (a 'dummy' project inserted to evaluate the alternative of rejection of all projects), made a total of six projects for evaluation. Table 18.4 shows the data used. Clearly, detailed examination of the computer output relating to each of the sixty-three possible combinations would have been potentially confusing. Fortunately such an examination was unnecessary because the additional summary information printed by the computer in this model permitted the rejection of the majority of combinations because they were dominated in all respects by other combinations. Only the two options shown in Table 18.5 were not so dominated. As can be seen, to select the preferred option management would have to trade off the present value of dividends (maximized by the combination of Projects 2, 3 and 6) and the maximization of dividend growth (that would be achieved by adopting only Project 2).

18.5 Conclusion

In the real world of imperfect markets and changing economic climates there is a cogent argument that managers should accord a central role to steady dividend growth. Although the costs associated with this strategy may be significant, and are greatly increased when firms experience capital rationing and conditions of portfolio imbalance, the expected future rate of dividend growth possible under alternative decisions seems to be information which should prove useful when choosing among possible outcomes. It can represent a proxy for profit and cash balances and may well indicate the likely direction of

Table 18.4

Projects available : 1 Dummy (= rejection of other alternatives)
2–6 Various options

Project combinations : 63 combinations of available projects

Number of years in evaluation: 15

Project forecasts

Project flow (£'000)	Project 1	2	3	4	5	6
Capital expenditure						
Year 1	Nil	50	100	200	200	70
Year 2	Nil	50	100	100	Nil	100
Year 3	Nil	50	Nil	Nil	Nil	200
Thereafter	Nil	Nil	Nil	Nil	Nil	Nil
Revenue						
Year 1	Nil	100	Nil	50	60	Nil
Year 2	Nil	50	50	70	100	20
Year 3	Nil	Nil	50	70	20	50
Years 4–10	Nil	Nil	50	70	20	100
Years 11–15	Nil	Nil	10	30	Nil	100
Depreciation						
Year 1	Nil	75	Nil	20	20	37
Year 2	Nil	75	20	20	20	37
Years 3–10	Nil	Nil	20	20	20	37
Year 11	Nil	Nil	20	20	Nil	Nil
Years 12–15	Nil	Nil	Nil	20	Nil	Nil
Terminal value						
Year 15 (end)	Nil	Nil	Nil	50	Nil	200

Existing business forecast flows (£'000) :	
Profit Years 1–15	: 200
Depreciation Years 1–15	: 50
Terminal value	Year 15 (end)
Other cash flows (not connected with existing business or projects) (£'000):	
Year 1	: 100
Year 2	: 200
Thereafter	: Nil
Existing capital	: £400 000
Existing shares issued	: 400 000
Last dividend declared (gross)	: £50 000
Corporation tax payable (Year 1)	: £50 000
Corporation tax rate	: 45%
Rate of interest for short term lending	: 10%
Rate of return on internal re-investment of cash surplus to project and dividend requirements	: 20%
Minimum dividend cover required	: 1.0

movement of share price attributable to the information which investors appear to believe they receive from dividend declarations.

Modern theoretical developments have emphasized the informational qualities enshrined in the dividend payout in an attempt to bridge a notorious gap between the theory and the practice of financial management. As we are unable to model realistically the strategic uncertainty experienced by the risk-averse working manager, we have attempted to reduce the problem to a simple formula addressed by a basic simulation. Given our qualitative explanation of managers' seeming preference for a theoretically sub-optimal dividend strategy, the model can be claimed to have relevance for financial managers in the 1980s.

Table 18.5 Capital rationing model output: specimen results

Project 2

	Unsmoothed dividends			Smoothed dividends		
Year	Profit	Dividends	Cash balance	Profit	Dividends	Cash balance
1	96 250	56 547	203 750	96 250	33 194	243 500
2	83 809	49 238	305 571	86 747	37 509	338 827
3	120 144	70 584	131 593	125 540	42 385	201 599
4	129 870	76 298	186 140	140 440	47 895	277 892
5	143 627	84 380	226 667	160 979	54 122	348 025
6	160 380	94 223	274 451	186 701	61 157	435 618
7	165 608	97 293	279 160	200 900	69 108	465 280
8	163 654	96 146	268 005	210 246	78 092	480 654
9	173 736	102 070	305 134	230 871	88 244	549 038
10	182 530	107 237	327 879	250 911	99 715	603 302
11	190 011	111 631	347 046	269 779	112 678	650 201
12	195 378	114 784	359 835	285 638	127 327	681 584
13	201 339	118 287	376 458	301 626	143 879	712 761
14	209 355	122 996	399 879	318 780	162 583	745 456

Present value of dividends at 0.10 rate Unsmoothed 2.2410 Smoothed 2.2475
Present value of dividends at 0.11 rate Unsmoothed 2.0600 Smoothed 2.0359
Present value of dividends at 0.12 rate Unsmoothed 1.8988 Smoothed 1.8492
Present value of dividends at 0.13 rate Unsmoothed 1.7549 Smoothed 1.6840
Present value of dividends at 0.14 rate Unsmoothed 1.6261 Smoothed 1.5377
Present value of dividends at 0.15 rate Unsmoothed 1.5106 Smoothed 1.4078
Maximum rate of compound growth = 0.13

Projects 2, 3 and 6 combined

Year	Unsmoothed dividends Profit	Dividends	Cash balance	Smoothed dividends Profit	Dividends	Cash balance
1	75 900	44 591	54 100	75 900	32 019	75 500
2	79 899	46 940	146 092	81 480	34 900	173 741
3	120 946	30 297	0	124 571	38 041	1 924
4	148 446	87 212	169 538	152 214	41 465	261 484
5	160 977	94 574	191 198	171 540	45 197	319 951
6	175 108	102 876	230 748	195 187	49 265	404 200
7	188 164	110 546	265 197	219 481	53 599	487 216
8	196 967	115 718	285 539	242 650	58 532	563 933
9	218 071	128 117	352 711	284 188	63 799	723 935
10	231 609	136 070	383 155	318 367	69 541	834 811
11	244 147	143 436	383 728	354 771	75 800	928 353
12	266 453	156 541	402 317	404 510	82 622	1 062 223
13	276 588	162 495	419 782	447 009	90 058	1 201 141
14	286 510	168 324	446 456	494 105	98 163	1 365 644

Present value of dividends at 0.10 rate Unsmoothed 2.5269 Smoothed 2.5046
Present value of dividends at 0.11 rate Unsmoothed 2.3096 Smoothed 2.2474
Present value of dividends at 0.12 rate Unsmoothed 2.1164 Smoothed 2.0220
Present value of dividends at 0.13 rate Unsmoothed 1.9443 Smoothed 1.8241
Present value of dividends at 0.14 rate Unsmoothed 1.7906 Smoothed 1.6500
Present value of dividends at 0.15 rate Unsmoothed 1.6531 Smoothed 1.4966
Maximum rate of compound dividend growth = 0.09

References

Albin, P. S. (1974). 'Information exchange in security markets and the assumption of "homogeneous beliefs"', *Journal of Finance*, **29**, 1217–27.

Anderson, G. J. (1983). 'The internal financing decisions of the industrial and commercial sector: a reappraisal of the Lintner model of dividend disbursements', *Economica*, **50**, 235–48.

Baker, H. J., Farrelly, G. E. and Edelman, R. B. (1985). 'A survey of management views on dividend policy', *Financial Management*, **14**, 78–84.

Bhattacharya, S. (1979). 'Imperfect information, dividend policy, and the "bird in the hand" fallacy', *Bell Journal of Economics*, **10**, 259–80.

Chambers, D. (1972). 'Dividend plans and balance sheet management', *Journal of Business Finance*, **4**, 17–25.

Darling, P. G. (1957). 'The influence of expectations and liquidity on dividend policy', *Journal of Political Economy*, **65**, 209–224.

Dhrymes, P. J. and Kurz, M. (1967). 'Investment, dividend and external finance behavior of firms', in *Determinants of Investment Behavior* (ed. R. Ferber), 427–65, Columbia University Press, New York.

Donaldson, G. (1961). *Corporate Debt Capacity. A Study of Corporate Debt Policy and the Determination of Corporate Debt Capacity*, Harvard Graduate School of Business Administration, Boston.

Donaldson, G. (1963). 'Financial goals: management vs. stockholders', *Harvard Business Review*, **53**, 116–129.

Donaldson, G. (1969). *Strategy for Financial Mobility*, Harvard Graduate School of Business Administration, Boston.

Gitman, L. J. and Forrester, J. R. (1977). 'A survey of capital budgeting techniques used by major U.S. firms', *Financial Management*, **6**, 66–71.

Gitman, L. J. and Mercurio, V. A. (1982). 'Cost of capital techniques used by major U.S. firms: survey and analysis of Fortune's 1000', *Financial Management*, **11**, 21–9.

Grinyer, J. R. (1973). 'Financial planning models incorporating dividend growth elements', *Accounting and Business Research*, **10**, 145–55.

Grinyer, J. R. (1986). 'An alternative to maximisation of shareholders' wealth in capital budgeting decisions', *Accounting and Business Research* (Autumn, 1986).

Jalilvand, A. and Harris, R. S. (1984). 'Corporate behaviour in adjusting to capital structure and dividend targets: an econometric approach', *Journal of Finance*, **39**, 127–45.

Kane, A., Lee, Y. K. and Marcus, A. (1984). 'Earnings and dividend announcements: is there a corroboration effect?', *Journal of Finance*, **39**, 1091–9.

Lintner, J. (1956). 'Distribution of incomes of corporations among dividends, retained earnings and taxes', *American Economic Review*, **46**, 97–113.

Lonie, A. A. (1978). 'High interest rates: the experience of the company sector of the United Kingdom, 1966–1975', in *Microeconomic Effects of Monetary Pclicy* (E. Miller with A. A. Lonie), Martin Robertson, London.

Miller, M. and Modigliani, F. (1961). 'Dividend policy, growth and the valuation of share', *Journal of Business*, **34**, 411–433.

Miller, M. and Rock, K. (1985). 'Dividend policy under asymmetric information', *Journal of Finance*, **40**, 1031–51.

Myers, S. C. (1984). 'The capital structure puzzle', *Journal of Finance*, **39**, 575–92.

Nickell, S. J. (1978). *The Investment Decisions of Firms*. Cambridge University Press, Cambridge.

Partington, G. H. (1985). 'Dividend policy and its relationship to investment and financing policies: empirical evidence', *Journal of Business Finance and Accounting*, **12**, 531–51.

Riding, A. L. (1984). 'The information content of dividends: another test', *Journal of Business Finance and Accounting*, **11**, 163–76.

Roe, A. R. (1973). 'The case for flow of funds and national balance sheet accounts', *Economic Journal*, **83**, 399–420.

Rosenhead, J., Elton, M. and Gupta, S. K. (1972). 'Robustness and optimality as criteria for strategic decisions', *Operational Research Quarterly*, **23**, 413–431.

Tarshis, L. (1956). 'Discussion' (of Lintner article cited above), *American Economic Review*, **46**, 118.

Taylor, P. A. (1979). 'The information content of dividends hypothesis: back to the drawing board', *Journal of Business Finance and Accounting*, **6**, 495–526.

Woolridge, J. R. and Ghosh, C. (1985). 'Dividend cuts: do they always signal bad news?', *Midland Corporate Finance Journal*, **3**, 20–34.

Financial Modelling in Corporate Management, 2nd Edition
Edited by J. W. Bryant

19

Financial Model Building in the Multinational Enterprise

JOHN HOLLAND

19.1 Introduction

In the case of the international manufacturing and trading firm the field of study of corporate finance has become very complex. In particular this is brought about because such firms operate within a range of different political, legal, taxation and cultural systems. They also manufacture and trade within a wide range of product and factor markets, each with differing levels of competition, and efficiency. This inevitably leads to transactions taking place in a wide range of currencies, and as a result the multinational company (MNC) has frequent resort to foreign exchange markets. The MNC also has access to a wide range of domestic capital markets and to unregulated international capital markets. These markets may exhibit differing degrees of efficiency and integration with each other.

This increased internationalization of the firm and its finance function, has accentuated the need for decision models to help managers cope with the attendant increased complexity in the following decision areas,

(1) Foreign exchange risk management.
(2) Capital Budgeting decisions in many overseas locations.
(3) Financing decisions in international capital markets.
(4) Cash and working capital management in many currencies, including intra-firm transfers of funds.

The issues of currency risk and political risk create both problems and opportunities for the financial model builder. These possibilities will be investigated by looking at financial model building in key decision areas for the MNC. At the operational level this will include models for the netting decision and for the broader liquidity management problem. Strategic modelling will focus on the international financing and capital budgeting decisions facing the MNC. Finally, the issue of financial modelling and financial planning in the MNC will be considered.

19.2 Operational Models

The Netting Decision

A MNC with many overseas subsidiaries and considerable internal trade will generate a large number of multi-currency payments and receipts between its units. These internal payments and receipts are expected to go through the foreign exchange markets *en route* to the relevant subsidiary. However, the costs of transferring funds between these units can be very high, depending upon transaction costs in foreign exchange markets (e.g. the buy/sell spread), the opportunity cost of unused or delayed funds and various other transfer costs.

Netting is the means by which the parent company and its subsidiaries periodically settle up the net amounts owed or owing as a result of trade within the firm. The objective of a centralized netting centre within a MNC is to reduce transfer costs and to speed up payments out of depreciating currencies. In the case of a MNC the central treasury will estimate the overall payments and receipts due in a period within the group. These will then be 'netted out' for each unit and its net payments or receipts position assessed. The basic idea behind netting is to transfer only these net amounts, usually within a short period. The problem then is to establish which unit transfers what amount to satisfy each unit's net expected payment or receipt position. Many transfer options will be feasible and the treasurer will have to identify the least cost combination; in particular one that reduces transfer costs and minimizes the number of foreign exchange conversions.

A key ingredient in successful netting is the information system supporting the decision. If a firm can centralize its information gathering on inter-unit transfers and can also centrally direct financial transfers, there may be opportunities to reduce the total funds transferred, the number of transfers and hopefully the cost of transfer. If the firm cannot centralize its information gathering it may still be able to acquire the necessary information from the banking system. Several of the major international commercial banks can provide a treasurer with information on the state of his companys' balances worldwide. These are usually the previous day's balances, for both internal and external transactions and can include information from all of the MNC's banks (Bickerstaffe, 1984).

Netting is often controlled by host governments and a firm may have to request permission to net. This may only be given if it involves real (as opposed to purely financial) transactions or if it is restricted to netting within the firm. In some cases, netting is not permitted at all, unless the MNC is home-based, or it can demonstrate that its imports and exports net out and do not have a negative impact on the country's balance of payments position of foreign exchange reserves.

Netting is therefore a significant problem area in the management of foreign exchange risks. It is also a problem area that lends itself well to analysis using formal model-building techniques. Netting will therefore be used here as a convenient means to demonstrate the benefits of model-building in the operational area of foreign exchange risk management.

In the following example concerning the role of modelling with respect to the MNCs netting problem, it is assumed that comprehensive information on inter-unit transfer options is available from the banking system or from the MNCs internal system. It is also assumed that netting takes place within the context of a financial planning and liquidity planning process.

Table 19.1 Netting in the MNC: specimen data

	Paying unit (£m)						
Receiving unit (£m)	UK	France	West Germany	Japan	Philippines	US	Total
UK	0	30	6	2	31	3	72
France	11	0	12	10	2	0	35
West Germany	22	6	0	14	0	0	42
Japan	14	4	22	0	36	30	106
Philippines	67	0	14	50	0	11	142
US	12	0	2	19	21	0	54
Total	126	40	56	95	90	44	451

In the netting example, in Table 19.1 our UK MNC has collected data on the residual payments and receipts expected within its worldwide operations over the next three days. All payments and receipts are expressed in £s. The exchange rates for conversion to £s are based upon forecasts for the three-day netting period.

Twenty-five payments totalling £451 millions are to be made between the subsidiaries. If we assume that the costs of transfer are approximately 0.1 per cent of the volume transferred then the total cost of transfers will be £451 000. As this is for a single three-day period it is clear that the annual costs of transferring funds in this way would be a very large sum. The firm must therefore decide how much each unit transfers to each of the other units, such that the net payments/receipts positions for each unit are satisfied and total costs are minimized. Table 19.2 illustrates the problem. In this table, X_1 to X_9 are the unknown sums to be transferred between units. Thus,

Table 19.2 MNC netting example: problem statement

	Paying unit (£m)			
Receiving unit (£m)	UK	France	West Germany	Total
Japan	0.100	0.100	0.110	
	X_1	X_2	X_3	11
Philippines	0.080	0.075	0.088	
	X_4	X_5	X_6	52
US	0.110	0.110	0.120	
	X_7	X_8	X_9	10
Total	54	5	14	73

X_1 = Amount transferred from UK to Japan,
X_5 = Amount transferred from France to the Philippines.

Transfers from a country must equal the net *payment* position for each unit. Thus in the case of West Germany,

$$X_3 + X_6 + X_9 = 14$$

In a similar fashion, transfers to a country must equal the net *receipt* position of that unit. Thus in the case of the Philippines,

$$X_4 + X_5 + X_6 = 52$$

Also included above each transfer quantity in Table 19.2 above, are transfer costs as a percentage of the quantity transferred. These are estimates of the transfer costs and they are assumed to be a linear function of the volume of funds transferred. This is likely to be a robust assumption if the volume range is narrow. This assumption much simplifies the netting problem in that the goal of minimizing transfer costs can be simply expressed as follows.

Minimize,

$$(0.001\,X_1 + 0.001\,X_2 + 0.0011\,X_3 + 0.0008\,X_4 + \\ 0.00075\,X_5 + 0.00088\,X_6 + 0.0011\,X_7 + 0.0011\,X_8 + 0.0012\,X_9)$$

The constraints on achieving this objective are created by the need for each unit to safisfy its total payments and receipts position. These constraints can be expressed as follows,

$$X_1 + X_2 + X_3 = 11$$
$$X_4 + X_5 + X_6 = 52$$
$$X_7 + X_8 + X_9 = 10$$
$$X_1 + X_4 + X_7 = 54$$
$$X_2 + X_5 + X_8 = 5$$
$$X_3 + X_6 + X_9 = 14$$
X_1 to X_9 are non-negative

The objective function and set of constraints identified above are a formulation of the netting problem as a linear programming (LP) problem. Shapiro (1978) has demonstrated the feasibility of the linear programming approach to the netting problem and this modelling technique can be used to search through all feasible solutions (i.e. those that satisfy the payment and receipt requirements for each unit) to find the least cost solution for the transfer of funds between units.

Table 19.3 MNC netting example: solution statement

	Paying unit (£m)			
Receiving unit (£m)	UK	France	West Germany	Total
Japan	$X_1 = 11$	$X_2 = 0$	$X_3 = 0$	11
Philippines	$X_4 = 33$	$X_5 = 5$	$X_6 = 14$	52
US	$X_7 = 10$	$X_8 = 0$	$X_9 = 0$	10
Total	54	5	14	73

The optimal solution to this problem has been found by running a linear programming package. The details of such a run are shown in Holland (1986). The final solution to this problem is given in Table 19.3. As can be seen in these results only five relatively small transfers are required to satisfy the payments and receipts outlined in Table 19.1. Total payments are reduced from £451 millions to £73 millions and the costs of transfer are £64 470.

The benefits to the treasurer in employing this modelling approach are threefold. First, this is the least cost solution (given the linearity assumptions built into the model). Secondly, the LP solution can produce dramatic savings over a solution produced by managerial 'inspection' of Table 19.1. Finally, the LP model provides some very valuable additional information. This includes a sensitivity analysis of the solution to changes in the net amounts to be paid/received by each unit and a sensitivity analysis of the solution to changes in the costs of transfer.

The use of the linear programming method and sensitivity analysis of the netting problem gives a valuable demonstration of the benefits of model-building in foreign exchange risk management. Many other model-building possibilities exist and for example, treasurers may find that a combination of a simulation and optimization model provide the most suitable decision aid for the netting problem. Such models could form a valuable netting information system for the treasurer especially if supported by an adequate system for collecting data on inter-unit payments and transfer costs. Given the general availability of financial modelling packages with some kind of optimization facility, it seems that the above model-building exercise is well within the capacity of most large MNCs.

Liquidity Planning

It should be noted that similarly sophisticated information systems and model-building approaches are required for other foreign exchange risk management problems. For example, simulation methods appear to be particularly suitable for investigating the implications of matching foreign currency assets and liabilities and also the decision problem of leading and lagging payments and receipts. Optimization models are also very useful for understanding the broader liquidity management decision problem and such a model will be briefly discussed in this section.

Operational models should be co-ordinated through a foreign exchange risk management planning process such that managerial action minimizes the impact of unexpected exchange rate changes on home currency returns. When planning foreign exchange risk management the MNC treasurer will have to clarify the goal of foreign exchange risk management to be adopted by the corporation and measure and define the nature of the firm's exposure to foreign exchange risks. He will then have to forecast exchange rates for the relevant currencies over the exposure management periods in question. Finally he will have to assess the appropriate foreign exchange risk management strategies under the expected economic conditions.

Corporate planners can provide the treasury with essential exposure management information from the long-term plans for further expansion and growth in the business in overseas territories. In the case of ICI, the large British MNC, the planners and treasury teams critically review aggregate cash forecasts from these plans (Hodgson, 1980). This in turn is used to identify the overall division expected between internal and external funds, as well as the operating strategies to combat economic exposure. From this assessment, the treasury should have a clear view on transfer pricing policy between subsidiaries, and other policies on fees for internal legal services, managerial services and technical knowledge. General policy on inter-subsidiary lending and dividends to the parent can also be established at this point.

The internal financial system of a MNC can be used to optimize the choice amongst these variables. Rutenberg (1970) has shown how this might be achieved when focusing on the liquidity aspects of these decisions. His model (Rutenberg, 1982) has the following simple linear programming structure:

Objective: Maximize the sum of liquid funds from all subsidiaries at the plan horizon. The pursuit of this objective has the same effect as minimizing world taxes paid less interest received.

Subject to constraints on:
Flows of funds for each subsidiary.
Minimum bank balances in the bank(s) servicing all subsidiaries.
Minimum dividend requirements from each subsidiary.

Decision variables include:
Transfer prices between subsidiaries.
Leading and lagging levels between subsidiaries.
Intersubsidiary lending.
Managerial and legal fees and royalties.
Dividend flows from subsidiary to parent or its other legal stockholder subsidiary.

This problem can be formulated as above, in a linear programming format, or alternatively as a generalized network. Rutenberg (1982) recommends the former for the earlier stages of modelling and the latter for more sophisticated models. This type of model has considerable potential for linking the foreign exchange management and the working capital management decision areas. It already contains many of the relevant decision variables for considering major interactions between these areas and could be adapted further. For example, additional exposure management constraints could be added to this model. These might include, government leading and lagging terms imposed on certain subsidiaries, and the level of funds required in specific subsidiaries to ensure matching.

Clearly, the possibilities for model-building in these joint decision areas are very large and are likely to be fruitful. The initial development and cautious implementation of a simple liquidity model along the lines suggested by Rutenberg is recommended. This could be followed by the development of more sophisticated models that exploit the information system associated with a MNC's internal financial transfer system.

19.3 Strategic Modelling

When investing overseas, the multinational enterprise finds its path strewn with many novel problems unique to the international arena. These include many different tax systems, a wide range of government grants and loans, risks of political interference and controls over the repatriation of overseas income. In addition the firm may face a variety of possible market imperfections in world product, factor and capital markets. These additional complexities in the international economic environment therefore stimulate a renewed look at model-building in this decision area.

International Capital Budgeting

The two central tasks in a capital budgeting exercise are firstly the development of a decision model or rules to value the risky cash flows emanating from a project, and secondly the prediction of the size and risk of the incremental after-tax cash flows of the project. In both cases the role of a computer-based project cash-flow model is essential. This can be used to simulate various economic conditions and to assess the sensitivity of cash flows to any changes. The focus of attention here is the simulation model. However, the decision model and cash flow issues will be briefly discussed.

Decision Model

The choices open to the international financial manager with respect to a decision model are limited to various forms of the net present value rule. This model is generally considered to be conceptually superior to both the internal rate of return model, and the payback model (1980). The latter models are, however, very popular with financial managers and form the heart of many a firm's capital budgeting model. If the net present value rule is used as the basic guideline in designing a capital budgeting model then these other 'rules' can easily be incorporated in a multi-criteria corporate model. This in turn may encourage managers to fully adopt the net present value rule by creating the opportunity to assess its advantages over the other rules.

The adjusted present value (APV) rule is a variant of the net present value rule ideally suited to the complexities of the international capital budgeting decision (Lessar, 1981). In this approach the value effects of the financing, investment, tax and remittance decisions are separated as follows.

APV = PV of capital outlays
+ PV of remittable after tax operating cash flows
+ PV of tax savings due to depreciation
+ PV of financial subsidies
+ PV of project contribution to corporate debt capacity

+ PV of other tax savings
+ PV of additional remittances
+ PV of residual plant and equipment

This method can be widened to include all important side-effects of accepting the project. The idea behind APV is to 'divide and conquer' this complex problem. No attempt is made to try and capture all effects in one calculation, especially when interactions between investment and financing decisions are expected to occur (Brealey and Myers, 1981). The APV rule therefore divides up the present value terms and focuses on each present value term to maximize the development and use of information. Each present value term employs a unique discount rate for its level of systematic risk.

A particularly important variable in the international capital budgeting decision model is tax. This is because the nature of the tax system and the tax rate can affect most of the individual present value terms in the APV model above. For example, the British Chancellor of the Exchequer announced major changes in the UK tax system from March 1984. This involves phasing out all capital allowances and lowering corporation tax, all over a three-year period to 1987. Both British and foreign multinationals had to assess how their capital budgeting calculations would change due to new interactions between the British tax system and other national tax systems.

Developing Cash-flow Information

Local subsidiary managers and parent MNC managers are likely to have relative advantages in developing information about particular sources of cash flows. Thus project-specific cash flows generated within the subsidiary's economic sphere of influence and activity may best be estimated from the subsidiary's viewpoint. In the same way, additional cash flows generated in the corporate system may best be estimated by senior head office managers with a broad view of the overall activities and position of the MNC.

Once this basic information on cash flows has been generated the firm needs to identify precisely which project- and system-dependent cash flows are incremental to the parent. The incremental funds to the parent are the funds ultimately available to the shareholders of the MNC and therefore form the basis for evaluating the project. Not all of the project cash flows generated at the level of the subsidiary may be available for return to the parent. For example government controls over dividends, fees and transfer pricing, may mean that only a portion of the local subsidiary's cash flows can be returned to the home country of the MNC. Also, system-dependent cash-flow changes may involve reductions in MNC parent cash flows as well as increases. Lost sales elsewhere in the MNC's worldwide business may result from the project and the MNC must take these negative incremental cash-flow changes into account when valuing project returns. This approach, identifying the incremental benefits and costs of the project, blends in well with the APV approach and can ensure that a corporate as opposed to a subsidiary view dominates the model-building and project evaluation process.

Model-building

Managers will be faced with the task of investigating many alternatives within the international capital budgeting problem. It is under these conditions that computer-based corporate cash-flow models become invaluable. The APV model can simplify the modelling design problems in international capital budgeting. Such a model will be described in this section and used in the following section to simulate in detail a capital budgeting example. This will be followed by a discussion of how sensitivity analysis can be performed on the problem using the computer-based model.

Figure 19.1 outlines the nature of the input, process logic, and output of this model, with some general examples of sensitivity questions likely to be asked by managers.

The logic of this model has been derived directly from the APV rule and it has been written in the BASIC programming language. A listing of the

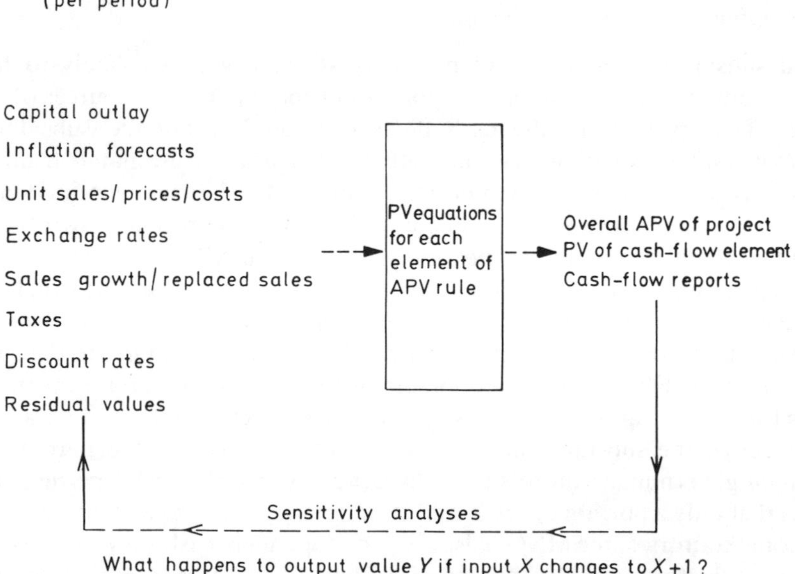

Figure 19.1 Capital budgeting model: outline structure

program is shown in Holland (1986). The model assumes very simple tax systems, nominal operating cash-flow calculations, nominal discount rates, one type of loan repayment schedule, and nine elements in the APV equation. In practice, financial managers will have to adapt their model to their unique and probably more complex circumstances. For example, expected corporate price deviations from overall price changes (across countries) may be seen as a crucial input. In addition a global tax model may be required to optimize corporate world tax payments. Further extensions to the model might include extra APV elements, a more sophisticated analysis of the operating cash flows, a wide range of loan calculations and many other features unique to a particular decision. For a more complete analysis of such design considerations in financial modelling, see Holland (1981). With these limitations of this model in mind the BASIC model will now be used to simulate an international capital budgeting problem.

Using the Computer-based Model

The first step in using the model involves inputting the data in response to questions prompted by the program. Once input is completed the program informs the user that it is calculating the elements of the APV equation. When the calculations finish, the user is presented with choice of output results ranging from operating cash flows, exchange rates, loan repayment schedules, and a summary report of present values. Finally, the user terminates the session. A typical run of the model is shown in Exhibit 19.1 in the Appendix to this chapter.

Sensitivity Analysis

Once the model has been constructed and tested, managers can use it to explore their views of the future. Thus sensitivity analysis of various input variables and their impact on APV values can be performed. For example, the impact of pessimistic values of exchange rates on the APV of the project can be compared with the impact of optimistic exchange rate forecasts. The model has a considerable capacity for sophisticated sensitivity analysis. For example, the following simulations can be performed.

(1) Pessimistic values for sales, sales growth, prices, costs, residual values, additional remittances and tax savings can be assumed. Optimistic values can also be assumed for the variables above.

(2) Another simulation could consider the impact of one overseas project on other existing overseas projects' business. This particular simulation demonstrates that the BASIC model can be employed for multicurrency as well as two-currency analyses.

(3) A real analysis could be adopted as opposed to the nominal analyses employed above.
(4) Another example could be where we simulate a situation where purchasing parity holds between Britain and France, but the firms' input and output prices are expected to deviate slightly from this.

It is clear that the development of a project or corporate cash-flow model is an essential ingredient in creating the cash-flow information for this complex capital budgeting decision area. The proposed marriage of orthodox theory with the appropriate technology can allow managers to grapple efficiently with a very difficult decision area. This approach will not remove or solve the fundamental difficulty of making long-term strategic decisions in a climate of high uncertainty. It does, however provide managers with a clearer perception of this problem area, and the means to efficiently develop and employ any available data. The strategy of this section has therefore been to try to combine the best insights of extant financial theory with the unique problems of overseas corporate investment. This has to be done in such a way as to produce usable decision rules that fully employ available information. As a result, the APV rules are ideal for sophisticated computer-based model-building. The approach adopted therefore provides managers with both the technology and a robust conceptual framework to tackle this complex decision area.

Overseas Financing

The overseas financing decision is a complex decision problem in its own right. For example, in the case of the MNC financing overseas subsidiaries it involves choices (for the parent company) between home currency financing (HC), local currency financing (LC) for subsidiaries, foreign currency financing (FC) (foreign to home and subsidiary) and internal transfers of funds.

The basic decision model for evaluating these choices is the conventional net present value model. The goal is therefore to maximize the net present value of a bond sale or debt issue. The single currency model can be expressed as follows,

Net present value of borrowed funds
= Present value of cash inflows − Present value of cash outflows

$$\text{Net present value} = B_0 - \sum \frac{RP_t}{(1 + r_t)^t}$$

where B_0 = amount borrowed (period 0), $RP_t = CR_t + I_t$, CR_t = capital repayments per period and I_t = interest payments per period. (All are expressed in nominal home currency terms.) r_t = opportunity cost of funds per period for this risk class.

The terms of various types of debt can vary considerably. In the case of a simple bond, the capital balance outstanding is generally constant over the term of the contract and interest is calculated on a fixed or varying percentage of the balance. As a result, CR_t is zero for every period except the final period when the total capital is repaid. In the case of a simple term loan, the capital balance declines each period by a known sum. Interest will be calculated on the balance outstanding and may be based on a fixed or floating interest rate. In this case CR_t will be positive for each period and will progressively reduce the balance to zero by the end of the term.

If taxes are included, then tax deductions may be allowed for interest charges and flotation costs. If not, the tax rate can be set to zero in the following equation.

$$RP_t = CR_t + (1 - T_t)I_t$$
$$T_t = \text{periodic tax rate}$$

If borrowing and repayments occur in a foreign currency then,

$$B_0 = B_{f0} * s_0$$
$$B_{f0} = \text{foreign currency borrowings}$$
$$s_0 = \text{spot rate in period 0 (HC per unit FC)}$$

and,

$$RP_t = RP_{ft} * s_t$$
$$RP_{ft} = CR_{ft} + (1 - T_{ft})I_{ft}$$
$$s_t = \text{spot rate in period } t$$

where the subscript '*ft*' refers to FC values per period.

If gains or losses on exchange rate changes are taxable or deductable, the tax effects will depend on the capital repayment pattern of the type of debt employed. In the case of a bond the capital gain or loss will occur at the end of the term when the total capital borrowed is repaid. In the case of the term loan, gains and losses can occur throughout the life of the loan. In general, the tax due or avoided can be calculated as follows,

Tax deduction or reduction per period

= Exchange gain or loss * Tax rate

$$TT_t = CR_{ft} *(s_t - s_0) * T_t$$

and TT_t included in the formula above to either increase or reduce RP_t.

In assessing the financing cost the corporate treasurer will have to forecast the expected path of exchange rates, interest rates, and changes in other key variables (e.g. tax rates), over the lives of FC loans. These can then be converted to after-tax expected home currency interest charges and principal repayments, and compared with the home currency alternatives.

Folks and Advani (1980) advocate the use of the IRR criteria (or yield to maturity) for this comparison. This equates the present value (HC) of these interest and principal payments with the (HC) value of the financing proceeds. The firm then chooses the source of funds with the lowest interest cost. This suffers from the conventional problems of IRR in that it is a single internal statistic of these cash flows and does not reflect the multi-period financing opportunities open to the firm.

As an alternative, if data on the term structure of interest rates for the HC funds of similar risk is available, then net present values can be calculated. It is important in this context to identify the additional net present value derived from the international dimensions of the financing decision. The reference point for this comparison is the domestic home country market of the MNC. In this case, if the (HC) capital market is efficient, then the HC funds will have a zero net present value, and the firm should therefore only consider those alternative funds that have positive net present values. Interest rates on Eurocurrencies denominated in the HC would be preferable here as a more accurate reflection of the opportunity cost of financing for the firm. Any difference in the net present values of the domestic and the equivalent offshore alternative, both assumed to be efficiently priced, should only reflect the difference in transaction costs between these markets.

When taxes enter the domestic scene and taxable profits exist, there may be positive net present values when the firm borrows in efficient domestic markets. As the capital structure debate demonstrates, these benefits are only likely to exist if the firm has unused debt capacity and if investors cannot obtain the tax benefits through personal borrowing. In addition, Miller (1972) has argued that these benefits are exaggerated if the corporate demand for debt increases and interest rates rise to offset the advantages of debt over equity. Masulis (1980) has, however, presented some empirical evidence for the tax benefits of domestic debt and it seems likely that as there are international differences in tax rates and systems (personal and corporate) the MNC may be in a position to increase its tax advantages by borrowing in the country with the most favourable tax system. The major differences in these tax systems include firstly, different corporate tax rates and systems. These affect the size of the tax relief or allowances on interest charges. Secondly, differential treatment of foreign exchange gains and losses on the capital repayments is of considerable significance. Some countries tax gains and disallow losses and vice versa.

Even if before-tax interest rates (adjusted or 'covered' for the exchange rate forward premium or discount) are equal in two capital markets there may be differences in their after-tax ('covered') interest rates. As a result the firm's choice of the currency of denomination of borrowing may have a significant affect on the net present value calculation. This may be accentuated if systematic covered interest rate deviations are assumed to exist between domestic capital markets. Further additions to net present value may therefore be gained by exploiting these differences in the pricing of risky debt in different capital markets.

If the financing opportunities open to the firm are analysed in the above way they can be ranked on a net present value basis and the highest net present value financing source chosen. Some important caveats have to be mentioned here. First, only external sources of funds have been considered here. The internal financing sources must also be analysed on the same basis and a choice made using the net present value criterion. Secondly, political risks of financing have been ignored. If the highest net present value financing opportunity also exposes the firm to increased political risks then the MNC may prefer to raise debt locally to counteract the risk of asset expropriation. These and other related issues, such as foreign exchange exposure avoidance, should be considered within the financial plans developed by the firm.

Financing Model

It is the existence of imperfections such as tax system asymmetries between countries, the availability of 'soft' loans from governments and deviations from ideal bond and debt pricing conditions that create positive financing net present values. The number of combinations here can be very large and this in turn creates complex computational and analytical problems for the treasurer of the MNC. Various model-building approaches have been suggested to solve these computational problems. For example, Vinso (1983) has proposed a goal programming approach to the financing problem. The particular virtue of this model is that it allows managers to assess the trade-offs between conflicting goals as well as seeking optimal financing combinations. However, such optimization models are generally too complex for practical application, Lessard and Shapiro (1984). Shapiro (1984) has also demonstrated the power of analytic models in assessing the impact of tax on long-term borrowing decisions. His models are particularly valuable in finding the interest rate, exchange rate and tax conditions which equate foreign and home currency borrowing. This analytic approach makes several simplifying but restrictive assumptions, such as constant appreciation or depreciation of the exchange rate over the life of the debt, and these may be inappropriate for corporate specific analyses. Despite the limitations, optimization and analytic models are of value in indicating the general features of a financing simulation model and the appropriate range for sensitivity analysis of key variables.

The basic structure of a simple simulation financing model can be illustrated as in Figure 19.2. The logic of this model has been derived from the equations outlined above on the debt financing decision and it has been written in the BASIC programming language. A listing of the program is shown in Holland (1986). This model has a similar design to the capital budgeting model previously demonstrated. In particular its design has been restricted in many

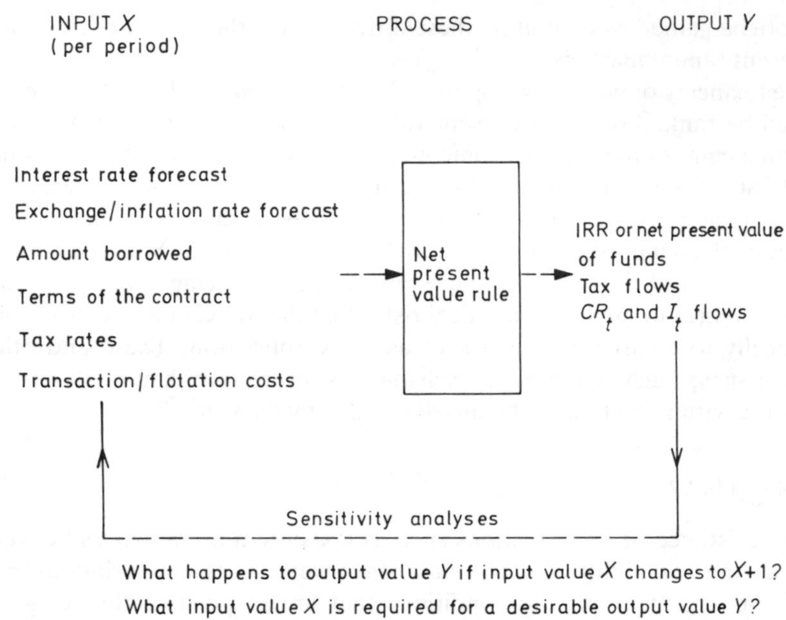

Figure 19.2 Financing model: outline structure

simplifying ways. The model logic is derived from the net present value rule and assumes nominal loan cash-flow calculations, nominal discount rates, two types of loan repayment schedules, and simple corporate income and capital tax systems. This financing model needs adaptation to become a practical decision aid for corporate treasurers. Corporate treasurers will have to adapt the model to their unique and probably more complex circumstances. For example, if major deviations from the interest rate and purchasing parity relationships are expected then the input to the model will have to vary to correspond to this situation. Further extensions to the model might include extra debt types, a more sophisticated analysis of the loan cash flows, and many other features unique to a particular decision.

The model takes a simplified view of the many choices facing a firm in its overseas debt financing decision. It is assumed that the financing problem has been identified in this simple form within the context of an explicit financing strategy and that simple heuristics have been employed to screen out unlikely sources of funds. In the model the firm has three major strategic choices. These are,

(1) The choice of the debt issuing unit. This is assumed to be the parent, a subsidiary, or an affiliated company that needs the funds. This choice

determines the jurisdiction within which the firm may face taxes on capital gains and tax deductions on interest expenses or capital losses.

(2) Two different types of debt arc included in the model: bonds and term loans. Many variations are possible on each of these themes. The choice between these debt forms will depend upon their relative availability, costs and perceived level of subordination in the firm's debt structure. This choice issue, should of course be clarified within the context of the firm's financing strategy. Taxes may play a role in the choice of debt types because of the way in which they affect the size and timing of the tax bill. Bonds will have deferred tax on capital gains (if they occur) and thus deferred tax bills, whereas term loans may have annual capital gains and therefore tax liabilities throughout the life of the loan.

(3) The choice of currency of financing is crucial, especially with respect to tax. Clearly, home currency (HC) financing, i.e. relative to a tax jurisdiction, will mean that there will be no capital gains or losses to consider. Foreign currency (FC) financing considerably complicates the tax issues involved, in that HC gains and losses due to exchange rate changes, have to be considered.

Given these design considerations for the financing model a simple problem is used to illustrate the debt financing decision and the use of the BASIC model in Exhibit 19.2 in the Appendix.

Sensitivity Analysis of the Results

Many variations are possible in the input data. For example, managers may vary some of the following input data (variable X in Figure 19.2), and the effect on output values can be assessed:

Corporate income tax rates
Life or horizon of the loan.
Inflation forecasts.
Currency of denomination may now include US dollars or French francs.
Amount of the loan or bond.
Deviations from parity, especially International Fisher.
Capital market segmentation as expressed in different real rates for identical risk securities.
The impact of interest rate subsidies.

As indicated previously, tax is likely to be a key variable affecting most of the model output and so sensitivity analysis of tax data may be a major preoccupation of the financial manager. Alternatively, one can reverse the sensitivity analysis and seek the appropriate tax system which provides a required level of net present value. Finally, small changes in the program logic may also be important in investigating issues such as the timing of tax payments and slightly different debt forms.

19.4 Coordinated Financial Planning

In the sections above the major international financial decisions have been viewed in isolation. This has been a necessary step in understanding the unique international features of these decision areas. However, the senior financial manager of the internationally involved enterprise has to plan the joint effects of investment, financing and exposure decisions. Brealey and Myers give three major reasons for developing financial plans:

(1) The central financial decision areas interact and should be made together.
(2) Integrated financial planning can help managers to avoid foreseeable 'surprises' and to think ahead about how they can react to unavoidable surprises.
(3) Financial planning helps establish concrete goals to motivate managers and provide standards for measuring performance.

In the international context, the major task for senior financial management is to identify value dependencies or interactions between investment, financing, exposure and tax decisions as part of a strategic analysis of the threats and opportunities facing the enterprise. Financial models are clearly an essential component in such financial planning.

The relationships between the use of these models and the overall financial goals of a MNC are shown in Figure 19.3.

The conventional goal of corporate finance, conceived within the field of domestic finance is to maximize shareholder wealth. In the field of international financial management and under the assumption of market imperfections, this is conventionally taken as an ideal. Shareholder wealth maximization is seen as a desirable target to move towards but not fully achievable with existing theoretical prescriptions. Movement towards this ideal is generally proposed in the international financial management literature by adopting the following approach.

(1) Identify operational goals for each major decision area that are deemed generally consistent with shareholder wealth maximization.
(2) Employ decision rules drawn from sound finance theory and use these to design financial models.
(3) Use the computer-based financial models to help analyse the trade-offs between the central decision areas such that progress towards shareholder wealth maximization is achieved.

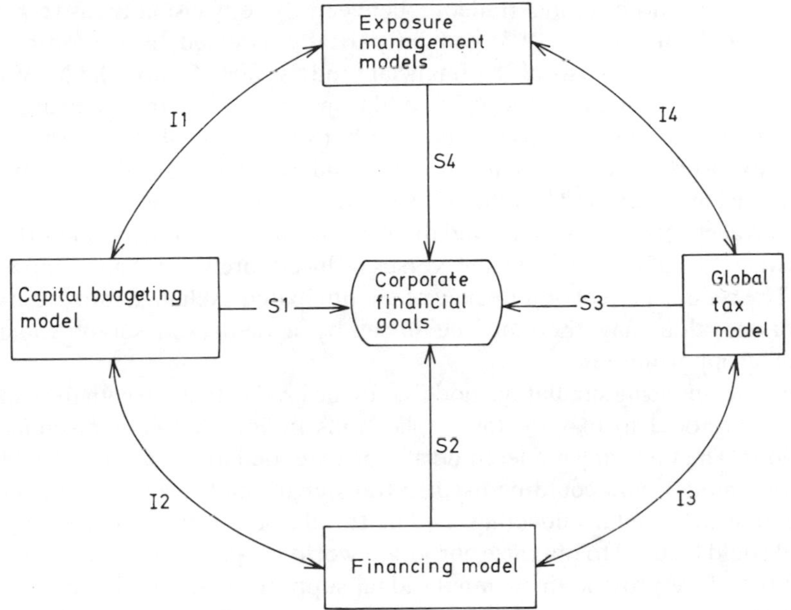

Figure 19.3 Financial planning in the MNC

In the overseas investment decision the goal was to accept positive net present value projects; for exposure decisions the goal was to minimize the impact of unexpected variations in exchange rate on the HC cash flows; and in financing it was to maximize additions to net present value. Tax was shown to be a key variable affecting the investment, financing and exposure decisions. Thus all four of these decision areas are assumed to affect net corporate cash flows and ultimately to affect net corporate cash flows and ultimately to affect the value of the firm. These sources of net present value (S1, S2, S3 and S4 in Figure 19.3) can be identified for each decision area and for each major interaction. For example, in capital budgeting, positive net present values stem both from firm-specific advantages such as unique firm knowledge, technology, or market power, and from location specific advantages (see Holland (1986) for details of the sources of positive net present value in the overseas financing and capital budgeting decisions).

In the foreign cash-flow exposure decision, potential losses of net present value can be identified in situations where purchasing parity holds generally between economies but where a firms' specific input/output prices deviate from parity. In the financing decision, additional sources of net present value were identified in government subsidized funds, tax asymmetries between countries and through internal transfers of funds.

Interactions and desirable tradeoffs between these decision areas (e.g. I1, I2, I3 and I4 in Figure 19.3) can be partially assessed by exploiting the common conceptual basis of the financial models. Specifically, the NPV rule has been used to identify the value additions from both the financing and investment decisions as well as including other sources of value from say, tax.

The exposure decision has also to be considered with both the investment and financing decision. Thus the decision to match assets and liabilities may affect project net present values and financing costs. The explicit trade-off here is between loss of net present value versus reduced foreign exchange exposure risk. The reduced effect or influence of unanticipated exchange rate events on corporate value may therefore be offset by a decreased set of valuable financing opportunities.

Thus the financing simulation model could be used in tandem with the capital budgeting model to explore the implications of joint investment-financing decisions. The financing model could also be extended to become a full liability portfolio model, and could be used to transfer to, and receive data from, a company-wide capital budgeting model. In addition a global corporate tax model could be used to optimize corporate world tax payments. These models could therefore provide the computational support for sensitivity analysis of corporate financial plans and a financing strategy. This in turn could provide the guidelines for the use of the foreign exchange risk management models. The models, taken together can form a very sophisticated information system for the MNC in producing detailed cash-flow forecasts for both the capital budgeting portfolio and the borrowing portfolio of the firm. This in turn could provide the basic data for the projection of pro-forma financial reports. The models outlined in this chapter therefore provide the basic building blocks of a corporate-wide financial model for the MNC. This implies a 'bottom up' strategy for model building in which each model is firmly embedded and tested out in a specific decision process. Hopefully by designing the models around a common conceptual base, the problems of implementing the models and integrating them within the corporate-wide planning decision process, will be somewhat alleviated.

References

Bickerstaffe, G. (1984). 'Banks start cashing in on faster money management', *International Management Europe (UK)*, **39**(7), 33–5.

Brealey, R. and Myers, S. (1981). *Principles of Corporate Finance*, McGraw-Hill.

Folks, W. and Advani, R. (1980). 'Raising funds with foreign currency', *Financial Executive* (February), 44–9.

Hodgson, M. (1980). 'The corporate treasurer and the international development of a group', *The Treasurer (UK)* (November/December), 5–12.

Holland, J. B. (1981). 'Problems in the development and use of managerial financial models', *Managerial and Decision Economics*, **2**(1), 40–48.

Holland, J. B. (1986). *International Financial Management*, Basil Blackwell, Oxford.
Lessard, D. (1981). 'Evaluating international projects: an adjusted present value approach', in *Capital Budgeting under Conditions of Uncertainty* (Eds R. L. Crum and F. G. Derkinderen) Martinus Nijhoff Publishing.
Lessard, D. and Shapiro, A. (1984). 'Guidelines for global financing choices', *Midland Corporate Finance Journal* (Spring).
Masulis, R. W. (1980). 'The effect of capital structure changes on security prices', *Journal of Financial Economics* (March).
Miller, M. (1972). 'Debt and taxes', *Journal of Finance*, **27** (May), 435–52.
Rutenberg, D. P. (1970). 'Maneuvering liquid assets in a multinational company: formulation and deterministic solution procedures', *Management Science*, **16**(10), 671–84.
Rutenberg, D. P. (1982). *Multinational Management*, Little Brown and Company, Boston.
Shapiro, A. (1978). 'Payments netting in international cash management', *Journal of International Business Studies* (Fall), 51–8.
Shapiro, A. (1984). 'The impact of taxation on the currency of denomination decision for long term foreign borrowing and lending', *Journal of International Business Studies*, (Spring/Summer), 15–25.
Vinso, J. (1983). Financial planning for the multinational corporation with multiple goals', *Journal of International Business Studies*, (Winter), 43–58.

Appendix to Chapter 19

Exhibit 19.1 Specimen run of capital budgeting model

The simulation is begun by the use of the BASIC command RUN

INTERNATIONAL CAPITAL BUDGETING MODEL	
LIFE OF PROJECT (years)?	6
CAPITAL OUTLAY (FC)?	20,000,000
ADDITIONAL & RESTRICTED FUNDS RELEASED BY PROJECT (FC)?	3000000
SPOT RATE FC per unit of HC?	12
INFLATION FORECASTS	
HOME COUNTRY?	.06
FOREIGN COUNTRY?	.09
PRODUCT SALES PER ANNUM?	75000
PRICE PER UNIT YEAR 1?	300
ANNUAL GROWTH RATE OF SALES?	.025
COST PER UNIT YEAR 1?	250
DISCOUNT RATE FOR OPERATING CASH FLOWS?	.18
PRODUCT SALES REPLACED DUE TO PROJECT?	20000
DECLINE IN REPLACED SALES (PER ANNUM)?	.15
HC PROFITS PER UNIT ON REPLACED SALES?	3
RESIDUAL VALUE OF PLANT, BUILDINGS & LAND IN HC & TODAYS' VALUES?	.05
DISCOUNT RATE FOR RESIDUAL VALUES?	.18
HOME COUNTRY CORPORATE TAX RATE?	.52
HOME COUNTRY CAPITAL GAINS TAX RATE?	.3
FOREIGN COUNTRY CORPORATE TAX RATE?	.5
DISCOUNT RATE FOR DEPRECIATION TAX ALLOWANCES?	.11
INCREASE IN CORPORATE BORROWING CAPACITY (HC)?	1000000
HC BORROWING RATE FOR THESE FUNDS?	.135
HC RISKLESS RATE?	.11
FC GOVERNMENT SUBSIDIZED LOAN?	5000000
FC BORROWING RATE?	.2
GOVERNMENT LOAN RATE?	.06
EXTRA TAX SAVINGS p.a. from deferrals & transfer pricing?	20000
DISCOUNT RATE FOR EXTRA TAX SAVINGS?	.18
ADDITIONAL REMITTANCES p.a. HC?	40000
DISCOUNT RATE?	.18

OUTPUT OF RESULTS
CHOOSE ONE OF THE FOLLOWING RESULTS BY INPUTTING THE APPROPRIATE RHS NUMBER

OPERATING CASH FLOWS	1
TAX ALLOWANCES FOR DEPRECIATION	2
INCREASES IN BORROWING CAPACITY	3
LOAN FROM GOVERNMENT	4
EXTRA TAX SAVINGS	5
EXTRA REMITTANCES	6
TOTAL OF NPVs	7
NO MORE RESULTS	8

? 1

PERIOD	EXCHANGE RATE	OPERATING (HC) CASH FLOWS	DISCOUNTED (HC) CASH FLOWS
1	12.33963	137026.1	116123.8
2	12.68887	153692.2	110379.4
3	13.04798	171323.8	104272.9
4	13.41727	190050.7	98026.02
5	13.79701	210011	91797.69
6	14.1875	231348.9	85698.88

NPV OF OPERATING CASH FLOWS IS 606298.6
PV OF RESIDUAL PLANT, BUILDINGS & LAND, AFTER CG TAX 367824.7

? 2

PERIOD	DEPRECIATION HC	TAX ALLOWANCES HC	DISCOUNTED ALLOWANCES
1	277777.8	144444.4	130130.1
2	277777.8	144444.4	117234.4
3	277777.8	144444.4	105616.5
4	277777.8	144444.4	95150.02
5	277777.8	144444.4	85720.74
6	277777.8	144444.4	77225.9

HC PV OF DEPRECIATION TAX ALLOWANCES 611077.6

? 3

PERIOD	TAX BENEFITS	DISC BENEFITS
1	70200	63243.24
2	70200	56975.9
3	70200	51329.64
4	70200	46242.92
5	70200	41660.28
6	70200	37531.79

HC PV OF INCREASE IN BORROWING CAPACITY 296983.8

? 4

		HC VALUES OF		
BALANCE DUE	CAPITAL REPAID	INTEREST PAID	TOTAL PAYMENTS	DISCOUNTED PAYMENTS
5000000	833333.3	300000	1133333	944444.3
4166667	833333.3	250000	1083333	752314.8
3333334	833333.3	200000	1033333	597993.8
2500000	833333.3	150000	983333.3	474215.5
1666667	833333.3	100000	933333.3	375085.7
833333.7	833333.3	50000.02	883333.3	295826.5

FC PV of loan int+cap rep = 3439881
FC NPV of loan = 1560120
HC NPV of loan = 130010

? 5

PERIOD	TAX SAVINGS	DISCOUNTED
1	20000	16949.15
2	21200	15225.51
3	22472	13677.15
4	23820.32	12286.25
5	25249.53	11036.8
6	26764.51	9914.413

HC PV of extra Tax savings due to deferrals/transfer pricing 79089.28

? 6

PERIOD	EXTRA REMITTANCES	DISCOUNTED
1	40000	33898.31
2	42400	30451.01
3	44944	27354.3
4	47640.64	24572.51
5	50499.07	22073.6
6	53529.01	19828.83

PV OF ADDITIONAL REMITTANCES 158178.6

PV SUMMARY

PV OF CAPITAL OUTLAY	1666667
PV OF RELEASED FUNDS	250000
NPV OF OPERATING CASH FLOWS IS	606298.6
PV OF RESIDUAL PLANT, BUILDINGS & LAND, AFTER CG TAX	367824.7
HC PV OF DEPRECIATION TAX ALLOWANCES	611077.6
HC PV OF INCREASE IN BORROWING CAPACITY	296983.8
HC NPV of loan	130010
HC PV of extra Tax savings due to deferrals/transfer pricing	79089.28
PV OF ADDITIONAL REMITTANCES	158178.6
TOTAL OF NPVs	£832,795.8

Exhibit 19.2 Specimen Use of Financing Model

WEST GERMAN TERM LOAN	
horizon?	5
CURRENCY OF DENOMINATION?	D-Marks
CURRENCY OF TRANSLATION?	£ Sterling
EXCHANGE RATE FORECAST, DIRECT OR VIA PP	
INPUT 1 or 2?	2
SPOT RATE D-Marks per units of £ Sterling?	4
INFLATION FORECASTS	
£ Sterling COUNTRY?	.06
D-Marks COUNTRY?	.02
CORPORATE TAX RATE?	.5
CAPITAL GAINS & LOSSES TAX RATE	
INPUT ZERO (0) IF NOT APPLICABLE	
ZERO IF GAIN NOT TAXED	
ZERO IF LOSS NOT ALLOWED	
ON GAINS?	.4
ON LOSSES?	.4
TERM LOAN or BOND ISSUE? (input 1 or 2)?	1
D-Marks LOAN AMOUNT?	250000
LOAN RATE?	.03
INITIAL FEE AS % OF LOAN?	.05

OUTPUT OF RESULTS

CHOOSE ONE OF THE FOLLOWING RESULTS BY INPUTTING THE APPROPRIATE RHS NUMBER

Exchange rate forecast	1
LOAN OR BOND CASH FLOWS	2
Tax details	3
IRR and NPV values	4
NO MORE RESULTS	5

? 1

PERIOD	EX. RATE D-Marks per £ Sterling
0	4
1	3.849057
2	3.70381
3	3.564044
4	3.429551
5	3.300134

	D-Mark VALUES OF			AFTER TAX
BAL. OUT	CAP. REP	INTEREST	TOT. REP	CASH FLOWS
250000	12500	0	12500	6250
200000	50000	7500	57500	53750
150000	50000	6000	56000	53000
100000	50000	4500	54500	52250
50000	50000	3000	53000	51500
0	50000	1500	51500	39982.97

PERIOD	TOTAL REPAY. D-Marks	TOTAL REPAY. £ Sterling	AFTER TAX TOTAL REPAY. £ Sterling
0	12500	3125	1562.5
1	57500	14938.72	13964.46
2	56000	15119.57	14309.59
3	54500	15291.62	14660.32
4	53000	15453.92	15016.55
5	51500	15605.43	12115.56

? 3

	D-Marks VALUES OF			
PERIOD	CAPITAL GAIN/LOSS +/−	TAX CHANGE	INTEREST TAX BENEFIT	TOTAL TAX CHANGE
0	0	0	6250	6250
1	−1886.788	754.7152	3750	4504.716
2	−3702.381	1480.953	3000	4480.953
3	−5449.456	2179.783	2250	4429.782
4	−7130.617	2852.247	1500	4352.247
5	−8748.326	3499.331	750	4249.331

? 4

	IRR VALUES	
	D-Marks	£ Sterling
BEFORE TAX	4.857999	8.970002
AFTER TAX	.9519998	4.910998

	NPV VALUES	
	D-Marks	£ Sterling
BEFORE TAX	0	0
AFTER TAX	24828.63	6207.059

Index